Praise for *Essential Windows Presentation Foundation*

"As one of the architects behind WPF, Chris Anderson skillfully explains not only the 'how,' but also the 'why.' This book is an excellent resource for anyone wanting to understand the design principles and best practices of WPF."

—*Anders Hejlsberg, technical fellow, Microsoft Corporation*

"If WPF stands as the user interface technology for the next generation of Windows, then Chris Anderson stands as the Charles Petzold for the next generation of Windows user interface developers."

—*Ted Neward, founding editor,* TheServerSide.NET

"This is an excellent book that does a really great job of introducing you to WPF, and explaining how to unlock the tremendous potential it provides."

—*Scott Guthrie, general manager, Developer Division, Microsoft*

"WPF is a whole new animal when it comes to creating UI applications, drawing on design principles originating from both Windows Forms and the Web. Chris does a great job of not only explaining how to use the new features and capabilities of WPF (with associated code and XAML based syntax), but also explains why things work the way they do. As one of the architects of WPF, Chris gives great insight into the plumbing and design principles of WPF, as well as the mechanics of writing code using it. This is truly essential if you plan to be a serious WPF developer."

—*Brian Noyes, chief architect, IDesign Inc.;*
Microsoft Regional Director; Microsoft MVP

"I was given the opportunity to take a look at Chris Anderson's book and found it to be an exceedingly valuable resource, one I can comfortably recommend to others. I can only speak for myself, but when faced with a new technology I like to have an understanding of how it relates to and works in relation to the technology it is supplanting. Chris starts his book by tying the WPF directly into the world of Windows 32-bit UI in C++. Chris demonstrates both a keen understanding of the underlying logic that drives the WPF and how it works and also a skill in helping the reader build on their own knowledge through examples that mimic how you would build your cutting edge applications."

—*Bill Sheldon, principal engineer, InterKnowlogy*

Essential
Windows
Presentation
Foundation

Microsoft .NET Development Series

John Montgomery, *Series Advisor*
Don Box, *Series Advisor*
Martin Heller, *Series Editor*

The Microsoft .NET Development Series is supported and developed by the leaders and experts of Microsoft development technologies including Microsoft architects. The books in this series provide a core resource of information and understanding every developer needs in order to write effective applications and managed code. Learn from the leaders how to maximize your use of the .NET Framework and its programming languages.

Titles in the Series

Brad Abrams, *.NET Framework Standard Library Annotated Reference Volume 1: Base Class Library and Extended Numerics Library*, 0-321-15489-4

Brad Abrams and Tamara Abrams, *.NET Framework Standard Library Annotated Reference, Volume 2: Networking Library, Reflection Library, and XML Library*, 0-321-19445-4

Chris Anderson, *Essential Windows Presentation Foundation (WPF)*, 0-321-37447-9

Keith Ballinger, *.NET Web Services: Architecture and Implementation*, 0-321-11359-4

Bob Beauchemin and Dan Sullivan, *A Developer's Guide to SQL Server 2005*, 0-321-38218-8

Don Box with Chris Sells, *Essential .NET, Volume 1: The Common Language Runtime*, 0-201-73411-7

Keith Brown, *The .NET Developer's Guide to Windows Security*, 0-321-22835-9

Eric Carter and Eric Lippert, *Visual Studio Tools for Office: Using C# with Excel, Word, Outlook, and InfoPath*, 0-321-33488-4

Eric Carter and Eric Lippert, *Visual Studio Tools for Office: Using Visual Basic 2005 with Excel, Word, Outlook, and InfoPath*, 0-321-41175-7

Mahesh Chand, *Graphics Programming with GDI+*, 0-321-16077-0

Steve Cook, Gareth Jones, Stuart Kent, Alan Cameron Wills, *Domain-Specific Development with Visual Studio DSL Tools*, 0-321-39820-3

Krzysztof Cwalina and Brad Abrams, *Framework Design Guidelines: Conventions, Idioms, and Patterns for Reusable .NET Libraries*, 0-321-24675-6

Len Fenster, *Effective Use of Microsoft Enterprise Library: Building Blocks for Creating Enterprise Applications and Services*, 0-321-33421-3

Sam Guckenheimer and Juan J. Perez, *Software Engineering with Microsoft Visual Studio Team System*, 0-321-27872-0

Anders Hejlsberg, Scott Wiltamuth, Peter Golde, *The C# Programming Language*, Second Edition, 0-321-33443-4

Alex Homer and Dave Sussman, *ASP.NET 2.0 Illustrated*, 0-321-41834-4

Joe Kaplan and Ryan Dunn, *The .NET Developer's Guide to Directory Services Programming*, 0-321-35017-0

Mark Michaelis, *Essential C# 2.0*, 0-321-15077-5

James S. Miller and Susann Ragsdale, *The Common Language Infrastructure Annotated Standard*, 0-321-15493-2

Christian Nagel, *Enterprise Services with the .NET Framework: Developing Distributed Business Solutions with .NET Enterprise Services*, 0-321-24673-X

Brian Noyes, *Data Binding with Windows Forms 2.0: Programming Smart Client Data Applications with .NET*, 0-321-26892-X

Brian Noyes, *Smart Client Deployment with ClickOnce: Deploying Windows Forms Applications with ClickOnce*, 0-321-19769-0

Fritz Onion with Keith Brown, *Essential ASP.NET 2.0*, 0-321-23770-6

Fritz Onion, *Essential ASP.NET with Examples in C#*, 0-201-76040-1

Fritz Onion, *Essential ASP.NET with Examples in Visual Basic .NET*, 0-201-76039-8

Ted Pattison and Dr. Joe Hummel, *Building Applications and Components with Visual Basic .NET*, 0-201-73495-8

Scott Roberts and Hagen Green, *Designing Forms for Microsoft Office InfoPath and Forms Services 2007*, 0-321-41059-9

Dr. Neil Roodyn, *eXtreme .NET: Introducing eXtreme Programming Techniques to .NET Developers*, 0-321-30363-6

Chris Sells and Michael Weinhardt, *Windows Forms 2.0 Programming*, 0-321-26796-6

Dharma Shukla and Bob Schmidt, *Essential Windows Workflow Foundation*, 0-321-39983-8

Guy Smith-Ferrier, *.NET Internationalization: The Developer's Guide to Building Global Windows and Web Applications*, 0-321-34138-4

Will Stott and James Newkirk, *Visual Studio Team System: Better Software Development for Agile Teams*, 0-321-41850-6

Paul Vick, *The Visual Basic .NET Programming Language*, 0-321-16951-4

Damien Watkins, Mark Hammond, Brad Abrams, *Programming in the .NET Environment*, 0-201-77018-0

Shawn Wildermuth, *Pragmatic ADO.NET: Data Access for the Internet World*, 0-201-74568-2

Paul Yao and David Durant, *.NET Compact Framework Programming with C#*, 0-321-17403-8

Paul Yao and David Durant, *.NET Compact Framework Programming with Visual Basic .NET*, 0-321-17404-6

For more information go to www.awprofessional.com/msdotnetseries/

Essential Windows Presentation Foundation

■ Chris Anderson

✦ Addison-Wesley

Upper Saddle River, NJ • Boston • Indianapolis • San Francisco
New York • Toronto • Montreal • London • Munich • Paris • Madrid
Capetown • Sydney • Tokyo • Singapore • Mexico City

Many of the designations used by manufacturers and sellers to distinguish their products are claimed as trademarks. Where those designations appear in this book, and the publisher was aware of a trademark claim, the designations have been printed with initial capital letters or in all capitals.

The .NET logo is either a registered trademark or trademark of Microsoft Corporation in the United States and/or other countries and is used under license from Microsoft.

The author and publisher have taken care in the preparation of this book, but make no expressed or implied warranty of any kind and assume no responsibility for errors or omissions. No liability is assumed for incidental or consequential damages in connection with or arising out of the use of the information or programs contained herein.

The publisher offers excellent discounts on this book when ordered in quantity for bulk purchases or special sales, which may include electronic versions and/or custom covers and content particular to your business, training goals, marketing focus, and branding interests. For more information, please contact:

U.S. Corporate and Government Sales
(800) 382-3419
corpsales@pearsontechgroup.com

For sales outside the United States, please contact:

International Sales
international@pearsoned.com

 This Book Is Safari Enabled

The Safari® Enabled icon on the cover of your favorite technology book means the book is available through Safari Bookshelf. When you buy this book, you get free access to the online edition for 45 days.

Safari Bookshelf is an electronic reference library that lets you easily search thousands of technical books, find code samples, download chapters, and access technical information whenever and wherever you need it.

To gain 45-day Safari Enabled access to this book:

- Go to http://www.awprofessional.com/safarienabled
- Complete the brief registration form
- Enter the coupon code XFJ8-G3GK-XH1A-NMKN-CFH9

If you have difficulty registering on Safari Bookshelf or accessing the online edition, please e-mail customer-service@safaribooksonline.com.

Visit us on the Web: www.awprofessional.com

Library of Congress Cataloging-in-Publication Data

Anderson, Chris, 1974-
  Essential Windows presentation foundation/Chris Anderson.
     p.   cm.
  Includes index.
  ISBN 0-321-37447-9 (pbk. : alk. paper) 1. Microsoft Windows
(Computer file) 2. Application software. I. Title.

    QA76.76.A65A54 2007
    005.4′46—dc22
                                              2006102505

ISBN 13: 978-0-321-37447-9
ISBN 10:   0-321-37447-9
Text printed in the United States on recycled paper at RR Donnelley in Crawfordsville, Indiana.
Second printing, July 2007

This book is dedicated to my wife Megan,
who has stood by me always,
supported me in all my endeavors,
and inspires me to achieve more.

Contents

Figures   *xv*
Foreword by Don Box   *xxv*
Foreword by Chris Sells   *xxvii*
Preface   *xxix*
About the Author   *xxxix*

1   **Introduction**   **1**
WPF as the New GUI   1
    User32, à la Charles Petzold   *1*
    HTML, a.k.a. the Web   *8*
A Brief Look at the XAML Programming Model   11
A Tour of WPF   17
    Getting Up and Running   *17*
    Moving to Markup   *19*
    The Basics   *21*
    Working with Data   *27*
    The Power of Integration   *30*
    Getting Some Style   *37*
Tools for Building Applications   39
Where Are We?   41

2　**Applications　43**

Application Principles　43
　　Scalable Applications　44
　　Web Style　48
　　Desktop Style　50

Application　52
　　Definition　53
　　Lifetime　55
　　Error Handling　57
　　Managing State　59

Resources and Configuration　60
　　Configuration State　61
　　Content State　64
　　Document State　71

Windows　71
　　Displaying a Window　74
　　Sizing and Position　77
　　Window and Application　78

User Controls　80

Navigation and Pages　83
　　Passing State between Pages　89
　　Controlling Navigation　94
　　Controlling the Journal　96
　　Functional Navigation and Page Functions　97

Hosting Applications in a Browser　103
　　HelloBrowser　104
　　Under the Covers　109
　　Loose Markup　111

Where Are We?　111

3　**Controls　113**

Control Principles　113
　　Content Model　116
　　Templates　121

Control Library　128
　　Buttons　129
　　Lists　130

Menus and Toolbars   138

Containers   143

Ranges   144

Editors   145

Document Viewers   160

Frame   160

Building Blocks   161

ToolTip   161

Thumb   163

Border   165

Popup   167

ScrollViewer   167

Viewbox   169

Where Are We?   171

4   **Layout   173**

Layout Principles   173

Layout Contract   174

Consistent Layout   176

No Built-In Layout   185

Layout Library   186

Canvas   186

StackPanel   189

DockPanel   190

WrapPanel   194

UniformGrid   194

Grid   196

Grid Concepts   196

Grid Layout   202

GridSplitter   205

Writing a Custom Layout   207

Where Are We?   215

5   **Visuals   217**

2D Graphics   218

Principles of 2D   218

Geometry   222

Color   225

Brushes   228

Pens   234

Drawings   237

Shapes   239

Images   241

Opacity   250

BitmapEffects   253

3D Graphics   254

Hello World, 3D Style   255

Principles of 3D   258

Documents and Text   267

Hello World, Text Style   268

Fonts   272

Text Layout   274

Advanced Typography   281

Animation   283

Animation as the New Timer   283

Time and Timelines   292

Defining an Animation   293

Animation Integration   296

Media   300

Audio   301

Video   303

Where Are We?   305

6   **Data   307**

Data Principles   307

The .NET Data Model   307

Pervasive Binding   308

Data Transformation   309

Resources   310

Binding Basics   316

Binding to CLR Objects   322

Editing   325

Binding to XML   331

XPath 101   *331*

XML Binding   *333*

Data Templates   338

Template Selection   *340*

Advanced Binding   342

Hierarchical Binding   *342*

Collection Views   *349*

Data-Driven Display   357

Where Are We?   363

7 Actions 365

Action Principles   365

Element Composition   *366*

Loose Coupling   *366*

Declarative Actions   *369*

Events   369

Commands   373

Commands and Data Binding   *380*

Triggers   383

Adding Triggers to Data   *384*

Adding Triggers to Controls   *387*

Triggers as the New "if"   *388*

Where Are We?   389

8 Styles 391

Style Principles   391

Element Composition   *392*

Unified Model for Customization   *393*

Optimization for Tools   *396*

Beginning Styles   397

Models, Display, and Styles   *401*

Themes   *405*

Skinning   *407*

Style Inheritance   *412*

Using Styles for Good, Not Evil   415

Build Themes, Not Styles   *417*

Consistency Is King   417

Have a Point   419

Where Are We?   419

Appendix Base Services   421

Threading and Dispatchers   421

Properties   427

.NET Properties   427

Property System 101   431

Metadata   434

Keyboards, Mice, and Styluses   437

InputBinding   438

Input Device Communication   441

Keyboard Focus   441

Where Are We?   442

Index   443

Figures

FIGURE 1.1: *Windows Forms controls overlapping. Notice that each control obscures the others.* 4

FIGURE 1.2: *WPF controls overlapping, with opacity set to semitransparency. Notice that all the controls compositing together are visible, including the background image.* 5

FIGURE 1.3: *Comparing vector and raster graphics. Notice that zooming in on a vector graphic does not reduce its crispness.* 6

FIGURE 1.4: *WPF controls with a variety of transformations applied. Despite the transformations, these controls remain fully functional.* 6

FIGURE 1.5: *WPF controls are built out of composition and containment. The button shown here contains both text and an image.* 7

FIGURE 1.6: *The power of composition, as revealed by zooming in on the composite button shown in Figure 1.5* 7

FIGURE 1.7: *Displaying a simple HTML document in Internet Explorer* 8

FIGURE 1.8: *Displaying a WPF document in Internet Explorer* 9

FIGURE 1.9: *Displaying a WPF document in Internet Explorer using controls and layout from WPF* 9

FIGURE 1.10: *Running an application authored in XAML. The program can be run in a top-level window or hosted in a browser.* 10

FIGURE 1.11: *Empty window created in an application* 19

FIGURE 1.12: *A simple button in a window* 21

FIGURE 1.13: *Two buttons inside of a stack panel* 22

FIGURE 1.14: *Several more controls added to a window* 23

FIGURE 1.15: *Several controls inside of a wrap panel 24*

FIGURE 1.16: *Clicking a button to cause changes in another element 27*

FIGURE 1.17: *Binding to a resource 29*

FIGURE 1.18: *Data binding between two controls 30*

FIGURE 1.19: *Rectangle filled with a gradient 31*

FIGURE 1.20: *Using a visual brush to fill a rectangle 32*

FIGURE 1.21: *Controls used as the material for a 3D shape 35*

FIGURE 1.22: *Adding rotation animation to our 3D scene 37*

FIGURE 1.23: *Buttons with a custom template, provided by a style 40*

FIGURE 2.1: *A very simple application in a browser 45*

FIGURE 2.2: *XAML Browser Application running in a browser 47*

FIGURE 2.3: *Desktop application 47*

FIGURE 2.4: *Desktop navigation-based application 49*

FIGURE 2.5: *Referencing a resource from the Internet 50*

FIGURE 2.6: *Running an application using configuration settings 63*

FIGURE 2.7: *Images loaded using a fully qualified path or URI 64*

FIGURE 2.8: *Structure of an application with various types of resources 67*

FIGURE 2.9: *Simple display: a window with a button 70*

FIGURE 2.10: *A boring window 73*

FIGURE 2.11: *Showing a window using multiple methods 76*

FIGURE 2.12: *Showing a window with the* Owner *property 77*

FIGURE 2.13: *Displaying the list of open windows 81*

FIGURE 2.14: *A window with two instances of a newly defined user control 82*

FIGURE 2.15: *Logical model of how referencing a user control works 83*

FIGURE 2.16: *Logical model for navigation 84*

FIGURE 2.17: *Initial navigation display 87*

FIGURE 2.18: *After navigating to page 2 87*

FIGURE 2.19: *Entering data in* name.xaml *90*

FIGURE 2.20: *Consuming the data from* name.xaml *91*

FIGURE 2.21: *The navigation flow that we want after the user has logged into our program 97*

FIGURE 2.22: *Logic flow of a console application 98*

FIGURE 2.23: *Our first page function: displaying "Welcome!" 100*

FIGURE 2.24: *Flow of navigation with page functions 101*

FIGURE 2.25: *Compiling an XBAP application: inputs and outputs 106*

FIGURE 2.26: *Internet Explorer displaying an HTML page*   107

FIGURE 2.27: *Internet Explorer displaying the download dialog for a XAML Browser Application*   108

FIGURE 2.28: *Internet Explorer displaying a XAML Browser Application*   109

FIGURE 2.29: *Browser hosting: PresentationHost view*   110

FIGURE 2.30: *Loose XAML hosted in the browser*   111

FIGURE 3.1: *The three principles of controls: element composition, rich content, and simple programming model*   114

FIGURE 3.2: *"Hello World" in a button*   116

FIGURE 3.3: *A button, with the elements generated to display it*   116

FIGURE 3.4: *Using several* ContentPresenter *objects to display different bits of data, and the corresponding display tree*   118

FIGURE 3.5: ListBox *containing several strings, and its display tree*   120

FIGURE 3.6: Button's *display tree (notice* ButtonChrome*)*   122

FIGURE 3.7: *A button templated with a rectangle, and its display tree*   123

FIGURE 3.8: *The button after the new template is applied, and its display tree*   125

FIGURE 3.9: *A button with a more artistic template, and its display tree*   126

FIGURE 3.10: *A button with a template that uses template binding*   127

FIGURE 3.11: *Making a window template can create a common style for an application's entire user interface.*   128

FIGURE 3.12: *The* Button *class hierarchy*   129

FIGURE 3.13: *Several button controls*   130

FIGURE 3.14: *The two basic list types:* ListBox *and* ComboBox   132

FIGURE 3.15: *Windows XP control panel in category mode: an example of a list box with custom layout*   133

FIGURE 3.16: ListBox *with a grid item layout*   133

FIGURE 3.17: *Using* ControlTemplate *to customize more than just the layout of a list box*   134

FIGURE 3.18: ListView *displaying items with the built-in* GridView   135

FIGURE 3.19: TreeView *displaying a hierarchy of lists*   137

FIGURE 3.20: *Making a list box into a radio button list*   138

FIGURE 3.21: *An alternative presentation for a menu*   139

FIGURE 3.22: *A window with a simple menu*   141

FIGURE 3.23: *Two toolbars—one with buttons, the other with a text box and a button*   142

FIGURE 3.24: *Toolbar with items in the overflow menu* 142

FIGURE 3.25: *Various containers nested* 143

FIGURE 3.26: *A slider control* 145

FIGURE 3.27: *An abstract text model* 148

FIGURE 3.28: RichTextBox *with some text selected* 150

FIGURE 3.29: TextOffset *example, showing how the start and end tokens of an element occupy space in the text object model* 150

FIGURE 3.30: *Simplified markup for text, with the corresponding offsets of each item* 151

FIGURE 3.31: *Incorrectly implemented find functionality* 152

FIGURE 3.32: *Working with the ink object model* 155

FIGURE 3.33: *Adjusting the display using additional properties from the ink object model* 156

FIGURE 3.34: InkCanvas *recognizing gestures* 159

FIGURE 3.35: *All the views of a document. Notice that* FlowDocumentReader *has a view control to let us see the document in either page mode or scrolling mode, and it provides search functionality.* 160

FIGURE 3.36: ToolTip *in action* 163

FIGURE 3.37: *Templated* ToolTip, *with transparency* 164

FIGURE 3.38: *Various borders created by adjusting the radius and thickness of the edges* 165

FIGURE 3.39: *A window with a pop-up over it* 166

FIGURE 3.40: *A dialog with the scrollbar appearing in the list box* 168

FIGURE 3.41: *A dialog with a scroll viewer at the root. Notice that the list box no longer has a scrollbar.* 170

FIGURE 3.42: Viewbox *scales the content inside of it to fit a space* 170

FIGURE 4.1: *Visible, collapsed, and hidden buttons. Notice that the collapsed button is completely missing.* 176

FIGURE 4.2: *Aligning buttons in a panel* 178

FIGURE 4.3: *Setting margins around buttons in a panel* 179

FIGURE 4.4: *Three buttons with no transforms applied* 181

FIGURE 4.5: *Applying* RenderTransform *to each button* 182

FIGURE 4.6: *Applying* LayoutTransform *to each button* 183

FIGURE 4.7: *Effects of the z-index on the layout of controls* 184

FIGURE 4.8: Canvas *using different origins for buttons* 187

FIGURE 4.9: *The magical missing canvas* 188

FIGURE 4.10: *Using* Canvas *to "float" controls out of the layout* 188

FIGURE 4.11: *Three stack panels nested together* 190

FIGURE 4.12: *Horizontal* StackPanel *clipping text instead of wrapping* 191

FIGURE 4.13: *Windows Explorer, a classic example of dock layout* 191

FIGURE 4.14: *Windows Explorer, with the four major parts highlighted* 192

FIGURE 4.15: *Using* DockPanel *to build the classic dock layout* 192

FIGURE 4.16: *Adjusting the order of children affects the layout* 193

FIGURE 4.17: WrapPanel *in action* 194

FIGURE 4.18: UniformGrid *with a 2×3 layout* 195

FIGURE 4.19: UniformGrid *with too many children* 195

FIGURE 4.20: *A simple use of the* Grid *layout* 196

FIGURE 4.21: *Star sizing allows for percentages.* 199

FIGURE 4.22: *Percentages in star sizing are weighted.* 199

FIGURE 4.23: Grid *sharing size information within a single column* 200

FIGURE 4.24: Grid *with and without shared sizing* 201

FIGURE 4.25: *Two* Grid *controls sharing sizing information* 202

FIGURE 4.26: *The grid layout of MSN Messenger* 204

FIGURE 4.27: *A mockup of the columns and rows that we want* 204

FIGURE 4.28: Grid *resizing the final layout* 205

FIGURE 4.29: *Resizing MSN Messenger using the splitter above the text area* 206

FIGURE 4.30: GridSplitter *in action* 207

FIGURE 4.31: *An example of algorithmic layout: a circle* 208

FIGURE 4.32: *A model for calculating the desired size of the circle layout* 209

FIGURE 4.33: *A model for arranging children in the circle layout* 211

FIGURE 5.1: *The four basic geometries* 218

FIGURE 5.2: *Close-up of rectangles with pixel snapping on and off. Notice how crisp the snapped version is, even though the actual rectangle doesn't exactly fit on pixel boundaries.* 221

FIGURE 5.3: *A complex path built from all the segments of multiple figures* 222

FIGURE 5.4: *A variety of ways to combine geometries* 224

FIGURE 5.5: *Various color profiles showing shades of gray* 227

FIGURE 5.6: *Basic attributes of the two types of gradient brushes* 228

FIGURE 5.7: *Effects of adjusting the attributes of* RadialGradient 229

FIGURE 5.8: *Effects of* SpreadMethod *on radial and linear gradient brushes* 230

FIGURE 5.9: RelativeToBoundingBox *and* Absolute *mapping modes compared* 230

FIGURE 5.10: *Close-up of the Windows XP–style border* 231

FIGURE 5.11: *Using the* Absolute *mapping mode to create a fixed-size gradient* 231

FIGURE 5.12: *Using* Viewbox, Viewport, *and* TileMode *to create a fill from a portion of an image* 232

FIGURE 5.13: *Using* VisualBrush *to fill several rectangles* 233

FIGURE 5.14: *Shapes drawn with a pen. Each shape is drawn with three different thicknesses of pens.* 235

FIGURE 5.15: *Shapes with different line joins applied* 235

FIGURE 5.16: *Shapes with different line caps applied* 236

FIGURE 5.17: *Shapes with different dash caps applied. All the various thicknesses are using the same dash style.* 237

FIGURE 5.18: *Using* DrawingBrush *in combination with* GeometryDrawing 238

FIGURE 5.19: *The drawing graph created to draw the display in Figure 5.18* 239

FIGURE 5.20: *Using* DrawingBrush *to fill a shape with a border* 240

FIGURE 5.21: *Using* Rectangle's *built-in stroke support* 241

FIGURE 5.22: *The* Image *control stretching a raster image. The control is the same size for each example.* 243

FIGURE 5.23: *Output of an image that has passed through the pipeline* 245

FIGURE 5.24: *Windows Vista properties dialog showing metadata about a picture* 246

FIGURE 5.25: *Rendering a visual into an image, and displaying it (on the right)* 248

FIGURE 5.26: *Rectangle filled with translucent white, on a checkered background* 250

FIGURE 5.27: *Rectangle filled with a gradient, with each stop having an alpha value* 251

FIGURE 5.28: *Several shapes with an opacity mask applied to their container* 251

FIGURE 5.29: *Several shapes with an image-based opacity mask* 252

FIGURE 5.30: *The image used for the opacity mask in Figure 5.29* 253

FIGURE 5.31: *Selection of* BitmapEffect *elements applied to images and controls* 254

FIGURE 5.32: *A simple 3D shape (triangle) being viewed* 257

FIGURE 5.33: *Partial construction of a 3D cube* 259

FIGURE 5.34: *First attempt at using a texture, without texture coordinates* 261

FIGURE 5.35: *The same rectangle, with a texture gradient applied to it* 262

FIGURE 5.36: *A three-faced cube, with a linear gradient texture applied* 263

FIGURE 5.37: *Spheres with different types of materials applied* 264

FIGURE 5.38: *Spheres with different types of brushes* 264

FIGURE 5.39: *Types of lights* 265

FIGURE 5.40: `AxisAngleRotation3D`*'s two components: a 3D axis and an angle around that axis* 266

FIGURE 5.41: *Effects of rotating a cone in 3D around different axes* 266

FIGURE 5.42: *Hello World in text* 268

FIGURE 5.43: *Hello World, multilingual and multiformat* 269

FIGURE 5.44: *Hello World, now with multiple paragraphs* 270

FIGURE 5.45: *Hello World, hosted in the* `FlowDocumentReader` *control* 270

FIGURE 5.46: *Hello World, now with UI controls hosted in-line* 271

FIGURE 5.47: *Hello World, printed as an XPS document being viewed in Internet Explorer* 273

FIGURE 5.48: *The block element's box model for layout* 275

FIGURE 5.49: `KeepWithNext` *prevents column and page breaks immediately following a heading* 276

FIGURE 5.50: *Two lists with different markers* 276

FIGURE 5.51: *Two tables with thick borders added around each table and thin borders around cells* 278

FIGURE 5.52: *Figures and floaters positioned in a paginated document, with marks for their anchors* 280

FIGURE 5.53: *Using document-level formatting, including automatic sizing, to control columns* 281

FIGURE 5.54: *A demonstration of several alternative forms of Palatino Linotype* 282

FIGURE 5.55: *Hyphenation and justification control the way in which words are broken and positioned in a paragraph.* 282

FIGURE 5.56: *A time hierarchy, with a double animation starting at 2 seconds and lasting 5 seconds* 293

FIGURE 5.57: *Key frames for two animations: the width and height of an ellipse* 295

FIGURE 5.58: *Using animation in a template to create an interactive button* 297

FIGURE 5.59: `TextEffects` *allows targeting of animation to individual characters.* 300

FIGURE 5.60: *Music playing (You didn't think that would require a picture, did you?)* 303

FIGURE 5.61: *Playing a video using* MediaElement *304*

FIGURE 5.62: *Using video as the foreground for a rich text box* *304*

FIGURE 6.1: *Overriding resources in the element hierarchy* *311*

FIGURE 6.2: *Binding from* TextBox *to* ContentControl *317*

FIGURE 6.3: *Binding* TextBox *to* FontFamily *318*

FIGURE 6.4: *The conceptual model of binding using a value converter* *318*

FIGURE 6.5: *Binding using a value converter* *320*

FIGURE 6.6: *Binding with a data template* *321*

FIGURE 6.7: *The object model of a* Person *object.* Person *has a single name and zero or more addresses.* *324*

FIGURE 6.8: *Complex binding paths* *325*

FIGURE 6.9: *Editing an object using two-way data binding* *328*

FIGURE 6.10: *Editing a list using two-way binding* *331*

FIGURE 6.11: *Selecting nodes from an XML document* *335*

FIGURE 6.12: *Binding using a template selector* *343*

FIGURE 6.13: *A list box displaying our one directory* *344*

FIGURE 6.14: *Simple hierarchical binding using nested data templates* *346*

FIGURE 6.15: *More hierarchy using more nested data templates* *346*

FIGURE 6.16: *Using* HierarchicalDataTemplate *to provide data to a* TreeView *control* *348*

FIGURE 6.17: *Using* ListBox *to show currency management* *350*

FIGURE 6.18: *Filtering items out of a view* *352*

FIGURE 6.19: *Sorting items in a view* *354*

FIGURE 6.20: *Grouping items in a view* *355*

FIGURE 6.21: *Displaying a bitmap image with* ContentControl *359*

FIGURE 6.22: *Displaying a bitmap image with a more interesting template* *359*

FIGURE 6.23: *Displaying a bitmap image with more chrome* *360*

FIGURE 6.24: *More complex chrome, including actions and additional binding* *361*

FIGURE 6.25: *Reusing a complex template in a list* *362*

FIGURE 7.1: *Display tree (left) of a button containing another button (right)* *367*

FIGURE 7.2: *Examples illustrating the spectrum of coupling actions* *367*

FIGURE 7.3: *Event tunneling and bubbling in an element tree* *371*

FIGURE 7.4: *Execution flow of a command using an event to route notifications* *378*

FIGURE 7.5: *Displaying the list of files* *381*

FIGURE 7.6: *Running the program with data-bound commands* 383

FIGURE 7.7: *Using* DataTrigger *to replace a value converter,
and setting multiple properties* 386

FIGURE 8.1: *Using property setters to apply styles
to UI, documents, and media* 394

FIGURE 8.2: *Our skinning application with no skin applied* 409

FIGURE 8.3: *Our skinning application with a custom skin applied* 412

FIGURE 8.4: *Property value precedence* 413

FIGURE 8.5: *Property value precedence with base styles* 414

FIGURE 8.6: *Using a* BasedOn *style to apply common
properties to multiple styles* 416

FIGURE 8.7: *Consistency in a theme is critical to building a usable application.* 418

FIGURE 8.8: *Consistency applies also to using a custom theme for all
the controls, or at least matching the existing ones.* 418

FIGURE A.1: *Downloading some HTML content asynchronously* 424

Foreword
By Don Box

WOW, I CAN'T believe that after all that time in the chute, .NET 3.0 and Windows Vista have finally shipped.

I vividly remember scrambling backstage at PDC 2003 with Chris trying to ready the first live demonstration of .NET 3.0 (then called WinFX) for the keynote speaker, Jim Allchin. It was an especially stressful keynote because Los Angeles was plagued with brush fires at the time and Chris Anderson's flight had been canceled; fortunately Chris Sells had already arrived and was ready to pinch-hit both in preparation and presentation if Chris Anderson, in fact, couldn't make it to LA in time. At the time, Chris' job at Microsoft was to make sure that Vista—including Windows Presentation Foundation (WPF)—was a smashing success. Little did he know it would take almost four years until the product actually shipped (which of course is a prerequisite for success).

So, what's the big deal with WPF?

Like its sister .NET 3.0 technology, Windows Workflow Foundation (WF), WPF embraces the "it takes a village" approach to software development and uses XAML to allow people with different skill sets to collaborate in the development process. In the case of WF, XAML lets high-level process and rule descriptions integrate with imperative code written in C# or Visual Basic. In the case of WPF, XAML is the bridge between us code monkeys and the beret-wearing, black-turtleneck set who design visuals that look like they weren't designed by, well, us code monkeys.

WPF really is an impressive piece of technology: documents, forms, and multimedia all wrapped up nicely in a markup- and code-friendly package.

What I find even more impressive is the fact that Chris found the time outside his day job to pull together the book you're holding in your hands right now, capturing those four-plus years of experience with WPF (including screenshots!) into a digestible and portable form.

I've had the good fortune of having many conversations with Chris over the years about the nuances of WPF—sometimes on the phone, sometimes in his office (it's across the hall from mine), and sometimes at the poker table.

This book has taught me a whole lot more.

Now that it's all shipped, let the light blinking begin!

Yarrow Point, WA
January 2007

Foreword
By Chris Sells

THANK GOD THERE weren't more people like Chris Anderson when I was making my living outside of Microsoft.

I work at Microsoft now (two doors down from Chris, in fact), but not all that long ago I was an instructor at a Windows developer training company. My brethren and I were led by a deep-thinking Ph.D. candidate who applied the same rigor at work that he applied to any scholarly pursuit that would have to stand up to the "crush or be crushed" mentality of academia. We learned how to think clearly as a defense mechanism and to communicate clearly as a survival technique. If we didn't do it to his exacting standards, he'd sweep us aside and redo our work before our eyes (we learned to call it "swooping," and we worked hard to avoid the phenomenon).

In a similar fashion, we learned to ignore the tutorial and reference materials produced by our vendor of choice because it was obvious that however clearly they might or might not be thinking inside their hallowed walls, it was certain that they weren't up to communicating it with the rest of us. Arguably, our whole job for close to a decade was "swooping" Microsoft itself, redoing its materials in the form of short courses, conference talks, magazine articles, and books. We called it the "Microsoft Continuing Employment Act," treating it like a pork barrel entitlement program that kept us in the style to which we had grown accustomed.

In fact, we made a nice living traveling the country saying things like, "Remember to call Release," "Avoid round-trips," and "Ignore aggregation," because these were clear guidelines that distilled for developers what Microsoft couldn't manage to say for itself. That's not to say that there weren't clear thinkers inside of Microsoft (Tony Williams and Crispin Goswell being two of my very favorites), but the gap between the beginner and the reader of such advanced writings was largely unfilled in those days.

With this book, that gravy train has run right off the track. Chris Anderson was one of the chief architects of the next-generation GUI stack, Windows Presentation Foundation, which is the subject of the book you're now holding in your hands. You might have thought that the very nature of the architecture job—that is, to make sure that the issues deep, deep inside are solved properly so that others can come along and build the trappings that make it into plain sight—would disqualify Chris from leading the developer from "go" to "whoa," but that's not the case. Chris's insight allows him to shine a light from the internals of WPF to those standing at the entrance, guiding you through the concepts that form the foundation of his creation (and the creation of more than 300 other people, too, let's not forget).

As the author of a competing book from another publisher, I can't say that this is the only book you'll ever need on WPF (or they'd have me in front of a firing squad), but I can say this with certainty: It belongs on your shelf within an easy reach. I know that's where my copy will be.

sellsbrothers.com
October 2006

Preface

OVER THE PAST nine years I have worked on many user interface (UI) projects at Microsoft. I have spent time working on Visual Basic 6.0, the version of Windows Foundation Classes that shipped with Visual J++ 6.0, Windows Forms for the .NET Framework, internal projects that never saw the light of day, and now, finally, Windows Presentation Foundation (WPF).

I started working on WPF about 18 months after the team was created, joining as an architect in the fall of 2002. At that time, and until late 2005, the team and technology were code-named *Avalon*. Early in 2003 I had the privilege of helping to redesign the platform, which we released as a technology preview for the Professional Developers Conference (PDC) 2003 in Los Angeles. WPF is the product of almost five years of work by more than 300 people. Some of the design ideas in WPF date back to products from as early as 1997 (Application Foundation Classes for Java was the beginning of some of the ideas for creating components in WPF).

When I joined the WPF team, it was still very much in research mode. The project contained many more ideas than could possibly ship in a single version. The primary goal of WPF—to replace all the existing infrastructure for building applications on the client with a new integrated platform that would combine the best of Win32 and the Web—was amazingly ambitious and blurred the lines between user interface, documents, and media. Over the years we have made painful cuts, added great features, and listened to a ton of feedback from customers, but we never lost sight of that vision.

A Brief History of GUI

Graphical user interfaces (GUIs) started in the early 1980s in the Xerox PARC laboratory. Since then, Microsoft, Apple, and many other companies have created many platforms for producing GUI applications. Microsoft's GUI platform began with Windows 1.0 but didn't gain widespread use until Windows 3.0 was released in 1990. The primary programming model for building GUI applications consisted of the two dynamic link libraries (DLLs): User and GDI. In 1991 Microsoft released Visual Basic 1.0, which was built on top of User and GDI, and offered a much simpler programming model.

Visual Basic's UI model, internally called *Ruby*,[1] was far simpler to use than were the raw Windows APIs. This simplicity angered the developers who felt that programming should be difficult. The early versions of Visual Basic were significantly limited, however, so most developers building "real" applications chose to program directly to User and GDI. Over time, that changed. By the time the Microsoft world moved to 32-bit with the release of Windows 95 and Visual Basic 4.0, the VB crowd was gaining significant momentum and was offering a much wider breadth of platform features.

At about the same time there was another big shift in the market: the Internet. Microsoft had been working on a replacement for the Visual Basic UI model that was internally called *Forms3*. For various reasons, Microsoft decided to use this model as the basis for an offering in the browser space. The engine was renamed *Trident* internally, and today it ships in Windows as `MSHTML.dll`. Trident evolved over the years to be an HTML-specific engine with great text layout, markup, and scripting support.

Also around the same time, another phenomenon appeared on everyone's radar: managed code. Visual Basic had been running in a managed environment for a long time (as had many other languages), but the introduction of Java by Sun Microsystems in 1994 marked the first time that many developers were exposed to the notion of a virtual machine. Over the next several years managed code became a larger and larger force in the market,

---

1. This code name has no relationship to the Ruby programming language.

and in 2002 Microsoft released its own general-purpose managed-code platform: the .NET Framework. Included in the .NET Framework was Windows Forms, a managed-code API for programming User32 and GDI+ (a successor to GDI32). Windows Forms was intended to replace the old Ruby forms package in Visual Basic.

As we entered the new millennium, Microsoft had four predominant UI platforms: User32/GDI32, Ruby, Trident, and Windows Forms. These technologies solve different sets of problems, have different programming models, and are used by different sets of customers. Graphics systems had also evolved: In 1995, Microsoft introduced DirectX, a graphics system that gave the programmer much deeper access to the hardware. But none of the four main UI technologies used this newfound power in a meaningful way.

There was a real problem to be solved here. Customers were demanding the richness of modern video games and television productions in their applications. Media, animation, and rich graphics should be everywhere. They wanted rich text support because almost every application displayed some type of text or documentation. They wanted rich widgets for creating applications, buttons, trees, lists, and text editors—all of which were needed to build the most basic application.

With these four major platforms a large percentage of the customers' needs were met, but they were all islands. The ability to mix and match parts of the platforms was difficult and error-prone. From a purely selfish point of view, Microsoft management (well, I'll name names: Bill Gates) was tired of paying four teams to build largely overlapping technologies.

In 2001, Microsoft formed a new team with a simple-sounding mission: to build a unified presentation platform that could eventually replace User32/GDI32, Ruby, Trident, and Windows Forms, while enabling the new scenarios that customers were demanding in the presentation space. The people who made up this team came largely from the existing presentation platform teams, and the goal was to produce a best-of-breed platform that could really be a quantum leap forward.

And so the Avalon team was formed. At PDC 2003, Microsoft announced Avalon (the code name at the time). Later the project was given the name Windows Presentation Foundation.

Principles of WPF

WPF has taken a long time to build, but for the entire life of this project, several guiding principles have remained constant.

Build a Platform for Rich Presentation

In descriptions of new technology, *rich* is probably one of the most over-used words. However, I can't think of a better term to convey the principle behind WPF. Our goal was to create a superset of features from all existing presentation technologies—from basic things like vector graphics, gradients, and bitmap effects, to more advanced things like 3D, animation, media, and typography. The other key part of the principle was the word *platform*. The goal was to create not merely a runtime player for rich content, but rather an application platform that people could use to build large-scale applications and even extend the platform to do new things that we never envisioned.

Build a Programmable Platform

Early on, the WPF team decided that both a markup (declarative) and code (imperative) programming model were needed for the platform. As we looked around at the time, it became clear that developers were embracing the new managed-code environments. Quickly, the principle of a programmable platform became a principle of a managed programming model. The goal was to make managed code the native programming model of the system, not a tacked-on layer.

Build a Declarative Platform

From the perspective of both customers and software developers, it seemed clear that the industry was moving to a more and more declarative programming model. We knew that for WPF to be successful, we needed a rich, consistent, and complete markup-based programming model. Again, a look at what was going on in the industry made it clear that XML was becoming the de facto standard for data interchange, so we decided to build an XML programming model, which became XAML (Extensible Application Markup Language).

Integrate UI, Documents, and Media

Probably the biggest problem facing customers who were building applications was the separation of pieces of functionality into isolated islands. There was one platform for building user interfaces, another for building a document, and a host of platforms for building media, depending on what the medium was (3D, 2D, video, animation, etc.). Before embarking on building a new presentation system, we set a hard-and-fast goal: The integration of UI, documents, and media would be the top priority for the entire team.

Incorporate the Best of the Web, and the Best of Windows

The goal here was to take the best features from the last 20 years of Windows development and the best features from the last 10 years of Web development and create a new platform. The Web offers a great simple markup model, deployment model, common frame for applications, and rich server connectivity. Windows offers a rich client model, simple programming model, control over the look and feel of an application, and rich networking services. The challenge was to blur the line between Web applications and Windows applications.

Integrate Developers and Designers

As applications become graphically richer and cater more to user experience, an entirely new community must be integrated into the development process. Media companies (print, online, television, etc.) have long known that a variety of designer roles need to be filled to create a great experience for customers, and now we are seeing that same requirement for software applications. Historically the tools that designers used were completely disconnected from the software construction process: Designers used tools like Adobe Photoshop or Adobe Illustrator to create rich designs, only to have developers balk when they tried to implement them. Creating a unified system that could natively support the features that designers required, and using a markup format (XAML) that would allow for seamless interoperability between tools, were two of the outcomes of this principle.

About This Book

Many books on WPF are, and will be, available. When I first thought of writing a book, I wanted to make sure that mine would offer something unique. This book is designed for application developers; it is intended as a conceptual reference book covering most of WPF.

I chose each word in the preceding statement carefully.

This book is about applications. There are really two types of software: software designed to communicate with people, and software designed to communicate with software. I use the term *application* to mean software written primarily for communication with people. Fundamentally, WPF is all about communication with people.

This is a book for *developers.* I wanted to present a very code-centric view of the platform. I'm a developer first and foremost, and in working as an architect on the WPF team I have always considered the external developer as my number one customer. This book focuses on topics primarily for the application developer. Although a control developer will also find a lot of useful information in this book, its purpose is not to present a guide for building custom controls.

This book is about *concepts,* not just APIs. If you want an API reference, use Google or MSN search features and browse the MSDN documentation. I want to raise the abstraction and present the hows and whys of the platform design and show how the various APIs of the platform work together to add value to developers.

This book is a reference; it is organized by technical topics so that you can flip back to a section later or flip forward to a section to answer a question. You do not need to read the book from cover to cover to gain value from it.

This book covers most of WPF, not all of it. When I started writing the book, Chris Sells gave me an important piece of advice: "What you leave out is as important as what you include." Because WPF is an immense platform, to present the big picture I had to omit parts of it. This book represents what I believe are the best landmarks from which to explore the platform.

My goal with this book is to provide a map of the core concepts, how they relate to each other, and what motivated their design. I hope you'll come away from this book with a broad understanding of WPF and be able to explore the depth of the platform yourself.

Prerequisites

Before reading this book, you should be familiar with .NET. You don't need to be an expert, but you should be familiar with the basics of classes, methods, and events. The book uses only C# code in its examples. WPF is equally accessible in any .NET language; however, C# is what I use primarily for my development.

Organization

This book is organized into eight chapters and a three-part appendix. My goal was to tell the story of the WPF platform in as few chapters as possible.

- **Introduction** (Chapter 1) briefly introduces the platform and explains how the seven major components of WPF fit together. This chapter also serves as a quick start for building applications with WPF, showing how to use the SDK tools and find content in the documentation.
- **Applications** (Chapter 2) covers the structure of applications built using WPF, as well as the application services and top-level objects used by applications.
- **Controls** (Chapter 3) covers both the major design patterns in WPF controls and the major control families in WPF. Controls are the fundamental building blocks of user interfaces in WPF; if you read only one chapter in the book, this is the one.
- **Layout** (Chapter 4) covers the design of the layout system, and an overview of the six stock layout panels that ship in WPF.
- **Visuals** (Chapter 5), provides an overview of the huge surface area that is the WPF visual system. The chapter covers typography, 2D and 3D graphics, animation, video, and audio.
- **Data** (Chapter 6) covers the basics of data sources, data binding, resources, and data transfer operations.
- **Actions** (Chapter 7) provides an overview of how events, commands, and triggers work to make things happen in your application.

- **Styles** (Chapter 8) covers the styling system in WPF. Styling enables the clean separation of the designer and developer by allowing a loose coupling between the visual appearance of a UI and the programmatic structure.
- The appendix, **Base Services,** drills down into some of the low-level services in WPF. Topics covered include threading model, the property and event system, input, composition, and printing.

Acknowledgments

This book has been a massive undertaking for me. I've worked on articles, presentations, and white papers before, but nothing prepared me for the sheer volume of work it takes to condense a platform the size of WPF into a relatively short book.

I've dedicated this book to my wife, Megan. She has been constantly supportive of this project (even when I brought a laptop on numerous vacations!) and everything else I do.

The entire Avalon team has been a huge help in the creation of this book (and the product!). My manager, Ian Ellison-Taylor, supported my working on this project. Sam Bent, Jeff Bogdan, Vivek Dalvi, Namita Gupta, Mike Hillberg, Robert Ingebretsen, David Jenni, Lauren Lavoie, Ashraf Michail, Kevin Moore, Greg Schechter—the team members who helped are too many to list. I thoroughly enjoyed working with everyone on the team.

I am grateful to Don Box for pushing me to write the book, and to Chris Sells for giving me sage advice even while we were creating competing books.

My developmental editor, Michael Weinhardt, deserves a huge amount of credit for the quality of this book. Michael read, reread, edited, and re-edited every section of this book. He pushed me to never accept anything that isn't great. All the errors and bad transitions in the book are purely my fault.

Joan Murray, Karen Gettman, Julie Nahil, and the entire staff at Addison-Wesley, have done an amazing job dealing with me on this book. Stephanie Hiebert, my copy editor, spent countless hours pouring over my poor spelling, grammar, and prose, turning my ramblings into the English language.

Finally, I want to thank the technical reviewers of this book. Erick Ellis, Joe Flanigan, Jessica Fosler, Christophe Nasarre, Nick Paldino, Chris Sells, and a host of others provided great feedback. Jessica gave me some of the deepest and most constructively critical feedback that I've ever received.

I'm sure I'm forgetting many other people, and for that I apologize.

Chris Anderson
November 2006
simplegeek.com

About the Author

Chris Anderson is an architect at Microsoft in the Connected Systems Division. Chris's primary focus is the design and architecture of .NET technologies used to implement the next generation of applications and services.

During his ten years at Microsoft, Chris has worked on Visual Basic 6.0, Visual J++ 6.0, .NET Framework 1.0 and 1.1, and most recently, Windows Presentation Foundation. Most of Chris's career has involved working on presentation technologies—building controls for Visual Basic, developing Windows Foundation Classes for Visual J++, and working on Windows Forms and ASP.NET in the .NET Framework.

In 2002, Chris joined the Windows Client team as lead architect for Windows Presentation Foundation. Through his experience and expertise, Chris has presented and been a keynote speaker at numerous conferences (PDC, Tech-Ed, Win-Dev, DevCon, etc.) worldwide. Chris also has published numerous articles in both print and online publications.

Chris's other "addictions" include digital photography, blogging, video games, scuba diving, powerboating, and home theaters—all of which his wife, Megan, patiently puts up with.

This is Chris Anderson's first book.

■ 1 ■

Introduction

WINDOWS PRESENTATION FOUNDATION (WPF) represents a major step forward in user interface technology. This chapter will lay out some of the basic principles of WPF and walk through a quick overview of the entire platform. You can think of this chapter as a preview of the rest of the book.

WPF as the New GUI

Before we dive into WPF proper, it is interesting to consider where we're coming from.

User32, à la Charles Petzold

Anyone programming to User32 has, at some point, read one of Petzold's "Programming Windows" books. They all start with an example something like this:

```
#include <windows.h>
LRESULT CALLBACK WndProc(HWND hwnd,
            UINT msg,
            WPARAM wparam,
            LPARAM lparam);
INT WINAPI WinMain(HINSTANCE hInstance, HINSTANCE hPrevInstance,
        LPSTR cmdline, int cmdshow) {
  MSG         msg;
  HWND        hwnd;
  WNDCLASSEX  wndclass = { 0 };
  wndclass.cbSize         = sizeof(WNDCLASSEX);
```

```
wndclass.style          = CS_HREDRAW | CS_VREDRAW;
wndclass.lpfnWndProc    = WndProc;
wndclass.hIcon          = LoadIcon(NULL, IDI_APPLICATION);
wndclass.hCursor        = LoadCursor(NULL, IDC_ARROW);
wndclass.hbrBackground  = (HBRUSH)GetStockObject(WHITE_BRUSH);
wndclass.lpszClassName  = TEXT("Window1");
wndclass.hInstance      = hInstance;
wndclass.hIconSm        = LoadIcon(NULL, IDI_APPLICATION);
RegisterClassEx(&wndclass);
hwnd = CreateWindow(TEXT("Window1"),
        TEXT("Hello World"),
        WS_OVERLAPPEDWINDOW,
        CW_USEDEFAULT,
        0,
        CW_USEDEFAULT,
        0,
        NULL,
        NULL,
        hInstance,
        NULL);

  if( !hwnd )
    return 0;
  ShowWindow(hwnd, SW_SHOWNORMAL);
  UpdateWindow(hwnd);
  while( GetMessage(&msg, NULL, 0, 0) ) {
    TranslateMessage(&msg);
    DispatchMessage(&msg);
  }
  return msg.wParam;
}
LRESULT CALLBACK WndProc(HWND hwnd, UINT msg,
        WPARAM wparam, LPARAM lparam) {
  switch(msg) {
    case WM_DESTROY:
      PostQuitMessage(WM_QUIT);
      break;
    default:
      return DefWindowProc(hwnd, msg, wparam, lparam);
  }
  return 0;
}
```

This is "Hello World" when talking to User32. There are some very interesting things going on here. A specialized type (Window1) is first defined by the calling of RegisterClassEx, then instantiated (CreateWindow) and displayed (ShowWindow). Finally, a message loop is run to let the window receive user input and events from the system (GetMessage, TranslateMessage, and `DispatchMessage`). This program is largely unchanged from the original introduction of User back in the Windows 1.0 days.

Windows Forms took this complex programming model and produced a clean managed object model on top of the system, making it far simpler to program. Hello World can be written in Windows Forms with ten lines of code:

```
using System.Windows.Forms;
using System;

class Program {
  [STAThread]
  static void Main() {
    Form f = new Form();
    f.Text = "Hello World";
    Application.Run(f);
  }
}
```

A primary goal of WPF is to preserve as much developer knowledge as possible. Even though WPF is a new presentation system completely different from Windows Forms, we can write the equivalent program in WPF with very similar code[1] (changes are in boldface):

```
using System.Windows;
using System;

class Program {
  [STAThread]
  static void Main() {
    Window f = new Window();
    f.Title = "Hello World";
    new Application().Run(f);
  }
}
```

In both cases the call to `Run` on the `Application` object is the replacement for the message loop, and the standard CLR (Common Language Runtime) type system is used for defining instances and types. Windows

---

1. As programs become more complex, the differences between WPF and Windows Forms become more apparent.

Forms is really a managed layer on top of User32, and it is therefore limited to only the fundamental features that User32 provides.

User32 is a great 2D widget platform. It is based on an on-demand, clip-based painting system; that is, when a widget needs to be displayed, the system calls back to the user code (on demand) to paint within a bounding box that it protects (with clipping). The great thing about clip-based painting systems is that they're fast; no memory is wasted on buffering the content of a widget, nor are any cycles wasted on painting anything but the widget that has been changed.

The downsides of on-demand, clip-based painting systems relate mainly to responsiveness and composition. In the first case, because the system has to call back to user code to paint anything, often one component may prevent other components from painting. This problem is evident in Windows when an application hangs and goes white, or stops painting correctly. In the second case, it is extremely difficult to have a single pixel affected by two components, yet that capability is desirable in many scenarios—for example, partial opacity, anti-aliasing, and shadows.

With overlapping Windows Forms controls, the downsides of this system become clear (Figure 1.1). When the controls overlap, the system needs to clip each one. Notice the gray area around the word *linkLabel1* in Figure 1.1.

WPF is based on a retained-mode composition system. For each component a list of drawing instructions is maintained, allowing for the system to automatically render the contents of any widget without interacting with

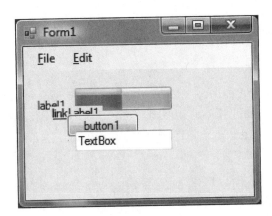

FIGURE 1.1: Windows Forms controls overlapping. Notice that each control obscures the others.

user code. In addition, the system is implemented with a **painter's algorithm,** which ensures that overlapping widgets are painted from back to front, allowing them to paint on top of each other. This model lets the system manage the graphics resource, in much the same way that the CLR manages memory, to achieve some great effects. The system can perform high-speed animations, send drawing instructions to another machine, or even project the display onto 3D surfaces—all without the widget being aware of the complexity.

To see these effects, compare Figures 1.1 and 1.2. In Figure 1.2 the opacity on all the WPF controls is set so that they're partially transparent, even to the background image.

WPF's composition system is, at its heart, a vector-based system, meaning that all painting is done through a series of lines. Figure 1.3 shows how vector graphics compare to traditional raster graphics.

The system also supports complete transform models, with scale, rotation, and skew. As Figure 1.4 shows, any transformation can be applied to any control, producing bizarre effects even while keeping the controls live and usable.

Note that when User32 and GDI32 were developed, there was really no notion of container nesting. The design principle was that a flat list of children existed under a single parent window. The concept worked well for

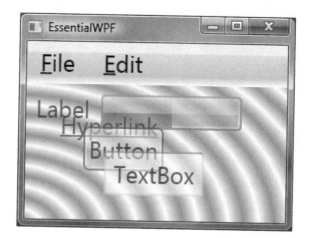

FIGURE 1.2: WPF controls overlapping, with opacity set to semitransparency. Notice that all the controls compositing together are visible, including the background image.

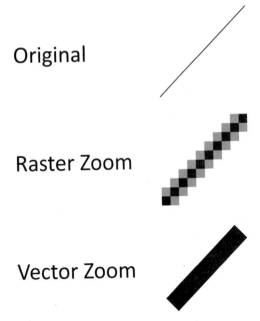

FIGURE 1.3: Comparing vector and raster graphics. Notice that zooming in on a vector graphic does not reduce its crispness.

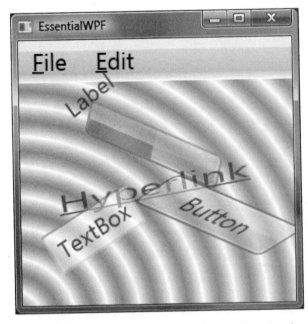

FIGURE 1.4: WPF controls with a variety of transformations applied. Despite the transformations, these controls remain fully functional.

FIGURE 1.5: WPF controls are built out of composition and containment. The button shown here contains both text and an image.

the simple dialogs of the 1990s, but today's complex user interfaces require nesting. The simplest example of this problem is the GroupBox control. In the User32 design, GroupBox is behind controls but doesn't contain them. Windows Forms does support nesting, but that feature has revealed many problems with the underlying User32 model of control.

In WPF's composition engine, all controls are contained, grouped, and composited. A button in WPF is actually made up of several smaller controls. This move to embrace composition, coupled with a vector-based approach, enables any level of containment (Figure 1.5).

To really see the power of this composition, examine Figure 1.6. At the maximum zoom shown, the entire circle represents less than a pixel on the original button. The button actually contains a vector image that contains a complete text document that contains a button that contains another image.

In addition to addressing the limitations of User32 and GDI32, one of WPF's goals was to bring many of the best features from the Web programming model to Windows developers.

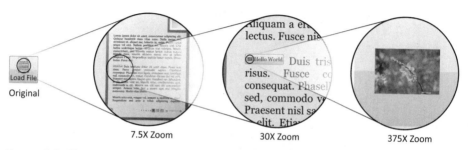

FIGURE 1.6: The power of composition, as revealed by zooming in on the composite button shown in Figure 1.5

HTML, a.k.a. the Web

One of the biggest assets of Web development is a simple entry to creating content. The most basic HTML "program" is really nothing more than a few HTML tags in a text file:

```html
<html>
  <head>
    <title>Hello World</title>
  </head>
  <body>
    <p>Welcome to my document!</p>
  </body>
</html>
```

In fact, all of these tags can be omitted, and we can simply create a file with the text "Welcome to my document!", name it `<something>.html`, and view it in a browser (Figure 1.7). This amazingly low barrier to entry has made developers out of millions of people who never thought they could program anything.

In WPF we can accomplish the same thing using a new markup format called **XAML** (Extensible Application Markup Language), pronounced "zammel." Because XAML is a dialect of XML, it requires a slightly stricter syntax. Probably the most obvious requirement is that the `xmlns` directive must be used to associate the namespace with each tag:

```xml
<FlowDocument
  xmlns='http://schemas.microsoft.com/winfx/2006/xaml/presentation'>

  <Paragraph>Welcome to my document!</Paragraph>
</FlowDocument>
```

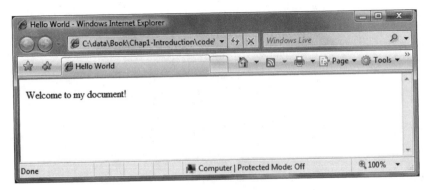

FIGURE 1.7: Displaying a simple HTML document in Internet Explorer

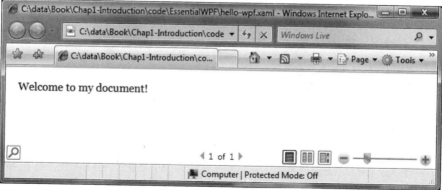

FIGURE 1.8: Displaying a WPF document in Internet Explorer

You can view the file by double-clicking `<something>.xaml` (Figure 1.8).

Of course, we can leverage all the power of WPF in this simple markup. We can trivially implement the button display from Figure 1.5 using markup, and display it in the browser (Figure 1.9).

One of the big limitations of the HTML model is that it really only works for creating applications that are hosted in the browser. With XAML markup, either we can use it in a loose markup format and host it in the

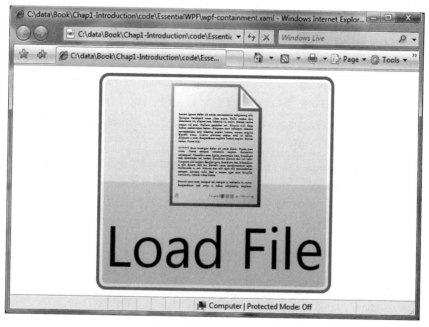

FIGURE 1.9: Displaying a WPF document in Internet Explorer using controls and layout from WPF

FIGURE 1.10: Running an application authored in XAML. The program can be run in a top-level window or hosted in a browser.

browser, as we have just seen, or we can compile it into an application and create a standard Windows application using markup (Figure 1.10):

```
<Window
   xmlns='http://schemas.microsoft.com/winfx/2006/xaml/presentation'
   Title='Hello World!'>

   <Button>Hello World!</Button>
</Window>
```

Programming capability in HTML comes in three flavors: declarative, scripting, and server-side. **Declarative programming** is something that many people don't think of as programming. We can define behavior in HTML with simple markup tags like <form /> that let us perform actions (generally posting data back to the server). **Script programming** lets us use JavaScript to program against the HTML Document Object Model (DOM). Script programming is becoming much more fashionable because now enough browsers have support for a common scripting model to make scripts run everywhere. **Server-side programming** lets us write logic on the server that interacts with the user (in the Microsoft platform, that means ASP.NET programming).

ASP.NET provides a very nice way to generate HTML content. Using repeaters, data binding, and event handlers, we can write simple server-side code to create simple applications. One of the more trivial examples is simple markup injection:

```
<%@ Page %>
<html>
  <body>
    <p><%=DateTime.Now().ToString()%></p>
  </body>
</html>
```

The real power of ASP.NET comes in the rich library of server controls and services. Using a single control like `DataGrid`, we can generate reams of HTML content; and with services like membership we can create Web sites with authentication easily.

The big limitation of this model is the requirement to be online. Modern applications are expected to run offline or in occasionally connected scenarios. WPF takes many of the features from ASP.NET—repeaters and data binding, for example—and gives them to Windows developers with the additional ability to run offline.

One of the primary objectives of WPF was to bring together the best features of both Windows development and the Web model. Before we look at the features of WPF, it is important to understand the new programming model in the .NET Framework 3.0: XAML.

A Brief Look at the XAML Programming Model

One of the major, and often misunderstood, features of .NET 3.0 is the new XAML programming model. XAML provides a set of semantics on top of raw XML that enables a common interpretation. To oversimplify slightly, XAML is an XML-based instantiation script for CLR objects. There is a mapping from XML tags to CLR types, and from XML attributes to CLR properties and events. The following example shows an object being created and a property being set in both XAML and C#:

```
<!-- XAML version -->
<MyObject
  SomeProperty='1' />

// C# version
MyObject obj = new MyObject();
obj.SomeProperty = 1;
```

XML tags are always defined in the context of a namespace. That namespace determines what tags are valid. In XAML we map XML namespaces to collections of CLR namespaces and assemblies. To make the simple example that was just illustrated work, we need to map in the required namespaces. In XML, we use the `xmlns` attribute to define new namespaces:

```
<!-- XAML version -->
<MyObject
  xmlns='clr-namespace:Samples'
  SomeProperty='1' />

// C# version
using Samples;

MyObject obj = new MyObject();
obj.SomeProperty = 1;
```

In C#, the list of assemblies where types are found is always determined by the project file or the command-line arguments to `csc.exe`. In XAML, we can specify the location of the source assembly for each namespace:

```
<!-- XAML version -->
<MyObject
  xmlns='clr-namespace:Samples;assembly=samples.dll'
  SomeProperty='1' />

// C# version
csc /r:samples.dll test.cs

using Samples;

MyObject obj = new MyObject();
obj.SomeProperty = 1;
```

In XML the world is divided into two spaces: elements and attributes. In terms of objects, properties, and events, the XAML model is more closely aligned with the CLR. The encoding to attributes or child elements for property values is flexible. We can rewrite the previous example using a child element instead:

```
<MyObject
  xmlns='clr-namespace:Samples;assembly=samples.dll'>
  <MyObject.SomeProperty>
    1
  </MyObject.SomeProperty>
</MyObject>
```

Every property element is qualified with the type that defines the property, allowing properties to contain arbitrarily complex structured data. For example, suppose we have a second property that takes a `Person` object with `FirstName` and `LastName` properties. We can easily write the code in XAML using the property element syntax:

```
<MyObject
  xmlns='clr-namespace:Samples;assembly=samples.dll'>
  <MyObject.Owner>
    <Person FirstName='Chris' LastName='Anderson' />
  </MyObject.Owner>
</MyObject>
```

XAML was created to be a markup language that integrated well with the CLR and provided for rich tool support. A secondary goal was to create a markup format that was easy to read and write. It may seem a little rude to design a feature of the platform that is optimized first for tools, then for humans, but the WPF team felt strongly that WPF applications would typically be authored with the assistance of a visual design tool like Microsoft Visual Studio or Microsoft Expression. To walk the line between tools and humans, WPF allows the type author to define one property to be the content property.[2]

In our example, if we make the `Owner` property of `MyObject` the content property,[3] then the markup can be changed to omit the property element tag:

```
<MyObject
  xmlns='clr-namespace:Samples;assembly=samples.dll'>

  <Person FirstName='Megan' LastName='Anderson' />
</MyObject>
```

For further readability, XAML has a feature known as **markup extensions.** This is a general way to extend the markup parser to produce simpler markup. Markup extensions are implemented as CLR types, and they work almost exactly like CLR attribute definitions. Markup extensions are enclosed in curly braces, { }. For example, to set a property value to the special value null, we can use the built-in `Null` markup extension:

```
<MyObject
  xmlns='clr-namespace:Samples;assembly=samples.dll'>

  <Person FirstName='Megan' LastName='{x:Null}' />
</MyObject>
```

Table 1.1 lists all of the built-in XAML features.

---

2. This is similar to the Visual Basic "default property" feature.
3. We can do this by adding `System.Windows.Markup.ContentPropertyAttribute` to the type.

TABLE 1.1: Built-in XAML Features

XAML Namespace Directive	Meaning	Example

x:Array	Creates a CLR array.	```<x:Array Type='{x:Type Button}'>`` `<Button />`
		`<Button />`
		`</x:Array>```

x:Class	Specifies the name of the type to define (used only in markup compilation).	`<Window`
		`x:Class='MyNamespace.MyClass'>...`
		`</Window>`

x:ClassModifier	Specifies the modifiers ("public," "internal," etc.) of the type to define (used only in markup compilation).	`<Window x:Class='...'`
		`  x:ClassModifier='Public'>`
		`...`
		`</Window>`

x:Code	Delineates a block of in-line code (used only in markup compilation).	`<Window x:Class='...'>`
		`  <x:Code>`
		`    public void DoSomething() {`
		`      ...`
		`    }`
		`  </x:Code>`
		`  ...`
		`</Window>`

x:Key	Specifies the key to use for an element (supported only on elements contained in a dictionary).	`<Button>`
		`  <Button.Resources>`
		`    <Style x:Key='Hi'>...</Style>`
		`  </Button.Resources>`
		`</Button>`

x:Name	Specifies the programmatic name of an element (typically used when an element doesn't have a built-in name property).	`<sys:Int32`
		`  xmlns:sys='clr-namespace:`
		`System;...'`
		`  x:Name='_myIntegerValue'>`
		`5</sys:Int32>`

x:Null	Creates a null value.	`<Button Content='{x:Null}' />`

x:Static	Creates a value by accessing a static field or property from a type.	`<Button`
		`  Command='{x:Static`
		`ApplicationCommands.Close}' />`

XAML Namespace Directive	Meaning	Example
x:Subclass	Provides a base type for markup compilation for languages that don't support partial types.	
x:Type	Provides a CLR type (equivalent to Type.GetType).	```<ControlTemplate` ` TargetType='{x:Type Button}'>` `...` `</ControlTemplate>```
x:TypeArguments	Specifies the generic type arguments for instantiating a generic type.	```<gc:List` `xmlns:gc='clr-` `namespace:System.Collections.` `Generic;...'` ` x:TypeArguments='{x:Type Button}' />```
x:XData	Delineates a block of in-line XML; may be used only for properties of type IXmlSerializable.	```<XmlDataSource>` ` <x:XData>` ` <Book xmlns='' Title='...' />` ` </x:XData>` `</XmlDataSource>```

Markup extensions are resolved exactly like object tags, which means that we must declare the "x" XML prefix for this markup to be parsed. XAML defines a special namespace for dealing with the parser built-in types:

```
<MyObject
  xmlns:x='http://schemas.microsoft.com/winfx/2006/xaml'
  xmlns='clr-namespace:Samples;assembly=samples.dll'>

  <Person FirstName='Megan' LastName='{x:Null}' />
</MyObject>
```

It is also possible for any CLR assembly (or set of assemblies) to define a URI-based name for a collection of CLR namespaces and assemblies. This is the equivalent of the old #include 'windows.h' statement that C/C++ developers know. The WPF assemblies use this mechanism, so we can use either format to import WPF into a XAML file:

```
<!-- option 1: import by CLR namespace -->
<Window
  xmlns:x='http://schemas.microsoft.com/winfx/2006/xaml'
  xmlns=
    'clr-namespace:System.Windows;assembly=presentationframework.dll'>
</Window>

<!-- option 2: import by URI -->
<Window
  xmlns:x='http://schemas.microsoft.com/winfx/2006/xaml'
  xmlns='http://schemas.microsoft.com/winfx/2006/xaml/presentation'>
</Window>
```

The nice thing about the URI-based method is that it imports several CLR namespaces and assemblies, meaning that your markup is more compact and easier to work with.

The final feature of XAML is the ability to extend types with properties provided by other types; we call this feature **attached properties.** In effect, attached properties are just type-safe versions of the JavaScript expando properties. In the WPF version of XAML, attached properties work only if the type defining the property and the type whose property is being set both derive from the DependencyObject type, but the specification for XAML doesn't have this requirement.

In the following example the property Dock is defined by the type Dock-Panel. Attached properties are always prefixed by the name of the type providing the property, even when they appear as attributes:

```
<Window
  xmlns:x='http://schemas.microsoft.com/winfx/2006/xaml'
  xmlns='http://schemas.microsoft.com/winfx/2006/xaml/presentation'>

  <DockPanel>
    <Button DockPanel.Dock='Top'>Top</Button>
    <Button>
      <DockPanel.Dock>Left</DockPanel.Dock>
      Left
    </Button>
    <Button>Fill</Button>
  </DockPanel>
</Window>
```

XAML is a fairly simple language with relatively few rules. In the .NET Framework 3.0 release of XAML, all the definitions for XAML tags are in

CLR types—the goal being to ensure that anything we can do in markup we can also do in code. Throughout this book I will switch back and forth between using markup[4] and using code, depending on whichever one more easily demonstrates a particular concept.

Now that we have a grounding of XAML under our belts, we can begin looking at the main parts of WPF itself.

A Tour of WPF

When I started writing this book, I wanted to make it as short as possible, but no shorter (my apologies to Dr. Einstein). Even with that philosophy, I wanted to give you, the reader, a quick overview of the platform to provide a grounding in all the basic concepts you need to get started.

Getting Up and Running

There are many ways to approach WPF: from the browser, from markup, or from code. I've been programming for so long that I can't help but start from a simple C# program. Every WPF application starts with the creation of an `Application` object. The `Application` object controls the lifetime of the application and is responsible for delivering events and messages to the running program.

In addition to the `Application` object, most programs want to display something to a human. In WPF that means creating a window.[5] We've already seen the basic WPF application source code, so this should come as no surprise to you:

```
using System.Windows;
using System;
```

---

4. After this chapter, I will omit the "…/xaml/presentation" and "…/xaml" namespaces from markup samples. I will consistently map the presentation (WPF) namespace to be the default XML namespace, and "x" as the prefix for the XAML namespace.
5. We will see later that even in navigation scenarios a window is created for page-based applications.

```
class Program {
  [STAThread]
  static void Main() {
    Application app = new Application();
    Window w = new Window();
    w.Title = "Hello World";
    app.Run(w);
  }
}
```

To compile this code, we need to invoke the C# compiler. We have two options; the first is to directly invoke the C# compiler on the command line. We must include three reference assemblies to compile against WPF. The locations of the tools for building WPF applications depend on how they were installed. The following example shows how to compile this program if the .NET Framework 3.0 SDK has been installed and we're running in the build window provided:

```
csc /r:"%ReferenceAssemblies%"\WindowsBase.dll
  /r:"%ReferenceAssemblies%"\PresentationCore.dll
  /r:"%ReferenceAssemblies%"\PresentationFramework.dll
  /t:winexe
  /out:bin\debug\tour.exe
  program.cs
```

Compiling with C# directly works great for a single file and a couple of references. A better option, however, is to use the new build engine included with the .NET Framework 3.0 SDK and Visual Studio 2005: MSBuild. Creating an MSBuild project file is relatively simple. Here we convert the command line into a project file:

```
<Project
  DefaultTargets='Build'
  xmlns='http://schemas.microsoft.com/developer/msbuild/2003'>

  <PropertyGroup>
    <Configuration>Debug</Configuration>
    <Platform>AnyCPU</Platform>
    <RootNamespace>Tour</RootNamespace>
    <AssemblyName>Tour</AssemblyName>
    <OutputType>winexe</OutputType>
    <OutputPath>.\bin\Debug\</OutputPath>
  </PropertyGroup>

  <ItemGroup>
    <Reference Include='System' />
    <Reference Include='WindowsBase' />
```

```
    <Reference Include='PresentationCore' />
    <Reference Include='PresentationFramework' />
  </ItemGroup>

  <ItemGroup>
    <Compile Include='program.cs' />
  </ItemGroup>

  <Import Project='$(MSBuildBinPath)\Microsoft.CSharp.targets' />
  <Import Project='$(MSBuildBinPath)\Microsoft.WinFX.targets' />
</Project>
```

To compile the application, we can now invoke MSBuild at the command line:

```
msbuild tour.csproj
```

Running the application will display the window shown in Figure 1.11.

With our program up and running, we can think about how to build something interesting. One of the most visible changes in WPF (at least to the developer community) is the deep integration of markup in the platform. Using XAML to build an application is generally much simpler.

Moving to Markup

To build our program using markup, we will start by defining the Application object. We can create a new XAML file, called App.xaml, with the following content:

```
<Application
  xmlns='http://schemas.microsoft.com/winfx/2006/xaml/presentation'
  />
```

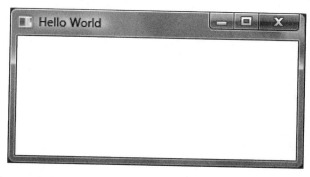

FIGURE 1.11: Empty window created in an application

As before, it isn't very interesting to run. We can define a window using the `MainWindow` property of `Application`:

```
<Application
  xmlns='http://schemas.microsoft.com/winfx/2006/xaml/presentation'>
  <Application.MainWindow>
    <Window Title='Hello World' Visibility='Visible' />
  </Application.MainWindow>
</Application>
```

To compile this code, we need to update our project file to include the application definition:

```
<Project ...>
  ...
  <ItemGroup>
    <ApplicationDefinition Include='app.xaml' />
  </ItemGroup>
  ...
</Project>
```

If we were to build now, we would get an error because, by including our application definition, we have automatically defined a "Main" function that conflicts with the existing `program.cs`. So we can remove `program.cs` from the list of items in the project, and we are left with just the application definition. At this point, running the application produces exactly the same result as Figure 1.11 shows.

Instead of defining our window inside of the application definition, it is normal to define new types in separate XAML files. We can move the window definition into a separate file, `MyWindow.xaml`:

```
<Window
  xmlns='http://schemas.microsoft.com/winfx/2006/xaml/presentation'
  Title='Hello World'
>
</Window>
```

We can then update the application definition to refer to this markup:

```
<Application
  xmlns='http://schemas.microsoft.com/winfx/2006/xaml/presentation'
  StartupUri='MyWindow.xaml'
  />
```

Finally, we need to add the window to the project file. For any compiled markup (except the application definition), we use the `Page` build type:

```
<Project ...>
  ...
  <ItemGroup>
    <Page Include='mywindow.xaml' />
    <ApplicationDefinition Include='app.xaml' />
  </ItemGroup>
  ...
</Project>
```

Now we have a basic program up and running, well factored, and ready to explore WPF.

The Basics

Applications in WPF consist of many controls, composited together. The `Window` object that we have already seen is the first example of one of these controls. One of the more familiar controls is `Button`:

```
<Window
  xmlns='http://schemas.microsoft.com/winfx/2006/xaml/presentation'
  Title='Hello World'
  >
  <Button>Howdy!</Button>
</Window>
```

Running this code will produce something like Figure 1.12. The first interesting thing to notice here is that the button automatically fills the entire area of the window. If the window is resized, the button continues to fill the space.

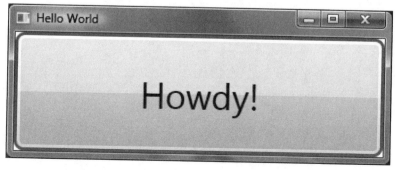

FIGURE 1.12: A simple button in a window

All controls in WPF have a certain type of layout. In the layout for a window, a single child control fills the window. To put more than one control inside of a window, we need to use some type of container control. A very common type of container control in WPF is a **layout panel.**

Layout panels accept multiple children and enforce some type of layout policy. Probably the simplest layout is the stack:

```
<Window
  xmlns='http://schemas.microsoft.com/winfx/2006/xaml/presentation'
  Title='Hello World'
  >
  <StackPanel>
    <Button>Howdy!</Button>
    <Button>A second button</Button>
  </StackPanel>
</Window>
```

StackPanel works by stacking controls one on top of another (shown in Figure 1.13).

A lot more controls, and a lot more layouts, are included in WPF (and, of course, you can build new ones). To look at a few other controls, we can add them to our markup:

FIGURE 1.13: Two buttons inside of a stack panel

```
<Window
  xmlns='http://schemas.microsoft.com/winfx/2006/xaml/presentation'
  Title='Hello World'
  >
  <StackPanel>
    <Button>Howdy!</Button>
    <Button>A second button</Button>
    <TextBox>An editable text box</TextBox>
    <CheckBox>A check box</CheckBox>
    <Slider Width='75' Minimum='0' Maximum='100' Value='50' />
  </StackPanel>
</Window>
```

Running this code shows that you can interact with all the controls (Figure 1.14).

To see different layouts, we can replace StackPanel. Here we swap in WrapPanel:

```
<Window
  xmlns='http://schemas.microsoft.com/winfx/2006/xaml/presentation'
  Title='Hello World'
  >
  <WrapPanel>
    <Button>Howdy!</Button>
    <Button>A second button</Button>
    <TextBox>An editable text box</TextBox>
    <CheckBox>A check box</CheckBox>
    <Slider Width='75' Minimum='0' Maximum='100' Value='50' />
  </WrapPanel>
</Window>
```

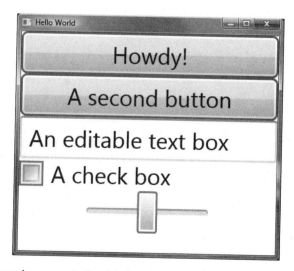

FIGURE 1.14: Several more controls added to a window

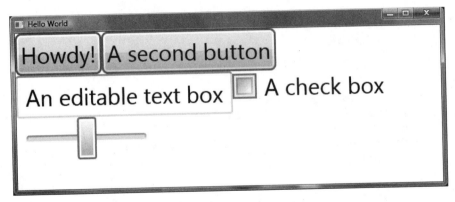

FIGURE 1.15: Several controls inside of a wrap panel

Running this code reveals a noticeable difference in the layout of the controls (Figure 1.15).

Now that we have seen some controls, let's write some code that interacts with the controls. Associating a markup file with code requires several steps. First we must provide a class name for the markup file:

```
<Window
    x:Class='EssentialWPF.MyWindow'
    xmlns:x='http://schemas.microsoft.com/winfx/2006/xaml'
    xmlns='http://schemas.microsoft.com/winfx/2006/xaml/presentation'
    Title='Hello World'
    >
    <WrapPanel>
      <Button>Howdy!</Button>
      <Button>A second button</Button>
      <TextBox>An editable text box</TextBox>
      <CheckBox>A check box </CheckBox>
      <Slider Width='75' Minimum='0' Maximum='100' Value='50' />
    </WrapPanel>
</Window>
```

It is also very common to use the C# 2.0 feature of partial types to associate some additional code with the markup file. To define a code-behind file, we need to create a C# class with the same name[6] that we specified in

---

6. The naming convention for code-behind files is "<markupfile>.cs", so for mywindow.xaml we would create a file called mywindow.xaml.cs.

the markup file. We must also call `InitializeComponent` from the constructor of our class:[7]

```
using System;
using System.Windows.Controls;
using System.Windows;

namespace EssentialWPF {
  public partial class MyWindow : Window {
    public MyWindow() {
      InitializeComponent();
    }
  }
}
```

To finish associating our code with the markup, we need to update the project file to include the newly defined C# file:

```
<Project ...>
  ...
  <ItemGroup>
    <Compile Include='mywindow.xaml.cs' />
    <Page Include='mywindow.xaml' />
    <ApplicationDefinition Include='app.xaml' />
  </ItemGroup>
  ...
</Project>
```

Because our code doesn't do anything interesting, there isn't a lot to see if we run the program. The most common link between a code-behind file and the markup file is an event handler. Controls generally expose one or more events, which can be handled in code. Handling an event requires only specifying the event handler method name in the markup file:

```
<Window
  x:Class='EssentialWPF.MyWindow'
  xmlns:x='http://schemas.microsoft.com/winfx/2006/xaml'
  xmlns='http://schemas.microsoft.com/winfx/2006/xaml/presentation'
  Title='Hello World'
  >
<WrapPanel>
  <Button Click='HowdyClicked'>Howdy!</Button>
  <Button>A second button</Button>
```

---

7. Chapter 2 will explain why this step is required.

```
      <TextBox>An editable text box</TextBox>
      <CheckBox>A check box </CheckBox>
      <Slider Width='75' Minimum='0' Maximum='100' Value='50' />
    </WrapPanel>
</Window>
```

We can then implement the method in the code-behind file:

```
using System;
using System.Windows.Controls;
using System.Windows;

namespace EssentialWPF {
  public partial class MyWindow : Window {
    public MyWindow() {
      InitializeComponent();
    }
    void HowdyClicked(object sender, RoutedEventArgs e) {
    }
  }
}
```

To access any control from the code-behind file, we must provide a name for the control:

```
<Window
  x:Class='EssentialWPF.MyWindow'
  xmlns:x='http://schemas.microsoft.com/winfx/2006/xaml'
  xmlns='http://schemas.microsoft.com/winfx/2006/xaml/presentation'
  Title='Hello World'
  >
  <WrapPanel>
    <Button Click='HowdyClicked'>Howdy!</Button>
    <Button>A second button</Button>
    <TextBox x:Name='_text1'>An editable text box</TextBox>
    <CheckBox>A check box </CheckBox>
    <Slider Width='75' Minimum='0' Maximum='100' Value='50' />
  </WrapPanel>
</Window>
```

We can then use the specified name in the code-behind file:

```
using System;
using System.Windows.Controls;
using System.Windows;

namespace EssentialWPF {
  public partial class MyWindow : Window {
```

```
    public MyWindow() {
      InitializeComponent();
    }
    void HowdyClicked(object sender, RoutedEventArgs e) {
      _text1.Text = "Hello from C#";
    }
  }
}
```

Running this application and clicking the **Howdy!** button reveals something like Figure 1.16.

Beyond the basics of controls, layout, and events, probably the most common thing to do is have an application interact with data.

Working with Data

WPF has a deep dependency on data and data binding. A look at one of the most basic controls shows many types of binding:

```
Button b = new Button();
b.Content = "Hello World";
```

At least three types of binding are occurring here. First, the way a button is displayed is determined by a type of binding. Every control has a `Resources` property, which is a dictionary that can contain styles, templates, or any other type of data. Controls then can bind to these resources.

Second, the data type of the content of a button is `System.Object`. `Button` can take any data and display it. Most controls in WPF leverage what is called the **content model,** which, at its core, enables rich content and data presentation. For example, instead of a string, we can create buttons with almost any content.

Third, the basic implementation of both the button's display and the core content model uses data binding to wire up properties from the control to the display elements.

FIGURE 1.16: Clicking a button to cause changes in another element

To get a feel for how binding works in WPF, we can look at a couple of scenarios. First let's consider setting the background of a button:

```
<Button
  Background='Red' />
```

If we want to share this background between multiple buttons, the simplest thing to do is to put the color definition in a common place and wire all the buttons to point at that one place. This is what the Resources property is designed for.

To define a resource, we declare the object in the Resources property of a control and assign x:Key to the object:

```
<Window
  x:Class='EssentialWPF.ResourceSample'
  xmlns:x='http://schemas.microsoft.com/winfx/2006/xaml'
  xmlns='http://schemas.microsoft.com/winfx/2006/xaml/presentation'
  Title='Hello World'
  >
  <Window.Resources>
    <SolidColorBrush x:Key='bg' Color='Red' />
  </Window.Resources>
  <!-- ... rest of window ... -->
</Window>
```

We can then refer to a named resource using the DynamicResource or StaticResource markup extension (covered in detail in Chapter 6):

```
<Window
  x:Class='EssentialWPF.ResourceSample'
  xmlns:x='http://schemas.microsoft.com/winfx/2006/xaml'
  xmlns='http://schemas.microsoft.com/winfx/2006/xaml/presentation'
  Title='Hello World'
  >
  <Window.Resources>
    <SolidColorBrush x:Key='bg' Color='Red' />
  </Window.Resources>
  <WrapPanel>
    <Button Background='{StaticResource bg}'
      Click='HowdyClicked'>Howdy!</Button>
    <Button Background='{StaticResource bg}'>A second button</Button>
    <TextBox x:Name='_text1'>An editable text box</TextBox>
    <CheckBox>A check box </CheckBox>
    <Slider Width='75' Minimum='0' Maximum='100' Value='50' />
  </WrapPanel>
</Window>
```

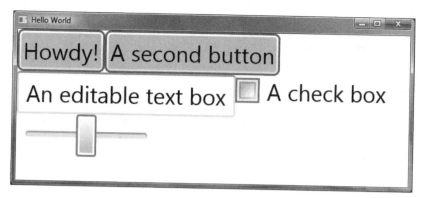

FIGURE 1.17: Binding to a resource

Running this program reveals that both buttons have the same color (Figure 1.17).

Resource binding is a relatively simple type of binding. We can also bind properties between controls (and data objects) using the data-binding system. For example, we can bind the text of TextBox to the content of CheckBox:

```
<Window
  x:Class='EssentialWPF.ResourceSample'
  xmlns:x='http://schemas.microsoft.com/winfx/2006/xaml'
  xmlns='http://schemas.microsoft.com/winfx/2006/xaml/presentation'
  Title='Hello World'
  >
  <Window.Resources>
    <SolidColorBrush x:Key='bg' Color='Red' />
  </Window.Resources>
  <WrapPanel>
    <Button Background='{StaticResource bg}'
      Click='HowdyClicked'>Howdy!</Button>
    <Button Background='{StaticResource bg}'>A second button</Button>
    <TextBox x:Name='_text1'>An editable text box</TextBox>
    <CheckBox Content='{Binding ElementName=_text1,Path=Text}' />
    <Slider Width='75' Minimum='0' Maximum='100' Value='50' />
  </WrapPanel>
</Window>
```

When we run this code, we can type in the text box and the content of the check box will be updated automatically (Figure 1.18).

Deep data integration with controls enables powerful data visualization. In addition to traditional controls, WPF provides seamless access to documents, media, and graphics.

FIGURE 1.18: Data binding between two controls

The Power of Integration

The visual system in WPF includes support for 2D vector graphics, raster images, text, animation, video, audio, and 3D graphics. All of these features are integrated into a single composition engine that builds on top of DirectX, allowing many features to be accelerated by hardware on modern video cards.

To start looking at this integration, let's create a rectangle. Instead of filling the rectangle with a solid color, we will create a gradient (blending from one color to another—in this case, from red to white to blue:

```
<Window ... >
  <Window.Resources>
    <SolidColorBrush x:Key='bg' Color='Red' />
  </Window.Resources>
  <DockPanel>
    <WrapPanel DockPanel.Dock='Top'>
      <Button Background='{StaticResource bg}'
        Click='HowdyClicked'>Howdy!</Button>
      <Button Background='{StaticResource bg}'>A second button</Button>
      <TextBox x:Name='_text1'>An editable text box</TextBox>
      <CheckBox  Content='{Binding ElementName=_text1,Path=Text}' />
      <Slider Width='75' Minimum='0' Maximum='100' Value='50' />
    </WrapPanel>
    <Rectangle Margin='5'>
      <Rectangle.Fill>
        <LinearGradientBrush>
          <GradientStop Offset='0' Color='Red' />
          <GradientStop Offset='.5' Color='White' />
          <GradientStop Offset='1' Color='Blue' />
        </LinearGradientBrush>
      </Rectangle.Fill>
    </Rectangle>
  </DockPanel>
</Window>
```

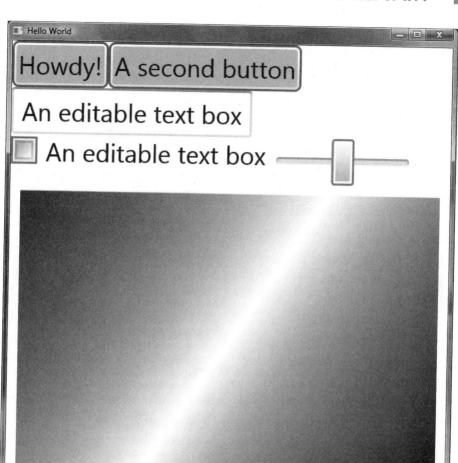

FIGURE 1.19: Rectangle filled with a gradient

Figure 1.19 shows the result. Resizing the window shows that the rectangle changes size and the gradient rotates such that it starts and ends at the corners of the rectangle. Clearly, 2D graphics integrate with the layout engine.

We can take this integration one step further, using a set of controls as the brush instead of filling the rectangle with a colored brush. In the following example, we will add a name to our wrap panel and use Visual-Brush to fill the rectangle. VisualBrush takes a control and replicates the

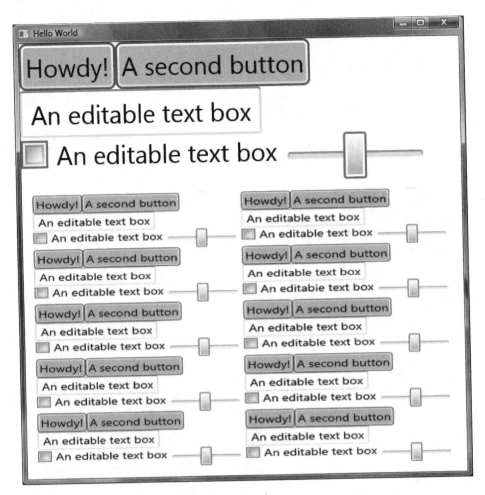

FIGURE 1.20: Using a visual brush to fill a rectangle

display of that control as the fill. Using the `Viewport` and `TileMode` properties, we can make the contents replicate multiple times:

```
<Window ... >
  <Window.Resources>
    <SolidColorBrush x:Key='bg' Color='Red' />
  </Window.Resources>
  <DockPanel>
    <WrapPanel x:Name='panel' DockPanel.Dock='Top'>
      <Button Background='{StaticResource bg}'
        Click='HowdyClicked'>Howdy!</Button>
      <Button Background='{StaticResource bg}'>A second button</Button>
      <TextBox x:Name='_text1'>An editable text box</TextBox>
      <CheckBox  Content='{Binding ElementName=_text1,Path=Text}' />
      <Slider Width='75' Minimum='0' Maximum='100' Value='50' />
```

```
    </WrapPanel>
    <Rectangle Margin='5'>
      <Rectangle.Fill>
        <VisualBrush
          Visual='{Binding ElementName=panel}'
          Viewport='0,0,.5,.2'
          TileMode='Tile' />
      </Rectangle.Fill>
    </Rectangle>
  </DockPanel>
</Window>
```

Running this code shows that, if we edit the controls on the top, the display in the rectangle is updated (Figure 1.20). We can see that not only can we use 2D drawings with controls, but we can use controls themselves as 2D drawings. In fact, the implementations of all controls are described as a set of 2D drawings.

We can go even further with this integration. WPF provides basic 3D support as well. We can take the same visual brush and use it as a texture in a 3D drawing. Creating a 3D scene requires five things: a model (the shape), a material (what to cover the shape with), a camera (where to look from), a light (so we can see), and a viewport (someplace to render the scene). In Chapter 5 we'll look at 3D scenes in detail, but for now the important thing to notice is that, as the material of the model, we use the same visual brush as before:

```
<Window ... >
  <Window.Resources>
    <SolidColorBrush x:Key='bg' Color='Red' />
  </Window.Resources>
  <DockPanel>
    <WrapPanel x:Name='panel' DockPanel.Dock='Top'>
      <Button Background='{StaticResource bg}'
        Click='HowdyClicked'>Howdy!</Button>
      <Button Background='{StaticResource bg}'>A second button</Button>
      <TextBox x:Name='_text1'>An editable text box</TextBox>
      <CheckBox  Content='{Binding ElementName=_text1,Path=Text}' />
      <Slider Width='75' Minimum='0' Maximum='100' Value='50' />
    </WrapPanel>
    <Viewport3D>
      <Viewport3D.Camera>
        <PerspectiveCamera
          LookDirection='-.7,-.8,-1'
          Position='3.8,4,4'
          FieldOfView='17'
          UpDirection='0,1,0' />
```

```
        </Viewport3D.Camera>
        <ModelVisual3D>
          <ModelVisual3D.Content>
            <Model3DGroup>
              <PointLight
                Position='3.8,4,4'
                Color='White'
                Range='7'
                ConstantAttenuation='1.0' />
              <GeometryModel3D>
                <GeometryModel3D.Geometry>
                  <MeshGeometry3D
                    TextureCoordinates=
                    '0,0 1,0 0,-1 1,-1 0,0 1,0 0,-1 0,0'
                    Positions=
                    '0,0,0 1,0,0 0,1,0 1,1,0 0,1,-1 1,1,-1 1,1,-1  1,0,-1'
                    TriangleIndices='0,1,2 3,2,1 4,2,3 5,4,3 6,3,1 7,6,1'
                  />
                </GeometryModel3D.Geometry>
                <GeometryModel3D.Material>
                  <DiffuseMaterial>
                    <DiffuseMaterial.Brush>
                      <VisualBrush
                        Viewport='0,0,.5,.25'
                        TileMode='Tile'
                        Visual='{Binding ElementName=panel}' />
                    </DiffuseMaterial.Brush>
                  </DiffuseMaterial>
                </GeometryModel3D.Material>
              </GeometryModel3D>
            </Model3DGroup>
          </ModelVisual3D.Content>
        </ModelVisual3D>
      </Viewport3D>
    </DockPanel>
  </Window>
```

Figure 1.21 shows what this looks like. Just as when the shape was a 2D rectangle, changing the controls will be reflected on the 3D object.

As the previous example shows, creating 3D scenes requires a lot of markup. I highly recommend using a 3D authoring tool if you intend to play with 3D.

Our last stop in looking at integration is animation. So far everything has been largely static. In the same way that 2D, 3D, text, and controls are integrated, everything in WPF supports animation intrinsically.

Animation in WPF allows us to vary a property value over time. To animate our 3D scene, we will start by adding a rotation transformation.

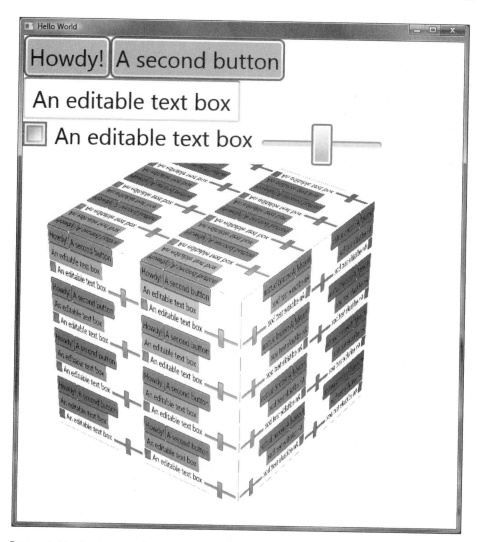

FIGURE 1.21: Controls used as the material for a 3D shape

Rotation will allow us to spin our 3D model by adjusting the angle. We will then be able to animate the display by adjusting the angle property over time:

```
<!-- ...rest of scene... -->
<GeometryModel3D>
  <GeometryModel3D.Transform>
    <RotateTransform3D
      CenterX='.5'
      CenterY='.5'
      CenterZ='-.5'>
```

```
    <RotateTransform3D.Rotation>
      <AxisAngleRotation3D
        x:Name='rotation'
        Axis='0,1,0'
        Angle='0' />
    </RotateTransform3D.Rotation>
  </RotateTransform3D>
</GeometryModel3D.Transform>
<!-- ...rest of scene... -->
```

Now we can define our animation. There are a lot of details here, but the important thing is DoubleAnimation, which allows us to vary a double value over time. (ColorAnimation would allow us to animate a color value.) We are animating the angle of the rotation from –25 to 25. It will automatically reverse and take 2.5 seconds to complete each rotation.

```
<Window ...>

<!-- ...rest of scene... -->
  <Window.Triggers>
    <EventTrigger RoutedEvent='FrameworkElement.Loaded'>
      <EventTrigger.Actions>
        <BeginStoryboard>
          <BeginStoryboard.Storyboard>
            <Storyboard>
              <DoubleAnimation
                From='-25'
                To='25'
                Storyboard.TargetName='rotation'
                Storyboard.TargetProperty='Angle'
                AutoReverse='True'
                Duration='0:0:2.5'
                RepeatBehavior='Forever'
                />
            </Storyboard>
          </BeginStoryboard.Storyboard>
        </BeginStoryboard>
      </EventTrigger.Actions>
    </EventTrigger>
  </Window.Triggers>
<!-- ...rest of scene... -->
```

Running this code produces something like Figure 1.22, but animated. (I tried to get the publisher to include a laptop in every copy of the book so you could see the animation, but they decided it wouldn't be cost-effective.)

The integration of UI, documents, and media runs deep in WPF. We can give buttons texture with 3D, we can use a video as the fill for text—almost

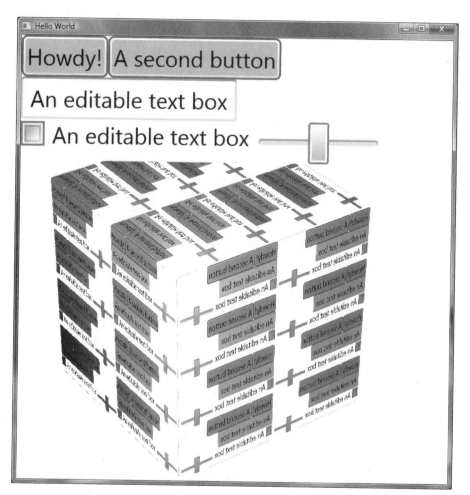

FIGURE 1.22: Adding rotation animation to our 3D scene

anything is possible. This flexibility is very powerful, but it can also lead to very unusable experiences. One of the tools that we can use to get a rich, but consistent, display is the WPF styling system.

Getting Some Style

Styles provide a mechanism for applying a set of properties to one or more controls. Because properties are used for almost all customization in WPF, we can customize almost every aspect of an application. Using styles, we can create consistent themes across applications.

To see how styles work, let's modify those two red buttons. First, instead of having each button refer to the resource, we can move the setting of the background to a style definition. By setting the key of the style to be the type Button, we ensure that that type will automatically be applied to all the buttons inside of this window:

```
<Window ... >
  <Window.Resources>
    <SolidColorBrush x:Key='bg' Color='Red' />

    <Style x:Key='{x:Type Button}' TargetType='{x:Type Button}'>
      <Setter Property='Background' Value='{StaticResource bg}' />
    </Style>
  </Window.Resources>

  <!-- ... rest of window ... -->

    <WrapPanel x:Name='panel' DockPanel.Dock='Top'>
      <Button Click='HowdyClicked'>Howdy!</Button>
      <Button>A second button</Button>
      <TextBox x:Name='_text1'>An editable text box</TextBox>
      <CheckBox  Content='{Binding ElementName=_text1,Path=Text}' />
      <Slider Width='75' Minimum='0' Maximum='100' Value='50' />
    </WrapPanel>

  <!-- ... rest of window ... -->

</Window>
```

Running this code will produce a result that looks indistinguishable from Figure 1.22. To make this more interesting, let's try customizing the Template property for the button. Most controls in WPF support templating, which means that the rendering of the control can be changed declaratively. Here we will replace the button's default appearance with a stylized ellipse.

ContentPresenter tells the template where to put the content of the button. Here we are using layout, controls, and 2D graphics to implement the display of a single button:

```
<Style x:Key='{x:Type Button}' TargetType='{x:Type Button}'>
  <Setter Property='Background' Value='{StaticResource bg}' />
  <Setter Property='Template'>
    <Setter.Value>
      <ControlTemplate TargetType='{x:Type Button}'>
        <Grid>
          <Ellipse StrokeThickness='4'>
            <Ellipse.Stroke>
              <LinearGradientBrush>
                <GradientStop Offset='0' Color='White' />
                <GradientStop Offset='1' Color='Black' />
              </LinearGradientBrush>
            </Ellipse.Stroke>
```

```
        <Ellipse.Fill>
          <LinearGradientBrush>
            <GradientStop Offset='0' Color='Silver' />
            <GradientStop Offset='1' Color='White' />
          </LinearGradientBrush>
        </Ellipse.Fill>
      </Ellipse>
      <ContentPresenter
        Margin='10'
        HorizontalAlignment='Center'
        VerticalAlignment='Center' />
    </Grid>
  </ControlTemplate>
 </Setter.Value>
 </Setter>
</Style>
```

Figure 1.23 (on page 40) shows what we get when we run this code. The buttons are still active; in fact, clicking the **Howdy!** button will still update the text box (remember, we wrote that code earlier in the tour).

We have now traveled through most of the areas of WPF, but we've only begun to scratch the surface of the concepts and features in this platform. Before we finish the introduction, we should talk about how to configure your computer to build and run all these wonderful programs that we're creating.

Tools for Building Applications

To compile and run any of the code in this book, you will need a basic set of tools and some understanding of how they work. You can build a complete development environment with little more than an Internet connection because the new Visual Studio Express products give you a great development environment at no cost!

- .NET Framework 3.0[8]
- Windows Software Development Kit[9]
- Code editor of your choice (Visual C# Express[10] is what I'm using right now)

---

8. The .NET Framework 3.0 redistributable is available at http://msdn.microsoft.com/windowsvista/downloads/products/default.aspx.

9. The Windows SDK is available at http://msdn.microsoft.com/windowsvista.

10. Visual C# Express is available at http://msdn.microsoft.com/vstudio/express/visualCsharp/default.aspx.

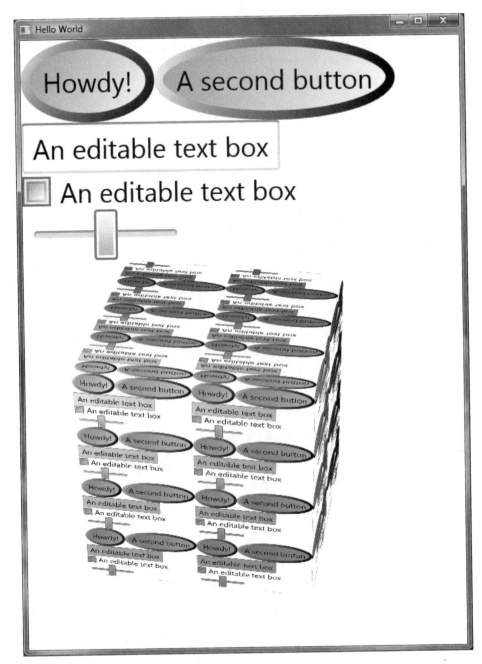

FIGURE 1.23: Buttons with a custom template, provided by a style

Optionally, you can get the .NET Framework 3.0 Extensions for Visual Studio (currently code-named *Orcas*), which right now is packaged as a community technology preview (CTP) of the next release of Visual Studio. Over time, though, this package will be replaced by a new release of Visual Studio that has native support for .NET Framework 3.0 development.

In our earlier tour of WPF, we walked through the basics of creating a project file for compiling WPF applications. With Visual Studio extensions installed, all the project file maintenance can be handled by Visual Studio. Alternatively, Microsoft's Expression Blend (code-named *Sparkle*) can be used to build projects.

The two most useful sources for API documentation are the Windows SDK documentation and an assembly browser tool like Reflector.[11]

WHERE ARE WE?

In this chapter we've seen why Microsoft built WPF, and we've taken a brief tour through the major areas of the platform. We've learned how to use the tools needed to build WPF applications, and we've received some pointers on where to find the needed software to get started.

---

11. Reflector is available at http://www.aisto.com/roeder/dotnet.

■ 2 ■
Applications

W E EACH HAVE our own definition of what an application is; my favorite is "a piece of software whose primary function is to communicate with a human." Windows Presentation Foundation is fundamentally about presenting information to humans, so it shouldn't be a surprise that I believe the right place to start digging into this enormous platform is at the application level.

WPF tries to walk a fine line with its application model, providing a set of flexible services for building applications without introducing such rigid rules that new solutions cannot be built. The model was to provide a set of integrated services that developers could take advantage of incrementally.

WPF applications consist of various pieces of user interface, resources, connections to services and data, and configuration information. In looking at the structure of an application, it is useful to understand the top-level building blocks of the user interface (windows, pages, and user controls), as well as the application-level services (navigation, resources, configuration, and hosting). We will cover all of these in this chapter.

Application Principles

When building WPF, we wanted to create a very light application model. We knew that the core platform should be as flexible as possible; however, we wanted to adhere to a few fundamental principles. We believed we should build a system that extended from lightweight Web applications up to full-blown desktop applications. Not only did we want this scalability, but we wanted to take the best features from Web- and desktop-style development and make them available regardless of the type of application being created.

Scalable Applications

One of the core principles of WPF was to offer scalability, making it possible for people to build a broad spectrum of application types—from lightweight applications that run in a browser, to applications that easily deploy to desktops, all the way to full-blown client applications that can install. So even though an `Application` object is created and eventually `Run` is called on that object, a simple WPF application can be written in a simple markup file.

Create a new file called `HelloWorld.xaml`, and put the following markup in it:

```
<Page
  xmlns='http://schemas.microsoft.com/winfx/2006/xaml/presentation'
  WindowTitle='Hello World'>

  <TextBlock FontSize='24'>Hello World</TextBlock>
</Page>
```

To run this application, we double-click the XAML file, and we see something like Figure 2.1. This very simple application is fairly limited; there is no code. We can create simple interaction using animation and data binding, but for real application logic we need to be able to put some code in the application.

To write some code to the page, we need to give the page a name in the CLR world, by adding the `x:Class` attribute. We can also add the `x:Name` attribute to `TextBlock` so that we can programmatically change it:

```
<Page
  x:Class='EssentialWPF.HelloWorld'
  xmlns='http://schemas.microsoft.com/winfx/2006/xaml/presentation'
  xmlns:x='http://schemas.microsoft.com/winfx/2006/xaml'
  WindowTitle='Hello World'>
  <TextBlock x:Name='text1' FontSize='24'>Hello World</TextBlock>
</Page>
```

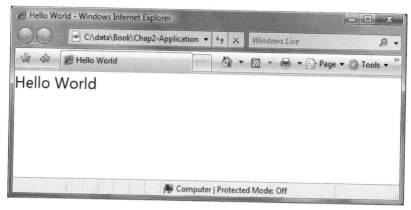

FIGURE 2.1: A very simple application in a browser

We can now write some code behind the page. Any .NET programming language can be used; in this case we'll use C#. We'll set the text to announce the current time:

```
using System;
using System.Windows;
using System.Windows.Controls;

namespace EssentialWPF {
  public partial class HelloWorld : Page {
    public HelloWorld() {
      InitializeComponent();

      text1.Text = "Now is: " + DateTime.Now.ToString();
    }
  }
}
```

Because we want to include code, we must compile the project. In any compiled project that we want to be executable (like our application), it is generally a good idea to include an application definition. To define our application, we will use the basic WPF `Application` object, and set `StartupUri` to be our XAML file:

```
<Application
  xmlns='http://schemas.microsoft.com/winfx/2006/xaml/presentation'
  StartupUri='helloworld.xaml' />
```

The final step in converting from a markup-only application to an application with code is to compile the project. For this we need a project file to instruct MSBuild how to compile the project. Most of the content of the project file[1] is boilerplate code (and will actually be generated automatically by a tool like Visual Studio); however, we need to include our three files:

```
<Project DefaultTargets="Build"
xmlns="http://schemas.microsoft.com/developer/msbuild/2003">
  <!-- ...rest of project file... -->
  <PropertyGroup>
    <HostInBrowser>true</HostInBrowser>
  </PropertyGroup>
  <ItemGroup>
    <Page Include="HelloWorld.xaml" />
    <ApplicationDefinition Include="App.xaml" />
    <Compile Include="HelloWorld.xaml.cs" />
  </ItemGroup>
  <!-- ...rest of project file... -->
</Project>
```

When we build the project, a file called `HelloWorld.xbap` will be created. Double-clicking the XBAP (XAML Browser Application) file, will result in something like Figure 2.2.

XBAPs allow a great deal more functionality than traditional HTML-based applications. They allow us to communicate with Web servers, access secure local storage, and leverage much of the power of the .NET Framework.[2] If a program needs more functionality than is available to browser applications, we can convert this program to a desktop application by changing the `HostInBrowser` attribute in the project file:

```
<Project DefaultTargets="Build" xmlns="http://schemas.microsoft.com/
developer/msbuild/2003">
  <!-- ...rest of project file... -->
  <PropertyGroup>
    <HostInBrowser>false</HostInBrowser>
  </PropertyGroup>
  <!-- ...rest of project file... -->
</Project>
```

---

1. The manifests for the project must also be signed, so `SignManifests`, `ManifestKeyFile`, and `ManifestCertificateThumbprint` must be included in the project file. The best way to enable signing is to check the **SignManifests** button on the **Signing** tab in Visual Studio's project properties view. It is unfortunate that browser-hosted applications require this complexity.

2. XBAPs normally run with "Internet" security, so they are limited in functionality to operations that are safe for partially trusted code.

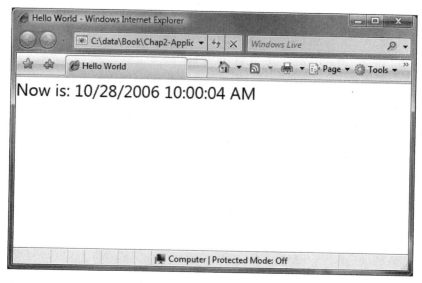

FIGURE 2.2: XAML Browser Application running in a browser

If we rebuild the project, we can now run HelloWorld.exe and we'll see something like Figure 2.3.

This design principle of scalable applications has several interesting aspects. For one thing, the deployment mechanism is scalable. Markup applications are deployed by a simple HTTP request, browser applications

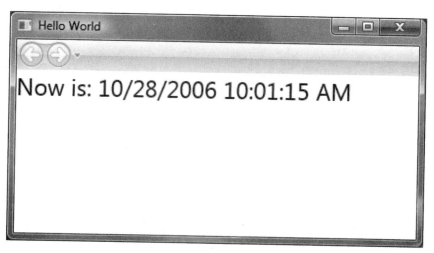

FIGURE 2.3: Desktop application

are temporarily deployed[3] using a form of ClickOnce, and desktop applications can use ClickOnce or MSI (Microsoft Installer) installation.

In addition to scalable deployment, scalable applications have scalable hosting. The application user interface can be hosted in the browser or a desktop window. A close look at Figure 2.3 shows that, even in a desktop window, navigation is supported. This brings up another core principle of the application model: the integration of Web concepts into desktop applications.

Web Style

A big push for the application model in WPF was to integrate the best of desktop programming with the best of Web programming. We've already seen some examples of this integration: browser hosting and Web deployment. WPF's application model goes deeper and has an integrated notion of navigation.

Whether an application is hosted in the browser or in a desktop window, we can easily add navigation. Building on the previous example, we can create a second page called `second-page.xaml`:

```
<Page
  xmlns='http://schemas.microsoft.com/winfx/2006/xaml/presentation'
  WindowTitle='Second Page'>
  <TextBlock FontSize='24'>Welcome to page 2</TextBlock>

</Page>
```

Using the `Hyperlink` control, we can add a link from the first page:

```
<Page ... WindowTitle='Hello World'>
  <StackPanel>
    <TextBlock x:Name='text1' FontSize='24'>Hello World</TextBlock>
    <TextBlock FontSize='24'>
      <Hyperlink NavigateUri='second-page.xaml'>
        Goto Page 2
      </Hyperlink>
    </TextBlock>
  </StackPanel>

</Page>
```

---

3. I say "temporarily deployed" because browser applications have no permanent presence on the local machine. They are actually deployed to the client, but put into a cache that will be purged just like the Internet Explorer cache.

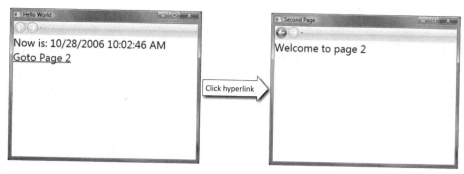

FIGURE 2.4: Desktop navigation-based application

Running this program (Figure 2.4) reveals that, even in a desktop window, we get the full power of a navigation system.

Notice that the URI for navigation was second-page.xaml. How was that URI determined? Web-style applications use URIs to reference any resources. In addition, Web-style applications have the the application root as a base; that is, relative URIs are relative to the application.

The WPF model for resource referencing borrows heavily from the Web style and takes it one step further, integrating compiled types (like the compiled version of the XAML files), loose resources (images on disk, Internet locations, etc.), and package resources (like resources embedded in an application).

For example, we can add an image to our second page and reference an image from an Internet site using a URI:

```
<Page
  xmlns='http://schemas.microsoft.com/winfx/2006/xaml/presentation'
  WindowTitle='Second Page'>
  <TextBlock FontSize='24'>Welcome to page 2
  <Image
    Source='http://blog.simplegeek.com/images/img_1476-small.png'  />
  </TextBlock>
</Page>
```

Running this code will show something like Figure 2.5, after the image is downloaded.

Web-based applications are becoming a bigger and bigger part of programming. WPF embraces this model by offering many of the advantages of the Web model for building rich desktop applications. However, one of the

FIGURE 2.5: Referencing a resource from the Internet

core principles of WPF is to incorporate the best attributes of desktop programming as well.

Desktop Style

Most of the concepts of desktop programming—multiple windows, tool tips, **Start** menu integration, clipboard control, offline support, file system integration, and so on—are so ingrained in developers that they don't even think about them.

One of the most visible stylistic elements of any desktop application is its windowing model. User32-based applications can easily implement single-document interface (SDI), multiple-document interface (MDI), dialogs, and wizard models (Table 2.1). Microsoft Office Word 2003 provides an SDI model: Each document is opened in a separate top-level window, and when the final document is closed the application shuts down. Adobe Photoshop CS uses an MDI model: there is a single top-level window, and multiple child windows represent views on an open document. Photoshop is terminated when the top-level window is closed.

TABLE 2.1: Windowing Models

Model	Definition	Common Uses
Single-document interface (SDI)	Each document is hosted in a separate top-level window. Users switch between documents using the system taskbar. The application is terminated when the final document is closed.	General-purpose editing applications that handle documents, spreadsheets, and e-mail (e.g., Microsoft Office Word 2003)
Dialog	The application is generally executed as one logical action. A single top-level window is created, and the application terminates when the logical action is completed.	Infrequently used customizations (e.g., to change display settings, add new users, install updates)
SDI navigation	Each distinct instance of the navigation window corresponds to a logical browsing session.	Infrequent tasks (e.g., travel booking, shopping)
Browser navigation	The application is started by clicking a link. The various parts of the application are activated by clicking links inside of a single browser instance. The application never appears to terminate, but the user can navigate away.	Navigating information spaces, such as encyclopedias or document repositories (e.g., www.msn. com)

As the Internet has evolved, we have seen a new application platform emerge: the browser. Browser-based applications have really only one windowing model option: navigation. A few examples of Web-based applications have implemented dialog, SDI, or even MDI models; however, they have had to re-create many of the platform services normally associated with these models.

WPF strives to unify these windowing models, allowing developers to easily mix and match models and create new models. Given the flexibility offered by WPF, the key is to understand when a given windowing model is appropriate.

MDI was intentionally omitted from WPF's windowing-model support. When WPF was started (late in 2000), there was a move away from

MDI-based applications. Implementing MDI support is a lot of work, and the WPF team decided it wasn't worth the investment, given the desire for new styles of applications (tabbed MDI as in Visual Studio 2005, navigation as in Internet Explorer, etc.). When the first preview of WPF was released in 2003, people started asking for MDI support, but at that point it was too late to integrate it into the product. There are two options for working around this problem: The first is to use the implementation of MDI offered by Windows Forms. The second is to write our own child window manager, which does not involve too much code but doesn't always yield a completely functional window manager (it's really easy to write 80 percent of the window manager, very hard to get to 100 percent). I would recommend using Windows Forms if your application needs MDI support.

Application authors do not have to limit themselves to a single model for their entire application. For example, an e-mail program might use browser or SDI navigation for browsing, but then switch to SDI for composing new messages. A shopping application might start as an SDI navigation application, letting a customer window-shop an online store; then at checkout time, a dialog might guide the customer through the final payment and shipping options.

These three principles—scalable applications, Web style, and desktop style—are integrated into most aspects of the application model. Now that we've reviewed the three core principles, we can start digging into some of the details that make it all work.

Application

The Application object is responsible for managing the lifetime of the application, tracking the visible windows, dispensing resources, and managing the global state of the application. A WPF application logically starts executing when the Run method is invoked on an instance of the Application object:

```
using System;
using System.Windows;

namespace EssentialWPF {
  static class Program {
```

```
        [STAThread]
        static void Main() {
          Application app = new Application();
          Window w = new Window();
          w.Title = "Hello World";
          w.Show();
          app.Run();
        }
      }
    }
```

In our simple Hello World example, we can see the application object get created and start running. The call to Run is normally the last line of the entry-point function.[4] Run starts sending events and messages to components in the WPF application.[5] Run will exit until the application is shutting down. Only one Application object at a time may be running (in fact, once an application has started, no new ones can be created). Using the Application.Current static property, we can access the current application from anywhere in the program.

Definition

To encapsulate startup logic, most WPF applications create a subclass of Application:

```
// program.cs
using System;
using System.Windows;

namespace EssentialWPF {
  static class Program {
    [STAThread]
    static void Main() {
      MyApp app = new MyApp();
      app.Run();
    }
  }
}
```

---

4. The [STAThread] marker on the entry-point function is required. Like Windows Forms and User32 before it, WPF requires the UI thread to be STA (single-threaded apartment) because many components that WPF uses (such as the Clipboard) require STA. To ensure consistent behavior, the WPF team decided to make STA a requirement at all times.

5. To be explicit, Run starts the dispatcher, which is responsible for sending events and messages. The dispatcher is covered in more detail in the appendix.

```
class MyApp : Application {
  public MyApp() {
    Window w = new Window();
    w.Title = "Hello World";
    w.Show();
  }
 }
}
```

One of the goals of WPF is to reduce the amount of boilerplate code that must be written. Another goal is to allow declarative programming wherever possible. When writing an application using WPF, we must always have a certain set of code in the `Main` function: setting the `STAThread` attribute, creating the `Application` object, and calling `Run`.

Rather than requiring this code to be rewritten for each application, WPF allows us to define the application in markup. Finally, we need to add two new files to the project file:

```
<!-- myapp.xaml -->
<Application x:Class='EssentialWPF.MyApp' ... />
```

```
// myapp.xaml.cs
using System;
 using System.Windows;

namespace EssentialWPF {
  partial class MyApp : Application {
    public MyApp() {
      Window w = new Window();
      w.Title = "Hello World";
      w.Show();
    }
  }
}
```

```
<!-- sample.csproj -->
<Project
  DefaultTargets='Build'
  xmlns='http://schemas.microsoft.com/developer/msbuild/2003'>
  ...
  <ItemGroup>
    <ApplicationDefinition Include='myapp.xaml' />
    <Compile Include='myapp.xaml.cs' />
  </ItemGroup>
  ...
</Project>
```

The build system takes this markup and generates the boilerplate code that we previously wrote. A snippet of the generated code is shown here:

```
namespace EssentialWPF {

    /// <summary>
    /// MyApp
    /// </summary>
    public partial class MyApp : System.Windows.Application {

        /// <summary>
        /// Application entry point
        /// </summary>
        [System.STAThreadAttribute()]
        [System.Diagnostics.DebuggerNonUserCodeAttribute()]
        public static void Main() {
            EssentialWPF.MyApp app = new EssentialWPF.MyApp();
            app.Run();
        }
    }
}
```

Note that the generated code replaces the handwritten `Main` function with a generated `Main`.[6]

Lifetime

The last line of our `Main` function was a call to `Application.Run`. At some point that method must return, or the application will run forever. One of the primary roles of the `Application` object is to control the lifetime of the process. The construction of the `Application` object signals the start of the application, and the completion of the `Run` method marks the end of the application. Between these two is where everything happens in the application. All WPF applications follow the same general pattern:

1. `Application` object is constructed.
2. `Run` method is called.
3. `Application.Startup` event is raised.
4. User code constructs one or more `Window` objects.

---

6. As we'll see later, `Application` is the only markup item that doesn't require a call to `InitializeComponent`.

5. `Application.Shutdown` method is called.

6. `Application.Exit` event is raised.

7. `Run` method completes.

We can initialize the application in one of two ways: (1) from the constructor of the `Application` object, or (2) by handling the `Startup` event. The `Startup` event is generally preferred, because `Application` has completed its internal initialization at this point (e.g., `Application.Current` will be not be set inside of the constructor):

```xml
<!-- myapp.xaml -->
<Application
  x:Class='EssentialWPF.MyApp'
  ...
  Startup='MyApp_Startup'
  />
```

```csharp
// myapp.xaml.cs
using System;
using System.Windows;

namespace EssentialWPF {
  partial class MyApp : Application {
    public MyApp() {
    }
    void MyApp_Startup(object sender, StartupEventArgs e) {
      Window w = new Window();
      w.Title = "Hello World";
      w.Show();
    }
  }
}
```

Eventually the `Run` method must return, and that happens only when `Application.Shutdown` is called. However, `Shutdown` can be made to work automatically, as we'll learn in a few pages, when we talk about `Window`.

In the general pattern of an application lifetime, you may have noticed something missing. As the saying goes, into each lifetime a little rain must fall. Most developers will eventually see an error occur—because the code contains a bug, a user is doing something weird, or (gasp!) the underlying platform has a bug. For this reason, we should always include code to handle any errors that are likely crop up.

Error Handling

Dealing with errors and exceptions in an application is a rich enough topic to fill an entire book. Application authors need to figure out how to deal with errors when they occur, and understanding the philosophy that guided the design and building of WPF might provide help on this front.

WPF attempts to be hardened to any type of recoverable exception. That is a bit of a circular argument, since *recoverable* limits the types of exceptions to something we are hardened against! The issue here is that there are certain types of exceptions from which we cannot recover; StackOverflow-Exception, OutOfMemoryException, and ThreadAbortException are the best examples.

A thread is aborted only when application code calls Thread.Abort, so if we don't call Thread.Abort we won't ever see ThreadAbortException. Stacks overflow most often when code is infinitely recursive, so StackOverflowException is also a bad bug. OutOfMemoryException is probably the most interesting of the gang. When the system runs low on memory—truly low—so few resources may be available that the CLR cannot allocate even a single byte more.[7] In such a case, no just-in-time code can be implemented, no variables can be boxed, and no objects can be allocated.

Except with these three special exceptions, in the WPF all code returns to a consistent state after an exception occurs. This means that developers can perform their own application recovery logic when an exception occurs, and can assume that the underlying platform is consistent.

When calling a method, it is simple to write exception-handling code. Using a try/catch/finally pattern, we can easily write code to handle any

---

7. The CLR provides a mechanism—the constrained execution region (CER)—that guarantees execution even when no memory is available. Code in a CER must not allocate memory, box values, or call methods that are not also part of a CER. The burden of writing CER code is extremely high, so CER code is generally reserved for only the deepest layers of the platform (fewer than a hundred methods in all of .NET use CER). WPF instead relies on memory gates that cause the system to fail with a recoverable exception before the system completely runs out of resources. Memory gates are predictive (evaluating system resources and failing before no memory is available), and as such they cannot guarantee success. The goal of memory gates is to reduce the likelihood of hitting a hard out-of-memory condition. Although we do everything we can to avoid these unrecoverable exceptions, they aren't as interesting; they are unrecoverable, and the process will simply terminate if any of these arise.

error condition. The problem is what happens when no one handles an exception—because either it happened asynchronously or it simply wasn't caught. WPF's default is that the application will fail if any asynchronous or uncaught exception occurs.

The `Application` object offers an event, `DispatcherUnhandledException`,[8] that corresponds to these circumstances. By listening to this event, an application can implement any policy for dealing with exceptions that bubble up to the application:

```
<!-- MyApp.xaml -->
<Application ... DispatcherUnhandledException='Failure' />

// MyApp.xaml.cs
void Failure(object sender, DispatcherUnhandledExceptionEventArgs e) {
  // your custom logic
}
```

The dispatcher is the part of the system that sends events and messages to components. This event is raised when the dispatcher sees an exception bubble up. `DispatcherUnhandledExceptionEventArgs` contains the exception that occurred, as well as a `Handled` flag that can be set to `true` to indicate that the exception should be ignored and the application should continue to run:

```
public class DispatcherUnhandledExceptionEventArgs
  : DispatcherEventArgs {

  public Exception Exception { get; }
  public bool Handled { get; set; }
}
```

Here we can implement a policy that any failure will be ignored but written out to a log, and request that the user submit the error to the system administrator:

```
void Failure(object sender, DispatcherUnhandledExceptionEventArgs e)
{
  using (StreamWriter errorLog =
      new StreamWriter("c:\\error.log", true))
```

---

8. *Dispatcher* here refers to the top-level messaging-handling object, which is the object that does the work inside of `Application.Run`.

```
    {
      errorLog.WriteLine("Error @ " + DateTime.Now.ToString("R"));
      errorLog.WriteLine(e.Exception.ToString());
    }
    e.Handled = true;
    MessageBox.Show("An error occured, please report this " +
            "to your system administrator with the " +
            "contents of the file 'c:\\error.log'");
  }
```

By the time an exception has percolated up to the `DispatcherUnhandled-`
`Exception` event, an application author has few options; very little is
known about the context of what happened (besides the exception object),
and the operation can't really be retried (unless an internal state identifies
what was being attempted). Basically, the application can report the exception somehow, ignore it, fail, or perform a combination of these three
options.

Error handling is a sometimes forgotten part of the application life cycle,
but a critical part. During all phases of the life cycle, state will accumulate
and need to be dealt with.

Managing State

State commonly spans top-level UI components; for example, we may
want to track the current list of open documents in an application, or the
current state of a network connection. The `Application` object is a convenient place to store state because it is available globally (through the
`Application.Current` static property) for the entire lifetime of the application.

The simplest way to store state on the application is using the `Properties`
property available on `Application`. `Properties` is typed as `System.Collec-`
`tions.IDictionary`, which allows us to store any object in it, keyed by any
other object; the most common key type is a string.

We can extend our error-handling example to cache the last error seen on
the application:

```
// myapp.xaml.cs
public partial class MyApp : Application {
  ..
  void Failure(object sender, DispatcherUnhandledExceptionEventArgs e) {
    using (StreamWriter errorLog =
        new StreamWriter("c:\\error.log", true)) {
```

```
        errorLog.WriteLine("Error @ " + DateTime.Now.ToString("R"));
        errorLog.WriteLine(e.Exception.ToString());
    }
    e.Handled = true;
    this.Properties["LastError"] = e.Exception;
  }
  ...
}
```

Because `Properties` is a simple object/object dictionary, we need to continually cast the data we store there. Alternatively, we can define a property or field on the application `Application` object:

```
// myapp.xaml.cs
public partial class MyApp : Application {
  private Exception _lastError;
  public Exception LastError {
    get { return _lastError; }
    set { _lastError = value; }
  }
  ...
  void Failure(object sender, DispatcherUnhandledExceptionEventArgs e) {
    using (StreamWriter errorLog =
            new StreamWriter("c:\\error.log", true)) {
      errorLog.WriteLine("Error @ " + DateTime.Now.ToString("R"));
      errorLog.WriteLine(e.Exception.ToString());
    }
    e.Handled = true;
    this.LastError = e.Exception;
  }
  ...
}
```

As we add more state to the application, some patterns will emerge. Is the state persistent across runs of the application? Is the state scoped per user? Is the state determined only at compile time (like an image)? Properties on the `Application` object will take us only so far; for many of these types of state, we need to leverage the available resources and configuration services.

Resources and Configuration

There are a dozen different ways to categorize application state, but I like to look at it as divided into three main categories: configuration, content, and document. .NET has support for all three of these models.

Configuration State

Configuration state consists of settings associated with a user or machine and can generally be modified by a user or administrator at runtime or deployment. The configuration runtime from .NET has been evolving since .NET 1.0, and we can look at how to integrate that into our WPF application.

For managing most of the persistent settings of an application, the System.Configuration APIs are the right thing to use. An in-depth review of the configuration system isn't the right subject for this book, but understanding how to plumb configuration into an Application object is.

To start using the configuration system, we need to define the object model for our settings. We can do this either using the Visual Studio 2005 settings designer, or by authoring the class in any .NET language. Here we will define the object model in C#, which we will use to track the number of times we run the program:

```
public class AppSettings {
  int _runCount;

  public int RunCount {
    get { return _runCount; }
    set { _runCount = value; }
  }
}
```

This initial code creates a property to track state information. To plug this into the configuration system, we need to derive our settings class from SettingsBase (or ApplicationSettingsBase) and provide some metadata about the property. Instead of using a local field to store the value, we must use the storage built into the SettingsBase type so that the system can track changes to the value:

```
public class AppSettings : ApplicationSettingsBase {
  public AppSettings() : base() {
  }

  [UserScopedSetting]
  [DefaultSettingValue("0")]
  public int RunCount {
    get { return (int)this["RunCount"]; }
    set { this["RunCount"] = value; }
  }
}
```

Settings can be either tailored to each user (**user-scoped**) or shared (**application-scoped**). In this case we made RunCount user-scoped by applying the UserScopedSetting attribute to the property.

Once we've defined the object model, we have two more things to do: set up the configuration file bindings and expose the settings through the Application object. The configuration file bindings provide the information to the configuration system about how to map from the configuration file to the object model that we just defined.

To set up the configuration file bindings, we need to register the AppSettings class with the configuration system by adding a section in the app.config file. The app.config file is a part of .NET that provides a common place for configuration information about an application. To include app.config in our project, we should add it as a None action (I know, very confusing):

```
<ItemGroup>
  <None Include='app.config' />
</ItemGroup>
```

The build system automatically converts app.config into <OurProgram-Name>.exe.config when we compile. The configuration file will look something like this after it is compiled:

```
<?xml version='1.0' encoding='utf-8' ?>
<configuration>
  <configSections>
    <sectionGroup
      name='userSettings'
      type='System.Configuration.UserSettingsGroup, System, Version=2.0.0.0,
Culture=neutral, PublicKeyToken=b77a5c561934e089'
      >
      <section
        name='EssentialWPF.AppSettings'
        type='System.Configuration.ClientSettingsSection, System,
Version=2.0.0.0, Culture=neutral, PublicKeyToken=b77a5c561934e089'
        allowExeDefinition='MachineToLocalUser'
        requirePermission='false'
        />
    </sectionGroup>
    ...
  </configSections>
  ...
</configuration>
```

At this point we can compile the application and use the new settings object. However, we like simpler access from within the application. To use the settings object, we only need to instantiate it. To expose it on the application object, we can create a public instance property:

```
public partial class MyApp : Application {
  AppSettings _settings = new AppSettings();
  public AppSettings Settings {
    get {
      return _settings;
    }
  }

  public MyApp() {
    this.Exit += MyApp_Exit;
    this.Startup += AppStartup;
  }

  void MyApp_Exit(object sender, ExitEventArgs e) {
    Settings.Save();
  }

  void AppStartup(object sender, StartupEventArgs args) {
    Window w = new Window();
    w.Title = "You ran this " + (Settings.RunCount++) + " times";
    w.Show();
  }

}
```

Running the application several times will produce a display similar to Figure 2.6. If we expose the settings directly from the Application object, any WPF object can easily access the settings. Calling the Settings.Save

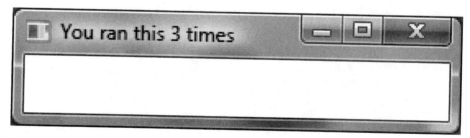

FIGURE 2.6: Running an application using configuration settings

method from the Exit event makes the settings persist every time the application is exited. We can call Settings.Save at any time; applications like Microsoft OneNote persist settings while the application is running, ensuring that even if the application crashes, the state will be saved.

Content State

Content state, also commonly called *resources* (links to images, media, documents, etc.), is determined at authoring time. WPF has a set of resource-loading APIs that allow us to access content associated with an application.

Using the configuration system, we are able to access state that persists and can be modified at runtime. For state that is determined at author time, such as images and user interface definitions, we use the resource system. In its simplest form, we can reference resources by using a fully qualified file path or HTTP URI (shown in Figure 2.7):

```
<!-- Window1.xaml -->
<Window ... >
  <StackPanel Orientation='Horizontal'>
    <Image
      Source='http://blog.simplegeek.com/images/img_1476-small.png' />
    <Image
      Source='C:\Users\Public\Pictures\Sample Pictures\Autumn Leaves.jpg'
      />
  </StackPanel>
</Window>
```

FIGURE 2.7: Images loaded using a fully qualified path or URI

TABLE 2.2: Types of Resources and How They Can Be Used

Build Action	API	Usable in Markup?	What It Does
`Content`	`Application.GetContentStream`	Yes	Copies each resource to the directory of the application.
`Resource`	`Application.GetResourceStream`	Yes	Embeds each resource in a common resource in the application.
`EmbeddedResource`	`Assembly.GetManifestResourceStream`	No	Embeds each resource in the application separately.

This works great when we need to reference only things that we can guarantee are on the user's machine or at a URL on the Web. In most cases we want to reference something either relative to the application or actually embedded in the application binary.

When adding an image (or other application resource) to an application, we have no shortage of options. Inside of the MSBuild project file[9] we can configure a resource[10] to be `Content`, `Resource`, or `EmbeddedResource`.[11] `EmbeddedResource` items are compiled into the .NET assembly as a manifest resource. `Content` is largely ignored by the build system, unless we set the `CopyToOutputDirectory` option to be either `PreserveNewest` or `Always`. When `CopyToOutputDirectory` is set, the resource is copied to the output directory mirroring the source structure. `Resource` items are embedded in the application as a named item inside of a generated resources file (Table 2.2).

---

9. Or using Visual Studio .NET's Solution Explorer.

10. Several other options—for example, `ApplicationDefinition`, `Compile`, or `Page`—don't relate to resources.

11. `Resource` and `EmbeddedResource` support localized loading. We can create specially named assemblies with alternate versions of the resources. See http://msdn.microsoft.com/library/default.asp?url=/library/en-us/cpguide/html/cpconcreatingusingresources.asp for more details.

To understand this better, let's look at an example. Suppose we have a simple project called ResourceTest that contains a `program.cs` file and three images: `content-image.jpg`, `resource-image.jpg`, and `embedded-image.jpg`:

```
<Project
  DefaultTargets='Build'
  xmlns='http://schemas.microsoft.com/developer/msbuild/2003'>
  ...
  <ItemGroup>
    <Content Include='images\content-image.jpg'>
      <CopyToOutputDirectory>Always</CopyToOutputDirectory>
    </Content>
    <Resource Include='images\resource-image.jpg' />
    <EmbeddedResource Include='images\embedded-image.jpg' />
    <Compile Include='program.cs' />
  </ItemGroup>
  ...
</Project>
```

Compiling this code using MSBuild will result in the following directory structure:

```
bin\debug\
      ResourceTest.application
      ResourceTest.exe
      ResourceTest.exe.manifest
      ResourceTest.pdb
bin\debug\images\
      content-image.jpg
```

What happened here is that `embedded-image.jpg` was embedded[12] in ResourceTest.exe, `resource-image.jpg` was placed inside of an embedded resource called `ResourceTest.g.resources`, and `content-image.jpg` was copied as a loose file into the debug directory. For all of these scenarios the directory name, `images`, was preserved in the name. Figure 2.8 shows this structure.

Now that we have followed this diversion down the road of resources, how would you use all of these resources inside of our WPF application?

---

12. To be 100 percent correct, the image was embedded into the assembly's resource section. This is often called a *manifest resource* because these resources appear in the assembly manifest.

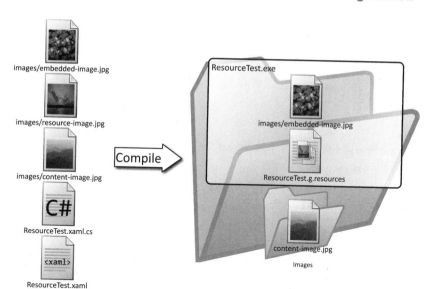

FIGURE 2.8: Structure of an application with various types of resources

```xml
<!-- Window1.xaml -->
<Window ... >
  <StackPanel Orientation='Horizontal'>
    <!-- These will work -->
    <Image Source='images/content-image.jpg'>
    <Image Source='images/resource-image.jpg'>

    <!-- This won't work!! -->
    <Image Source='images/embedded-image.jpg'>
  </StackPanel>
</Window>
```

For either a resource or copied content, we can simply refer to the resource from markup as a relative path. EmbeddedResource items are not accessible directly through markup. From within code, most WPF components natively support URI referencing:

```csharp
Image img = new Image();
img.Source = new BitmapImage(
    new Uri("images/content-image.jpg", UriKind.Relative));
```

All of these higher-level APIs eventually call into the Application resource APIs. Using a relative URI, we can access resources associated with the application:

```
public class Application : DispatcherObject, IResourceHost {
   ...
  public static StreamResourceInfo GetContentStream(Uri uriContent);
  public static StreamResourceInfo GetRemoteStream(Uri uriRemote);
  public static StreamResourceInfo GetResourceStream(Uri uriResource);
   ...
}
```

The three APIs for accessing resources from the application map to three different logical stores:

1. GetContentStream maps to resources that are known to the application manifest, which we specify using the MSBuild Content option. These resources are loose files on the disk.

2. GetResourceStream maps to resources embedded inside of the executable, which we specify using the MSBuild Resource option.

3. GetRemoteStream maps to any arbitrary content available on the site of origin for the application. The site of origin is the directory or Web server from which the application was started. Typically this is used for larger resources, or resources that are decoupled from the application itself.

Open Packaging Conventions

Content and resources both use an underlying mechanism called **packages**. To understand this better, you may want to look into the Open Packaging Conventions, or OPC. The COM world contained a notion of structure storage, exposed through a set of interfaces, of which IStorage and IStream are the most fundamental types. Through .NET 2.0 there was no successor to this technology. At its heart, structured storage enabled the consistent access of a structured file system. The structure storage interfaces could be implemented on top of any packaging model, the most popular of which was a binary file format commonly referred to as *OLE compound files*, which was Microsoft Office's native file format.

.NET 3.0 contains the logical successor to structured storage and the OLE compound file format. In the same way that IStorage and IStream provided a set of interfaces that could be implemented on any packaging format, the `System.IO.Packaging` namespace defines a set of interfaces and types that can be used to access any packaging format. And in the same way that OLE compound files provided a reference implementation of structured storage, `ZipPackage` provides a reference implementation of an OPC package (using ZIP compression with XML metadata).

It is important to understand OPC only in that it provides an abstract way to access a structured file system, regardless of packaging model. All WPF resource references effectively become OPC part references.

The OPC model provides for three main concepts: package, parts, and relationships. A single *package* consists of multiple *parts* that have *relationships* with each other. The relationships are encoded in a specially named part. This entire model is well documented in the OPC specification, available from www.microsoft.com/whdc/xps/downloads.mspx.

In addition to resource loading, the `Application` object provides direct access to loading components defined in markup:

```
public class Application : DispatcherObject, IResourceHost {
  ...
  public static object LoadComponent(Uri resourceLocator);
  public static void LoadComponent(object component,
                Uri resourceLocator);
  ...
}
```

The two overloads of `LoadComponent` are used for loading and parsing XAML-authored components. The first overload uses `GetResourceStream` and loads the embedded XAML into an object. Probably the most common use of `LoadComponent` is to load a piece of user interface.

Any component authored in XAML has two names: a URI and a CLR-type name. When we instantiate a type defined with markup using `new`, the constructor for that type calls `InitializeComponent`, which in turn loads the XAML. Up to now `InitializeComponent` has been a little magical; let's take a few seconds to peer under the covers at how this function actually works.

FIGURE 2.9: Simple display: a window with a button

We will start with a basic UI definition of a button in a window that, when run, looks like Figure 2.9:

```
<!-- LoadTest.xaml -->
<Window x:Class='EssentialWPF.LoadTest'
  xmlns='http://schemas.microsoft.com/winfx/2006/xaml/presentation'
  xmlns:x='http://schemas.microsoft.com/winfx/2006/xaml'
  Title='EssentialWPF'
  >
  <Button>Hello World</Button>
</Window>

// LoadTest.xaml.cs
public partial class LoadTest : Window {
  public LoadTest() {
    InitializeComponent();
  }
}
```

What happens if we comment out InitializeComponent? Go ahead and try; I'll wait.

An empty window is shown, right? The issue is that, inside of its implementation, InitializeComponent calls LoadComponent, which does the work of loading the XAML and generating the visuals. We can simulate the situation by calling LoadComponent ourselves:

```
public partial class LoadTest : Window {
  public LoadTest() {
    Application.LoadComponent(this,
            new Uri("LoadTest.xaml", UriKind.Relative));
  }
}
```

InitializeComponent also defines member variables and hooks up events, so generally I wouldn't recommend skipping calling it, but it's good to understand what's going on.

The other overload of LoadComponent is identical to calling new on the CLR type. The two overloads of LoadComponent are very different, so it is unfortunate that they have the same name. Both of the following lines will produce exactly the same result:

```
LoadTest load;

load = (LoadTest)Application.LoadComponent(
        new Uri("LoadTest.xaml", UriKind.Relative));
load = new LoadTest();
```

The two names for LoadTest—the URI and the CLR type—are clear here.

Document State

Document state is the set of data associated with a user document (like a Microsoft Word document or image file). Although .NET has some services for creating and manipulating documents, WPF provides no default framework for managing document state. This is something that application authors must integrate on their own.

Now that we've covered the basics of the Application object, we can start venturing into putting some pixels on the screen. At the top level of an application are three types of building blocks: windows, user controls, and pages.

Windows

User32 called it HWND, Microsoft Foundation Classes (MFC) called it CWnd, and Windows Forms called it Form. No matter what it's called, most UI frameworks eventually want to create a top-level visual element that end users can manipulate. In WPF we call it Window.

The base type for all windows in WPF is System.Windows.Window. Window is generally used for SDI windows and dialogs. Window is really nothing more than a control designed for hosting top-level content in an application. Typically we define a window using a combination of markup and code:

```
<!-- Window1.xaml -->
<Window   ...
   x:Class='EssentialWPF.Window1'
   Visibility='Visible'
   Title='This is a Window!'
   >
</Window>

// Window1.cs
namespace EssentialWPF {
   public partial class Window1 : Window {
     public Window1() {
        InitializeComponent();
     }
   }
}
```

Running this code will produce the boring window in Figure 2.10.

Note that even the life of a boring window like this has many phases, the most important of which are outlined here:

1. Constructor is called.
2. `Window.Initialized` event is raised.
3. `Window.Activated` event is raised.[13]
4. `Window.Loaded` event is raised.
5. `Window.ContentRendered` event is raised.
6. User interacts with the window.
7. `Window.Closing` event is raised.
8. `Window.Unloaded` event is raised.
9. `Window.Closed` event is raised.

`Activated` and `Deactivated` occur many times over the life of a window as the user switches between multiple windows running on the system. The `ContentRendered` event maps to the first time that the window is completely rendered. To make something happen immediately before anything is displayed to the user, we use `Loaded`; to make something happen immediately after something is displayed to the user, we use `ContentRendered`.

---

13. There is a `Window.Deactivated` event as well, which is raised when the window ceases to be the focused window—typically during phase 6 in this list.

FIGURE 2.10: A boring window

Probably the three most commonly used events are Loaded, Closing, and Closed. Loaded is generally where we initialize the default state of the window. Here we set the title of the window; running this code shows that the title of the window is always set before the window is visible:

```
<!-- Window1.xaml -->
<Window ...
  Loaded='WindowLoaded'
  >
</Window>

// Window1.xaml.cs
...
  void WindowLoaded(object sender, RoutedEventArgs e) {
    Title = "This window was loaded at " + DateTime.Now;
  }
...
```

The Closing event is raised before the window is actually closed. Because this event can be canceled, we can prevent the window from closing. Often this capability is used to implement features like user confirmation:

```
<!-- Window1.xaml -->
<Window ...
  Closing='WindowClosing'
  >
</Window>

// Window1.xaml.cs
...
  void WindowClosing(object sender, CancelEventArgs e) {
```

```
if (MessageBox.Show("Are you sure you want to close?",
    "Confirmation",
    MessageBoxButton.YesNo) == MessageBoxResult.No) {
  // prevent the window from closing
  e.Cancel = true;
}
else {
  // window will close
}
}
...
```

This window will close only if the user selects **Yes** when prompted by the message box on the screen.

Finally, the `Closed` event will fire only when the window is, in fact, closed (no longer visible to the user). I won't show an example, however, because only rarely should this event be used. If we try to save the document that a user is editing in the `Closed` event, what happens if we can't save the file? The window is already closed. It's best to save all work in the `Closing` event, so that if there's a problem it might be possible to stop the window from closing.

Displaying a Window

There are three primary methods for displaying a window: `Show`, `ShowDialog`, and the `Visibility` property. Calling `Show` and setting the `Visibility` property to `Visible` have exactly the same result: to display a window without mode.[14] People wanting to programmatically display a window expect a `Show` method, but for data binding and declarative programming people expect a property, so the WPF team provided both. Modeless windows are the best method for implementing the SDI windowing model.

We call `ShowDialog` to display the dialog modally. Modal dialogs allow us to implement the dialog windowing model:

---

14. *Modality* is a fancy word for describing a window's behavior with respect to other windows in the application. Windows that block all other windows are said to be *modal*. When a modal window is displayed, the window must be closed before the user can interact with any other window. *Modeless* windows are the opposite: they do not block other windows, and therefore the user can interact with any window while any number of other modeless windows are displayed.

```
<!-- Window1.xaml -->
<Window ... Title='Starter Window' >
  <StackPanel>
    <Button Click='ShowMethod'>Show</Button>
    <Button Click='UseVisibilityProperty'>Visibility = Visible</Button>
    <Button Click='ShowDialogMethod'>ShowDialog</Button>
  </StackPanel>
</Window>
```

```
// Window1.xaml.cs
...
  void ShowMethod(object sender, RoutedEventArgs e) {
    Window w = new Window();
    w.Title = "Show";
    w.Show();
  }
  void UseVisibilityProperty(object sender, RoutedEventArgs e) {
    Window w = new Window();
    w.Title = "Visibility = Visible";
    w.Visibility = Visibility.Visible;
  }
  void ShowDialogMethod(object sender, RoutedEventArgs e) {
    Window w = new Window();
    w.Title = "ShowDialog";
    w.Owner = this;
    w.WindowStartupLocation = WindowStartupLocation.CenterOwner;
    w.ShowInTaskbar = false;
    w.ShowDialog();
  }
...
```

Clicking either of the first two buttons will yield the same result, including the ability to select the original window and create any number of windows. Clicking the third button will block the ability to select the original window (Figure 2.11). The purpose of modal dialogs is to prohibit users from selecting other windows, although this behavior is often frustrating for people using the software because users want to be in control of the application, not be controlled by the application! Generally we try to limit modal dialogs to only the things that absolutely must be modal. (Yes, I know this is circular reasoning.)

Besides these normal ways of displaying a window, we want to be able to create a window that floats in front of another window while still allowing the user to select the parent window. Generally this feature would be used for modeless dialogs or floating tool windows. We can implement

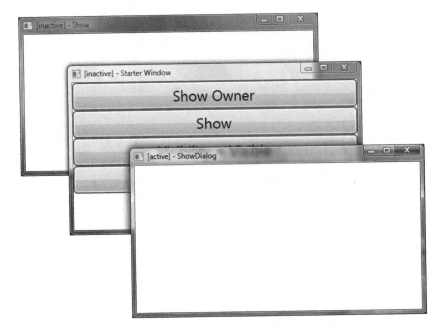

FIGURE 2.11: Showing a window using multiple methods

such a floating window by using the Show method but setting the Owner property (Figure 2.12). Owned windows are always displayed in front of their owner; however, they don't prevent the user from selecting the owner:

```
<!-- Window1.xaml -->
<Window ... Title='Starter Window' >
  <StackPanel>
    <Button Click='ShowOwner'>Show Owner</Button>
    <Button Click='ShowMethod'>Show</Button>
    <Button Click='UseVisibilityProperty'>Visibility = Visible</Button>
    <Button Click='ShowDialogMethod'>ShowDialog</Button>
  </StackPanel>
</Window>

// Window1.xaml.cs
...
  void ShowOwner(object sender, RoutedEventArgs e) {
    Window w = new Window();
    w.Owner = this;
    w.Title = "Show Owner";
    w.Show();
  }
...
```

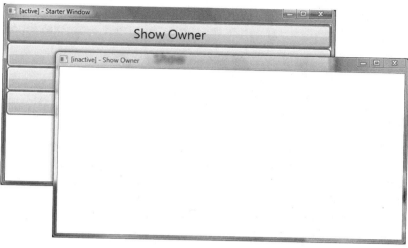

FIGURE 2.12: Showing a window with the Owner property

Owned windows have a couple other specific behaviors. They don't appear in the **Alt+Tab** window list, although they can optionally appear in the taskbar. In addition, they are automatically closed when the owning window is closed, and hidden when the owner is minimized.

Sizing and Position

Now that we know how to display a window, let's look at how to control where it is on the screen. There are three main types of control that we can exert on a window's size and position: startup behavior, user interactivity, and current values.

Startup behavior can be divided into two parts: where will the window be placed, and how big will it be? To determine where it will be, we use the `WindowStartupLocation` property, combined with the `Top` and `Left` properties. To determine how big it will be, we use the `SizeToContent` property in combination with the `Width` and `Height` properties. `SizeToContent` works as long as `Width` and `Height` are set to `Double.NaN` (auto) and the user has not resized the window.

After the desired location and dimensions for the window have been determined, what can the user do with the window? User interactivity is dictated by the `ResizeMode` property, which determines whether the user is allowed to resize the window at all. In addition, we can use the `MinWidth`, `MaxWidth`, `MinHeight`, and `MaxHeight` properties to control the amount by which the user can resize the window. Using the constraints and size modes, we can create windows that provide boundaries. In the following example, the window cannot be made smaller than 500 pixels, so all the content will remain readable:

```
<Window ...
  Title='EssentialWPF'
  MinWidth='500'
  >
  ...
</Window>
```

Finally, the current values of the window's position and size can be accessed with the Width, Height, Top, and Left properties. We can update the size or position of the window (or query what the current size or position is) at any time using these properties. Window sizing is strongly related to layout, which we will cover in Chapter 4.

Users have different expectations about the behavior—sizing, startup location, and ownership—of different window styles. For example, a dialog is expected to be displayed with code something like this:

```
void ShowDialogMethod(object sender, RoutedEventArgs e) {
  Window w = new Window();
  w.Title = "ShowDialog";
  w.Owner = this;
  w.SizeToContent = SizeToContent.WidthAndHeight;
  w.WindowStartupLocation = WindowStartupLocation.CenterOwner;
  w.ShowInTaskbar = false;
  w.ShowDialog();
}
```

This code ensures that the dialog is centered on the owner, does not appear in the taskbar, and resizes automatically to fit the content.

Window and Application

Once we have a window (or windows) up and running, visible, positioned, and sized, we often want to find all the open windows. Most applications that allow multiple top-level windows (such as Microsoft Office Word 2003) provide a Window menu to navigate to the other open documents. One way to implement this feature is to create a global variable to which each window is added as it is shown and closed. The WPF team, however, chose to build this feature into the Application object, so in WPF

TABLE 2.3: Shutdown Behavior

ShutdownMode Value	Defined	Common Uses
OnLastWindowClose (default)	The application will shut down when the windows collection is empty. Each window is created after the application is added to the list, and removed when it is closed.	SDI applications that create multiple top-level windows—for example, Microsoft Internet Explorer.
OnMainWindowClose	The application will shut down when the window assigned to the MainWindow property on the application is closed.	SDI applications with a primary window—for example, an application with one document window and a collection of floating tool windows (such as Adobe Photoshop)
OnExplicitShutdown	The application will shut down only when the ShutDown method is called by user code.	Any scenario in which custom logic is required for shutdown. For example, an application might have no open windows but instead use a tray icon to show presence (e.g., MSN Messenger).

the Application object is automatically notified whenever a window is created or closed.

Because the Application object is informed about all windows, it can automatically shut down when the last window is closed (or for other reasons). The call to Shutdown is often performed automatically in response to the value of the ShutdownMode property on the Application object. Table 2.3 lists the possible values.

We can also enumerate all the currently open windows using the Application.Windows property. To demonstrate, we can create a window with two buttons. The first button will create a new window; the second will display a list of all the open windows:

```
<!-- WindowList.xaml -->
<Window ... x:Class='EssentialWPF.WindowList'
  Title='Window List'
  SizeToContent='WidthAndHeight'
  >
```

```
<StackPanel>
  <Button Click='NewWindowClicked'>Create New Window</Button>
  <Button Click='ListOpenWindows'>List Open Windows</Button>
</StackPanel>
</Window>
```

To make it obvious that we're creating several windows, we will use a static variable and increment it so that each window has a different caption. In the `NewWindowClicked` event handler we can simply create a new window and show it:

```
// WindowList.xaml.cs
public partial class WindowList : Window {
  static int _createCount;
  public WindowList() {
    InitializeComponent();
    Title = "Window List " + _createCount;
    _createCount++;
  }
  void NewWindowClicked(object sender, RoutedEventArgs e) {
    new WindowList().Show();
  }
}
```

Finally, to implement the `ListOpenWindows` event handler, we can simply iterate through the windows collection on our `Application` object and build a string with all the titles. When we run this code, we end up with something like Figure 2.13:

```
void ListOpenWindows(object sender, RoutedEventArgs e) {
  StringBuilder sb = new StringBuilder();
  foreach (Window openWindow in Application.Current.Windows) {
    sb.AppendLine(openWindow.Title);
  }
  MessageBox.Show(sb.ToString(), "Open Windows");
}
```

User Controls

In the previous section we learned how to create windows. An interesting aspect of defining windows is that they define an encapsulated set of functionality. Windows are also isolated, both because a new CLR type is defined and because a top-level window that is visually isolated is created. Often we want to break our UI definition down into smaller chunks that

FIGURE 2.13: Displaying the list of open windows

are encapsulated, but we don't necessarily want each of these to be a new window. This is the role that user controls play.

There are two primary kinds of control developers: user controls and custom controls. The names are slightly arbitrary—they date back to Visual Basic 5.0, which introduced a simple way to build controls—but they are used to convey the two different scenarios. My definition is that **user controls** are used as a way of encapsulating parts of the UI, and **custom controls** are used as a way to build reusable controls for other applications to consume. The gray area between the two is the source of much debate.

Defining a user control is exactly like defining a new window, except that the base class can be any class. In reality, creating a window is like creating a user control. The typical base class for a user control is ContentControl:

```
<ContentControl ...
  x:Class='EssentialWPF.MyUserControl'
  >
  <Button Click='ButtonClicked'>Hello World</Button>
</ContentControl>
```

Just as we do with windows, we can put logic in a code-behind file:

```
public partial class MyUserControl : ContentControl {
  public MyUserControl() {
    InitializeComponent();
  }
```

```
void ButtonClicked(object sender, RoutedEventArgs e) {
  MessageBox.Show("Howdy!");
}
}
```

Now we can use the new control anywhere in an application, but first we must create an XML namespace for the application. Using the clr-namespace scheme, we can associate any CLR namespace with an XML namespace in XAML:

```
<Window ... x:Class='EssentialWPF.UserControlHost'
  xmlns:l='clr-namespace:EssentialWPF'
  Title='User Controls'
  >
  ...
</Window>
```

Voilà! Now we can use the user control in our window (Figure 2.14):

```
<Window ...
  x:Class='EssentialWPF.UserControlHost'
  xmlns:l='clr-namespace:EssentialWPF'
  Title='User Controls'
  >
  <StackPanel>
    <l:MyUserControl />
    <l:MyUserControl />
  </StackPanel>
</Window>
```

FIGURE 2.14: A window with two instances of a newly defined user control

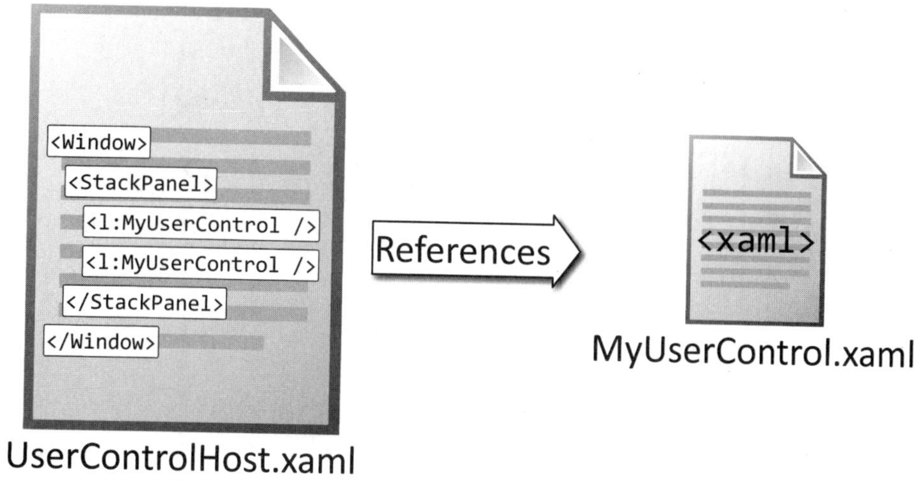

FIGURE 2.15: Logical model of how referencing a user control works

What's happening here is that the two custom tags `<l:MyUserControl />` are referring to a component defined in `MyUserControl.xaml` (Figure 2.15). If we update the definition in `MyUserControl.xaml`, both uses will be updated.

User controls are designed to be used as a way of dividing an application into components. When we want to move into the realm of creating a complete custom control (defining a theme, supporting content, etc.), we should think about building a custom control. Building a custom control requires a deeper understanding of the control model in WPF, and that depth is beyond the scope of this book.

Looking back at this section, notice that creating a custom window is really just a special case of creating a user control. Another way of factoring an application into manageable chunks is to use pages, which are part of the WPF navigation framework.

Navigation and Pages

HTML is often credited with introducing navigation into applications, but lots of examples of navigation date much further back in history. Every wizard, gopher screen, or bulletin board system is an example of early navigation. HTML popularized the notion of navigation through a series of pages connected through hyperlinks. Because of the popularity of the Web,

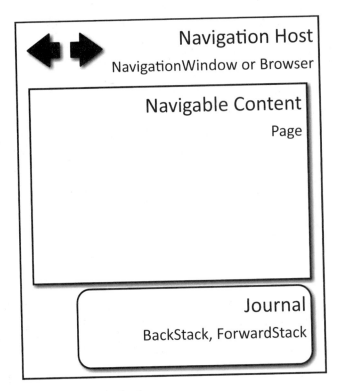

FIGURE 2.16: Logical model for navigation

almost every user immediately understands how to use links to navigate through information or an application.

To make it easy to build applications that leverage this navigation model, WPF has a built-in navigation framework. The three basic concepts are navigation hosts (NavigationWindow), navigable content (Page), and the journal (Figure 2.16).[15] The journal is responsible for tracking the navigation actions for the application, but it is not a public class in the framework.

NavigationWindow is the default host for navigation in WPF. Navigation-Window derives from Window and adds a default navigation UI (back button, etc.) and the necessary infrastructure to enable navigation. NavigationWindow has access to all the same application-level features as

---

15. It is important not to confuse *history* with the *journal*. The Internet Explorer team refers to the two concepts as History and TravelLog, respectively. History is a persistent list of sites visited, a type of automatic bookmark list created on the basis of time. The journal, or TravelLog, is the list of sites visited in this session. This is a subtle difference, but it's important when we're thinking about a navigation framework.

`Window`. Using `NavigationWindow`, we can implement the SDI navigation windowing model.

In WPF we can navigate to any content: data objects, primitive types like strings, or pages. `Page` is nothing more than a convenient class that has helper methods for making content easier to navigate.

Before we jump into a complete markup-based solution for navigation, let's look at a simple example of navigation that uses only code, to make it clear how things fit together. To start, we will create a new window. Because we want to support navigation, we will derive this window from `NavigationWindow` instead of `Window`:

```
public class NavExample : NavigationWindow {
  public NavExample() { }
}
```

`NavigationWindow` is a navigation host, which means it can host navigable content. We can define a new piece of navigable content by deriving from `Page`. Creating a new page is just like defining a `Window` or user control:

```
public class Page1 : Page {
  public Page1() {
    this.WindowTitle = "Page 1";
  }
}
```

Now we need to tell `NavigationWindow` to display our first page (`Page1`):

```
public class NavExample : NavigationWindow {
  public NavExample() {
    Navigate(new Page1());
  }
}
```

Fabulous! We have a navigation host displaying some navigable content. However, it isn't very interesting yet, because we don't have the user navigating to anything. In fact, running this code as it stands produces a blank window. Let's define a second page:

```
public class Page2 : Page {
  public Page2() {
    WindowTitle = "Page 2";
  }
}
```

Then we can make the first page more interesting by adding some content, including a hyperlink:[16]

```
public class Page1 : Page {
  public Page1() {
    TextBlock block = new TextBlock();
    Hyperlink link = new Hyperlink();
    link.Inlines.Add("Click for page 2");
    block.Inlines.Add(link);
    Content = block;
    WindowTitle = "Page 1";
  }
}
```

The final step is to handle the Click event on Hyperlink to navigate to the next page. The NavigationService object provides host-independent access to navigation operations. NavigationService will work for navigation regardless of whether the page is hosted in the browser or in NavigationWindow:

```
public class Page1 : Page {
  public Page1() {
    TextBlock block = new TextBlock();
    Hyperlink link = new Hyperlink();
    link.Click += LinkClicked;
    link.Inlines.Add("Click for page 2");
    block.Inlines.Add(link);
    Content = block;
    WindowTitle = "Page 1";
  }
  void LinkClicked(object sender, RoutedEventArgs e) {
    NavigationService.Navigate(new Page2());
  }
}
```

Running this code will produce something like Figure 2.17. Clicking the link should bring up the second page, which is blank except for the caption change in the window (Figure 2.18).

---

16. All this code of blocks and inlines will be explained in more detail in Chapter 5. For now you'll have to trust me when I say that this is adding a couple bits of text with a hyperlink.

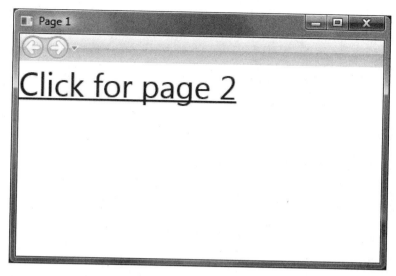

FIGURE 2.17: Initial navigation display

All the basics of navigation are here now. We have a host, some content, a journal tracking everything, and even a basic UI for moving forward and back. Clicking the link enables the back button, which takes the user back to the previous page, after which the forward button becomes enabled.

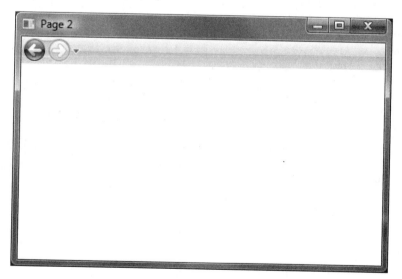

FIGURE 2.18: After navigating to page 2

All of this is provided by the journal. NavigationWindow provides the default navigation UI (back button, title bar, etc.) and automatically hooks up the journal.

If we convert this example to markup, it should look like possibly familiar HTML. We can leverage the fact that Hyperlink natively supports navigation to a URI-based component, which lets us replace all of the code we saw previously with this markup:

```
<!-- page1.xaml -->
<Page ...
  WindowTitle='Page 1'>
  <TextBlock>
    <Hyperlink NavigateUri='page2.xaml'>
      Click for page 2
    </Hyperlink>
  </TextBlock>
</Page>

<!-- page2.xaml -->
<Page ...
  WindowTitle='Page 2'>
</Page>

<!-- navexample.xaml -->
<NavigationWindow ...
  x:Class='EssentialWPF.NavExample'
  Source='page1.xaml'>
</NavigationWindow>
```

NavigationWindow's Source property can be set to the URI-based name of the first page—Page1.xaml—to avoid having to create an instance of the type. Hyperlink's NavigateUri property likewise can be set to the URI Page2.xaml, which is the URI-based name of the second page, so that no code has to be written to handle the Click event.

When we don't want to customize the look of the basic navigation window, as is often the case, we can skip defining it altogether. Using the StartupUri property on Application, we can launch the page directly:

```
<!-- app.xaml -->
<Application ...
  x:Class='EssentialWPF.App'
  StartupUri='page1.xaml'>
</Application>
```

Passing State Between Pages

What we've accomplished so far is all fine and good when we have just one page or the second page doesn't do anything, but once we start doing more, we need to be able to transfer data between pages. In HTML we transfer data typically by storing state on the server, or possibly using a cookie on the client. One simple option for transferring data in WPF is to leverage the `Properties` dictionary on `Application`.

For this example, let's write two pages: the first will accept a user's name, and the second will greet that person. The first page will have a text box to accept user input and a hyperlink to navigate to the next page:

```
<Page ...
  x:Class='EssentialWPF.Name'
  WindowTitle='Who are you?'
  >
  <StackPanel>
    <Label>What is your name?</Label>
    <TextBox Name='_nameBox'/>
    <TextBlock>
      <Hyperlink NavigateUri='hello.xaml'>Continue</Hyperlink>
    </TextBlock>
  </StackPanel>
</Page>
```

The second page will simply have a label that should display the name the user entered:

```
<Page ...
  x:Class='EssentialWPF.Hello'
  WindowTitle='Hello!'
  >
  <StackPanel>
    <TextBlock>Hello!</TextBlock>
    <Label Name='_name' />
  </StackPanel>
</Page>
```

The first step is to copy the data out of the text box on the name page and push it into the application. Then we can update the navigation logic to use the property to store the necessary data. By hooking the `RequestNavigate` event, we can stuff the name into the application object right before the navigation occurs (Figure 2.19):

```
<!-- name.xaml -->
<Page ...
  x:Class='EssentialWPF.Name'
  WindowTitle='Who are you?'
  >
  <StackPanel>
...
    <Hyperlink
      NavigateUri='hello.xaml'
      RequestNavigate='Page_RequestNavigate'
      >
      Continue
    </Hyperlink>
...
  </StackPanel>
</Page>

// name.xaml.cs
public partial class Name : Page {
  ...
  void Page_RequestNavigate(object sender,
                RequestNavigateEventArgs e) {
    Application.Current.Properties["Name"] = _nameBox.Text;
  }
}
```

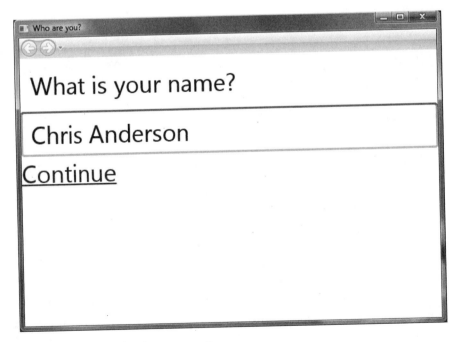

FIGURE 2.19: Entering data in name.xaml

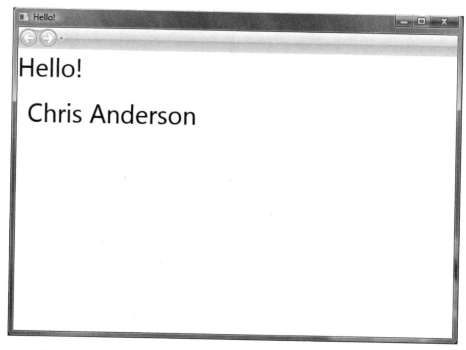

FIGURE 2.20: Consuming the data from name.xaml

On the second page we need to hook the Loaded event, grab the data from the application, and display it (Figure 2.20):

```
<!-- hello.xaml -->
<Page ...
  x:Class="EssentialWPF.Hello"
  Text="Hello!"
  Loaded="PageLoaded"
  >
...
</Page>

// hello.xaml.cs
using System;
using System.Windows;
using System.Windows.Navigation;
using System.Windows.Controls;

namespace EssentialWPF {
  public partial class Hello : Page {
    public Hello() {
      InitializeComponent();
    }
```

```
    void PageLoaded(object sender, EventArgs e) {
      _name.Content = Application.Current.Properties["Name"];
    }
  }
}
```

This approach works great for simple scenarios, but in the end, using the Application object like this is really nothing more than using a global variable. My object-oriented spider sense tingles when I see code using global variables. Remember that we don't always have to navigate via URI; instead we can create the second page programmatically and set properties just as we do for any other object. Thus we can keep the communication between the two pages isolated:

```
<!-- hello.xaml -->
<Page ...
  x:Class='EssentialWPF.Hello'
  Text='Hello!'
  >
...
</Page>

// hello.xaml.cs
...
public partial class Hello : Page {
  public string Name {
    set { _name.Content = value; }
  }
}
...

<!-- name.xaml -->
<Page ...>
...
  <Hyperlink Click='Navigate'>Continue</Hyperlink>
...
</Page>

// name.xaml.cs
...
void Navigate(object sender, RoutedEventArgs e) {
  Hello hello = new Hello();

  hello.Name = _nameBox.Text;
  NavigationService.Navigate(hello);
}
...
```

A promising option for passing state between pages is the navigation-State argument on Navigate:

```
public class NavigationService {
...
  public bool Navigate(object root);
  public bool Navigate(Uri source);
  public bool Navigate(object root, object navigationState);
  public bool Navigate(Uri source, object navigationState);
...
}
```

It's a little tricky to get to, but we can capture the data by using the LoadCompleted event on NavigationService. First we can change the caller to put the extra data in the Navigate call:

```
void Navigate(object sender, RoutedEventArgs e) {
  Hello hello = new Hello();
  NavigationService.Navigate(hello, _nameBox.Text);
}
```

In our "hello" page, we can listen to the LoadCompleted event. NavigationService for a page has a null value until the Loaded event is raised, so we must do the hookup for the LoadCompleted event[17] in the event handler for the Loaded event (I said it was slightly tricky):

```
void PageLoaded(object sender, EventArgs e) {
  NavigationService.LoadCompleted += LoadCompleted;
}
void LoadCompleted(object sender, NavigationEventArgs e) {
  _name.Content = e.ExtraData;
  NavigationService.LoadCompleted -= LoadCompleted;
}
```

There are a lot of ways to hook up the LoadCompleted event, and they all have pros and cons. Using the Application object introduces some global

---

17. Notice also that we had to unhook from LoadCompleted in our handler. LoadCompleted is a NavigationService event; that is, it will fire for every page that is loaded in NavigationService. By unhooking after we are notified of the page being loaded, we avoid getting extra notifications. It is also important to unhook from the event to prevent NavigationService from keeping our page in memory for the lifetime of the service.

state that can often be tricky to deal with in larger applications. Setting properties on pages removes the ability to declare navigation in XAML. Using the navigationState argument on Navigate has the same problem.

The method that I found works best for pages with parameters is to create a command for the navigation (because commands support parameters) and style a button (which supports commands) to look like a hyperlink.[18] It's not particularly elegant, but it works.

Controlling Navigation

One problem with the previous example is that the user can navigate away without filling out the name field. When working with a Window object, to prevent the user from dismissing a dialog without completing the required fields, we can use the Closing event (or any other validation to determine if we want to close the window).

The equivalent functionality is found on NavigationService:

```
public class NavigationService
{
   ` ...
    public event LoadCompletedEventHandler LoadCompleted;
    public event NavigatedEventHandler Navigated;
    public event NavigatingCancelEventHandler Navigating;
    public event NavigationProgressEventHandler NavigationProgress;
    public event NavigationStoppedEventHandler NavigationStopped;
    ...
}
```

Using Navigating, we can cancel navigation in the same way that we cancel the closing of a window. Because there isn't a simple event like Window.Closing on Page, we have to do a little bit of work. The reason is subtle, but important. When we add a listener to the Navigating event, we are putting a pointer to our object in NavigationService, which is part of the navigation host. If we don't sever this link, the page will be kept in memory forever. This gets a bit more complicated because once the navigation is completed, we no longer have access to NavigationService, so we must cache it.

---

18. For an example, see http://blog.simplegeek.com/book.

Let's walk through the code for adding validation to our page. First we will hook the Loaded event on Page. Loaded will be raised every time a user navigates to the page:

```
<!-- name.xaml -->
<Page ...
  x:Class='EssentialWPF.Name'
  Text='Who are you?'
  Loaded='PageLoaded'
  >
...
</Page>
```

Now, in Loaded we need to do two things: attach listeners to the correct events, and cache NavigationService:

```
NavigationService _navigation;

void PageLoaded(object sender, EventArgs e) {
  _navigation = this.NavigationService;
  _navigation.Navigating += Page_Navigating;
  _navigation.Navigated += Page_Navigated;
}
```

We have hooked the Navigated event simply to do the needed unhooking of the events and clearing of our references to prevent the leak:

```
void Page_Navigated(object sender, NavigationEventArgs e) {
  _navigation.Navigating -= Page_Navigating;
  _navigation.Navigated -= Page_Navigated;
  _navigation = null;
}
```

Finally we get to the Navigating event handler, where we can perform the actual validation:

```
void Page_Navigating(object sender, NavigatingCancelEventArgs e) {
  if (_nameBox.Text.Length == 0) {
    e.Cancel = true;
  }
}
```

This code will prevent navigation unless the name is filled in. If you try this out, try clicking the forward button in the navigation window after clicking back from the "hello" page. When you click back, the name is empty, at which point clicking forward on the navigation bar won't work. Because we want the forward button to move to the page where you were, we shouldn't do our validation. With a slight change, we can catch this case:

```
void Page_Navigating(object sender, NavigatingCancelEventArgs e) {
  if (e.NavigationMode == NavigationMode.New &&
    _nameBox.Text.Length == 0) {
    e.Cancel = true;
  }
}
```

Controlling the Journal

We have navigation under control now; we can choose when to navigate and where to go. The next problem that application authors typically face with navigation applications is controlling the journal. Because the journal is the service responsible for tracking where a user has been, and for populating the back and forward buttons, there are many scenarios for how it should be controlled. Probably the two most common scenarios are shopping-cart applications (once the purchase has been completed, removing all the entries from the journal that were part of the purchase process to prevent people from accidentally resubmitting the same order) and login pages (once the user has logged in, having the back button return to the home page, not the login screen) (Figure 2.21).

To see how to control the journal, let's update the example from the previous section to include a home page:

```
<!-- home.xaml -->
<Page ...
  x:Class='EssentialWPF.Home'
  WindowTitle='Home'
  >
  <TextBlock>
    Welcome to the application. I can say
    <Hyperlink NavigateUri='name.xaml'>hello</Hyperlink>
    to you.
  </TextBlock>
</Page>

<!-- app.xaml -->
<Application ...
  x:Class='EssentialWPF.App'
  StartupUri='home.xaml'
  >
</Application>
```

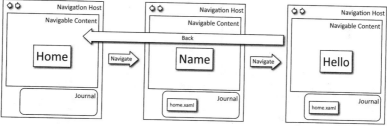

FIGURE 2.21: The navigation flow that we want after the user has logged into our program

Next we want to update our login page (name.xaml) to remove itself from the journal once it has succeeded in getting the user's name. The entire API for working with the journal is on `NavigationService`:

```
public sealed class NavigationService {
  public bool CanGoBack { get; }
  public bool CanGoForward { get; }

  public void AddBackEntry(CustomContentState state);
  public void GoBack();
  public void GoForward();
  public JournalEntry RemoveBackEntry();
}
```

Looking back at Figure 2.21, notice that we don't want `name.xaml` to be put into the journal, because we want to make sure that the back button from the "hello" page goes back to the home page. To remove the entry, we simply call `RemoveBackEntry` after the navigation is completed:

```
void Page_Navigated(object sender, NavigationEventArgs e) {
  _navigation.RemoveBackEntry();
  ...
}
```

In addition to controlling the journal, we may want to simply query the journal. The most common reason for wanting to do this is to put a custom back button on the page. This is a trivial task: the `CanGoBack` property is used to enable or disable the button, and the `GoBack` method is used to perform the operation.

Functional Navigation and Page Functions
Traditional navigation today is unstructured. It is much like programming in BASIC in the 1960s: arbitrary goto statements jumping between parts of

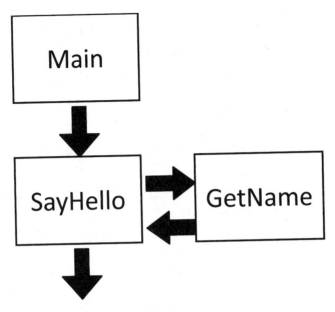

FIGURE 2.22: Logic flow of a console application

an application, global variables tracking state, and line numbers needing to be fixed whenever something is changed. Today we call them *hyperlinks, session states* or *cookies,* and *URIs,* but the same problems are still there. Web sites are brittle, difficult to change in terms of flow, and hard to encapsulate functionality.

WPF introduces a new, more functional form of navigation, in which navigation is modeled much more like a function call. To understand what I mean by *functional navigation,* let's walk through a simple example. Suppose we want to create a program that greets the user, asks the user's name, and says hello. Figure 2.22 shows the rough flow of logic.

Implementing this as a standard console application is trivial. Obviously this is a simple example, but by encapsulating the functionality in methods, we could reuse it in later parts of the application:

```
// program.cs
using System;
static class Program {
  static void Main() {
    Console.WriteLine("Welcome to my program");
    SayHello();
  }
```

```
static void SayHello() {
  string name = GetName();
  Console.WriteLine("Hello {0}!", name);
}
static string GetName() {
  Console.Write("What is your name? ");
  string name = Console.ReadLine();
  return name;
}
}
```

Running this code produces a simple user experience:

```
C:\projects\ConsoleFunction> program.exe
Welcome to my program
What is your name? chris
Hello chris!
```

The nice thing about the console application is that everything is synchronous. When we ask the user for a piece of information, we sit and wait for it. In a GUI application we could implement the same model using a series of modal dialogs, but that doesn't fit in the context of a navigation application.

To translate this to a navigation model, we need to embrace asynchronicity. Navigating to a new page may take any amount of time, and we can't block the application while we wait for the user to respond (remember, this is a single-threaded application, so if we block on the UI thread, the user won't even be able type into a text box!).

To start, we can build our welcome page as a `PageFunction` object. Every instance of `PageFunction` has a return type; in this case we aren't really returning anything from our welcome page, so we don't care what type it is. We'll use `Object`:

```
public class Welcome : PageFunction<object> {
  public Welcome() {
    TextBlock text = new TextBlock();
    text.FontSize=24;
    text.Inlines.Add("Welcome!");
    Content = text;
  }
}
```

We will then need to create a UI to display to the user. The details of how to program the UI will be covered in Chapter 3.

FIGURE 2.23: Our first page function: displaying "Welcome!"

PageFunction derives from Page, so anywhere that we can navigate to Page we can also navigate to PageFunction. To display our welcome page, we need to create a navigation window and navigate to it (Figure 2.23):

```
public class Program {
  [STAThread]
  static void Main() {
    Application app = new Application();
    NavigationWindow w = new NavigationWindow();
    w.Show();
    w.Navigate(new Welcome());
    app.Run();
  }
}
```

In our original logic flow and the console program, the welcome was followed with a call to SayHello. Encapsulation of logic is one of the big benefits of functional programming, so we don't want the welcome page to have any knowledge of how SayHello will be implemented. We need to do two things then: first, create the new PageFunction for SayHello; and second, put a link between Welcome and SayHello:

```
public class Welcome : PageFunction<object> {
  public Welcome() {
    TextBlock block = new TextBlocks();
    block.FontSize=24;
    block.Inlines.Add("Welcome!");

    Hyperlink link = new Hyperlink();
    link.Inlines.Add("Next");
    link.Click += DoSayHello;
    block.Inlines.Add(link);

    Content = block;
  }
```

```
    void DoSayHello(object sender, RoutedEventArgs e) {
      NavigationService.Navigate(new SayHello());
    }
  }
}
public class SayHello : PageFunction<object> {
  public SayHello() {
  }
}
```

Our first method call is completed. So far, this is exactly the same model that we would expect for traditional navigation: In response to a click, we navigate to the next page. GetName is more interesting; it has a return parameter. We know that the first thing that SayHello needs to do is get the name from the user. However, we've already navigated to SayHello.

There are two important things to note about how to call PageFunction with a return value. First, because of the asynchronous nature of navigation, the completion of the function is modeled as an event. We attach a listener to the GetName.Return event to perform actions after the function is complete. Second, when we navigate to PageFunction, we are navigating away from the current object. That may seem obvious, but if you think about it, it means that SayHello must be unloaded for GetName to display. To make this simple to implement, we can use the KeepAlive property to keep the instance of SayHello alive in memory, so that when GetName is completed the exact same instance of SayHello will be activated. Keep-Alive can be used for any page.

Figure 2.24 illustrates this navigation flow. The Welcome object is created, and then we navigate to SayHello. At this point the Welcome object is destroyed. When we navigate to SayHello, the first thing it does is navigate to GetName, but because KeepAlive is set to true, the instance of Say-Hello is kept in the journal (not just the URI, which is what the journal normally keeps). When GetName returns, SayHello is displayed again.

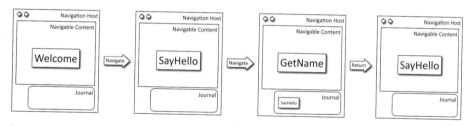

FIGURE 2.24: Flow of navigation with page functions

To implement this navigation flow in code, we will update SayHello to call GetName. The call to NavigationService.Navigate must be made after the object is initialized; during the constructor call there is no NavigationService:

```
public class SayHello : PageFunction<object> {
  public SayHello() {
    // We need to be kept alive, so that we can listen
    // to the return of GetName
    //
    this.KeepAlive = true;

    // When this page is initialized, we first need to get
    // the name from the user
    //
    this.Initialized += DoGetName;
  }

  void DoGetName(object sender, EventArgs e) {
    // To get the name from the user, we navigate to
    // GetName, and listen for GetName to complete (Return)
    //
    GetName get = new GetName();
    get.Return += GetNameReturned;
    NavigationService.Navigate(get);
  }
  void GetNameReturned(object sender, ReturnEventArgs<string> e) {
    // When GetName returns, we can update the content
    // of this page to say hello to the user
    //
    Label label = new Label();
    label.Content = string.Format("Hello {0}", e2.Result);
    Content = label;
  }
}
```

Finally, we need to implement GetName. Since GetName returns a string, we will define it as PageFunction<string>. We will add a label to prompt the user, a text box for the user to enter a name, and finally a button to click to finish. If we call OnReturn, the page function framework will automatically raise the Return event and navigate back to the caller of this function:

```
public class GetName : PageFunction<string> {
  public GetName() {
    StackPanel stack = new StackPanel();

    Label label = new Label();
    label.Content = "What is your name?";
    stack.Children.Add(label);
```

```
    TextBox nameBox = new TextBox();
    stack.Children.Add(nameBox);

    Button done = new Button();
    done.Content = "Done";
    done.Click += ReturnName;
    stack.Children.Add(done);

    Content = stack;
  }
  void ReturnName(object sender, RoutedEventArgs e) {
    OnReturn(new ReturnEventArgs<string>(nameBox.Text));
  }
}
```

Note that, in the implementation of GetName, there is no mention of SayHello. GetName is just like a function in any programming language, it can be called from any number of pages, and it will always return to the correct page.

Page functions are by far the biggest navigation innovation that WPF introduces. Once we have shifted to thinking about method calls as navigation and we are returning results as events, we can begin to approach building navigation-based applications using many of the same models as in writing object-oriented code. Sometimes simple page links are adequate, but for many programming tasks, using a function-oriented model for navigation is far more productive.

Hosting Applications in a Browser

When people think about navigation, typically they think of an application hosted inside of the Web browser, such as www.msn.com. WPF applications support running either in a stand-alone window or inside the browser. XAML Browser Applications (XBAPs) allow us to run an application inside the browser frame; they have no permanent presence on the user's machine, and they normally run in a .NET-enforced partial-trust sandbox.

There is no cut-and-dried answer to the question of when it's preferable to write an XBAP instead of creating a standard application. First there's the issue of the user model. Browser applications tend to be a lighter experience for the user (the user navigates to and away from them, instead of launching a separate application), and they tend to be more integrated into the user's workflow (the user decides when to navigate to and away from an application). Traditional applications generally have a more modal feeling (the user is either running the application or not) and tend to put the application more in control (an explicit exit action is typically required from the user).

In addition to the user model question is the question of whether the application can function properly with the restrictions of running in a browser. Browser applications cannot put icons in the start menu, install file extension handlers, or in any other way leave a permanent mark on the user's machine. In addition, they normally run in a partial-trust environment, where only a subset of the functionality of .NET Framework is available.[19] For example, when running in an XBAP, we can't use the latest Web service protocols provided by the Windows Communication Foundation, but rather are limited to the Web service support offering in .NET 2.0.

As a general recommendation, users prefer browser-based applications for applications they use occasionally, and stand-alone applications for applications they use every day. Luckily, it is relatively easy to switch between the two, so you can try both.

HelloBrowser

An application that is hosted in a browser must have at least one page, must have `Application.StartupUri` set, and must have the `HostIn-Browser` property set in the project file. One of the restrictions of partial trust is that new windows cannot be created and displayed; all visuals must be displayed in pages:

```
<!-- HelloBrowser.csproj -->
<Project
  DefaultTargets='Build'
  xmlns='http://schemas.microsoft.com/developer/msbuild/2003'>
  <PropertyGroup>
    ...
```

---

19. There is no complete list of functionality available in partial trust; rather, the SDK documentation for .NET Framework 3.0 states whether each function is available in partial trust.

```
    <HostInBrowser>True</HostInBrowser>
  </PropertyGroup>
  ...
</Project>

<!-- App.xaml -->
<Application ... x:Class='HelloBrowser.MyApp'
  StartupUri='Page1.xaml'
  />

<!-- page1.xaml -->
<Page ... x:Class='HelloBrowser.Page1'>
  <TextBlock FontSize='24pt'>Hello Browser!</TextBlock>
</Page>
```

If only it were this easy, but that's not the case. Unfortunately, we must sign the application manifest[20] to create a browser-hosted application; I hope this limitation will be removed in the future (we don't have to sign HTML and JavaScript files, after all!). If you happen to be using Visual Studio, it is relatively straightforward to create a test signature:

```
<Project DefaultTargets='Build'
  xmlns='http://schemas.microsoft.com/developer/msbuild/2003'>
  <PropertyGroup>
    ...
    <HostInBrowser>True</HostInBrowser>
    <SignManifests>True</SignManifests>
    <ManifestCertificateThumbprint>X</ManifestCertificateThumbprint>
    <ManifestKeyFile>HelloBrowser_TemporaryKey.pfx</ManifestKeyFile>
  </PropertyGroup>
  ...
</Project>
```

Once we set the manifest to be signed, we can compile the application. Now a new output file will be created with the extension XBAP. Figure 2.25 (on page 106) shows all the files.

The XBAP file is an XML file containing deployment information, exactly the same as the deployment manifest[21] used for desktop applications.

---

20. Complete information on ClickOnce application manifests is included in the WinFX SDK.
21. Complete information about ClickOnce deployment manifests is included in the WinFX SDK.

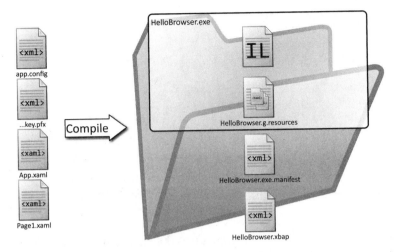

FIGURE 2.25: Compiling an XBAP application: inputs and outputs

The two most important pieces of information here are the `deployment` and `assemblyIdentity` tags:

```
<!-- HelloBrowser.xbap -->
<?xml version='1.0' encoding='utf-8'?>
<asmv1:assembly
  xsi:schemaLocation='urn:schemas-microsoft-com:asm.v1
  assembly.adaptive.xsd'
  manifestVersion='1.0' ...>

  <assemblyIdentity
    name='HelloBrowser.application'
    version='1.0.0.0'
    publicKeyToken='7038621db733f8fe'
    language='neutral'
    processorArchitecture='msil'
    xmlns='urn:schemas-microsoft-com:asm.v1' />

  <description
    asmv2:publisher='Microsoft'
    asmv2:product='HelloBrowser'
    xmlns='urn:schemas-microsoft-com:asm.v1' />

  <deployment install='false' />

  <dependency>
    <dependentAssembly
      dependencyType='install'
      codebase='HelloBrowser.exe.manifest'
      size='10037'>
```

```
<assemblyIdentity
  name='HelloBrowser.exe'
  version='1.0.0.0'
  publicKeyToken='7038621db733f8fe'
  language='neutral'
  processorArchitecture='msil'
  type='win32' />

<hash>
  ...
</hash>
    </dependentAssembly>
  </dependency>

<publisherIdentity
  name='CN=XXX'
  issuerKeyHash='XXX'
  />

<Signature
  Id='StrongNameSignature'
  xmlns='http://www.w3.org/2000/09/xmldsig#'>
  ...
</Signature>
</asmv1:assembly>
```

The deployment tag specifies that the application will not be installed, which prevents the creation of a start menu icon for the application or entries in add/remove programs. The only evidence left on a machine that a user navigated to a Web browser application will be the entry in the

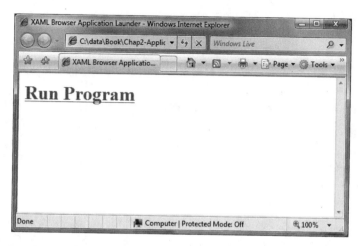

FIGURE 2.26: Internet Explorer displaying an HTML page

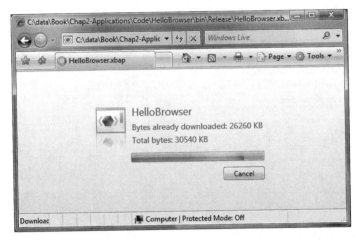

FIGURE 2.27: Internet Explorer displaying the download dialog[22] for a XAML Browser Application

browser's history, any cookies sent down from a Web server, files in the user's temporary Internet files directory, and possibly some data in the CLR's isolated store—all of which are automatically purged from the machine periodically, using the same OS features as Web sites use.

The `assemblyIdentity` tag tells the system where the implementation of the program is—something important for actually running it!

The most common way that a Web browser application is launched is that a user clicks a link. In this case, let's create a small HTML page with a link to the XBAP file. We will put it in the same directory as the XBAP file:

```
<h1>
  <a href='hellobrowser.xbap'>Run Program</a>
</h1>
```

Navigating the browser to this HTML file will display a standard HTML view (Figure 2.26 on page 107).

When the user clicks the link, the browser navigates to the XBAP, which causes the application to run inside of the browser. Depending on whether the application is already cached, the downloading page may be visible (Figure 2.27).

---

22. Astute readers might notice that the download size of this application is huge (30MB). In reality, the compiled application is so small that I couldn't get a screen capture of the download dialog. To make this picture I added a bunch of junk data to the program to make it take a few seconds to download.

FIGURE 2.28: Internet Explorer displaying a XAML Browser Application

Once the application is downloaded, you should see the UI in Figure 2.28. The goal is a seamless user experience with no additional windows being created, dialogs being displayed, or any other interruption to the flow.

Under the Covers

WPF hosts applications by implementing an ActiveX DocObject (or OLE DocObject, depending on when you learned about this stuff). Any application that supports hosting DocObjects can host WPF applications. When the .NET Framework 3.0 runtime is installed, a mime handler is registered for the XBAP extension, which loads up WPF. WPF runs all browser-hosted applications out of process, using a host application called PresentationHost.

From a high-level view, the rendering is split between two applications: Internet Explorer and PresentationHost.[23] All of the Internet Explorer UI

---

23. There is a very subtle, but important detail about the security ramifications of how PresentationHost is run. On Windows XP, presentationhost.exe is launched with modified NT permissions; effectively we strip the admin token off whatever permission iexplore.exe is running with. This provides an additional security level on top of the CLR code access security model. On Windows Vista, the Limited User Access feature provides this same type of security model globally for all applications running on the system.

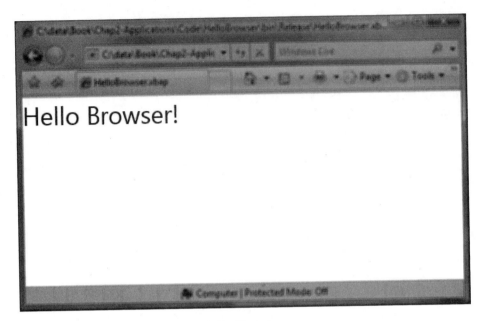

FIGURE 2.29: Browser hosting: PresentationHost view

(address bar, toolbar, title, etc.) is rendered in the iexplore.exe process. Those UI elements are controlled by IE and can be customized only using the existing COM-based interfaces (IHtmlWindow, etc.).

Figure 2.29 shows the UI provided by WPF. When running inside the browser, a special top-level window, called the **root browser window,** is created to host the pages navigated to. Remember that, when we talked about creating a browser-hosted application, we said that we must set Application.StartupUri to point to a page; that's because the navigation framework will automatically create this special navigation window and navigate it to the specified page.

When an application is hosted in older browsers, a second row of navigation buttons is sometimes present. If the browser doesn't support the new navigation APIs, the root browser window will automatically display a navigation UI.

Any WPF content viewed in the browser uses this same underlying mechanism. Several different types of content can be viewed in this way: XBAPs, XML Paper Specification (XPS) documents, and just plain XAML text files.

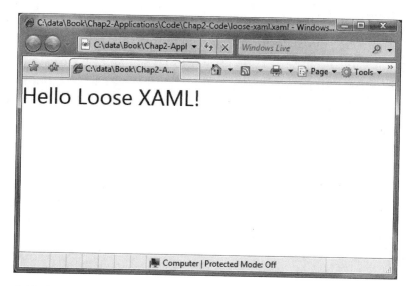

FIGURE 2.30: Loose XAML hosted in the browser

Loose Markup

In addition to compiling an application into an XBAP to run in the browser, we can take loose XAML files and view them in the browser. We are restricted to using the same set of elements that would be allowed in an XBAP, and we cannot have code behind. For publishing small documents or simple navigation-based content, however, we can use this technique to produce a very simple no-compile development model.

Because loose XAML doesn't support code behind, we cannot use the x:Class tag that we had in our page for the XBAP, but otherwise we can just take the same page and save it as a XAML file, double-click on it, and see it appear in the browser (Figure 2.30):

```
<Page
  xmlns='http://schemas.microsoft.com/winfx/2006/xaml/presentation'>
  <TextBlock FontSize='24pt'>Hello Loose XAML!</TextBlock>
</Page>
```

WHERE ARE WE?

In this chapter we've looked at the center object of an application—the Application object—and the main components that make up an application: windows, pages, and user controls. Using Windows, we can implement a variety of windowing models, and by leveraging pages and the navigation framework, we can easily build applications that support traditional or functional navigation. Managing state throughout any type of application is made easier with the services provided by the WPF application model. WPF attempts to have a lightweight application model that is flexible enough to build most types of applications, while still offering enough services to make it easy to build them.

3

Controls

C HAPTER 2 DESCRIBED how an application is built, the main UI components, application services, and options for hosting the application. Although the UI of an application is built from windows, user controls, and pages, the top-level parts of the UI are built out of smaller components, **controls.**

For as long as there have been UI toolkits, there have been controls. Whether they were called *widgets, gadgets, VBXs, OCXs, components, CWnds, elements,* or another name, there has always been some notion of a component that encapsulates a particular behavior, object model, and display. Windows Presentation Foundation is no exception.

In this chapter we can begin to dig into controls, which are the real meat of WPF. To start, we will walk through the key new concepts for controls in WPF: content model and templates. These two concepts are the core of the entire control model and, once understood, provide a context for understanding the WPF control library. In addition, we explore a few of the deeper building-block controls that we can use to create new controls of our own.

Control Principles

The team assembled to begin working on the control library for WPF had worked on many frameworks before. We had a list of mistakes and limitations that we had encountered in the past and did not want to repeat.

In addition, we knew that WPF needed to provide an integrated platform for UI, documents, and media.

One of the key issues with the previous frameworks was a lack of consistent flexibility. To create a customized list in Win32 requires a programming model that is totally different from using a control. In today's Windows, every place that needs a button has a different implementation: The scrollbar buttons behave differently from the close button on a window, which behaves differently from a standard button in a dialog. The WPF team wanted to build a system in which one button could be used everywhere. For this reason, **element composition** is a key principle in WPF.

To integrate the worlds of UI, documents, and media, we felt we needed a design principle around **rich content** everywhere. Early versions of HTML allowed rich text with multiple fonts, sizes, colors, and weight to be included almost anywhere—except inside a button. Even just making a button a different color required creating an image for people to click. Win32 was much the same way; the RichEdit control was the only control that could contain richly formatted text. The principle of rich content says that any place where text is allowed should support rich text, media, and other controls.

A pervasive characteristic of .NET is a **simple programming model,** so we adopted this principle for the WPF controls. A model that is easy to program is a critical component of a set of controls that developers can actually use.

One of the early issues in the building of WPF was (we thought) a simple problem: What is the object model for Button? A clickable button control is one of the most basic controls; it has been part of the Windows UI since Windows 1.0, and part of the Macintosh UI since Mac OS 1.0. It's a pretty basic thing! But the WPF team hit a snag.

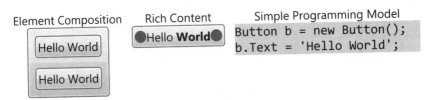

FIGURE 3.1: The three principles of controls: element composition, rich content, and simple programming model

Figure 3.1 shows a button containing two other buttons, a button containing rich content, and the simple programming model that we want. Initially, we looked at element composition and rich content and decided that if our rich content in fact consisted of elements, then we just needed element composition. The programming model we developed looked something like this:

```
Button b = new Button();
Ellipse left = new Ellipse();
TextBlock text  = new TextBlock();
text.Text = "Hello World";
Ellipse right = new Ellipse();

b.Children.Add(left);
b.Children.Add(text);
b.Children.Add(right);
```

This doesn't look too bad, but we're missing one thing: What if we want the word *World* in "Hello World" to be bold?

```
Button b = new Button();
Ellipse left = new Ellipse();
TextBlock text  = new TextBlock();
text.Inlines.Add(new Run("Hello "));
text.Inlines.Add(new Bold("World"));
Ellipse right = new Ellipse();

b.Children.Add(left);
b.Children.Add(text);
b.Children.Add(right);
```

If we wanted something very simple, on the other hand—for example, a button that said just "OK"—here's what the code would look like:

```
Button b = new Button();
Text text  = new Text();
text.Text = "OK";

b.Children.Add(text);
```

At this point you should be wondering what happened to the tenet of a simple programming model. The kind of code we really wanted to write should look like this:

```
Button b = new Button();
b.Text = "OK";
```

Hello World

FIGURE 3.2: "Hello World" in a button

Here we're adding content to the button using a single property, but the content can be only a string. Instead, we wanted all the richness to support the more complex content in a button.

Enter the content model.

Content Model

In Win32 programming, controls (e.g., ListBox, Button, and Label) traditionally defined their data model as a simple string. The WPF design team wanted to allow for both rich content everywhere and the separation of data from visualization. Many systems incorporate complex ways of separating models, views, and controllers, requiring developers to understand a data model for each control. WPF instead uses a model already familiar to many developers: the CLR type system.

Let's start by setting the content of a button:

```
Button b = new Button();
b.Content = "Hello World";
```

This code will create a simple button with the text "Hello World" inside of it, just as we would expect (Figure 3.2). Note that the property type of Content for Button is System.Object, not a string.

To understand what happened here, let's investigate the display that was created. We know there's a button at the root, but somewhere there has to be something that displays the text. Because we believe in element composition, we use other elements to render the button. Figure 3.3 shows

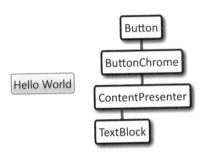

FIGURE 3.3: A button, with the elements generated to display it

the hierarchy of elements, also known as the **display tree,** created to display the button.

Dissecting the display elements in Figure 3.3 reveals a ButtonChrome element, which displays the nice background of the button, and two other interesting elements: ContentPresenter and TextBlock. We've seen Text-Block before; it is the type that displays basic text. But what about this ContentPresenter thing?

ContentPresenter

ContentPresenter is the workhorse of the content model. It will happily take whatever data we stuff into the Content property and create a corresponding visual tree to display it. For example, ContentPresenter can be used to display a number, a date and time, or a button:

```
public Window1() {
  StackPanel panel = new StackPanel();

  ContentPresenter intPresenter = new ContentPresenter();
  intPresenter.Content = 5;
  panel.Children.Add(intPresenter);

  ContentPresenter datePresenter = new ContentPresenter();
  datePresenter.Content = DateTime.Now;
  panel.Children.Add(datePresenter);

  ContentPresenter elementPresenter = new ContentPresenter();
  elementPresenter.Content = new Button();
  panel.Children.Add(elementPresenter);

  Content = panel;
}
```

Running this code shows that all the various types of data display something (Figure 3.4).

Now the big question: How? The object model for ContentPresenter provides some hints:

```
public class ContentPresenter : FrameworkElement {
  ...
  public object Content { get; set; }
  public string ContentSource { get; set; }
  public DataTemplate ContentTemplate { get; set; }
  public DataTemplateSelector ContentTemplateSelector { get; set; }
  ...
}
```

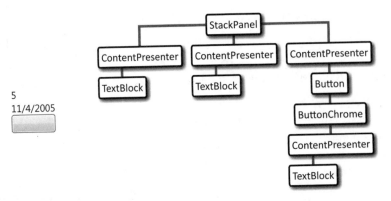

FIGURE 3.4: Using several `ContentPresenter` objects to display different bits of data, and the corresponding display tree

The first thing that the presenter looks at is the data type of the content. If the content is already of type `System.Windows.UIElement` (the base type of controls), then no more work is needed and the content can be added directly to the display tree. `ContentPresenter` then tries to find alternative ways to convert the content to a display, using the following logic:

1. If `Content` is of type `UIElement`, then add it to the display tree.
2. If `ContentTemplate` is set, use that to create a `UIElement` instance and add it to the display tree.
3. If `ContentTemplateSelector` is set, use that to find a template, use the template to create a `UIElement` instance, and add it to the display tree.
4. If the data type of `Content` has a data template[1] associated with it, use that to create a `UIElement` instance.
5. If the data type of `Content` has a `TypeConverter` instance associated with it that can convert to type `UIElement`, convert `Content` and add it to the display tree.
6. If the data type of `Content` has a `TypeConverter` instance associated with it that can convert to a string, wrap `Content` in `TextBlock` and add it to the display tree.
7. Finally, call `ToString` on `Cotent`, wrap it in `TextBlock`, and add it to the display tree.

---

1. Data templates will be covered in Chapter 6.

TABLE 3.1: Content Property Naming Pattern

Plurality	Object(s)	Element(s)
Single	Content	Child
Multiple	Items	Children

Obviously the presenter tries very hard to create something that can be displayed. The only value that is guaranteed not to display is null; everything else will, at worst, display the value returned by the content's ToString method. By encapsulating the logic for presenting content into a simple, composable element, we established a high degree of reusability.

So far we've seen how a control, such as Button, uses a content presenter to enable a simple programming model, while still allowing rich content and element composition. There are four general patterns for the content model, based on what the control does (e.g., can it consume any data, or just elements?) and whether the model is single or multiple. Each pattern is encapsulated as a property, as Table 3.1 shows.

We've already seen how the Content property is used to display content, so let's look at the Items, Child, and Children properties.

Items

If ContentPresenter is good for a single item, we should be able to use it as the basis for a list of items. The multiple-content pattern is very similar to the single-content pattern, but instead of the object-valued Content property, we have a list-valued Items property:

```
ListBox l = new ListBox();
l.Items.Add("Hello");
l.Items.Add("There");
l.Items.Add("World");
```

The resulting display tree (Figure 3.5) inspires a simple "Wow!"

There's a lot of stuff here. The visual tree for ListBox contains several presenters. Starting from the bottom (the items in the larger font), we see the familiar Button pattern: a ContentPresenter object containing a TextBlock element. ListBoxItem fits the single-content pattern: a control with the Content property, just like Button.

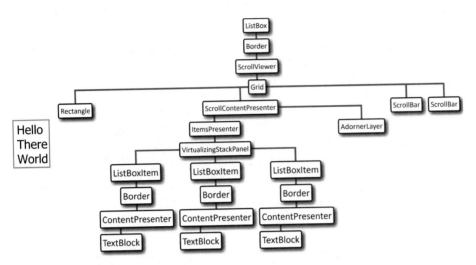

FIGURE 3.5: ListBox **containing several strings, and its display tree**

Working up the stack, we come to `ItemsPresenter`. Where `Content-Presenter` is the workhorse for displaying items composed of single pieces of content, `ItemsPresenter` is the workhorse for displaying items composed of multiple pieces of content. This presenter works in concert with several other classes to dynamically generate the necessary items, each of which uses an instance of `ContentPresenter`.

The final element that carries the *presenter* name is `ScrollContent-Presenter`, which enables scrolling within the list box. `ScrollContent-Presenter` is not part of the core content model, but rather an implementation of the `ScrollViewer` primitive control, which is used to implement scrolling.

Children and Child

Instead of supporting arbitrary objects as content (as `Button` and `ListBox` do), some controls support only `UIElement` children—which brings us to the final two patterns for content: `Child` and `Children`.

Before we dive into the element content models, it is interesting to quickly talk about the types of controls. Jeff Bogdan, another WPF architect, is often quoted as saying, "The key to factoring is knowing when to stop." Element composition is a great feature, but eventually someone needs to do some real work. WPF divides most controls into three categories: content controls, layout controls, and render controls.

Content controls like `ListBox` and `Button` don't do much work; they are composed of other elements that do work. For example, the display tree for `Button` (see Figure 3.3) shows that `ButtonChrome` and `Content-Presenter` do most of the work for `Button`.

On the other hand, **layout controls** are responsible for positioning other controls; `StackPanel` is the primary example that we've seen so far in this book. Generally, layout controls aren't visible themselves; rather we see their effects on other controls. Layout controls comprise the majority of the controls that support the multiple-element content pattern. All of the layout panels other than `FlowDocumentViewer`[2] implement the multiple-element content model by deriving from `Panel`:

```
public class Panel : FrameworkElement {
  public UIElementCollection Children { get; }
}
```

Render controls are the controls that actually put pixels on the screen. `Rectangle` and `Ellipse` are examples of render controls. Some render controls also support containing a control; probably the best example is the `Border` class. This type takes a single element and adds a border around it:

```
public class Border : Decorator {
  public UIElement Child { get; set; }
}
```

The content model helps solve the problem of rich content for controls with a simple programming model. Another big problem for writing controls is figuring out how to render everything that's not content: How did that `ButtonChrome` appear inside of the button?

Templates

Customizing the appearance of controls can be fairly problematic. With Windows Forms or User32 today, changing the look of a button requires overriding `OnPaint` or handling `WM_PAINT` and writing code to draw some pixels. Using HTML requires either creating a control using several images to look like a button, or writing customized HTML. A problem with all of

---

2. It seems there's always an exception.

these models is that their programming model for creating and modifying the look of a control is substantially different from the programming model for using a control.

Instead of requiring a new display to be written, another common solution is to enable customization of the display using properties. In HTML, Cascading Style Sheets (CSS) can be used to adjust the look of an element in HTML. A problem with this model is that it requires the author of the control to expose every possible customization point of the display as a property that CSS can style. Today's CSS provides a rich library of properties for adjusting the borders, fill, and text formatting of components, but it doesn't allow the person customizing the display to inject arbitrary content.

WPF controls offer a great deal of control over the visual display through the use of properties, but it is also possible to completely customize the look of any control. In WPF we wanted the entire spectrum of customization to be declarative and provide a consistent programming model experience. Our solution was the templating system. The display tree for Button (Figure 3.6) shows the ButtonChrome control that is not the button, the content presenter, or the content. This control was created by the template for the button.

The preceding discussion of the content model introduced the three types of controls: render, layout, and content controls. Besides implementing the content pattern, all content controls also support templates. A template allows the creation of a particular set of elements (such as ButtonChrome) to implement their display. Content controls derive from Control and inherit a common property named Template.

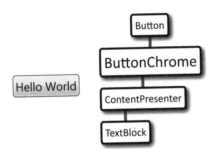

FIGURE 3.6: Button's display tree (notice ButtonChrome)

FIGURE 3.7: A button templated with a rectangle, and its display tree

To start, we can look at the code for a simple button, which will display the same button that we've already seen several times:

```
<Button>
  My Button
</Button>
```

If we wanted to change the look of the button without affecting the content, we could define a new template. Templates are a factory for creating a new display tree. Templates come in two varieties: `ControlTemplate` (which creates a display tree for a control) and `DataTemplate` (which creates a display tree for a piece of data, as will be described in Chapter 6).

To define a new control template, we must provide a target type and a display tree. We must also always set the target type for the template, which provides the template with information about the type to which it will be applied:

```
<Button>
  <Button.Template>
    <ControlTemplate TargetType='{x:Type Button}'>
      <Rectangle Fill='Red' Width='75' Height='23' />
    </ControlTemplate>
  </Button.Template>
  My Button
</Button>
```

The display tree in this example is a single red rectangle, and the code generates the element and display tree shown in Figure 3.7.

Notably, the `ButtonChrome`, `ContentPresenter`, and the `TextBlock` objects that we saw earlier are all missing. Yet the button is still functional. To demonstrate, let's use code to change the template when the button is clicked. To start, we will define an event handler that creates a new template and assigns it to the button:

```
void ChangeIt(object sender, RoutedEventArgs e) {
  ControlTemplate template = new ControlTemplate(typeof(Button));
  // The "do nothing" template
  ((Button)sender).Template = template;
}
```

Now that we have our template, we need to fill in the display tree. The VisualTree property on ControlTemplate defines the display tree, but notice that the type of the property is FrameworkElementFactory. Templates can be applied to more than one control, but controls can appear in the display tree only once. To address this problem, FrameworkElementFactory constructs a new instance of the display tree for every control that uses the template. Here we will set the button to be displayed as an ellipse:

```
void ChangeIt(object sender, RoutedEventArgs e) {
  ControlTemplate template = new ControlTemplate(typeof(Button));
  // The "create an invisible ellipse" template
  template.VisualTree = new FrameworkElementFactory(typeof(Ellipse));
  ((Button)sender).Template = template;
}
```

Next we want to set some of the ellipse's properties. We must use the SetValue syntax for setting properties because we are effectively creating a list of properties to set *when the ellipse is created*:

```
void ChangeIt(object sender, RoutedEventArgs e) {
  ControlTemplate template = new ControlTemplate(typeof(Button));
  // The "create a blue ellipse" template
  template.VisualTree = new FrameworkElementFactory(typeof(Ellipse));
  template.VisualTree.SetValue(Ellipse.FillProperty, Brushes.Blue);
  template.VisualTree.SetValue(Ellipse.WidthProperty, 75);
  template.VisualTree.SetValue(Ellipse.HeightProperty, 23);
  ((Button)sender).Template = template;
}
```

At this point you may notice that, by not tying markup to the object model, we are going against one of the tenets of the XAML language design. In this case the code equivalent of defining a template is very different from the markup. We decided here to go against the tenet of making the markup more usable. We effectively rerun the markup every time the template is used.

The final step in our example is to wire the event handler to the button:

```
<Button ... Click='ChangeIt'>
  ...
</Button>
```

The result after the click is shown in Figure 3.8.

FIGURE 3.8: The button after the new template is applied, and its display tree

With a little more artistic work, and including a content presenter, we can make a button that looks like a button:

```
<ControlTemplate TargetType='{x:Type Button}'>
  <Border CornerRadius='4' BorderThickness='3'>
    <Border.BorderBrush>
      <LinearGradientBrush EndPoint='0,1'>
        <LinearGradientBrush.GradientStops>
          <GradientStop Offset='0' Color='#FFFFFFFF' />
          <GradientStop Offset='1' Color='#FF777777' />
        </LinearGradientBrush.GradientStops>
      </LinearGradientBrush>
    </Border.BorderBrush>
    <Border.Background>
      <LinearGradientBrush EndPoint='0,1'>
        <LinearGradientBrush.GradientStops>
          <GradientStop Offset='0' Color='#FF777777' />
          <GradientStop Offset='1' Color='#FFFFFFFF' />
        </LinearGradientBrush.GradientStops>
      </LinearGradientBrush>
    </Border.Background>
    <ContentPresenter
      HorizontalAlignment='Center'
      VerticalAlignment='Center' />
  </Border>
</ControlTemplate>
```

Notably, a content presenter is introduced into the template and, by default, looks for a property called Content on the templated control, whose value it then displays. For the surrounding visuals, we have replaced the default ButtonChrome element from the button with a generic Border control. Running this code will produce something much more buttonlike (Figure 3.9).

With the richer template in place, what happens if we change the background property of the button?

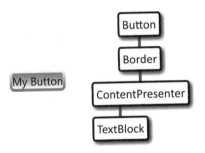

FIGURE 3.9: A button with a more artistic template, and its display tree

Template Binding

Think back to the three principles of controls: element composition, rich content everywhere, and simple programming model. Templates provide great support for element composition and rich content; however, requiring a a template to be defined just to change the color of a button may not always be the simplest programming model.

Ideally, we want to be able to add parameters to templates, or further customize them, by using properties from the template control. With this capability, a template author could bind to properties on the template control, letting the control user adjust properties on the control and customize the template:

```
<ControlTemplate TargetType='{x:Type Button}'>
  <Border CornerRadius='4'
    BorderThickness='{TemplateBinding Property=BorderThickness}'
    BorderBrush='{TemplateBinding Property=BorderBrush}'
    Background='{TemplateBinding Property=Background}'
    >
    <ContentPresenter />
  </Border>
</ControlTemplate>
```

This markup binds the `BorderThickness`, `BorderBrush`, and `Background` properties from `Border` to those same properties on the templated `Button`. Once this is done, we can create a button like that shown in Figure 3.10 simply by setting properties on `Button`:

```
<Button
  BorderThickness = '4'
  BorderBrush = 'Orange'
  Background = 'Yellow'
  >
  <Button.Template>...</Button.Template>
</Button>
```

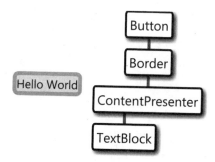

FIGURE 3.10: A button with a template that uses template binding

In this case the property names all match, but we could just as easily go back and use template binding on our original `Rectangle`-based style:

```
<ControlTemplate TargetType='{x:Type Button}'>
  <Rectangle Fill='{TemplateBinding Property=Background}' />
</ControlTemplate>
```

Both of these markup examples accomplish the same thing: allowing a developer to customize the look of the control by using only properties. Incremental customization is another important part of the philosophy of WPF. We start by customizing an application using basic elements and their properties (setting `Button`'s `Background` property). Then we move to composing elements within each other (putting an image inside of a button). Then we can create a custom template for a control, or go so far as to write a custom control if needed.

Thinking about Templates

WPF uses templates all over the place. Our goal is to make every piece of user interface customizable, allowing the creation of completely new models for interaction. Perhaps unexpectedly, `Window` is a control that supports the content model. We can make a template for `Window`:

```
<ControlTemplate TargetType='{x:Type Window}'>
  <Grid>
    <!-- background -->
    <Rectangle>
      ...
    </Rectangle>
    <!-- title overlay -->
    <Rectangle ...>
      ...
```

FIGURE 3.11: Making a window template can create a common style for an application's entire user interface.

```
      </Rectangle>
      <TextBlock ... Text='{TemplateBinding Property=Title}' />
      <!-- window content -->
      <ContentControl
        Margin='40,70,40,40' />
      ...
    </Grid>
  </ControlTemplate>
```

Here we use multiple visuals and several controls as the template for `Window`, so instead of the standard white background, the default window can look much more interesting (Figure 3.11) without our having to create a new base class or change the content of `Window`.

Using this technique, we can create a unique appearance for every aspect of an application!

Control Library

With two critical concepts—content model and templates—under our belts, we can start the tour of the control library that WPF provides. WPF offers the majority of the standard controls that we would expect in any UI package (with a few exceptions, such as `DataGrid`). Because the content model and

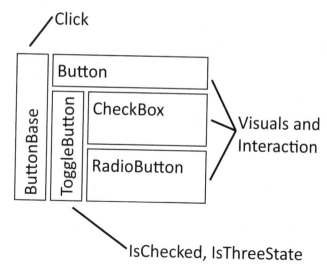

FIGURE 3.12: The Button class hierarchy

templates make visualization so customizable, the important description of a control is the data model and interaction model that it offers.

Buttons

For our tour of controls, it seems appropriate to start with Button. Fundamentally, buttons are "clickable" things.[3] Beyond the Click event from ButtonBase, Button doesn't add anything significant except the default look and feel of a standard button.

CheckBox and RadioButton both represent toggle buttons that support IsChecked (data model) and IsThreeState (interaction model) properties. IsThreeState is interesting, in that it controls only the user interaction model. When IsThreeState is True, the user can click the check box to toggle from Checked to Unchecked to Indeterminate. When IsThreeState is False, no matter what the user does the Indeterminate state will not appear; however, the state can be programmatically set to be indeterminate.

Figure 3.12 shows the Button class hierarchy. Both ButtonBase and ToggleButton are building-block types that aren't typically directly used. Button, CheckBox, and RadioButton customize these building-block classes

---

3. Originally the WPF team toyed with the idea of naming the ButtonBase class System.Windows.Controls.Clickable, but then we thought better of it!

FIGURE 3.13: Several button controls

by providing user interaction policy (like RadioButton enforcing a model that only one button is checked) and visuals (making radio buttons look like radio buttons).

The example that follows shows the default look for all three button controls:

```
<StackPanel Orientation='Horizontal'>
  <Button Margin='5' VerticalAlignment='Top'>Click</Button>
  <StackPanel Margin='5' VerticalAlignment='Top'>
    <CheckBox IsChecked='True'>Click</CheckBox>
    <CheckBox IsChecked='False'>Click</CheckBox>
    <CheckBox IsChecked='{x:Null}'>Click</CheckBox>
  </StackPanel>
  <StackPanel Margin='5' VerticalAlignment='Top'>
    <RadioButton>Click</RadioButton>
    <RadioButton IsChecked='True'>Click</RadioButton>
    <RadioButton>Click</RadioButton>
  </StackPanel>
</StackPanel>
```

As Figure 3.13 reveals, these controls look just like the built-in Windows controls,[4] and running this code shows that all the interaction logic is identical. For base-level controls, the goal of WPF was to be a pixel-perfect copy of the built-in controls.[5]

Lists

One of the most common tasks in an application is to display a list of data. The list controls in WPF provide two main pieces of functionality: displaying

---

4. Interestingly, WPF controls change the keyboard accelerator notation from "&" to "_". So if we wanted a button with the content "OK" and wanted "O" to be the accelerator, we would specify <Button>_OK</Button>. This change was introduced primarily because the XML rules around "&" would have required a very verbose "&" to be used everywhere an accelerator was needed.

5. Well, as close as possible.

lists of data, and allowing the selection of one or more list items. During the development of WPF, the number of list controls to ship was a question of considerable debate. Because of WPF's rich template support, ListBox, ComboBox, DomainUpDown, and even something like a radio button list are differentiated only by different templates on top of a base control. In the end, the WPF team decided to ship with the expected controls but generally favor templates instead of new controls (this is why the RadioButtonList control that was in the initial beta release was cut). WPF has four standard list controls: ListBox, ComboBox, ListView, and TreeView.

All list controls can be filled with items from one of two sources: the ItemsSource property or the Items property. The Items property adds data to the list's internal list of data items:

```
ListBox list = new ListBox();
list.Items.Add("a");
list.Items.Add("b");
```

The ItemsSource property provides the list control with a collection of data items, which the list displays:

```
string[] items = new string[] { "a", "b" };

ListBox list = new ListBox();
list.ItemsSource = items;
```

The difference between the two is subtle but important: using Items-Source lets us maintain the data external to the list control.

ListBox and ComboBox

Figure 3.14 (on page 132) shows the two basic list types: ListBox and ComboBox. ComboBox is really a different view on ListBox, but from an object model view the two controls are nearly identical. Initially we implemented the drop-down part of ComboBox with ListBox.

It is preferable to use the ItemsSource property. Although we can use any type that implements IEnumerable as the source for a list, .NET 3.0 provides a new collection designed specifically for use in these scenarios: ObservableCollection<T>. ObservableCollection<T> implements several interfaces for tracking changes that make it work much better as a source for data in list scenarios (this is covered in detail in Chapter 6).

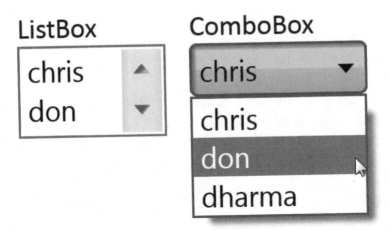

FIGURE 3.14: The two basic list types: ListBox and ComboBox

As you might have guessed from looking back at the two core control concepts—content model and templates—we can put any type of data into the list controls and change the entire look of the control using a template. In addition, ListBox and ComboBox offer a set of properties to adjust the look of the control without having to write an entirely new template.

The most commonly used property for customizing a list is probably ItemsPanel. ItemsPanel can provide a template for creating the layout panel that will be used to display the items in the list. We will cover layout in detail in Chapter 4.

To understand how to use this property, think about the Windows XP control panel (Figure 3.15). It's a ListBox object (well, selection isn't necessarily required, so we could also use the base ItemsControl), with a grid layout.

ItemsPanel takes ItemsPanelTemplate (not the normal Control-Template), which requires that the template build a panel. We can use UniformGrid for the layout of a list, which will produce something very close to the control panel shown in Figure 3.16:

```
<ListBox ...>
  <ListBox.ItemsPanel>
    <ItemsPanelTemplate>
      <UniformGrid Columns='2'/>
    </ItemsPanelTemplate>
  </ListBox.ItemsPanel>
</ListBox>
```

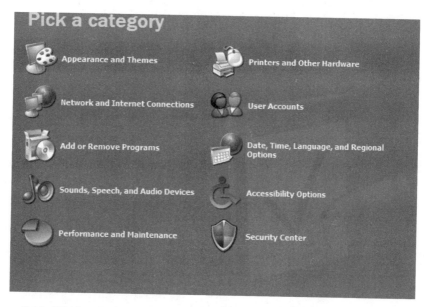

FIGURE 3.15: Windows XP control panel in category mode: an example of a list box with custom layout

Customizing the list using the `ItemsPanel` property can take us only so far; eventually we may want to build a custom template for the list. Building a template for a list control is just like building a template for any other control, with one notable exception: The list control needs a place to put

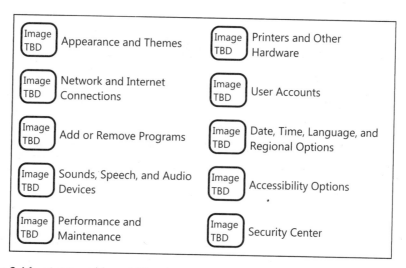

FIGURE 3.16: `ListBox` with a grid item layout

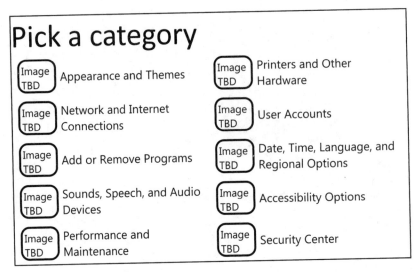

FIGURE 3.17: Using `ControlTemplate` to customize more than just the layout of a list box

the displayed items. When we use `ItemsPanel` to customize the list, the list control knows where to put the items. When we use the `Template` property, the list control has to search the display tree to find the panel where the displayed items should be put. We identify the correct panel by setting the `IsItemsHost` property on one or more panels:[6]

```
<ControlTemplate TargetType='{x:Type ListBox}'>
  <Border BorderBrush='Black' BorderThickness='1'>
    <!-- other elements -->
    <UniformGrid IsItemsHost='True' Columns='2' />
  </Border>
</ControlTemplate>
```

By adding more to the template, we can get even closer to the control panel (Figure 3.17).

Building templates is a great way to customize a list display. As you build more and more complex list templates, you may want to package these templates for reuse in other applications. Templates work great, until we need to define some properties to associate with them. For example, if we wanted to create a template for a list that shows multiple columns of data,

---

6. The default template for `ListBox` uses `ItemsPresenter`, which works as an item host by default, and honors the `ItemsPanel` property on `ListBox`.

we would need somewhere to store the column information. We can easily define a new control that derives from ListBox and adds the additional data.

Another way to accomplish this is to use the ListView control, which has built-in features to enable this type of separation.

ListView

ListView derives from ListBox and adds one feature: the ability to separate view properties (such as column information for a grid display) from control properties (such as the selected item). For example, we can build a display like the one shown in Figure 3.18. To create this display, first we need to define some custom objects with the needed data:

```
class Person
{
  string _name;
  bool _canCode;

  public Person(string name, bool canCode)
  {
    Name = name;
    CanCode = canCode;
  }

  public string Name
  {
    get { return _name; }
    set { _name = value; }
  }
  public bool CanCode
  {
    get { return _canCode; }
    set { _canCode = value; }
  }
}
```

There are no properties to set on ListView to control the number of columns, what the headers are, or anything else about the view. Instead,

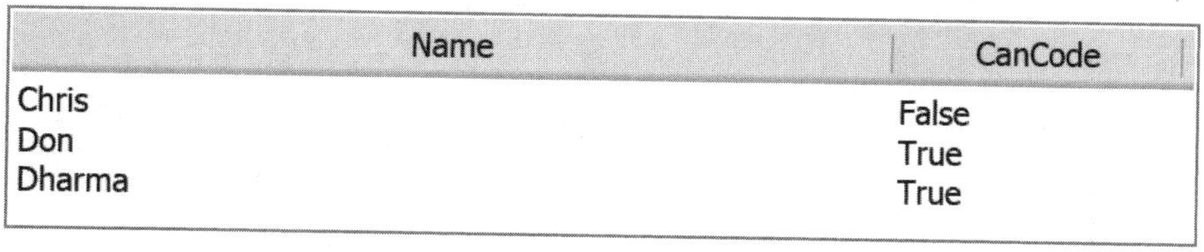

Name	CanCode
Chris	False
Don	True
Dharma	True

FIGURE 3.18: ListView displaying items with the built-in GridView

we must set the `ListView.View` property to `GridView`, and set properties on that object. `GridView` requires the use of binding (which will be covered in more detail in Chapter 6) to get data from the items in the list:

```
<ListView>
  <ListView.View>
    <GridView>
      <GridView.Columns>
        <GridViewColumn
          Width='300'
          Header='Name'
          DisplayMemberBinding='{Binding Path=Name}' />
        <GridViewColumn
          Width='100'
          Header='CanCode'
          DisplayMemberBinding='{Binding Path=CanCode}' />
      </GridView.Columns>
    </GridView>
  </ListView.View>
</ListView>
```

This separation between control properties and display properties makes `ListView` probably the most powerful list control.

Creating a new view for the `ListView` control (something to replace `GridView`), involves deriving from the deceptively simple `ViewBase` type. The essence of a custom view is actually simple: We override `PrepareItem` and adjust any properties needed:

```
public class MyView : ViewBase {
  private double angle;

  public double Angle {
    get { return angle; }
    set { angle = value; }
  }

  protected override void PrepareItem(ListViewItem item) {
    item.LayoutTransform = new RotateTransform(angle);
    base.PrepareItem(item);
  }
}
```

This is just the beginning, though. The real power of building a custom view comes from coupling it with the styling system. Overriding the `ItemContainerDefaultStyleKey` property allows a custom view to define all aspects of the resulting display, as `GridView` indicates.

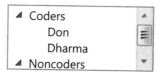

FIGURE 3.19: TreeView displaying a hierarchy of lists

All the list controls that we've seen so far present a flat list of data; often, however, the data that we want to display is hierarchical.

TreeView

TreeView adds the ability to display a hierarchy like that shown in Figure 3.19. One way to think about a tree is that it is just a list box in which each item is another list box; this is basically how TreeView works. TreeView is probably the best example of element composition; each TreeViewItem object is a control. To create the display in Figure 3.19, we can define the hierarchy of items:

```
<TreeView>
  <TreeViewItem Header='Coders'>
    <TreeViewItem Header='Don' />
    <TreeViewItem Header='Dharma' />
  </TreeViewItem>
  <TreeViewItem Header='Noncoders'>
    <TreeViewItem Header='Chris' />
  </TreeViewItem>
</TreeView>
```

Like the other list controls, TreeView supports getting items either by directly adding them to the Items property (which we did in the previous example) or by using the ItemsSource property. There are some very interesting aspects about exposing a hierarchy of data to TreeView, but we will leave that discussion to Chapter 6.

Creating New Lists Using Templates

At the beginning of the lists discussion, the ill-fated RadioButtonList was mentioned as one of the specialty lists that was cut from WPF, in favor of using templates. A radio button list is a list box that uses radio buttons to show the items and selection (Figure 3.20 on page 138).

Implementing the style for a radio button list doesn't require a lot of markup, although it does use some complex data-binding syntax. The binding syntax will be covered in detail later; for now, all we need to know is that

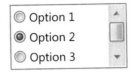

FIGURE 3.20: Making a list box into a radio button list

we're binding the IsChecked property from RadioButton to the IsSe-lected property from ListBoxItem:

```
<ListBox>
  <ListBox.ItemContainerStyle>
    <Style TargetType='{x:Type ListBoxItem}'>
      <Setter Property='Template'>
        <Setter.Value>
          <ControlTemplate TargetType='{x:Type ListBoxItem}'>
            <RadioButton
              IsChecked='{Binding
Path=IsSelected,RelativeSource={RelativeSource TemplatedParent}}'
              Content='{TemplateBinding Property=Content}' />
          </ControlTemplate>
        </Setter.Value>
      </Setter>
    </Style>
  </ListBox.ItemContainerStyle>
  <sys:String>Option 1</sys:String>
  <sys:String>Option 2</sys:String>
  <sys:String>Option 3</sys:String>
  <sys:String>Option 4</sys:String>
</ListBox>
```

This example just begins to show the power of the templating system coupled with the right selection of base controls.

Menus and Toolbars

Up to this point I've carefully omitted two very interesting list controls: MenuItem and ToolBar. It may seem strange at first, but a menu is logically nothing more than a TreeView control with a very special template. Digging into the object model reveals that TreeViewItem and MenuItem derive from the same base type: HeaderedItemsControl. The reasons for using these controls are very different from the reasons we use standard list boxes, but it's important to remember that all the features of the content model and templates are available for menus and toolbars.

Menus and toolbars go hand in hand. Both provide effectively the same functionality: the ability to execute one or more commands. The primary differences between the two are visual space and interaction model. Toolbars consume a lot more visual space to represent the same commands, but they allow easy user access. Generally, toolbars are shortcuts to commands already present in the menu structure. Menus provide a rich hierarchy and occupy minimal screen real estate, but users have more difficulty finding commands within them. Menus and toolbars are typically paired with commands, which we will discuss in Chapter 7.

Menus

Menus consist of a series of `MenuItem` controls hosted within either `Menu` or `ContextMenu`. Menus are always displayed and, in any Windows application, are typically located at the top of the window. Context menus are displayed only when the user requests them, typically by right-clicking, pressing **Shift+F10,** or, on newer keyboards, pressing the context menu key.

In User32, menus were relegated to the top of the window; in WPF that restriction has been removed. We can put menus anywhere we want. Figure 3.21 shows an alternative menu display—something that we can accomplish with a set of templates. Keep in mind, though, the amount of training that users will need to use a new interaction model. For most applications, keeping menus where users expect them is a good thing.

To create a menu, we add a hierarchy of `MenuItem` controls to a `Menu` object, which we typically host within `DockPanel` to make it easy to display the menu at the top of the window:

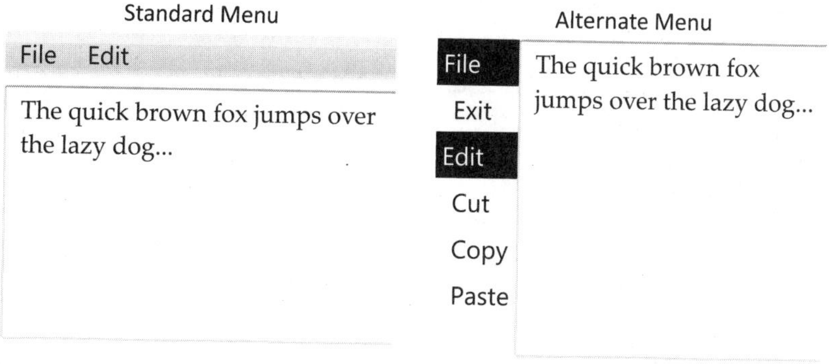

FIGURE 3.21: An alternative presentation for a menu

```
<Window x:Class='EssentialWPF.MenusAndToolbars'
  xmlns='http://schemas.microsoft.com/winfx/2006/xaml/presentation'
  xmlns:x='http://schemas.microsoft.com/winfx/2006/xaml'
  Title='Menus and Toolbars'
  >
  <DockPanel LastChildFill='False'>
    <Menu DockPanel.Dock='Top'>
      <MenuItem Header='_File'>
        <MenuItem Header='E_xit' Click='ExitClicked' />
      </MenuItem>
      <MenuItem Header='_Edit'>
        <MenuItem Header='_Cut' />
        <MenuItem Header='C_opy' />
        <MenuItem Header='_Paste' />
      </MenuItem>
    </Menu>
  </DockPanel>
</Window>
```

Users interact with a menu by clicking an item contained within it, causing an associated functionality to be executed. We detect the clicking of a menu item by handling its `Click` event:

```
<!-- MenusAndToolbars.xaml -->
...
<MenuItem Header="E_xit" Click="ExitClicked" />
...

// MenusAndToolbars.xaml.cs
...
void ExitClicked(object sender, RoutedEventArgs e) {
  Close();
}
...
```

Running this application yields the display in Figure 3.22, which shows exactly what we would expect: a drop-down menu containing options that the user can select with the mouse. Choosing **File** and then **Exit** will cause the application to terminate.

The notion that `MenuItem` is derived from `HeaderedItemsControl` should make some sense. The caption "Edit" is the **header,** and the three child menu items are the **items.** `ToolBar`, however, is a slightly bigger leap.

Toolbars

Like menus, toolbars have a host type (`ToolBarTray`) and an item type (`ToolBar`). The big difference between menus and toolbars is that menus

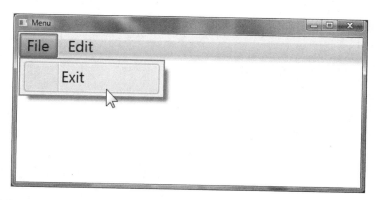

FIGURE 3.22: A window with a simple menu

support arbitrary hierarchies (through submenus), while toolbars provide only one level of nesting.

Each toolbar has a set of items and a header. In most examples of toolbars today, the header is blank and the items are buttons. The content model, however, allows us to add anything as an item in the toolbar:

```
<Window x:Class='EssentialWPF.MenusAndToolbars'
  xmlns='http://schemas.microsoft.com/winfx/2006/xaml/presentation'
  xmlns:x='http://schemas.microsoft.com/winfx/2006/xaml'
  Title='Menus and Toolbars'
  >
  <DockPanel LastChildFill='False'>
    ...
    <ToolBarTray DockPanel.Dock='Top'>
      <ToolBar>
        <Button>A</Button>
        <Button>B</Button>
        <Button>C</Button>
        <Button>D</Button>
      </ToolBar>
      <ToolBar Header='Search'>
        <TextBox Width='100' />
        <Button Width='23'>Go</Button>
      </ToolBar>
    </ToolBarTray>
  </DockPanel>
</Window>
```

Running this application yields the window shown in Figure 3.23 (on the next page). The toolbars can be moved within the toolbar tray (but not pulled

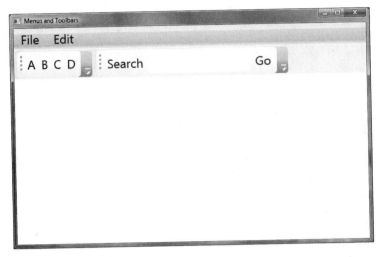

FIGURE 3.23: Two toolbars—one with buttons, the other with a text box and a button

out to be a floating toolbar). In addition, if we resize the window smaller, the items move to an overflow menu (Figure 3.24). We can control how items are moved to the overflow menu by using the `ToolBar.OverflowMode` property.

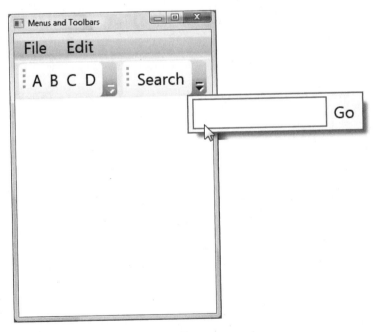

FIGURE 3.24: Toolbar with items in the overflow menu

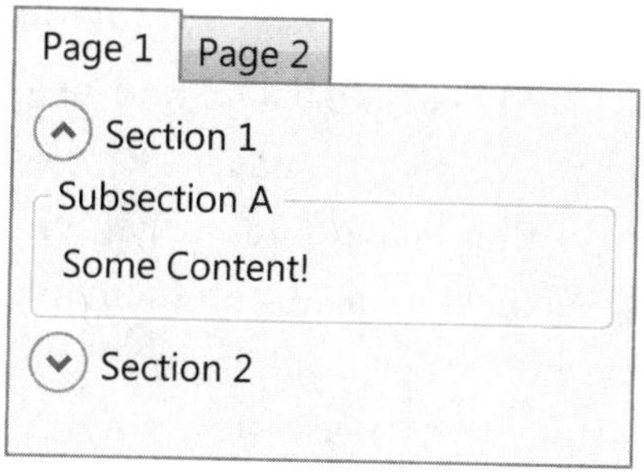

FIGURE 3.25: Various containers nested

Toolbars are frequently used as general control containers—for example, text boxes (such as a search box) or combo boxes (such as the address bar in most Web browsers). WPF has a number of general-purpose control containers as well.

Containers

For grouping and hiding parts of a user interface, WPF has three main built-in controls: TabControl, Expander, and GroupBox. TabControl provides the traditional tab-style UI, Expander offers the Windows XP–style expansion functionality that we see in the file explorer, and GroupBox provides a simple visual containment for separating parts of the UI. All of these are shown here and illustrated in Figure 3.25:

```
<TabControl>
  <TabItem Header='Page 1'>
    <StackPanel>
      <Expander Header='Section 1' IsExpanded='True'>
        <GroupBox Header='Subsection A'>
          <Label>Some Content!</Label>
        </GroupBox>
      </Expander>
      <Expander Header='Section 2'>
        <GroupBox Header='Subsection A'>
          <Label>Some Content!</Label>
        </GroupBox>
      </Expander>
    </StackPanel>
  </TabItem>
  <TabItem Header='Page 2' />
</TabControl>
```

There are some interesting things to note about the derivation hierarchy of these controls. First, `TabItem`, `Expander`, and `GroupBox` all derive from `HeaderedContentControl`. Effectively, `HeaderedContentControl` is a generic base type for any control that has a data model with a single header and single content model. At first this might seem wrong, since `Expander`, `TabItem`, and `GroupBox` most often contain multiple items. These controls are able to hold multiple items because a single layout container, like `StackPanel` or `Grid`, can be the root of that content.

The second interesting observation about the derivation hierarchy is that `TabControl` derives from `Selector` (and therefore `ItemsControl`). This means that `TabControl` is really a type of list. All the data model, templating, and selection events associated with lists are available to `TabControl`.

The last group of container controls consists of the layout controls, such as `WrapPanel`. These will be covered in detail in Chapter 4.

Ranges

Range controls allow the selection of a value between upper and lower bounds (a valid range of values, which is where the name comes from). WPF provides three range controls: `Slider`, `ScrollBar`, and `ProgressBar`. `ScrollBar` is considered a building-block control because using a scrollbar for anything other than scrolling is generally thought to be bad UI design.

All the range controls work in the same way: We specify a range by assigning minimum and maximum values using the `Minimum` and `Maximum` properties, and we specify or determine the current value within the range through the `Value` property. Or we can specify `SmallChange` and `LargeChange` to control how quickly the value changes when the user clicks on different parts of the control.

To see how a slider works, we can handle the `ValueChanged` event on the slider and update the text of a text block:

```
<!-- RangeControls.xaml -->
<Window x:Class='EssentialWPF.RangeControls'
  xmlns='http://schemas.microsoft.com/winfx/2006/xaml/presentation'
  xmlns:x='http://schemas.microsoft.com/winfx/2006/xaml'
  Title='Range Controls'
  SizeToContent='WidthAndHeight'
  >
```

```
<StackPanel Orientation='Horizontal' Margin='5'>
  <TextBlock
    Name='_value'
    Margin='10'
    />
  <Slider
    Name='_slider'
    Width='75'
    Minimum='0' Maximum='255' Value='255'
    ValueChanged='SliderChanged'
  />
</StackPanel>
</Window>

// RangeControls.xaml.cs
public partial class RangeControls : Window {
  public Window1() {
    InitializeComponent();
  }
  void SliderChanged(object sender,
          RoutedPropertyChangedEventArgs<double> e) {
    _value.Text = _slider.Value.ToString();
  }
}
```

Running this code produces the window shown in Figure 3.26, which allows users to adjust the value displayed in the text area by moving the sliders. Another really common use for a slider is to implement the zoom control for a piece of user interface. By listening to the change notification (or better yet, using data binding, which we'll learn about in Chapter 6), we can easily add a user-configurable zoom option to any application.

Editors

WPF offers several editors: PasswordBox, TextBox, RichTextBox, and InkCanvas.

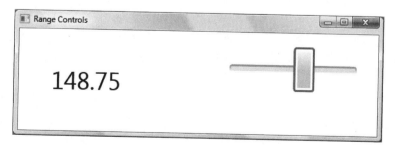

FIGURE 3.26: A slider control

PasswordBox is the outlier here, so let's talk about it first. PasswordBox provides the all-too-familiar function of a text box, except that it replaces what the user types with a series of dots or asterisks. The implementation of this control is interesting, in that it doesn't actually support the text object model. PasswordBox provides an island of functionality, with the password stored opaquely inside of it. Security is improved because walking the text tree will not accidentally disclose the password.

TextBox and RichTextBox are very similar to each other, except that TextBox turns off the ability to host rich text and offers many "simple" text-editing services (maximum length, character casing, etc.). Because TextBox supports only plain text, the API is much simpler, so we don't need to understand the text object model for simple scenarios. The globalization, text editing, IME (input method editor) support, spell checking (yes, built-in spell checking for all text editors!), and other features of the platform are otherwise identical between the two controls.

RichTextBox is the granddaddy text editor. Out of the box, it supports about 84 commands that are accessible via keyboard shortcut keys (did you know that **Ctrl+[** and **Ctrl+]** modify the font size of a selection?), and dozens more are available programmatically. RichTextBox is really a FlowDocument editor, which we will talk about in Chapter 5.

InkCanvas is to ink what RichTextBox is to text. The default behavior will support writing, erasing ink, selecting ink, and gestures[7] with no additional code.

Both ink editing and text editing have a corresponding object model for inspecting and modifying the native data types.

Text Data

There are two ways to deal with text data in WPF: streaming and collections. For most scenarios of building text dynamically and inspecting text, the collection model is simpler. Dealing with rich text editing (and selection) requires understanding some of the core parts of the streaming text model.

---

7. **Gestures** are a Tablet PC concept that converts a pen "gesture" (like making a check mark, or drawing a circle) into a programmatic command (like "check" or "circle"). Gesture recognition is a type of handwriting recognition.

The collection model for text manipulation works just like any of the control properties we've seen so far: We construct text elements and add them to collections on other text elements:

```
FlowDocument document = new FlowDocument();
Paragraph para = new Paragraph();
para.Inlines.Add(new Run("Hello World"));
document.Blocks.Add(para);
```

Note that `FlowDocument` has a `Blocks` property, while `Paragraph` has an `Inlines` property. The universe of text elements is divided into two main concepts: block elements and inline elements. **Block elements** occupy a rectangle of space; they start on a new line and are contiguous. Effectively, block elements are just like WPF controls, except they can break across page boundaries. Examples of block elements are `Paragraph` or `Table`. **Inline elements** can span lines. Examples of inline elements are `Span`, `Run`, and `Bold`.

The text object model enforces a strict set of rules about text containment, in order to allow for a very predictable model for text, that enables the building of editors and object models that behave regularly. The rules for text are fairly simple:

1. `Run` is the only element that contains strings of text (the real content).
2. `Paragraph` is the only block element that contains inline elements (and it can contain only inline elements).
3. `Table` contains one or more `TableRowGroup` objects, each of which contains one or more `TableRow` objects, which each contains one or more `TableCell` objects. `TableCell` is the only table element that contains block elements.
4. `List` contains one or more `ListItem` objects, which in turn can contain block elements.
5. Block containers (`Section`, etc.) contain only other block elements (this is really a repeat of rule 2).
6. Inline containers (`Span`, `Bold`, etc.) contain only other inline elements (this is really a repeat of rule 1).

Figure 3.27 illustrates this set of rules.

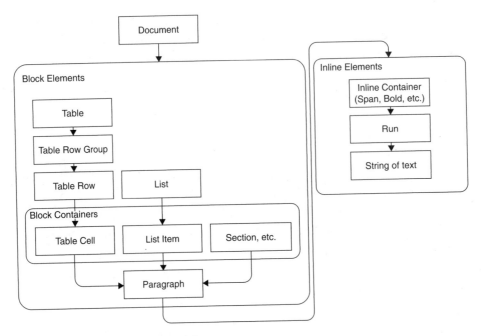

FIGURE 3.27: An abstract text model

The collection-based text object model directly reflects these rules. Some objects have helper methods (e.g., a `Paragraph` object of type `string` has a `Text` property) that create the appropriate elements under the covers.

The final two interesting text elements are `BlockUIContainer` and `InlineUIContainer`. These two types take an arbitrary `UIElement`-derived type and host it in the text flow in much the same way that `TextFlow` and `RichTextBox` host text flow content in the `UIElement` tree.

In Chapter 5 we will dive into the details of what all these text elements do.

So far we have looked at the collection-based text object model. The streaming model is used for manipulating text as a stream of elements. It is important to understand that text is sequential. That may sound obvious, but in the design of WPF it was a pretty difficult issue. Typically, UI libraries (User32, Windows Forms, Abstract Window Toolkit [AWT], Swing, etc.) represent their objects as a tree of elements. Each element has a parent and some children. It's a pretty simple model to grasp.

Typical text or document libraries (Internet Explorer, for example) represent their objects as a stream of text. Because the building block of the library is a stream of characters, everything can be equated back to that stream of text.

For a moment, consider the object model required to represent the following completely valid HTML: `<b>hello <i>there</b> reader</i>`.

The WPF development team was faced with the dilemma of how to represent objects. We knew that rich typography and documents were a core part of the platform, but dealing with everything as a stream of text means some cost in performance and complexity. In addition, the platform was intended to have a rich control framework, but concepts like partial selection cannot be easily represented in a simple tree model. Our solution was to do both. When rich text is added into the tree, a streaming model is used (hence the text object model), and a simple hierarchy is used for controls (which we've already seen).

`TextPointer` objects are the main building blocks in the streaming text object model. A **text pointer** can be thought of as a finger pointing right between two characters. A text pointer can represent the caret position, or the start and end of a selection, or the beginning of a word.

`TextRange` is used to represent the entire selection (or any range of text); it consists of simply two text pointers.[8] Formatting and visual effects can be applied to arbitrary ranges. This is a critical point, so let me repeat it: *formatting can be applied to arbitrary ranges.* We can re-create that nasty overlapping bold and italic HTML example by using ranges. However, if we attempt to save the generated markup, we'll find that the overlapping tags have been removed and something more reasonable has been created:

```
<Bold>hello </Bold><Inline
FontWeight='Bold'
FontStyle='Italic'> there</Inline><Italic>reader</Italic>.
```

The `Xml` property on `TextRange` returns a very verbose XAML string. The `Xml` property captures all information (including defaults) about the text range, and it is therefore useful for Clipboard operations or other cases of extracting part of a document.

---

8. `TextRange` can also be used to save and load sections of rich formatting. Using `TextRange.Save`, we can write out all or part of a document as RTF or XAML. Using `TextRange.Load`, we can read all or part of a document as RTF or XAML.

FIGURE 3.28: RichTextBox with some text selected

Using RichTextBox

To use RichTextBox, we must start with the Document property. Rich-TextBox allows the editing of a single FlowDocument object. Using the text object model, we can initialize the document for RichTextBox with some formatted text:

```
<Window ... Title='RichTextBox'>
  <RichTextBox Name='_rtb'>
    <FlowDocument FontSize='24'>
      <Paragraph>Hello</Paragraph>
    </FlowDocument>
  </RichTextBox>
</Window>
```

At runtime the editor is fully functional (Figure 3.28) and supports all the common editing commands.

The next big concepts to understand for RichTextBox are the notions of a caret and selection. The **caret** is the blinking line that represents the

FIGURE 3.29: TextOffset example, showing how the start and end tokens of an element occupy space in the text object model

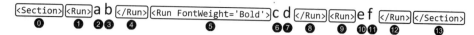

FIGURE 3.30: Simplified markup for text, with the corresponding offsets of each item

current insertion point, and it is generally the start or end of the **selection.** Three `TextPointer` objects are used to track caret positions and selections: `CaretPosition`, `Selection.Start`, and `Selection.End`.

Dealing with `TextPointer` objects isn't always the most intuitive thing, primarily because they expose the details of the underlying text storage. When dealing with programmatic manipulation of a selection, it is necessary to understand some of these details also. In the text store, start and end elements are represented by tokens in the stream, which means that `GetPositionAtOffset` will be able to see those start and end tokens:

```
public class TextOffset : Window {
  RichTextBox _rtb = new RichTextBox();
  public TextOffset() {
    Content = _rtb;
    _rtb.SelectionChanged += new RoutedEventHandler(Changed);
  }
  void Changed(object sender, RoutedEventArgs e) {
    Title = _rtb.Document.ContentStart
        .GetOffsetToPosition(
          _rtb.CaretPosition).ToString();
  }
}
```

When we run this code (Figure 3.29), we can type the characters and use **Ctrl+B** to make the center two characters boldface. (See Figure 3.30, which shows the offsets for each element.) Putting the caret before the letter *a* shows that the offset is actually 2. This is because `Section` and `Run` elements start before the *a*. As we move to the right, the title changes: 2, 3, 4, 7, 8, 11, 12.[9] The jumps (from 4 to 7, and from 8 to 11) occur right after *b* and *d*. Again, this is because there are end and corresponding start elements.

---

9. If we move left through the text, we see different numbers. Why? Because of a concept called **gravity.** The system tries to guess the element into which we want to insert text. If the caret is currently between *c* and *d* and we move to the right, we probably want to insert text into the boldface element. However, if the caret is between the *e* and *f* and we move left, we probably want to insert the text into the nonboldface element. This idea of gravity is common in text editors, and for users typing into the editor it normally "just works."

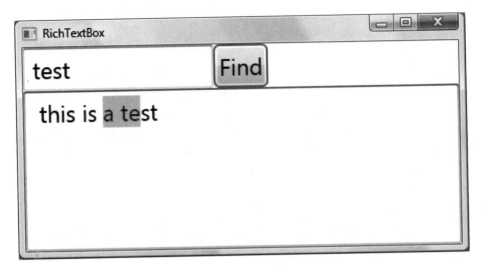

FIGURE 3.31: Incorrectly implemented find functionality

Offsets are important when we're dealing with RichTextBox because they must be taken into account when the caret or selection is being moved. My first attempt at writing a simple find method for RichTextBox missed this crucial point (Figure 3.31):

```xml
<!-- RichTextBoxWork.xaml -->
<Window x:Class='EssentialWPF.RichTextBoxWork'
  xmlns='http://schemas.microsoft.com/winfx/2006/xaml/presentation'
  xmlns:x='http://schemas.microsoft.com/winfx/2006/xaml'
  Title='RichTextBox'
  >
  <DockPanel>
    <WrapPanel DockPanel.Dock='Top' >
      <TextBox Width='100' Name='_toFind' />
      <Button Click='Find'>Find</Button>
      <TextBlock Name='_offset' />
    </WrapPanel>
    <RichTextBox Name='_rtb' />
  </DockPanel>
</Window>
```

```csharp
// richtextboxwork.xaml.cs
public partial class RichTextBoxWork : Window {
  public RichTextBoxWork() {
    InitializeComponent();
  }
```

```
// This doesn't work correctly!
//
void Find(object sender, RoutedEventArgs e) {
  FlowDocument doc = _rtb.Document;
  string text = new TextRange(doc.ContentStart,
              doc.ContentEnd).Text;
  int index = text.IndexOf(_toFind.Text);
  TextPointer start = doc.ContentStart.GetPositionAtOffset(index);
  TextPointer end =
        start.GetPositionAtOffset(_toFind.Text.Length);
  _rtb.Selection.Select(start, end);
  }
}
```

In this example the selection will always be off because of the start element tokens for Section and Run. The fix is to move a text pointer through the document searching for the match:

```
void Find(object sender, RoutedEventArgs e) {
  FlowDocument doc = _rtb.Document;
  TextPointer cur = doc.ContentStart;
  while (cur != null) {
    TextPointer end = cur.GetPositionAtOffset(_toFind.Text.Length);
    if (end != null) {
      TextRange test = new TextRange(cur, end);
      if (test.Text == _toFind.Text) {
        _rtb.Selection.Select(test.Start, test.End);
        break;
      }
    }
    cur = cur.GetNextInsertionPosition(LogicalDirection.Forward);
  }
}
```

The final big concept with RichTextBox is undo. All operations performed on RichTextBox can be undone (and redone) on command. Undo units are hierarchical also, which means that we can create groups of operations that will be treated as a single change. We can use either BeginChange/ EndChange or DeclareChangeBlock; however, using DeclareChangeBlock is generally preferred because it returns an IDisposable object that can be used in a using statement.

Consider the code to add two paragraphs to a rich text box. If we run this code, the user will have to run undo twice to remove both paragraphs:

```
_rtb.Document.Blocks.Add(new Paragraph(new Run("One")));
_rtb.Document.Blocks.Add(new Paragraph(new Run("Two")));
```

Instead, we can surround the programmatic changes to the document with a change block, making them both into a single undo unit:

```
using (_rtb.DeclareChangeBlock("add two")) {
    _rtb.Document.Blocks.Add(new Paragraph(new Run("One")));
    _rtb.Document.Blocks.Add(new Paragraph(new Run("Two")));
}
```

When making programmatic changes to the content of `RichTextBox`, we are expected to wrap them in a call to `DeclareChangeBlock` so that the end user can easily undo all the operations.

Using TextBox

`TextBox` is a simplification of most of the features of `RichTextBox`. Because `TextBox` supports only a single format, it is easy to expose selection as two integers that represent the offset into the text (no need to deal with the start/end token issues), and text is exposed as a simple string value. On top of this simplification, `TextBox` offers some additional functionality, such as the ability to easily limit the length of text or modify the casing of the text.

Ink Data

The base data type of ink is `Stroke`, defined in the `System.Windows.Ink` namespace. In some ways ink data is much simpler than rich text; it is effectively a series of packets received from the digitizer.

Ink was introduced in the Tablet PC version of Windows XP (if you ignore the fabled Pen Windows releases), with a binary persistence format (called *ink serialized format,* or *ISF*), COM programming model, and .NET programming model. The WPF development team wanted to have ink completely integrated into the platform. The binary format of ink is largely unchanged, but the programming model has undergone some changes to integrate it with the rest of the platform.

We can safely ignore the binary format, other than to know that the `Stroke` object model is implemented on top of this very efficient binary stream. This detail explains some of the oddity in the object model that `Stroke` exposes. In most cases we can get all needed data using the simple `StylusPoint` API, but when we really need access to all the data we can dive down into the `StylusPointDescription` API to gain access to

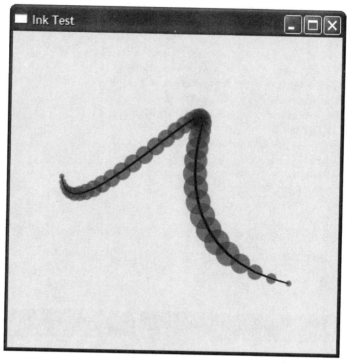

FIGURE 3.32: Working with the ink object model

everything.[10] To see how to work with ink, we can use InkCanvas and handle the InkCollected event (Figure 3.32):

```
<!-- inktest.xaml -->
<Window ... x:Class='EssentialWPF.InkTest'
  Title='Ink Test'
  Visibility='Visible'
  >
  <Grid>
    <InkCanvas
      Name='_ink'
      StrokeCollected='Collected'
      Background='Beige' />
    <Canvas Name='_overlay' />
  </Grid>
</Window>
```

---

10. You don't need a Tablet PC to try this example. By default, WPF will let a mouse act as a pen on InkCanvas. Mice today don't send pressure data, so the lines will be of uniform thickness, but hey, you could always convince your boss to buy you a Tablet, right?

```
// inktest.xaml.cs
void Collected(object sender, InkCanvasStrokeCollectedEventArgs e) {
  _overlay.Children.Clear();
  Brush fill = new SolidColorBrush(Color.FromArgb(120, 255, 0, 0));
  foreach (StylusPoint pt in e.Stroke.StylusPoints) {
    double markerSize = pt.PressureFactor * 35.0;
    Ellipse marker = new Ellipse();
    Canvas.SetLeft(marker, pt.X - markerSize / 2);
    Canvas.SetTop(marker, pt.Y - markerSize / 2);
    marker.Width = marker.Height = markerSize;
    marker.Fill = fill;
    _overlay.Children.Add(marker);
  }
}
```

Three sets of data are associated with a stroke: digitizer packets (called *stylus packets*), drawing attributes, and application-defined data. The application-defined data allows ink-optimized applications to annotate the ink data with

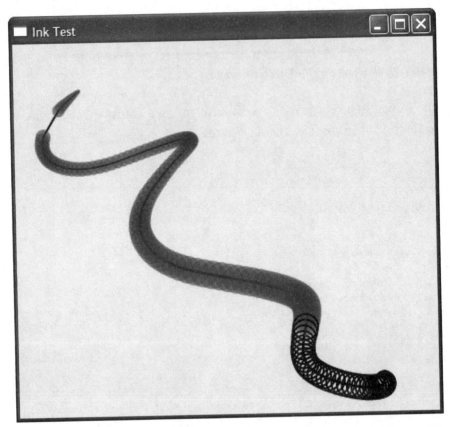

FIGURE 3.33: Adjusting the display using additional properties from the ink object model

special information. Drawing attributes control how the ink will be rendered. We can control drawing attributes on each stroke using the Drawing-Attributes property, or on InkCanvas with the DefaultDrawingAttributes property.

As we have started to see, stylus packets are somewhat complex beasts. A key reason for this complexity is that the ink stream can be extended by hardware manufacturers. Multiple buttons are very common extensions that digitizer manufacturers use. Other examples include pen tilt data, or even the rotation of the pen. The long-term goal of ink is to be able to capture all the information about someone's writing or drawings in order to accurately create a digital experience that matches or exceeds pen on paper.

To query this additional data, we need to tell the ink object model which data we want transferred from the packets into the object model. We can request the data either globally (by specifying the DefaultStylus-PointDescription value on InkCanvas) or per stroke (by using the Reformat method on StylusPointCollection).

Many newer tablets support XTilt and YTilt, which open up possibilities for very interesting visualizations. For this example, however, I'll stick with BarrelButton, which most tablets have. X, Y, and NormalPressure must be the first three properties in the query. When the barrel button is pressed, we will display an alternate circle (Figure 3.33):

```
public InkTest() {
  InitializeComponent();
  _ink.DefaultStylusPointDescription = new StylusPointDescription(
    new StylusPointPropertyInfo[]
    {
    new StylusPointPropertyInfo(StylusPointProperties.X),
    new StylusPointPropertyInfo(StylusPointProperties.Y),
    new StylusPointPropertyInfo(StylusPointProperties.NormalPressure),
    new StylusPointPropertyInfo(StylusPointProperties.BarrelButton),
    });
}

void Collected(object sender, InkCanvasStrokeCollectedEventArgs e) {
  _overlay.Children.Clear();
  Brush fill = new SolidColorBrush(Color.FromArgb(120, 255, 0, 0));
  Brush altFill = new SolidColorBrush(Color.FromArgb(120, 0, 255, 0));
  foreach (StylusPoint pt in e.Stroke.StylusPoints) {
    double markerSize = pt.PressureFactor * 35.0;
```

```
    Ellipse marker = new Ellipse();
    Canvas.SetLeft(marker, pt.X - markerSize / 2);
    Canvas.SetTop(marker, pt.Y - markerSize / 2);
    marker.Width = marker.Height = markerSize;
    marker.Fill = fill;
    if (pt.GetPropertyValue(StylusPointProperties.BarrelButton)
      != 0) {
      marker.Fill = null;
      marker.Stroke = Brushes.Black;
      marker.StrokeThickness = 2.0;
    }
    _overlay.Children.Add(marker);
  }
}
```

Using InkCanvas

We've already seen the basics of using the InkCanvas control, but there is a lot more there. With RichTextBox we have all the functionality needed to implement the WordPad application included in Windows; with InkCanvas we can implement Journal. All the basics are there: ink selection, erasing, highlighting, tip specification, and so on. Probably the most interesting feature is the new gesture support.

The gesture recognizer analyzes the ink data and determines whether the user tried to input one of 41 gestures (everything from Check to Double-Curlicue is included). Enabling gestures requires two critical steps: First, we must set EditingMode on InkCanvas to InkAndGesture. Second, we must call SetEnabledGestures on InkCanvas to tell the recognizer which gestures to look for:

```
<!-- InkCanvasTest.xaml -->
<Window ... x:Class='EssentialWPF.InkCanvasTest'
  Title='EssentialWPF'
  >
  <StackPanel>
    <InkCanvas Height='200' Name='_ink'
      Gesture='InkGesture'
      EditingMode='InkAndGesture' />
    <ListBox Name='_seen' />
  </StackPanel>
</Window>

// InkCanvasTest.xaml.cs
public partial class InkCanvasTest : Window {
  public InkCanvasTest() {
```

```
  InitializeComponent();
  _ink.SetEnabledGestures(new ApplicationGesture[] {
    ApplicationGesture.AllGestures,
  });
}

void InkGesture(object sender, InkCanvasGestureEventArgs e) {
  _seen.Items.Add(
    e.GetGestureRecognitionResults()[0].ApplicationGesture);
}
}
```

When we run the application, we can try several different gestures
(Figure 3.34) to see how close our writing is to what the recognizer expects.
Using gestures is a great way to ink-enable an application.

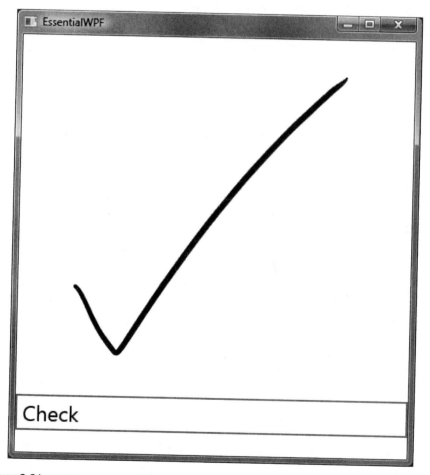

FIGURE 3.34: InkCanvas recognizing gestures

Document Viewers

For displaying a document, WPF offers several options. The simplest is to use the basic `FlowDocumentScrollViewer` (read-only scrolling view) and `RichTextBox` (editable scrolling view) controls to display the document. To present a reading experience to the end customer, however, the platform offers several options.

Effectively there are two building blocks: `FlowDocumentScrollViewer` and `FlowDocumentPageViewer`. `FlowDocumentScrollViewer` provides a scrollable viewer with standard end user chrome (zoom controls, etc.). `FlowDocumentPageViewer` provides a paginated view, one page at a time, with standard end user chrome.

The optimal control, though, is `FlowDocumentReader`, which offers a single control that users can select if they want a single-page view, multiple-page view, or scrolling view. The reader is the recommended control for viewing a document. Figure 3.35 shows all three.

Document viewers are one type of host for content—in this case, documents. The other common host is a frame.

Frame

Using `Frame` in an application allows an island of navigation to be placed anywhere. There are two interesting models for hosting navigable content: isolated hosting and integrated hosting.

With **isolated hosting** the content is not trusted and is run in a completely isolated (sandboxed) environment. This is how WPF content is

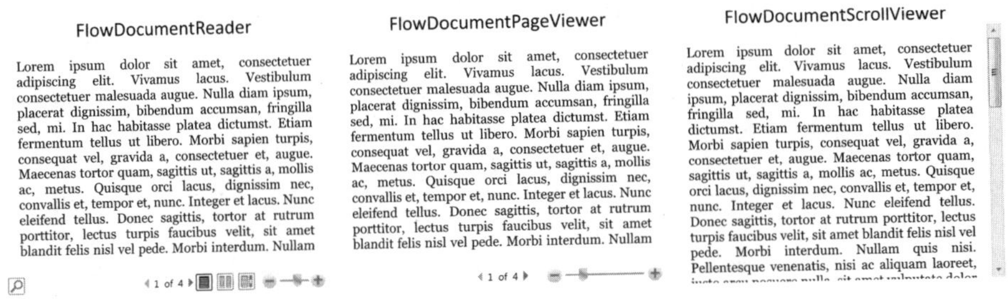

FlowDocumentReader

Lorem ipsum dolor sit amet, consectetuer adipiscing elit. Vivamus lacus. Vestibulum consectetuer malesuada augue. Nulla diam ipsum, placerat dignissim, bibendum accumsan, fringilla sed, mi. In hac habitasse platea dictumst. Etiam fermentum tellus ut libero. Morbi sapien turpis, consequat vel, gravida a, consectetuer et, augue. Maecenas tortor quam, sagittis ut, sagittis a, mollis ac, metus. Quisque orci lacus, dignissim nec, convallis et, tempor et, nunc. Integer et lacus. Nunc eleifend tellus. Donec sagittis, tortor at rutrum porttitor, lectus turpis faucibus velit, sit amet blandit felis nisl vel pede. Morbi interdum. Nullam

FlowDocumentPageViewer

Lorem ipsum dolor sit amet, consectetuer adipiscing elit. Vivamus lacus. Vestibulum consectetuer malesuada augue. Nulla diam ipsum, placerat dignissim, bibendum accumsan, fringilla sed, mi. In hac habitasse platea dictumst. Etiam fermentum tellus ut libero. Morbi sapien turpis, consequat vel, gravida a, consectetuer et, augue. Maecenas tortor quam, sagittis ut, sagittis a, mollis ac, metus. Quisque orci lacus, dignissim nec, convallis et, tempor et, nunc. Integer et lacus. Nunc eleifend tellus. Donec sagittis, tortor at rutrum porttitor, lectus turpis faucibus velit, sit amet blandit felis nisl vel pede. Morbi interdum. Nullam

FlowDocumentScrollViewer

Lorem ipsum dolor sit amet, consectetuer adipiscing elit. Vivamus lacus. Vestibulum consectetuer malesuada augue. Nulla diam ipsum, placerat dignissim, bibendum accumsan, fringilla sed, mi. In hac habitasse platea dictumst. Etiam fermentum tellus ut libero. Morbi sapien turpis, consequat vel, gravida a, consectetuer et, augue. Maecenas tortor quam, sagittis ut, sagittis a, mollis ac, metus. Quisque orci lacus, dignissim nec, convallis et, tempor et, nunc. Integer et lacus. Nunc eleifend tellus. Donec sagittis, tortor at rutrum porttitor, lectus turpis faucibus velit, sit amet blandit felis nisl vel pede. Morbi interdum. Nullam quis nisi. Pellentesque venenatis, nisi ac aliquam laoreet,

FIGURE 3.35: All the views of a document. Notice that `FlowDocumentReader` has a view control to let us see the document in either page mode or scrolling mode, and it provides search functionality.

hosted when running in the system Web browser as a XAML Browser Application. For navigation to another application or HTML content, this isolated hosting model is supported with a `Frame` object.

Integrated hosting, in which we want the content to behave as part of our application, is not supported at all in the system. When `Frame` navigates to content within the application, we get an odd hybrid of isolated and integrated behavior. `Frame` isolates its content from its style (and its parent's style), but not from the application's style. Events don't bubble from the content in `Frame`; however, the objects are accessible from the `Content` property (meaning that they aren't isolated in a security sense).

For all these reasons, `Frame` is most useful when we're working with external content, but it can be carefully used for application content.

Building Blocks

WPF's control model is built around the idea of element composition. We build up larger controls (such as `ListBox`) by using smaller controls (`StackPanel`, `ScrollViewer`, etc.). Although in most scenarios we don't need to dig into these building-block controls, it's good to know what services can be leveraged to build custom controls. The `System.Windows.Controls.Primitives` namespace contains many of the smaller components from which larger controls are built.

ToolTip

Generally we access tool tip functionality using the `ToolTip` property on elements:

```
<Button ToolTip='Click this button to do cool things!'>
  OK
</Button>
```

There are two common ways to adjust the behavior of tool tips. First, we can use `ToolTipService` to adjust more tool tip properties. An advantage of using the service is that only a single `ToolTip` control is created (this is useful when we have lots of tips on lots of controls). For more advanced scenarios we can create an instance of `ToolTip` directly on a control:

```xml
<!-- ToolTipTest.xaml -->
<Window ... x:Class='EssentialWPF.ToolTipTest'
  Title='Tool Tips'
  ToolTipService.InitialShowDelay='0'
  ToolTipService.ShowDuration='500000'
  >
  <Window.ToolTip>
    <ToolTip
      x:Name='_theTip'
      Placement='RelativePoint'
      VerticalOffset='10'
      />
  </Window.ToolTip>
  <UniformGrid Rows='3' Columns='3'>
    <Button Margin='5'>1</Button>
    <Button Margin='5'>2</Button>
    <Button Margin='5'>3</Button>
    <Button Margin='5'>4</Button>
    <Button Margin='5'>5</Button>
    <Button Margin='5'>6</Button>
    <Button Margin='5'>7</Button>
    <Button Margin='5'>8</Button>
    <Button Margin='5'>9</Button>
  </UniformGrid>
</Window>
```

```csharp
// ToolTipTest.xaml.cs
public partial class ToolTipTest : Window {
  public ToolTipTest() {
    InitializeComponent();
    this.MouseMove += ToolTipTest_MouseMove;
  }
  void ToolTipTest_MouseMove(object sender, MouseEventArgs e) {

    // Hit test to find the element that is directly
    // under the mouse.
    //
    PointHitTestResult hit =
      VisualTreeHelper.HitTest(
        this, e.GetPosition(this)) as PointHitTestResult;

    if (hit != null && hit.VisualHit != null)
    {
      _theTip.Content = hit.VisualHit.ToString();
      _theTip.PlacementRectangle =
              new Rect(e.GetPosition(this), new Size(0, 0));
    }
  }
}
```

If we run this example (Figure 3.36), we never see a window appear as one of the visuals to mouse over. Because the default template for Window

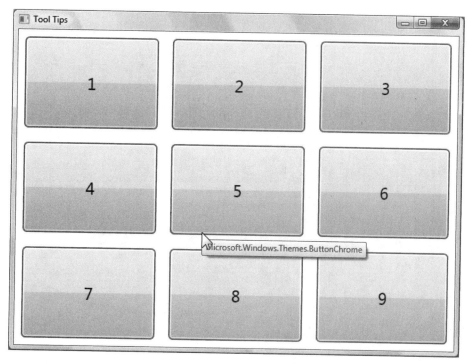

FIGURE 3.36: `ToolTip` **in action**

includes a border around the content presenter that hosts the content, the system will never detect a mouse hit on the window itself.[11] The same is true for `Button`: The button chrome and text block will appear, but not the button. This is another reason we often talk about controls not having a visual display of their own.

Of course, we can provide a custom template for the `ToolTip` control and give it any appearance and shape that we want (Figure 3.37 on page 164).

Thumb

`Thumb` provides a region that can be moved. More specifically, it provides the ability to get events when a user drags this region, the **thumb,** around. Using this control, we can easily create resize handles or splitter controls.

---

11. In fact, the outermost window display (the title bar, minimize and maximize buttons, etc.) are not accessible via any API in WPF. To customize the outermost part of the window (or receive events from it), we must either use P/Invoke or turn off the default window display (`WindowStyle.None`) and draw our own borders.

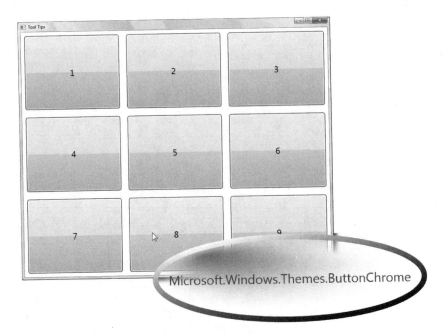

FIGURE 3.37: Templated `ToolTip`, with transparency

In this example we will simply have the thumb move when it is dragged. The `DragStarted` event lets us capture the start location, and then in `DragDelta` we can move the thumb by the appropriate amount:

```
<!-- window1.xaml -->
<Window ... x:Class='EssentialWPF.ThumbSample'
  Text='Thumb'
  >
  <Canvas>
    <Thumb
      Canvas.Top = '5'
      Canvas.Left = '5'
      Width = '10'
      Height = '10'
      Name='_thumb1'
      DragStarted='ThumbStart'
      DragDelta='ThumbMoved' />
  </Canvas>
</Window>

// window1.xaml.cs
...
double _originalLeft;
double _originalTop;
void ThumbStart(object sender, DragStartedEventArgs e) {
```

```
    _originalLeft = Canvas.GetLeft(_thumb1);
    _originalTop = Canvas.GetTop(_thumb1);
}
void ThumbMoved(object sender, DragDeltaEventArgs e) {
    double left = _originalLeft + e.HorizontalChange;
    double top = _originalTop + e.VerticalChange;
    Canvas.SetLeft(_thumb1, left);
    Canvas.SetTop(_thumb1, top);
    _originalLeft = left;
    _originalTop = top;
}
...
```

Border

Border is an amazing simple yet useful control for creating visual effects. Effectively, Border is a rectangle that can contain a child. This is handy because most render elements (Rectangle, Ellipse, etc.) don't support children. The typical workaround is to put the render elements into a layout container (like Grid or Canvas). Because enclosing an element in a rectangle is so common, Border is there to do just that.

Border actually does one better than a rectangle, though, allowing for variable thickness and corner radius around the border, which enables some unusual borders (Figure 3.38):

```
<Canvas>
  <Border
    Canvas.Left='15'
    Canvas.Top='15'
    BorderThickness='3'
    CornerRadius='0'
```

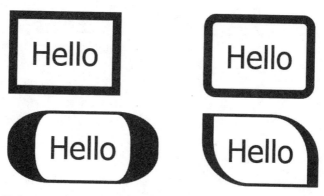

FIGURE 3.38: Various borders created by adjusting the radius and thickness of the edges

```
      BorderBrush='Black'
      Padding='5'>
<TextBlock>Hello</TextBlock>
</Border>
<Border
    Canvas.Left='85'
    Canvas.Top='15'
    BorderThickness='3'
    CornerRadius='3'
    BorderBrush='Black'
    Padding='5'>
    <TextBlock>Hello</TextBlock>
</Border>
<Border
    Canvas.Left='15'
    Canvas.Top='50'
    BorderThickness='10,1,10,1'
    CornerRadius='10'
    BorderBrush='Black'
    Padding='5'>
    <TextBlock>Hello</TextBlock>
</Border>
<Border
    Canvas.Left='85'
    Canvas.Top='50'
    BorderThickness='4,1,4,1'
    CornerRadius='0,15,0,15'
    BorderBrush='Black'
    Padding='5'>
    <TextBlock>Hello</TextBlock>
</Border>
</Canvas>
```

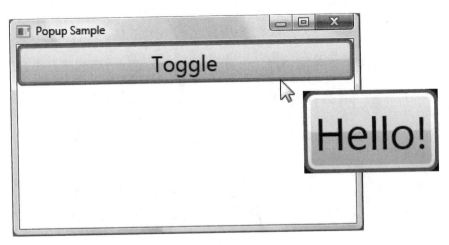

FIGURE 3.39: A window with a pop-up over it

Popup

One of the difficulties that faced UI developers in the past was creating floating windows. A big problem was how to manage the top-level window to host their content. In WPF, we ran into this problem while trying to implement tool tips, menus, and the combo box drop-down. In the spirit of creating reusable controls, the WPF team created a class called Popup that encapsulates all of the necessary behavior:

```
<!-- PopupSample.xaml -->
<Window ... x:Class='EssentialWPF.PopupSample'
  Text='EssentialWPF'
  >
  <StackPanel>
    <Button Click='ToggleDisplay'>Toggle</Button>
    <Popup PopupAnimation='Fade'
        Placement='Mouse'
        Name='_popup' >
      <Button>Hello!</Button>
    </Popup>
  </StackPanel>
</Window>

// PopupSample.xaml.cs
...
void ToggleDisplay(object sender, RoutedEventArgs e) {
  _popup.IsOpen = !_popup.IsOpen;
}
...
```

Running this example will display a window like the one in Figure 3.39.

ScrollViewer

Wherever scrolling is needed, the building-block control ScrollViewer can do it. You may have noticed that scrollbars are actually listed in the Primitives namespace; that's because scrollbars should be used only for scrolling, and the only component that needs to implement scrolling is ScrollViewer.

ScrollViewer must be used with caution because combining it with layout controls can have very unexpected results. One of the biggest confusions is that, in order for ScrollViewer to calculate the size of the scrollbar, it needs to know how big its children are. But ScrollViewer creates layout child elements that have an infinite size (in the directions that are scrollable),

thereby wreaking havoc on various controls—for example, FlowDocument-
ScrollViewer and, oddly enough, other ScrollViewer controls.

ScrollViewer can be found in the visual style of most lists and editors—
any control that by default will display a larger area than may be visible. It
is probably most common to want to place a scroll viewer on the window,
as the root element. You might think such placement would nicely enable a
dialog that, once sized to small, would automatically scroll. This does
work, provided that the size is set to Auto for any child content controls.
Consider, for example, the dialog in Figure 3.40.

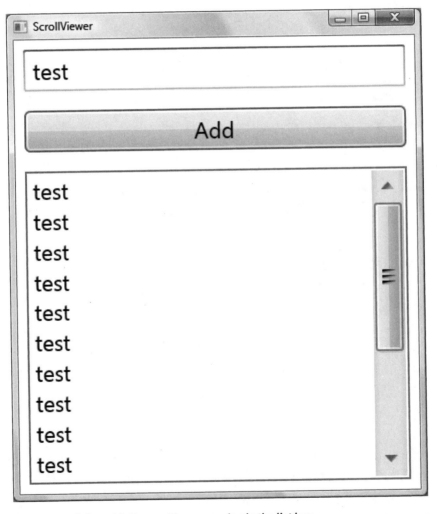

FIGURE 3.40: A dialog with the scrollbar appearing in the list box

This dialog has a simple grid with three rows (Grid will be covered in depth in Chapter 4). When we make the dialog too small, we want scrollbars to appear (not just for the list box). The simple solution is to surround the grid with a scroll viewer:

```
<Window ... x:Class='EssentialWPF.ScrollViewerTest'
  Title='ScrollViewer'
  >
  <ScrollViewer
      HorizontalScrollBarVisibility='Auto'
      VerticalScrollBarVisibility='Auto'
      >
    <Grid>
      <Grid.RowDefinitions>
        <RowDefinition Height='Auto' />
        <RowDefinition Height='Auto' />
        <RowDefinition />
      </Grid.RowDefinitions>
      <TextBox Margin='5' Grid.Row='0' Name='_toAdd' />
      <Button Margin='5' Grid.Row='1' Click='AddIt'>Add</Button>
      <ListBox Margin='5' Grid.Row='2' Name='_list' />
    </Grid>
  </ScrollViewer>
</Window>

void AddIt(object sender, RoutedEventArgs e) {
  _list.Items.Add(_toAdd.Text);
}
```

Because the list box itself uses a scroll viewer, we end up with unexpected results. Notice in Figure 3.41 (on page 170) that the scrollbar appears in the window, not in the list box as expected. There is no workaround for this problem. ScrollViewer is very powerful, but we must understand its impact on layout to fully utilize it.

ScrollViewer allows us to "fit" any content into a space by adding scrolling when the content is too large. The other control that helps with this problem is Viewbox.

Viewbox

Viewbox takes a single child and stretches it to fit by applying rendering transforms (stretching the content), as shown in Figure 3.42 (on page 170). Using the Stretch and StretchDirection properties, we can control how the content is sized.

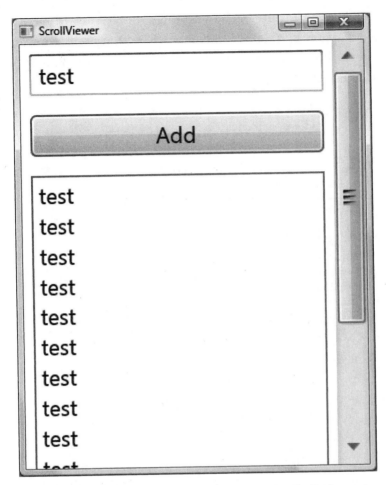

FIGURE 3.41: A dialog with a scroll viewer at the root. Notice that the list box no longer has a scrollbar.

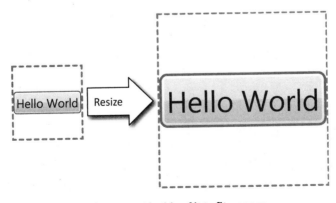

FIGURE 3.42: Viewbox scales the content inside of it to fit a space

WHERE ARE WE?

Three main principles underlie all the controls of WPF: element composition, rich content everywhere, and a simple programming model. This chapter has delved into the core concepts of WPF's controls that enable these three principles: the content model and templates. With these two concepts in mind, we have walked through a brief overview of the controls that ship with WPF.

▪4▪
Layout

C HAPTER 3 GAVE an overview of the control library in Windows Presentation Foundation that can be used to build UIs for applications. A real application needs more than one control, which means we have to figure out how to position all of those controls.

Although controls have been part of every major UI framework for the past 15 years, the notion of layout being a core part of a UI framework has lagged behind. For Win32 developers, layout is built on a simple 2D coordinate system that starts in the upper left corner of each window. On the other hand, HTML authors have been able to use a combination of flowing text, tables, and absolute positioning to create displays.

In WPF, layout is a pervasive concept that is deeply integrated into all WPF controls. WPF's layout engine is divided into two parts: a contract for specifying how components participate in layout, and a set of implementations of that contract.[1] There is no built-in layout; rather, all layouts are built using the platform extensibility mechanisms.

Layout Principles

The developers of WPF knew that layout was going to be an intrinsic part of the system. The goal was to define a single layout system that could span from

---

1. This chapter omits one large component of layout: text. Text layout presents an interesting set of challenges around pagination, columns, and reading optimizations (like hyphenation and justification). Text layout is implemented as just another extension of the base layout model. It is covered in detail in Chapter 5.

paginated documents to traditional application UIs. Eventually we realized that a single, monolithic system for this wide span of scenarios was impossible[2] (or at least very difficult) and moved to a model of layout composition. We ended up solving the bulk of the layout problems in the same way that we tackled the control library: by allowing layouts to be nested inside of other layouts.

Given this approach, it seemed that the most critical thing to determine was how a child control would communicate with the parent layout. This "contract" between the parent and child would, we hoped, enable any control to be hosted in any layout.

Layout Contract

The **layout contract** defines the way that a layout and child controls communicate. The goal in defining the layout contract was to keep it as simple as possible while still enabling various layout implementations to interoperate. Although some layouts have complex semantics that need deep knowledge of their child controls, the WPF team felt that the parts common to all layout implementations were fairly basic. A layout needs to be able to determine the size of the child controls, and then needs to tell its parent layout how big it wants to be. This concept boils down to two simple ideas: size to content, and two-phase layout.

Size to Content

Size to content, as the name implies, is the idea that each control is expected to determine its size on the basis of its content. This concept applies to all levels of the UI: Windows can resize to fit the controls inside them, buttons can resize to fit the text inside them, and text boxes can resize to fit the characters inside them. To enable size to content, each element must be asked what size it would prefer to be.

Two-Phase Layout

We determine a control's preferred size in two distinct phases: measure and arrange. This **two-phase layout** model enables both the parent and the child

---

2. The problems with creating a single engine are varied. Pagination is one of the most obvious examples. In a document-focused layout engine, all components must be aware of pagination (the idea that something can be broken across page boundaries). Pagination introduces a large amount of complexity into every control, making it very difficult to create controls that behave correctly in all situations. As a result, systems tend to create a closed set of things that can be paginated, and then everything else is treated as a black box that cannot be split across pages.

elements a chance to attempt to reach an agreement about the eventual size of an element.

The **measure phase** consists of walking the entire display and asking each element to determine its desired size, given a constraint. Elements must return a valid desired size, even if the constraint provided is infinite in size (e.g., when placed in a scrolling container). After all the elements have been asked to measure themselves, we move on to the **arrange phase,** during which each element is told by its parent to size itself to a specific size and location.

This two-phase model enables the parent and child to coordinate and negotiate about how much space is needed. Three interesting sizes are negotiated: available size, desired size, and actual size. **Available size** is the initial constraint used in the measure phase, typically the maximum amount of space that a parent is willing to give the child element. **Desired size** is the size that the child control wants to be. **Actual size** is the final size that the parent allocates to the child. In a perfect world, the three conform to this equation:

```
desiredSize ≤ actualSize ≤ availableSize
```

Layout is introduced in the WPF class hierarchy in the `UIElement` type. The layout-related object model on `UIElement` is fairly simple. `Measure`, `MeasureCore`, `Arrange`, and `ArrangeCore` implement the two phases of layout; and `Visibility` is the one layout-affecting property that controls whether an element will be displayed or included in layout:[3]

```
public class UIElement : Visual {
    ...
    public bool Visibility Visibility { get; set; }

    public void Arrange(Rect finalRect);
    protected virtual void ArrangeCore(Rect finalRect);
    public void Measure(Size availableSize);
    protected virtual Size MeasureCore(Size availableSize);
    ...
}
```

---

3. The rationale for the two sets of methods is to separate the method that we override to implement layout (`ArrangeCore` and `MeasureCore`) from the methods that can be called publicly (`Arrange` and `Measure`). For example, in the implementation of a layout panel, `Arrange` and `Measure` should always be called on the children; `ArrangeCore` and `MeasureCore` should never be called directly. This separation was created to allow the system to perform work (like caching, or updating the display) during the measure and arrange phases.

FIGURE 4.1: Visible, collapsed, and hidden buttons. Notice that the collapsed button is completely missing.

Visibility provides three ways of controlling how a child participates in layout. By default, elements are tagged as Visible; they will be displayed and will occupy space in layout. Controls may also be designated as Hidden (not displayed, but occupying space in layout) or Collapsed (neither displayed nor occupying space in layout). Figure 4.1 shows three buttons representing each type of visibility. The dotted border was added to illustrate where each control is occupying space in the layout.

The base layout contract is designed to be as flexible as possible, avoiding putting undue restrictions on implementations. Using this basic contract, the WPF team found it possible to implement rich typographic layout and a variety of 2D layout[4] implementations. This basic model is a great building block; in fact, many common patterns appeared in the 2D layout domain.

Consistent Layout

To make it simple to create layouts that implement these patterns consistently, WPF has a layer on top of the layout contract. The properties to control these common layout patterns are defined on System.Windows. FrameworkElement.

Probably the most common pattern that we found was the notion of layout constraints. When building a UI, it is very common to want to set minimums and maximums on control sizing, or even to set a specific size (effectively preventing size to content).

---

4. 3D layout is a very interesting problem space; at this time, however, it is a problem best left to researchers.

Layout Constraints

To control layout constraints, FrameworkElement introduces six properties: MinWidth, MinHeight, MaxWidth, MaxHeight, Width, and Height:

```
public class FrameworkElement : UIElement {
  public double Height { get; set; }
  public double MaxHeight { get; set; }
  public double MaxWidth { get; set; }
  public double MinHeight { get; set; }
  public double MinWidth { get; set; }
  public double Width { get; set; }
  // rest of FrameworkElement ...
}
```

Usually Width and Height are not set directly, because if they were, size to content would be disabled. MinWidth, MaxWidth, MinHeight, and MaxHeight, on the other hand, allow us to put constraints on layout without disabling size to content. For example, instead of setting a button to be a specific width, we can set MinWidth to be the desired width. If someone then entered a very long string, the button would grow to display the entire string, but it would normally be the desired size.

The properties ActualHeight and ActualWidth are the only output properties; they report the final size of the element. Note that they are not valid until a layout pass (measure and arrange) is complete.

The data type of Width and Height was one of the most hotly contested layout questions in WPF. The big debate centered on how to deal with percentages and automatic sizing.[5] Specifying automatic width or height signals the layout system to size the element to its content. Given that size to content is the default, the WPF developers chose to make the absence of a specified width or height mean automatic sizing.[6] Percentage sizing wasn't so easy to solve. Some controls (e.g., Grid or Table) natively have a notion of percentage size. Others (e.g., Canvas) can't really support percentage sizing (we'll see why later).

---

5. A smaller debate focused on how to deal with physical units (inches, centimeters, etc.). Because all lengths in WPF are 1/96 inch, however, trivial math can be used to support any units desired.

6. The value Double.NaN can also be used.

Slot Model

If percentage sizing is fairly control-specific, what we really need is a way for a control to determine its behavior when used in a parent. Interestingly enough, the solution helped the WPF development team deal with another common pattern: margins.

Although the various size properties can control the dimensions of the area that a parent allocates for an element, the design often introduces spacing around elements. If you've used CSS, you may be familiar with the box model, which allows for a margin, padding, and a border for each element. In WPF we moved to a simpler model, embracing the composition nature of the layout system.

Conceptually, the model for framework layout is that a parent allocates a *slot* of space for a child element. That child is free to occupy any portion of the space in the slot. This flexibility enables a compromise between the child and parent when conflicts arise. The parent sets boundaries, and the child can choose to use those boundaries as it sees fit. In the programming model, this functionality is exposed through three properties: `Margin`, `HorizontalAlignment`, and `VerticalAlignment`.

`Margin` lets a child put a buffer of space around itself inside of the slot, but outside of the content of the control. `HorizontalAlignment` and `VerticalAlignment` determine how the child occupies the remaining space

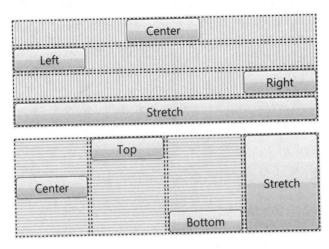

FIGURE 4.2: Aligning buttons in a panel

in the slot (alignment is determined with respect to the area inside of the margins):

```
public class FrameworkElement : UIElement {
  public HorizontalAlignment HorizontalAlignment { get; set; }
  public Thickness Margin { get; set; }
  public VerticalAlignment VerticalAlignment { get; set; }
  // rest of FrameworkElement ...
}
```

Figure 4.2 shows two different `StackPanel` objects. The top panel has a vertical orientation (buttons are stacked on top of each other from top to bottom), the bottom panel has a horizontal orientation (buttons are stacked from left to right). The dotted borders represent the slots that the panel allocated for each element. Using `HorizontalAlignment` and `VerticalAlignment`, we can control how much of the slot each button occupies:

```
<StackPanel Orientation='Vertical' Background='...'>
  <Button HorizontalAlignment='Center'>Center</Button>
  <Button HorizontalAlignment='Left'>Left</Button>
  <Button HorizontalAlignment='Right'>Right</Button>
  <Button HorizontalAlignment='Stretch'>Stretch</Button>
</StackPanel>
<StackPanel Orientation='Horizontal' Background='...'>
  <Button VerticalAlignment='Center'>Center</Button>
  <Button VerticalAlignment='Top'>Top</Button>
  <Button VerticalAlignment='Bottom'>Bottom</Button>
  <Button VerticalAlignment='Stretch'>Stretch</Button>
</StackPanel>
```

Using `Margin`, we can offset the slot for each edge. `Margin` supports different insets for top, left, right, and bottom. As Figure 4.3 shows, it is also

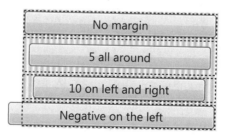

FIGURE 4.3: Setting margins around buttons in a panel

possible to have negative margins (again, dotted lines represent the slots allocated by the parent):

```
<StackPanel Orientation='Vertical' Background='...'>
  <Button Margin='0' HorizontalAlignment='Stretch'>No margin</Button>
  <Button Margin='5' HorizontalAlignment='Stretch'>5 all around</Button>
  <Button Margin='10,0,10,0' HorizontalAlignment='Stretch'>
10 on left and right</Button>
  <Button Margin='-15,0,0,0' HorizontalAlignment='Stretch'>
Negative on the left</Button>
</StackPanel>
```

Figure 4.3 shows something else that is subtle but important: Clipping is not the default. What does that mean? Notice that the last button in the figure extends outside the boundaries of the parent panel. In Win32 the default was to clip, or trim, the parts of controls that extended beyond their parent containers; only rarely could a child control paint outside the bounds of its parent. And if a child did paint outside of its parent, even more rarely would it produce the correct results.

As mentioned in Chapter 1, WPF uses a composition engine that employs the *painter's algorithm* (painting from back to front). Clipping is an expensive operation: Whenever we paint a pixel, we have to check its boundaries with the clip region to determine if we should actually light the pixel. Clipping has the benefit of being able to repaint a single control. In a world without clipping, we never know if a control has decided to draw outside the lines and affect us.

WPF takes the performance hit of always compositing, but that enables much richer visualizations. In addition, with today's video cards and CPUs, compositing is not so taxing. In a fully composited world, however, clipping is expensive.

In WPF, most controls use layout to ensure that they will fit within the bounds of their parent, so we can avoid clipping. You will notice that some controls (like Button) do turn on clipping, to ensure that its content will not leak outside of the control.

This discussion brings us to another interesting layout pattern: transforms. Negative margins allow us to move an element outside of the bounds that the parent intended for it. Transforms allow us to make these kinds of changes in a much more flexible fashion.

FIGURE 4.4: Three buttons with no transforms applied

Transforms

When all else fails, there's always the sledgehammer. To adjust the final position of a control, two properties are available for making an arbitrary transformation: RenderTransform and LayoutTransform:

```
public class FrameworkElement : UIElement {
  public Transform LayoutTransform { get; set; }
  public Transform RenderTransform { get; set; }
  // rest of FrameworkElement ...
}
```

Both properties are of type System.Windows.Media.Transform, which we will cover in depth in Chapter 5. For now, think about Transform from the view of the most common subclasses: ScaleTransform, RotateTransform, TranslateTransform, and TransformGroup. ScaleTransform allows us to perform an x/y zoom, RotateTransform allows us to rotate around a point, and TranslateTransform allows us to reposition something by a specified offset. Finally, TransformGroup allows us to group and combine these three primitives in any way.

The only difference between RenderTransform and LayoutTransform is the point at which the transform is applied. RenderTransform is applied immediately before rendering[7] (therefore affecting only rendering), and LayoutTransform is applied before layout (therefore affecting the layout of the component). To understand how these two properties interact, let's start with a simple stack panel containing three buttons (Figure 4.4):

```
<StackPanel Background='...' Orientation='Horizontal'>
  <Button Width='75'>
    15
  </Button>
```

---

7. It's a bit of a misnomer to talk about "before" and "after" with rendering. Because WPF is a retained-mode system we are actually talking about before and after with respect to generating the list of drawing instructions. RenderTransform introduces the transform into the drawing instruction list but never tells the layout system about that transform. LayoutTransform puts the same transform in the drawing instruction list but also applies that transform to the measure calculation for the control.

```
<Button Width='75'>
  45
</Button>
<Button Width='75'>
  65
</Button>
</StackPanel>
```

If we want to rotate each of these buttons by a particular angle, we can use layout, render, or both types of transforms. Adding `RotateTransform` to the `RenderTransform` property for each button illustrates the effect (Figure 4.5):

```
<StackPanel Background='...' Orientation='Horizontal'>
  <Button Width='75'>
    <Button.RenderTransform>
      <RotateTransform Angle='15' />
    </Button.RenderTransform>
    15
  </Button>
  <Button Width='75'>
    <Button.RenderTransform>
      <RotateTransform Angle='45' />
    </Button.RenderTransform>
    45
  </Button>
  <Button Width='75'>
    <Button.RenderTransform>
      <RotateTransform Angle='65' />
    </Button.RenderTransform>
    65
  </Button>
</StackPanel>
```

Notice in Figure 4.5 that the buttons overlap and extend outside the bounds of the panel. Because the transform is being applied after layout, the layout system has no knowledge that the display of each button is being manipulated; effectively the controls lie to the parent layout, saying that

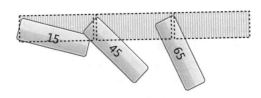

FIGURE 4.5: Applying `RenderTransform` to each button

FIGURE 4.6: Applying LayoutTransform to each button

they occupy their untransformed locations. Switching to LayoutTransform yields a much different effect (Figure 4.6):

```
<StackPanel Background='...' Orientation='Horizontal'>
  <Button Width='75'>
    <Button.LayoutTransform>
      <RotateTransform Angle='15' />
    </Button.LayoutTransform>
    . 15
  </Button>
  <Button Width='75'>
    <Button.LayoutTransform>
      <RotateTransform Angle='45' />
    </Button.LayoutTransform>
    45
  </Button>
  <Button Width='75'>
    <Button.LayoutTransform>
      <RotateTransform Angle='65' />
    </Button.LayoutTransform>
    65
  </Button>
</StackPanel>
```

As Figure 4.6 shows, now the buttons don't overlap and the panel has resized to fit the contained buttons completely. Because LayoutTransform is applied before layout, the system has complete knowledge of the effect. Generally it's a good idea to use the render transform for effects (such as an entrance animation). Because render transforms do not affect layout, they can run on the video card and avoid layout calculation while the effect is being created.

Z-Index

Controls that overlap (as we can see, just barely, in Figure 4.5) carry with them the notion of a specific ordering, or **z-index.** By default, all controls have a z-index of 0. The order of the children in the Panel.Children collection defines how they overlap. Using the `Panel.ZIndex` property, we can define "layers" for children. Within a layer, the order of children determines their rendering order; however, we can define multiple layers to control how children overlap.

To demonstrate, we can create several buttons, each with a negative margin to ensure that they all overlap:

```
<WrapPanel>
    <Button Margin='-5'>Button One</Button>
    <Button Margin='-5'>Button Two</Button>
    <Button Margin='-5'>Button Three</Button>
    <Button Margin='-5'>Button Four</Button>
</WrapPanel>
```

Running this code produces something like the top picture shown in Figure 4.7. The first control is at the bottom of the visual stack. By setting the z-index for several controls, we can alter the display:

```
<WrapPanel>
    <Button Panel.ZIndex='2' Margin='-5'>Button One</Button>
    <Button Margin='-5'>Button Two</Button>
    <Button Panel.ZIndex='1' Margin='-5'>Button Three</Button>
    <Button Margin='-5'>Button Four</Button>
</WrapPanel>
```

Notice that we can have several controls at any given z-index (in this case **Button Two** and **Button Four** are both at z-index 0). The result is a display like the bottom picture shown in Figure 4.7.

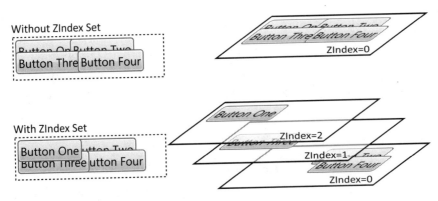

FIGURE 4.7: Effects of the z-index on the layout of controls

Implementing Consistent Layout

We've seen many of the layout properties that `FrameworkElement` introduces. Using these properties, we can greatly affect layout without needing to author a new panel. But if we do need to implement a new panel, it may seem a daunting task, given all of the behaviors we've seen up to now. Luckily, all of this behavior is hidden behind the scenes:

```
public class FrameworkElement : UIElement {
  public void Arrange(Rect finalRect);
  protected override sealed void ArrangeCore(Rect finalRect);
  protected virtual Size ArrangeOverride(Size finalSize);
  public void Measure(Size availableSize);
  protected override sealed Size MeasureCore(Size availableSize);
  protected virtual Size MeasureOverride(Size availableSize);
}
```

`FrameworkElement` overrides `ArrangeCore` and `MeasureCore`, replacing them with new versions: `ArrangeOverride` and `MeasureOverride`. To implement a custom layout that supports all the layout patterns that we've seen, we only have to override `ArrangeOverride` and `MeasureOverride`.[8] We can ignore all the rest of the layout properties.

No Built-In Layout

At this point you might be thinking that every layout property is baked into the base types of the system. With all the sizing properties, alignment, margins, and transforms, it's easy to see why you might get that impression. Remember, though, most of these properties were introduced on `FrameworkElement`, not on the base type `UIElement`. The goal was to clearly separate the contract of layout—measure and arrange—from the implementation of layout in the rest of the framework.

Early in the development of WPF, a topic of raging debate was how to implement layout. We felt it was critical to have a rich layout system.

---

8. Remember that we talked about `Measure`/`Arrange` versus `MeasureCore`/`ArrangeCore`, and how indirect use of the latter provides the system the ability to implement features around the measure and arrange phases. In the case of `FrameworkElement`, we wanted to add a lot more features (slot model, etc.). By overriding the "core" methods and providing new entry points, a developer can derive from `FrameworkElement`, override `MeasureOverride` and `ArrangeOverride`, and ignore the rest of these layout features.

We wanted a composition-based layout system that was extensible. For these reasons we didn't want to bake in knowledge about every layout into every element.

The best example of a rich, composition-based, extensible layout system is probably Windows Forms. Windows Forms 1.0 had a simple layout model using the Layout event. Each control in the system had two properties—Dock and Anchor—that were used for the default layout implementation. To implement a custom layout, however, we would have to figure out a new mechanism (maybe using IExtenderProvider?) to get the new layout properties to appear on elements. Windows Forms 2.0 has a more extensible layout system with better support for adding properties to other controls; however, the old Dock and Anchor properties are still around.

To avoid having so many properties on controls, all the properties specific to layout implementation are implemented as attached properties (like Canvas.Left, which we'll discuss next). **Attached properties** allow one object to offer a property for another object. Support for attached properties is implemented by DependencyObject, from which almost all types in WPF derive.

With this basic understanding of the principles of layout, we can walk through the library of layouts provided by WPF.

Layout Library

On top of the basic layout control and the more complete framework layout model, WPF provides a suite of layout panels. These panels implement a set of basic layouts that tries to represent the most common needs for layout. We will cover some of the more common layout panels: Canvas, StackPanel, DockPanel, and UniformGrid. The most complex layout, Grid, will be covered next, in a section all to itself.

Canvas

Canvas is the simplest layout included in WPF. Canvas offers four properties: Top, Left, Right, and Bottom. Canvas lets us position its child elements at any offset from one corner of the panel. Notice that I said "position"; Canvas does not introduce any sizing constraints on child elements. Canvas simply takes the desired size from an element and positions it relative to

FIGURE 4.8: Canvas using different origins for buttons

one of the four corners. Only two properties can be used: one horizontal coordinate and one vertical coordinate. If more are specified, the extra properties will be ignored.

To demonstrate, we can add several buttons to a Canvas with various offsets. Figure 4.8 shows that the offset is applied to the appropriate corner of the child control; for example, if we use Canvas.Right and Canvas.Top, the offset is applied from the top right corner of the child:

```
<Canvas Width='200' Height='100' Background='...' >
  <Button Canvas.Right='2' Canvas.Top='2'>
    Top, Right
  </Button>
  <Button Canvas.Left='2' Canvas.Top='2'>
    Top, Left
  </Button>
  <Button Canvas.Right='2' Canvas.Bottom='2'>
    Bottom, Right
  </Button>
  <Button Canvas.Left='2' Canvas.Bottom='2'>
    Bottom, Left
  </Button>
  <Button
    Canvas.Left='20'
    Canvas.Bottom='20'
    Canvas.Right='20'
    Canvas.Top='20'
    >
    All Four
  </Button>
</Canvas>
```

Canvas doesn't place any interesting constraints on the width or height of the layout slot, so the HorizontalAlignment and VerticalAlignment properties are irrelevant. Margins are still honored, but they are behaviorally identical to setting the Canvas layout properties. For this reason, Canvas is sometimes referred to as the "slotless" layout panel.

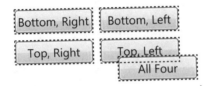

FIGURE 4.9: The magical missing canvas

There is one other interesting aspect to the Canvas control. Recall from the discussion of RenderTransform that, by default, we do not clip children. Because child controls can be oriented to any of the four corners of the canvas, it is impossible for Canvas to determine a desired width and height. This means that we can easily create the situation of a canvas with no width and height but all its child controls visible. Although this may seem an odd behavior, it is a pretty useful way to inject controls that float above the layout of the rest of the UI.

To see this, we can put Canvas inside of StackPanel and remove the Width and Height properties (setting the horizontal and vertical alignments will ensure that our canvas is sized to content in both directions):

```
<StackPanel>
  <Canvas
    HorizontalAlignment='Center'
    VerticalAlignment='Center'
    Background='...' >
    <Button ...>Top, Right</Button>
    <Button ...>Top, Left</Button>
    <Button ...>Bottom, Right</Button>
    <Button ...>Bottom, Left</Button>
    <Button ...>All Four</Button>
  </Canvas>
</StackPanel>
```

When we run this code (Figure 4.9), the canvas is nowhere to be seen, and the buttons seem to have scattered.

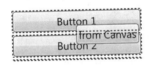

FIGURE 4.10: Using Canvas to "float" controls out of the layout

What has happened is that the canvas is actually zero height and is being stretched by StackPanel to the full width of the display. To see a bit more how this feature may be used practically, we can add some buttons to the stack panel:

```
<StackPanel>
  <Button>Button 1</Button>
  <Button>Button 2</Button>
  <Canvas
    HorizontalAlignment='Center'
    VerticalAlignment='Center' >
    <Button Canvas.Right='4' Canvas.Bottom='18'>from Canvas</Button>
  </Canvas>
</StackPanel>
```

As Figure 4.10 shows, the **from Canvas** button is floating above the other controls. The dotted lines represent the slots for the stack panel; the canvas has a zero height slot. Using this trick, we can inject controls into a panel and not affect the layout of the other components.

StackPanel

Up to this point in the book, StackPanel is the only layout panel that we've seen, so you've probably figured out how it works by now, but it's still useful to talk about it. As the name implies, StackPanel stacks things up in a row. Through the Orientation property we can control whether the stack is horizontal or vertical.

The slot for each child in StackPanel is given the entire width or height of the control (depending on its orientation), and StackPanel determines its preferred size according to the maximum size of its children. To show this, we can nest a couple of StackPanel controls and see how they behave. The outermost instance has a border around it (so that it's visible), and each inner panel has a background:

```
<Border BorderBrush='Black' BorderThickness='2'
  HorizontalAlignment='Center' VerticalAlignment='Center'>
  <StackPanel Orientation='Vertical'>
    <StackPanel Margin='5' Background='...'
      Orientation='Horizontal'>
      <Button Margin='2'>One</Button>
      <Button Margin='2'>Two</Button>
      <Button Margin='2'>Three</Button>
    </StackPanel>
```

```
        <StackPanel Margin='5' Background='...' Orientation='Vertical'>
          <Button Margin='2'>One</Button>
          <Button Margin='2'>Two</Button>
          <Button Margin='2'>Three</Button>
        </StackPanel>
      </StackPanel>
    </Border>
```

Figure 4.11 shows that the horizontal panel puts each button end to end. The buttons are stretched so that they're all the same height. The vertical panel stacks each button on top of the other, and all of the buttons have the same width (because we aren't setting their alignment). The reason that the buttons are so wide is that the outer panel forces the two inner panels to be the same width. As far as the complexities (and power) of layout composition go, this just touches the surface.

StackPanel must be used carefully because it measures children using an infinite width or height based on the orientation. This lack of a control on size can break other child layout panels, specifically causing problems for TextBlock with wrapping (Figure 4.12) and ScrollViewer:

```
    <StackPanel Background='...' Width='85' Orientation='Horizontal'>
      <TextBlock FontSize='18pt' TextWrapping='Wrap'>
        this is a test of stack panel wrapping
      </TextBlock>
    </StackPanel>
```

There is no way to avoid this problem with StackPanel. The most common workaround is to use DockPanel instead.

DockPanel

DockPanel is fairly similar to StackPanel, except that it allows mixing of stacking from different edges within the same layout container. In addition,

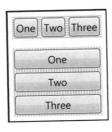

FIGURE 4.11: Three stack panels nested together

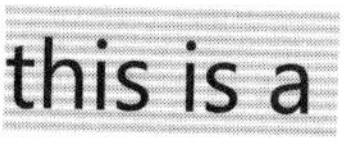

this is a

FIGURE 4.12: Horizontal StackPanel clipping text instead of wrapping

the LastChildFill property allows the last child to consume all the remaining space (like DockStyle.Fill in Windows Forms).

DockPanel is probably one of the most common UI layouts today. Windows Forms natively supported docking, and Java supports docking with its BorderLayout class. Docking allows elements to be stacked at any edge of a container, with the final element filling the remaining space. Windows Explorer (Figure 4.13) is a familiar application that benefits from dock layout.

We can break down Windows Explorer into its major structural elements: menu, toolbar, folder list, and details pane (Figure 4.14 on page 192).

Implementing this layout in WPF is relatively simple: The DockPanel offers a single property, Dock, which allows us to specify the edge to which a control is docked. The declaration order of the elements determines the order in which they're placed, and by default the last child fills the remaining space.

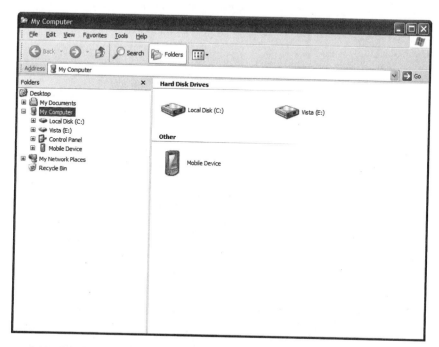

FIGURE 4.13: Windows Explorer, a classic example of dock layout

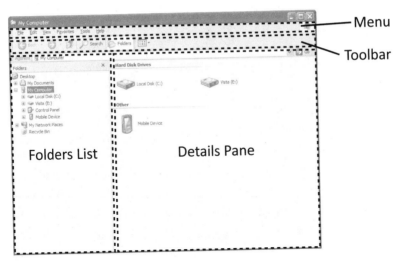

FIGURE 4.14: Windows Explorer, with the four major parts highlighted

We can use a dock panel to recreate the basic structure of Windows Explorer (Figure 4.15), using buttons to show the major elements:

```
<DockPanel>
    <Button DockPanel.Dock='Top'>Menu Area (Dock=Top)</Button>
    <Button DockPanel.Dock='Top'>Toolbar Area (Dock=Top)</Button>
    <Button DockPanel.Dock='Left'>Folders (Dock=Left)</Button>
    <Button>Content (Fills remaining space because
LastChildFill='true')</Button>
</DockPanel>
```

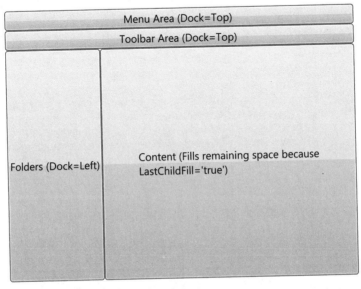

FIGURE 4.15: Using DockPanel to build the classic dock layout

We can change the relationships of the parts (e.g., suppose we want the folders section to extend the entire length of the left edge except for the menu area) by reordering the elements:

```
<DockPanel>
    <Button DockPanel.Dock='Top'>Menu Area (Dock=Top)</Button>
    <Button DockPanel.Dock='Left'>Folders (Dock=Left)</Button>
    <Button DockPanel.Dock='Top'>Toolbar Area (Dock=Top)</Button>
    <Button>Content (Fills remaining space because
LastChildFill='true')</Button>
</DockPanel>
```

As each slot is allocated by DockPanel, the remaining space is used to calculate the next slot, so no two slots will overlap. Moving the folders section immediately after the menu area will mean that its slot will be allocated immediately after the menu area (Figure 4.16).

Note that DockPanel has no default support for user modification of the layout (e.g., using a splitter between the folders section and the content to allow the user to resize the folder list). The only splitter that is part of WPF is GridSplitter, which relies on the Grid control, which we will learn about shortly.

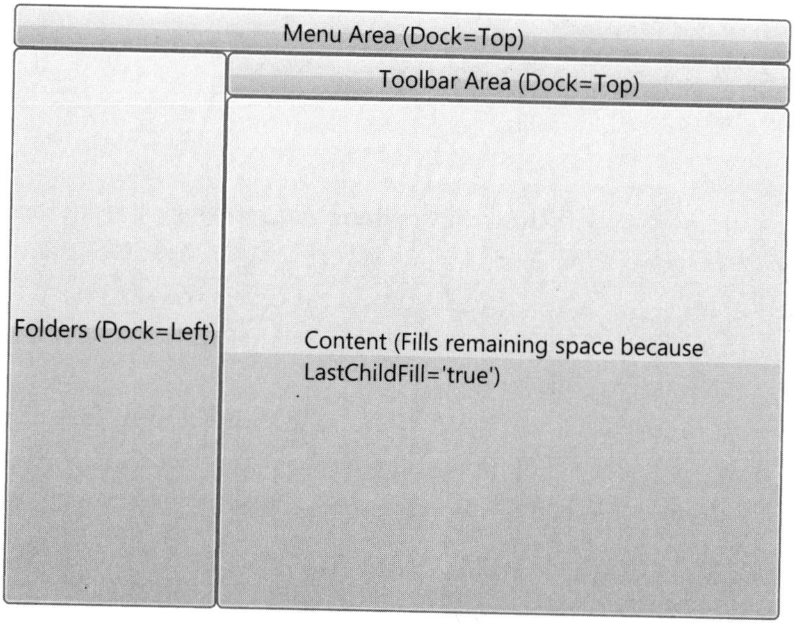

FIGURE 4.16: Adjusting the order of children affects the layout

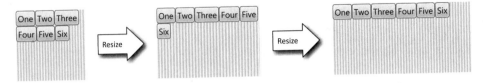

FIGURE 4.17: WrapPanel in action

WrapPanel

If DockPanel is a stack panel with multiple edges, then WrapPanel is a stack panel with wrapping support. Remember that StackPanel positions elements with infinite width or height (depending on the orientation), allowing any number of elements, stacked one after the other. WrapPanel, on the other hand, uses the available space and fits elements to it; and when it runs out of room, it wraps to the next line. The classic example of a wrap panel is toolbar layouts.

By default, WrapPanel simply sizes all the children to fit their content (see Figure 4.17), although we can fix the width and height of the children by using the ItemWidth and ItemHeight properties:

```
<WrapPanel Background='...'>
    <Button>One</Button>
    <Button>Two</Button>
    <Button>Three</Button>
    <Button>Four</Button>
    <Button>Five</Button>
    <Button>Six</Button>
</WrapPanel>
```

UniformGrid

The final basic layout, which is really nothing like StackPanel, is UniformGrid. UniformGrid hides in the System.Windows.Controls.Primitives namespace and provides a very basic grid layout: Each cell is the same size (hence *uniform*), and the locations of the items are determined simply by their order in the children collection.

To use UniformGrid, we specify the number of columns and rows we want. If we specify only columns, then rows will be calculated as the number of children divided by the number of columns, and vice versa:

```
<UniformGrid Columns='2' Rows='3' Background='...'>
    <Button>One</Button>
    <Button>Two</Button>
```

FIGURE 4.18: UniformGrid with a 2×3 layout

```
      <Button>Three</Button>
      <Button>Four</Button>
      <Button>Five</Button>
      <Button>Six</Button>
    </UniformGrid>
```

Running this code yields the grid illustrated in Figure 4.18.

The width of each cell is calculated as the maximum of all child widths, and the height of each cell is the maximum of all child heights. If we provide more children than can be displayed (e.g., adding a seventh button to the preceding example), it will be positioned as if the grid had infinite height (the **Seven** button will be directly below the **Five** button):

```
    <UniformGrid Columns='2' Rows='3' Background='...'>
      <Button>One</Button>
      <Button>Two</Button>
      <Button>Three</Button>
      <Button>Four</Button>
      <Button>Five</Button>
      <Button>Six</Button>
      <Button>Seven</Button>
    </UniformGrid>
```

Running this code produces something like Figure 4.19. The dark black border represents the bounds of the grid. It is important, but odd, that UniformGrid has positioned the last child outside the bounds of the control.

UniformGrid completes our tour of the basic layouts in WPF. Next we will dive into the most complex, but powerful, layout control: Grid.

FIGURE 4.19: UniformGrid with too many children

Grid

UniformGrid offers a basic grid, but for most scenarios it doesn't go far enough. People want grids with items that span cells, nonuniform row and column spacing, and so on. Grid is by far the most power, flexible, and complex of the UI layouts. On the surface, Grid is simple: Elements are positioned within grid cells defined by a series of rows and columns. Easy, right?

The simplest use of Grid is to set the RowDefinitions and Column-Definitions properties, add some children, and use the Grid.Row and Grid.Column attached properties to specify which child goes in which slot (Figure 4.20):

```
<Grid>
  <Grid.RowDefinitions>
    <RowDefinition />
    <RowDefinition />
  </Grid.RowDefinitions>
  <Grid.ColumnDefinitions>
    <ColumnDefinition />
    <ColumnDefinition />
  </Grid.ColumnDefinitions>
  <Button Grid.Row='0' Grid.Column='0' >One</Button>
  <Button Grid.Row='0' Grid.Column='1' >Two</Button>
  <Button Grid.Row='1' Grid.Column='0' >Three</Button>
  <Button Grid.Row='1' Grid.Column='1' >Four</Button>
</Grid>
```

Grid Concepts

Figure 4.20 shows the basic grid layout, but it doesn't adequately show three big concepts associated with Grid: (1) separation of layout from structure, (2) flexible sizing models, and (3) shared size information.

FIGURE 4.20: A simple use of the Grid layout

Separation of Layout from Structure

In all of the layout panels that we've covered up to now, we must change the structure of the element tree to change the layout. First we have to inject the layout panel into the display tree to plug in the layout algorithm, and then often we must change the order of controls to affect the layout (which we saw in the DockPanel example).

Injecting the layout panel as the parent of an element is a requirement with Grid too, but Grid's flexibility generally requires many fewer nested layout panels to accomplish a complex result.

Because the row and column information for Grid is based on property values, we can greatly modify the layout without changing the order of the elements. Therefore, not only is it much easier to change the layout, but the order of the elements does not depend on the layout order, so it is also much easier to control overlapping and predict what overlapping will do.

Both of these benefits serve a greater good: the ability to define layout without affecting the programming model. Using DockPanel and Stack-Panel, a graphic designer who wanted to change the layout of a window or page would be required to change the element hierarchy, and in so doing, could break the code. With Grid, it is much easier to adjust the layout without affecting code.

Finally, because the structure is separate, we can create the control structure (e.g., I want three buttons and a text box) and then apply layout (e.g., I want them positioned next to each other).

Flexible Sizing Models

Most layout panels partition the space using either the content size of the child, or the absolute value of the size of the child. In addition to these common modes, Grid introduces the notion of **percentage sizing,** in which the width or height of a column or row can be specified with a star (*) unit. Stars allow columns and rows to occupy a percentage of the space in the grid, after any size to content or absolute sizing of columns and rows is done.

The simplest way to understand stars is to see them in action. By adjusting the Width and Height properties on the definitions, we can adjust how the slots resize:

```
<Grid>
  <Grid.RowDefinitions>
    <RowDefinition Height='50' />
    <RowDefinition Height='1*' />
  </Grid.RowDefinitions>
  <Grid.ColumnDefinitions>
    <ColumnDefinition Width='50' />
    <ColumnDefinition Width='1*' />
  </Grid.ColumnDefinitions>
  <Button Grid.Row='0' Grid.Column='0' MinWidth='0'>One</Button>
  <Button Grid.Row='0' Grid.Column='1' MinWidth='0'>Two</Button>
  <Button Grid.Row='1' Grid.Column='0' MinWidth='0'>Three</Button>
  <Button Grid.Row='1' Grid.Column='1' MinWidth='0'>Four</Button>
</Grid>
```

As Figure 4.21 shows, the star-size row and column use all the remaining space after the fixed-size row and column.

To see the real flexibility offered by star sizing, let's change all of the slots to use stars. We'll make both the first row and the first column "2*". Since there are no fixed-size rows or columns, the two rows and columns will effectively be the same as items sized at 66.66 . . . percent and 33.33 . . . percent:

```
<Grid>
  <Grid.RowDefinitions>
    <RowDefinition Height='2*' />
    <RowDefinition Height='1*' />
  </Grid.RowDefinitions>
  <Grid.ColumnDefinitions>
    <ColumnDefinition Width='2*' />
    <ColumnDefinition Width='1*' />
  </Grid.ColumnDefinitions>
  <Button Grid.Row='0' Grid.Column='0' MinWidth='0'>One</Button>
  <Button Grid.Row='0' Grid.Column='1' MinWidth='0'>Two</Button>
  <Button Grid.Row='1' Grid.Column='0' MinWidth='0'>Three</Button>
  <Button Grid.Row='1' Grid.Column='1' MinWidth='0'>Four</Button>
</Grid>
```

This example demonstrates something interesting about stars: They represent weighted percentages (Figure 4.22). By adding up all the star units, we can determine what percentage each represents. In the preceding example, using "20*" and "10*" would achieve exactly the same results for the layout.

In addition to star sizing, column and row sizes can be expressed in absolute units (pixels) or left as Auto. The Auto option allows for controls to size to content and affect the size of the column or row.

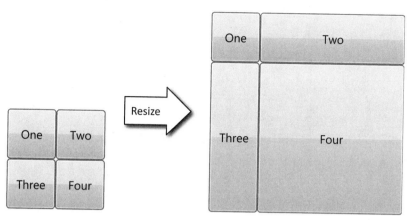

FIGURE 4.21: Star sizing allows for percentages

Automatically sized rows and columns introduce an interesting problem: Once we have a column or row in which the size is calculated (from the size of the children), we may often want *another* column or row to be the same size.

Shared Size Information

Shared sizing is the last major capability that is built into Grid. A grid shares sizing information among all the controls that are positioned in the

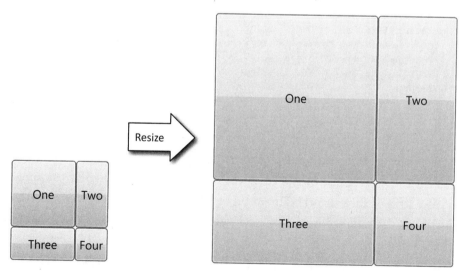

FIGURE 4.22: Percentages in star sizing are weighted

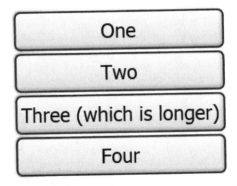

FIGURE 4.23: Grid sharing size information within a single column

same column. In the simplest form, this allows a set of controls to all have the same size, but be wide enough for the largest control. To demonstrate, we will adjust our example to have a longer string for one of the buttons, and put all the buttons in a single column (Figure 4.23):

```
<Grid>
  <Grid.RowDefinitions>
    <RowDefinition />
    <RowDefinition />
    <RowDefinition />
    <RowDefinition />
  </Grid.RowDefinitions>
  <Grid.ColumnDefinitions>
    <ColumnDefinition Width='Auto' />
  </Grid.ColumnDefinitions>
  <Button Grid.Row='0'>One</Button>
  <Button Grid.Row='1'>Two</Button>
  <Button Grid.Row='2'>Three (which is longer)</Button>
  <Button Grid.Row='3'>Four</Button>
</Grid>
```

If we set the column width to Auto, the column will size to content. Because each button has the default behavior, which is to stretch to fill the total space of the column (HorizontalAlignment.Stretch), the buttons will fill the total space of the column—which is determined by the maximum width of the buttons. This type of shared sizing is very powerful for laying out dialogs, where we might have multiple buttons or labels that we want to line up.

The other type of shared sizing is to size groups explicitly. Shared sizing allows two different columns or rows (even in different grids) to share

FIGURE 4.24: Grid with and without shared sizing

the same size. The two-row, two-column layout that we saw earlier illustrates what shared sizing does for us (see Figure 4.24).

To enable shared sizing we need to do two things: first, set the Shared-SizeGroup property on more than one column or row; and second, set the IsSharedSizeScope property on a control. In this first example we will share the sizing information between two columns in the same grid:

```
<Grid IsSharedSizeScope='true'>
  <Grid.RowDefinitions>
    <RowDefinition />
    <RowDefinition />
  </Grid.RowDefinitions>
  <Grid.ColumnDefinitions>
    <ColumnDefinition Width='Auto' SharedSizeGroup='a' />
    <ColumnDefinition Width='Auto' SharedSizeGroup='a' />
  </Grid.ColumnDefinitions>
  <Button Grid.Row='0' Grid.Column='0'>One</Button>
  <Button Grid.Row='0' Grid.Column='1'>Two</Button>
  <Button Grid.Row='1' Grid.Column='0'>Three (which is longer)</Button>
  <Button Grid.Row='1' Grid.Column='1'>Four</Button>
</Grid>
```

Finally, to see the real power of shared sizing, we can have sizing information span multiple Grid controls. IsSharedSizeScope can be set locally on Grid or used as an attached property on any element. To share the sizing information, we will set the parent StackPanel in the example to be the scope, and then have two Grid controls that use the same name for a size group:

```
<StackPanel Orientation='Vertical' Grid.IsSharedSizeScope='true'>
  <Grid>
    <Grid.RowDefinitions>
      <RowDefinition />
      <RowDefinition />
    </Grid.RowDefinitions>
    <Grid.ColumnDefinitions>
      <ColumnDefinition Width='Auto' SharedSizeGroup='a' />
      <ColumnDefinition Width='Auto' />
    </Grid.ColumnDefinitions>
```

```
  <Button Grid.Row='0' Grid.Column='0'>One</Button>
  <Button Grid.Row='0' Grid.Column='1'>Two</Button>
  <Button Grid.Row='1' Grid.Column='0'>Three (which is longer)</Button>
  <Button Grid.Row='1' Grid.Column='1'>Four</Button>
</Grid>

<Border ...>
  <Grid>
    <Grid.RowDefinitions>
      <RowDefinition />
      <RowDefinition />
    </Grid.RowDefinitions>
    <Grid.ColumnDefinitions>
      <ColumnDefinition Width='Auto' SharedSizeGroup='a' />
      <ColumnDefinition Width='Auto' />
    </Grid.ColumnDefinitions>
    <Button Grid.Row='0' Grid.Column='0'>a</Button>
    <Button Grid.Row='0' Grid.Column='1'>b</Button>
    <Button Grid.Row='1' Grid.Column='0'>c</Button>
    <Button Grid.Row='1' Grid.Column='1'>d</Button>
  </Grid>
</Border>
</StackPanel>
```

When we run this code (Figure 4.25), we can see that the second grid (with buttons **a** through **d** and a thick black border) has the same width for the first column as the first grid has. This powerful concept is used in controls like ListView to enable the column header to have the same size as the rows in the data section.

Grid Layout

Grid layout consists of two distinct phases: (1) defining the rows and columns, and (2) assigning the children to slots.

To define rows and columns we use the RowDefinition and Column-Definition objects, which support a subset of the standard framework layout properties:

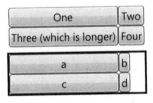

FIGURE 4.25: Two Grid controls sharing sizing information

```
public class ColumnDefinition : DefinitionBase {
    public string SharedSizeGroup { get; set; }

    public double MinWidth { get; set; }
    public double MaxWidth { get; set; }
    public GridLength Width { get; set; }

    ...
}

public class RowDefinition : DefinitionBase {
    public string SharedSizeGroup { get; set; }

    public double MinHeight { get; set; }
    public double MaxHeight { get; set; }
    public GridLength Height { get; set; }

    ...
}
```

These properties generally behave exactly like their counterparts on `FrameworkElement`, with the exception that `GridLength` allows the `Width` and `Height` properties to contain the additional sizing types that `Grid` supports. By using the `MinWidth`, `MaxWidth`, `MinHeight`, and `MaxHeight` properties, we can constrain the size of a column without having to set properties on every child element in the grid.

Before defining columns and rows, it's often best to start with a sketch of what we want to create. Suppose we want to clone a bit of the UI from MSN Messenger (Figure 4.26 on page 204). To start, we can create a mockup of what we want to create. We'll begin by drawing some boxes and using a dashed line to indicate where we want row and column boundaries (Figure 4.27 on page 205).

We need two rows and two columns. The first row should take up the majority of the space, but we know that the text entry area might grow to give people more space to type. To support this flexibility, we'll make the second row size to fit but put constraints on it to ensure that it doesn't consume all available space:

```
<Grid.RowDefinitions>
  <RowDefinition Height='*' />
  <RowDefinition Height='Auto' MinHeight='50' MaxHeight='150' />
</Grid.RowDefinitions>
```

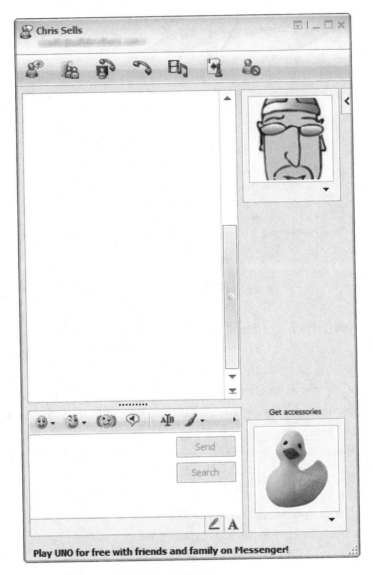

FIGURE 4.26: The grid layout of MSN Messenger

The first column should take up the bulk of the space, leaving just enough room for the second column to show the **Send** button:

```
<Grid.ColumnDefinitions>
  <ColumnDefinition Width='*' />
  <ColumnDefinition Width='Auto' />
</Grid.ColumnDefinitions>
```

Now that we've defined the rows and columns, we need to position the controls. The first thing to notice is that the conversation area spans multiple

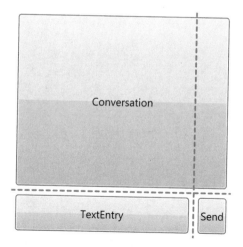

FIGURE 4.27: A mockup of the columns and rows that we want

columns. Grid defines four attached properties for child elements: Row, RowSpan, Column, and ColumnSpan. Using RowSpan and ColumnSpan, we can specify that any element be able to span multiple rows or columns:

```
<Button Grid.ColumnSpan='2' MinWidth='0'>Conversation</Button>
<Button Grid.Row='1' MinWidth='0'>TextEntry</Button>
<Button Grid.Row='1' Grid.Column='2' MinWidth='0'>Send</Button>
```

This combination of setting layout constraints on the definitions and the elements within the layout allows us to get the desired behavior. Not only is the initial state correct, but as we resize the display, the rows and columns size intelligently (Figure 4.28).

GridSplitter

If you've used MSN Messenger before, you may have noticed that the text entry area is resizable; a little splitter there allows the user to make more

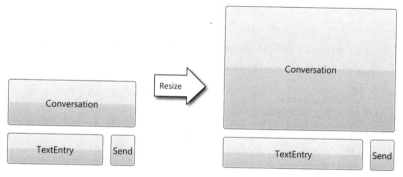

FIGURE 4.28: Grid resizing the final layout

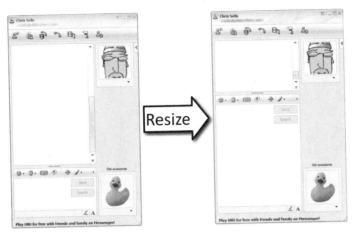

FIGURE 4.29: Resizing MSN Messenger using the splitter above the text area

space for typing (Figure 4.29). When we set up the rows and columns in our example, we specified a maximum and a minimum for the size of the second row, but we didn't provide the end user with any way of changing the size.

GridSplitter is a normal control (supporting templates, etc.) that allows the user to edit the layout of a row or column at runtime. In our example we can easily add it to the layout with no changes other than adding the control and setting some properties:

```
<GridSplitter
  Margin='0,0,0,-2.5'
  Height='5'
  ResizeDirection='Rows'
  ResizeBehavior='CurrentAndNext'
  Grid.Row='0'
  Grid.ColumnSpan='2'
  VerticalAlignment='Bottom'
  HorizontalAlignment='Stretch' />
```

ResizeDirection controls whether the splitter is editing rows or columns, and ResizeBehavior determines which rows or columns are being edited. There are two types of resize behavior: implicit and explicit. Using GridResizeBehavior.BasedOnAlignment will provide the implicit behavior; the splitter will use the vertical and horizontal alignment to "guess" which columns or rows should be edited. The other three values (CurrentAndNext, PreviousAndCurrent, and PreviousAndNext) allow us to specify explicitly which columns or rows should be edited.

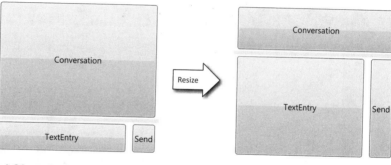

FIGURE 4.30: GridSplitter in action

Because we didn't create a new row for the splitter, it is occupying one of the rows that we want to edit (the first row), so we need to edit the "current" column. The splitter is at the bottom of the slot, and we want to edit the next row (the second row), so we need to use the CurrentAndNext value for ResizeBehavior (Figure 4.30). Of course, since the splitter's alignments are all set correctly, this example would work equally well with the BasedOnAlignment behavior.

Grid is a very powerful, but complex, layout. With effective use of Grid, we can build a complex UI without having to nest a lot of controls or create a custom layout logic. Sometimes, however, we really do need to write a custom layout.

Writing a Custom Layout

To write a custom layout, generally we build a new class deriving from Panel. Before we dive into implementing a layout, though, let's digress for a moment and talk about why we would build a custom layout.

The two most common reasons are "algorithmic layout" (the desire to position controls along a curve, for example) and performance. Be careful with the performance argument; remember the first rule of performance: test. People often jump to the conclusion that something is slow (or fast) without adequately testing it. Performance was one of the reasons that UniformGrid was created; for a uniform distribution of elements, the overhead of Grid was not needed.

Algorithmic layout is more interesting. Suppose we want to lay out a set of controls along a circular path (something like what's shown in Figure 4.31 on page 208). Obviously none of the existing layouts would handle this case.

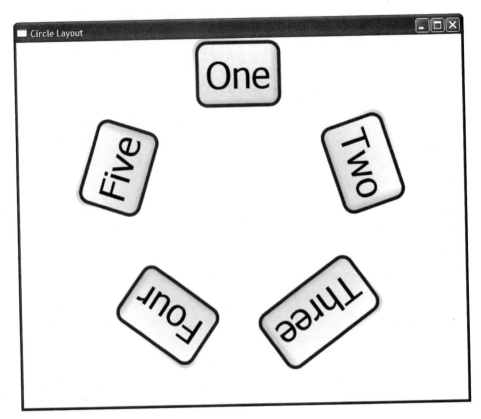

FIGURE 4.31: An example of algorithmic layout: a circle

With the two-phase model for layout in WPF, we should start by calculating the desired layout size. There are some complexities in calculating the desired size of this layout, mostly because of the math involved. We will simplify the algorithm a bit and use the model shown in Figure 4.32.

To calculate the desired size, we will check the size of each child and determine the maximum height and width. It is critical to call Measure on each child,[9] or else that child will not be rendered:

```
protected override Size MeasureOverride(Size availableSize) {
    double maxChildWidth = 0.0;
    double maxChildHeight = 0.0;
```

---

9. Notice that we're using the InternalChildren property; this property is intended for layout authors. The InternalChildren property is required if you intend to use the panel inside of an ItemsControl object or in another context that generates children (we'll talk more about this in Chapter 6).

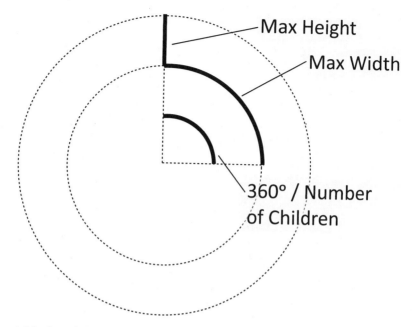

FIGURE 4.32: A model for calculating the desired size of the circle layout

```
// Measure each child; in this case we will not
// constrain them.
//
foreach (UIElement child in InternalChildren) {
  child.Measure(availableSize);
  maxChildWidth = Math.Max(child.DesiredSize.Width, maxChildWidth);
  maxChildHeight = Math.Max(child.DesiredSize.Height, maxChildHeight);
}
// more to come...
}
```

Knowing the maximum width and height, we can calculate the ideal size of the panel by computing the radius of a circle required to produce a circumference long enough for all the controls. We are cheating here a little, because we are evenly spacing the controls instead:

```
protected override Size MeasureOverride(Size availableSize) {
  double maxChildWidth = 0.0;
  double maxChildHeight = 0.0;

  // Measure each child; in this case we will not
  // constrain them.
  //
```

```
foreach (UIElement child in InternalChildren) {
  child.Measure(availableSize);
  maxChildWidth = Math.Max(child.DesiredSize.Width, maxChildWidth);
  maxChildHeight = Math.Max(child.DesiredSize.Height, maxChildHeight);
}

// Not a perfect algorithm for size, but we compute the desired
// radius for a circle that could fit all the widths,
// and then offset by the height.
//
double idealCircumference = maxChildWidth * InternalChildren.Count;
double idealRadius =
  (idealCircumference / (Math.PI * 2) + maxChildHeight);

Size ideal = new Size(idealRadius * 2, idealRadius * 2);
// more to come...
}
```

The final step is to attempt to "fit" into the available size. Because we are willing to overlap the controls as needed, we can fit in any size. However, in some cases (e.g., when contained in a stack panel), either width or height (or both) is infinite. It is important to take this possibility into account, because it is an error to return infinity as the desired size:

```
protected override Size MeasureOverride(Size availableSize) {
  double maxChildWidth = 0.0;
  double maxChildHeight = 0.0;

  // Measure each child; in this case we will not
  // constrain them.
  //
  foreach (UIElement child in InternalChildren) {
    child.Measure(availableSize);
    maxChildWidth = Math.Max(child.DesiredSize.Width, maxChildWidth);
    maxChildHeight = Math.Max(child.DesiredSize.Height, maxChildHeight);
  }

  // Not a perfect algorithm for size, but we compute the desired
  // radius for a circle that could fit all the widths,
  // and then offset by the height.
  //
  double idealCircumference = maxChildWidth * InternalChildren.Count;
  double idealRadius =
    (idealCircumference / (Math.PI * 2) + maxChildHeight);

  Size ideal = new Size(idealRadius * 2, idealRadius * 2);

  // Compute our size; keep in mind, we might get infinity in either
```

```
// direction. In this case we will return *up to* our ideal, but
// fit within whatever constraint we are given.
//
Size desired = ideal;
if (!double.IsInfinity(availableSize.Width)) {
  if (availableSize.Width < desired.Width) {
    desired.Width = availableSize.Width;
  }
}
if (!double.IsInfinity(availableSize.Height)) {
  if (availableSize.Height < desired.Height) {
    desired.Height = availableSize.Height;
  }
}
return desired;
}
```

Our arrange implementation will be a little more tricky. Because we want the layout to be circular (not elliptical), we need to calculate the largest square that can fit in the available size. We can use `RotateTransform` to do the heavy lifting of rotating the control, but we do have to calculate the center point. All of this together gives us the model shown in Figure 4.33.

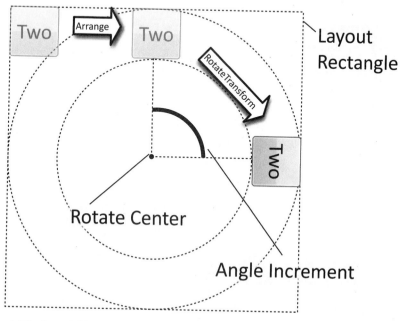

FIGURE 4.33: A model for arranging children in the circle layout

The first step is to calculate the bounds of our uniform circle:

```
protected override Size ArrangeOverride(Size finalSize) {
  // Compute the "uniform" fill of the circle.
  //
  Rect layoutRect;
  if (finalSize.Width > finalSize.Height) {
    layoutRect = new Rect(
                   (finalSize.Width - finalSize.Height) / 2
                   ,0
                   ,finalSize.Height
                   ,finalSize.Height);
  }
  else {
    layoutRect = new Rect(
                   0
                   ,(finalSize.Height - finalSize.Width) / 2
                   ,finalSize.Width
                   ,finalSize.Width);
  }

  // more to come...
}
```

Computing the angle increment is trivial; just divide the total number of degrees by the number of children:

```
protected override Size ArrangeOverride(Size finalSize) {
  // Compute the "uniform" fill of the circle.
  //
  Rect layoutRect;
  if (finalSize.Width > finalSize.Height) {
    layoutRect = new Rect(
                   (finalSize.Width - finalSize.Height) / 2
                   ,0
                   ,finalSize.Height
                   ,finalSize.Height);
  }
  else {
    layoutRect = new Rect(
                   0
                   ,(finalSize.Height - finalSize.Width) / 2
                   ,finalSize.Width
                   ,finalSize.Width);
  }

  double angleInc = 360.0 / InternalChildren.Count;
  // more to come...
}
```

We'll do two interesting things to each child. First we must call `Arrange` on the child. If we omit this call, the child will not render. `Arrange` takes a rectangle, which defines the final size and position of the child. In this case we'll center the control in the middle of the layout rectangle:

```
protected override Size ArrangeOverride(Size finalSize) {
  // Compute the "uniform" fill of the circle.
  //
  Rect layoutRect;
  if (finalSize.Width > finalSize.Height) {
    layoutRect = new Rect(
                    (finalSize.Width - finalSize.Height) / 2
                    ,0
                    ,finalSize.Height
                    ,finalSize.Height);
  }
  else {
    layoutRect = new Rect(
                    0
                    ,(finalSize.Height - finalSize.Width) / 2
                    ,finalSize.Width
                    ,finalSize.Width);
  }

  double angleInc = 360.0 / InternalChildren.Count;
  double angle = 0;

  foreach (UIElement child in InternalChildren) {
    Point childLocation = new Point(
    layoutRect.Left + ((layoutRect.Width - child.DesiredSize.Width) / 2)
    ,layoutRect.Top);

    child.Arrange(new Rect(childLocation,child.DesiredSize));
  }
  // more to come...
}
```

With our child positioned, we can now apply `RotateTransform` to spin it around the center of the layout rectangle:

```
protected override Size ArrangeOverride(Size finalSize) {

  if (InternalChildren.Count == 0) { return finalSize; }

  // Compute the "uniform" fill of the circle.
  //
  Rect layoutRect;
```

```
if (finalSize.Width > finalSize.Height) {
  layoutRect = new Rect(
                    (finalSize.Width - finalSize.Height) / 2
                    ,0
                    ,finalSize.Height
                    ,finalSize.Height);
}
else {
  layoutRect = new Rect(
                    0
                    ,(finalSize.Height - finalSize.Width) / 2
                    ,finalSize.Width
                    ,finalSize.Width);
}

double angleInc = 360.0 / InternalChildren.Count;
double angle = 0;

foreach (UIElement child in InternalChildren) {
  Point childLocation = new Point(
  layoutRect.Left + ((layoutRect.Width - child.DesiredSize.Width) / 2)
  ,layoutRect.Top);

  // Transform origin is 0,0 relative to the child's
  // arranged location.
  //
  child.RenderTransform = new RotateTransform(
                    angle,
                    child.DesiredSize.Width / 2,
                    finalSize.Height / 2 - layoutRect.Top);

  angle += angleInc;

  child.Arrange(new Rect(childLocation,child.DesiredSize));
}

return finalSize;
}
```

Although writing a circular layout is not the most common thing, this example has illustrated many of the interesting aspects of writing a custom layout.[10]

---

10. The only other feature related to custom layout that is worth mentioning is having layout that depends on a property (or set of properties) like DockPanel.Dock. When defining custom properties, we can specify that they affect arrange, measure, and render. This topic is covered in more depth in the appendix.

WHERE ARE WE?

In this chapter we've covered the basic principles of layout and the library of layout controls. We've seen how applications are built out of controls, and how layout plays a critical role in positioning and sizing those controls. Having a rich layout system enables a UI that can dynamically resize on the basis of user input, screen size, or changes to content.

5

Visuals

I N COVERING THE concepts of Windows Presentation Foundation, we've looked at applications and how UIs are built from a set of controls, as well as how we can use layout to determine the positioning of those controls. The next step on our journey is to talk about the inner workings of the controls—specifically, how the display is created for those controls. Eventually all controls boil down to creating a set of visuals that display pixels on the screen.

A fundamental design principle in the development of WPF was integration. We wanted a single stack of technology that could solve a broad range of customer scenarios—from traditional user interfaces, to documents, to media. We can see this tenet woven throughout the stack, but it comes into even sharper focus at the visual layer of the system.

In the tour of the WPF visuals that we'll take in this chapter, we'll start by looking at 2D graphics and then move on to 3D. After covering these basics, we'll move on to exploring documents, covering basic text, typography, and text flow. Once we understand all the fundamental ways of rendering pixels (2D, 3D, and text), we can talk about animation—how to add life to visuals. The final stop on our tour of visuals will be the land of media, which is an interesting combination of 2D and animation.

2D Graphics

WPF has three layers of 2D graphics: shapes, drawings, and drawing instructions. **Drawing instructions** are the low-level commands to the composition system, **drawings** provide a thin wrapper over these drawing commands, and **shapes** are direct elements that represent drawings. In other words, drawings provide an object-oriented view of drawing instructions, and shapes provide object identity, interactivity, and styling to drawings.

All 2D operations boil down to a geometry, a brush, and a pen. **Geometries** define the shape, **brushes** define the fill (contents), and **pens** define the stroke (edge) of the shape. There are four basic geometries: line, rectangle, ellipse, and path (Figure 5.1). Path is the most complex of these, enabling us to describe an arbitrarily complex path containing lines and curves. With a path we can describe any of the other geometries.

Principles of 2D

Common to all the layers of the composition system is a set of principles. In a system that is constructed like WPF, with higher layers like controls building directly on lower layers, these principles are evident in the high layers.

Composite Rendering

In building a graphics engine, two basic options are available to provide support for cooperative rendering: clipping and compositing. GDI and

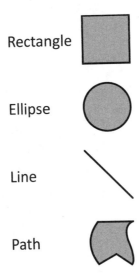

Rectangle

Ellipse

Line

Path

FIGURE 5.1: The four basic geometries

User32 previously were based on a **clipping system.** Each element would get its box of space, and all the rendering would be confined to that box. Clipping has some nice performance optimizations—mainly, that we can render an element with very little knowledge of the other elements. When Windows was created, this was a critical optimization: A window could paint without having to repaint any other window on the system.

A **compositing system,** on the other hand, allows elements to paint on top of each other. In the GDI/User32 world, we could accomplish this effect to some degree with CS_PARENTDC. Instead of clipping the rendering instructions, we perform a back-to-front paint operation, allowing elements at a lower z-index to paint and having the next layer of elements paint over them. In this world we can easily implement things like opacity and irregular-shaped elements.

WPF provides a fully composite rendering system for all elements; at a top level, however, we must create a User32 window handle to interoperate with the rest of the system. Using the layered window feature of the operating system, we can support some amount of compositing, and on Windows Vista this capability is greatly improved.

Resolution Independence

A pixel by any other name is not a pixel. In WPF there is no way to specify a real pixel. One of WPF's design principles is that applications should be resolution-independent; that is, an application should run the same regardless of device resolution, and it should look the best it can in all circumstances. Resolution independence comes in many forms—from the heavy use of vector graphics, to layout engine, and so on. One of the most basic ways that resolution independence is implemented in WPF is that all WPF coordinates are based on resolution-independent coordinates, not physical pixels.

The GDI coordinate system is based on pixels: When we say that something is 5 pixels away from something else, on the output device the system will put exactly 5 pixels between the objects. Of course, we can opt into other models in GDI—using himetric or other coordinate systems[1]—but at the end of the day, everything is resolved to pixels.

---

1. Visual Basic uses a system called *twips,* which is based on the typographic unit of points. *Points* are roughly defined as 1/72 of an inch, and a twip is 1/20 of a point or 1/1440 of an inch.

WPF uses **logical pixels,** which equate to 1/96 of an inch, as the native coordinate system. The first question everyone asks is, why 1/96 of an inch? Certainly 1 centimeter or 1 inch could have made a lot more sense. However, developers have been using GDI pixels for a very long time, and most output devices are 96 dpi (dots per inch), so using 1/96 of an inch as the native coordinate system matches not only most developers' intuition, but also the physical devices that are available today. As monitor resolutions improve,[2] I'm sure that this decision will seem increasingly arbitrary.[3]

To accomplish this logical view of the world, everything is rendered in WPF at effectively infinite resolution. This means that, for example, text will render identically regardless of size or output resolution, because the internal computations are done with infinite precision. (OK, not quite infinite, but pretty high!) But there are problems with relatively low-resolution devices like computer screens.

There are two common ways to create good-looking images on the relatively low-resolution displays that most users have. **Anti-aliasing** computes everything at a high resolution, and when it renders to the screen it determines how much of each logical line is on each pixel, and it lights it that amount. **ClearType** improves on this basic model, by taking into account the alignment of individual colored segments on LCD panels, yielding three times the number of addressable pixels on the output device, but effectively it is the same trick of "weighing" the line.

Both of these approaches have a problem: Things often look blurry. For text and vector graphics, this is generally what you want. Using ClearType on text makes it significantly more readable because the shapes of the letters are much smoother. However, for UI elements, like a button in a grid, we don't want blurry edges. To solve this problem, WPF introduced a concept called **pixel snapping.** We still render with the logical system, but then when we translate to the output device, we can ensure that the lines fall exactly on pixels (Figure 5.2).

---

2. The original Macintosh monitors were 72 dpi, to make them line up with the point measurement.
3. Today the typography *point* is treated as exactly 1/72 of an inch on most computer-based typesetting applications, even though the original point was slightly smaller.

Snapping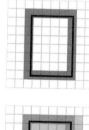

Not Snapping

FIGURE 5.2: Close-up of rectangles with pixel snapping on and off. Notice how crisp the snapped version is, even though the actual rectangle doesn't exactly fit on pixel boundaries.

Generally we don't need to adjust the defaults for pixel snapping; however, we can turn this feature on and off using the SnapsToDevicePixels property.

Transforms

At the base level in WPF's rendering system, there is no "position" for elements. Instead of having x and y coordinates, the system is based on transforms. Transforms allow for mathematical adjustments to the points associated with a geometry (remember, everything boils down to a geometry). The three most common transforms are TranslateTransform, ScaleTransform, and RotateTransform. With these three we can position, size, and rotate any element. Under the covers, WPF translates any position information on elements into TranslateTransform.

Transforms can also be combined. We can effectively chain one transform after another—for example, to shift an element 5 pixels to the right, then scale it by a factor of 2, then rotate it 15 degrees:

```
<Button>
  <Button.RenderTransform>
    <TransformGroup>
      <TranslateTransform X='5' />
      <ScaleTransform ScaleX='2' ScaleY='2' />
      <RotateTransform Angle='15' />
    </TransformGroup>
  </Button.RenderTransform>
</Button>
```

Geometry

Before we get too far into the discussion of geometries, brushes, pens, and other details about how to paint pixels on the screen, let's address the question of why we would care about any of this. For me it's a matter of understanding the grammar of a language. With a native language—the one we grew up speaking—we generally don't fully understand the minutiae of the grammar rules; we just know what sounds right. When I learned my first foreign language, I discovered a bunch about English also. I began to understand how the rules worked. Understanding the basic UI building blocks is important for the same reason: You've probably worked with other UI systems in the past—each with certain features, rules, and capabilities that you don't even think about anymore.

Geometries are the basic building block of all 2D graphics in WPF. Everything breaks down into a series of geometries that we can render. Therefore, it is useful to understand how that underlying system works. PathGeometry is effectively a superset of all other geometries, so it makes sense to spend our time looking at paths.

A path is defined as a series of figures. Each figure, in turn, is constructed out of a set of segments. Segments roughly equate to the "turtle graphics" program that I used on my old Apple II (MoveTo, LineTo, etc.). Segments instruct the pen to move around the screen. To understand this, let's walk through each type of segment that makes up a figure and produces a drawing like the one in Figure 5.3.

To begin, we need to specify a starting point for the figure. The simplest segment is LineSegment, which draws a line from the current position (labeled "StartPoint" in Figure 5.3) to the specified point ("Line.Point").

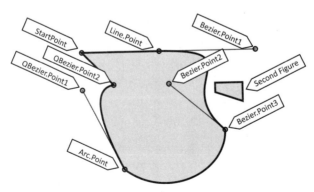

FIGURE 5.3: A complex path built from all the segments of multiple figures

To see this, we'll use a `Path` shape to contain the geometry that we're defining. By marking the figure with `IsClosed`, we ensure that the shape will always have a stroke line going from the last point to the starting point:

```
<Path Width='200' Height='200' Fill='#111111' Stroke='Black'
StrokeThickness='2'>
  <Path.Data>
    <PathGeometry>
      <PathGeometry.Figures>
        <PathFigure StartPoint='5,5' IsClosed='True'>
          <LineSegment Point='90,5' />
        </PathFigure>
      </PathGeometry.Figures>
    </PathGeometry>
  </Path.Data>
</Path>
```

The next interesting segment is `BezierSegment`, which lets us define a Bezier curve using two control points (`Point1` and `Point2`) and an end point (`Point3`), labeled "Bezier.Point1" and so on in Figure 5.3:

```
<PathFigure StartPoint='5,5' IsClosed='True'>
  <LineSegment Point='90,5' />
  <BezierSegment Point1='195,5' Point2='100,40' Point3='160,90' />
</PathFigure>
```

`ArcSegment` defines an arc to the specified point ("Arc.Point" in Figure 5.3), around an ellipse of the given size:

```
<PathFigure StartPoint='5,5' IsClosed='True'>
  <LineSegment Point='90,5' />
  <BezierSegment Point1='195,5' Point2='100,40' Point3='160,90' />
  <ArcSegment Point='50,130' Size='65,55' IsLargeArc='false'
SweepDirection='Clockwise' />
</PathFigure>
```

And finally, `QuadraticBezierSegment` ("QBezier" in Figure 5.3) is a simplified form of `BezierSegment` that uses an algorithm requiring only a single control point (`Point1`):

```
<PathFigure StartPoint='5,5' IsClosed='True'>
  <LineSegment Point='90,5' />
  <BezierSegment Point1='195,5' Point2='100,40' Point3='160,90' />
  <ArcSegment Point='50,130' Size='65,55' IsLargeArc='false'
SweepDirection='Clockwise' />
  <QuadraticBezierSegment Point1='5,45' Point2='40,40' />
</PathFigure>
```

In addition to any number of segments, we can include multiple figures in a single path. This capability is especially useful because any brush fills the entire path, so we can have smooth gradients go through multiple figures:

```
<Path ...>
  <Path.Data>
    <PathGeometry>
      <PathGeometry.Figures>
        <PathFigure StartPoint='5,5' IsClosed='True'>

          ...

        </PathFigure>

        <PathFigure StartPoint='150,40' IsClosed='True'>
          <LineSegment Point='180,40' />
          <LineSegment Point='180,60' />
          <LineSegment Point='150,50' />
        </PathFigure>

      </PathGeometry.Figures>
    </PathGeometry>
  </Path.Data>
</Path>
```

Two final geometries are the two combining geometries: CombineGeometry and GeometryGroup. GeometryGroup takes a list of children and composites them. The FillRule property determines what parts of the resulting geometry are filled. GeometryGroup can contain any number of child geometries, and under all conditions each geometry will be independently stroked.

CombinedGeometry allows us to merge exactly two geometries, with GeometryCombineMode determining how the system should create the new merged geometry (Figure 5.4 illustrates the options). Because CombinedGeometry

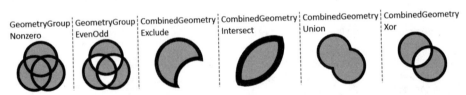

FIGURE 5.4: A variety of ways to combine geometries

actually creates a new single geometry, only the outside of the resulting geometry will be stroked.

Typically, complex geometries are created with a tool because anything beyond the simplest of shapes is nearly impossible to write and becomes unmaintainable. Understanding the basics of the platform helps us know what's possible, and what effects we can create.

Color

Now that we understand how to create shapes, we need to figure out how to paint the pixels. If 2D drawing is made up of geometries, brushes, and pens, we must first cover the basic concept of color.

What Color Is Green?

How can we talk about what a specific color is? In Webspeak it's "Green" or "#00FF00". In GDI-speak its "32768". In puppetspeak it's "the color of Kermit." These are all valid encodings of a color, but none tell me what color it really is.

Let's try this from another approach: How can we show someone green? We can go outside and point to a blade of grass. Of course, the color of that grass will be tinted by the daylight; it will look brighter on sunny days. We could point to the color on a computer monitor. Computer monitors (actually all color-reproduction devices) can display only a limited number of colors. The fundamental physical model of the device causes this limitation. Monitors, printers, televisions, digital cameras, scanners—anything that reads or displays a color—have some type of limitation.

So neither do we have a mechanism for accurately encoding the color, nor can we display the color. Now we're beginning to see how hard the problem of color is. A large portion of any book about high-end image-editing software (like Adobe Photoshop) talks about color—color spaces, models, working models, and so on.

Why do we care?

As more of our decisions are made through computers, the ability to preserve the color of something becomes more important. If we print the company logo on a Web site, shouldn't the color of the logo match the color on the printout? In another example, how close to the "real world" should the colors in a photograph be? If we then incorporate that picture into a document, should the colors still be the same? This problem of color work flow, and being able to maintain all the color information, is becoming an important issue for people dealing with digital media of any kind.

Color Description

As we've discussed, to describe a color we need some type of encoding. In addition, we need information about the profile of that encoding. A color profile provides information that enables software to convert from one encoding to another. Today most colors eventually are rendered on a device like a computer monitor (CRT or LCD) or a printer (with a wide variety of ink technologies).

The most popular color description is **sRGB.**[4] sRGB is the native color model for most monitors, and it is the default color model for the Web. sRGB allows for three channels of data, each at 8 bits, providing a 24-bit color description, or about 16.7 million colors. Given that the human eye can discern only about 8 million colors, it seems a shame to waste all that extra space. The problem with sRGB is that it has a compact gamut.[5]

Each encoding has a specific gamut that can be expressed. How black is black, how white is white? With sRGB we can express 16.7 million possible colors, but the total range of colors is relatively small.[6] So we have fairly fine-grained colors; that is, the steps between shades of colors are small. If we stretched the sRGB gamut to express a broader range of colors, then the steps between shades would be too large.

---

4. The *s* is for *standard*, *RGB* for *red-green-blue*. This color model is documented by the W3C (World Wide Web Consortium) at: www.w3.org/Graphics/Color/sRGB.

5. *Gamut* refers to the number of colors that can be expressed. There's a gamut that the human eye can perceive, there's a gamut that a display device can produce, and there's a gamut that a color encoding can represent. Saying that something has a "compact gamut" means that it can represent only a small spectrum of all possible colors.

6. The typical grading scale used in schools provides another example of gamut. This scale has a gamut of A through F, with only five distinct values: A, B, C, D, F. We can increase the precision of this scale by adding more values: A, A–, B+, B, B–, and so on. We can also increase the gamut, the actual range of possible values, by adding A+ or F–. By increasing the gamut, we can capture grades outside the bounds of A–F.

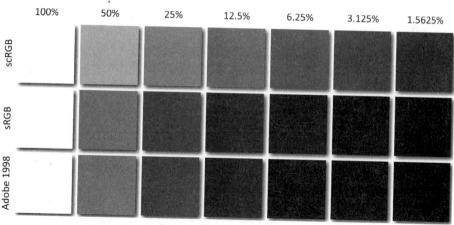

| 100% | 50% | 25% | 12.5% | 6.25% | 3.125% | 1.5625% |

scRGB

sRGB

Adobe 1998

FIGURE 5.5: Various color profiles showing shades of gray

To help address this problem, there is **scRGB**.[7] scRGB is a variable-sized floating-point encoding for color. It supports 64 or 128 bits of data to encode color (instead of sRGB's 24). In addition, the scRGB gamut is extremely large (extending far outside the range of human sight). The reason why scRGB allows for such precision on color, and such a large gamut, takes us back to the color work-flow problem. Because of the extra precision, we can perform color transformations (darkening a picture, for example) without leaving important data out of the picture.

WPF natively supports both sRGB and scRGB. In addition, we can use any ICC[8] color profile. Figure 5.5 shows scRGB, sRGB, and a custom profile,

---

7. The origin of the *sc* in *scRGB* is shrouded in mystery. Officially it stands for nothing. According to Michael Stokes (the national and international leader of the International Electrotechnical Commission, or IEC, group working on scRGB), the name appeared when the Japanese national committee requested a name change from the earlier *XsRGB* (*excess RGB*). The two leading candidates for meaning are "specular RGB" because scRGB supports whites greater than the diffuse 1.0 values, and "standard compositing RGB" because the linearity, floating-point support, HDR (high dynamic range) support, and wide gamut support are ideally suited for compositing. This meaning also implicitly emphasizes that scRGB is not intended to be directly supported in devices or formats, since by definition scRGB encompasses values that are beyond both the human visual system and (even theoretically) realizable physical devices.

8. The International Color Consortium (www.color.org) defines a common format for color profiles.

the Adobe 1998 color profile (which is remarkably similar to sRGB)—all showing the encoding of "White":

```
<Rectangle Fill='sc# 1.0,1.0, 1.0, 1.0' />
<Rectangle Fill='#FFFFFFFF' />
<Rectangle
  Fill='ContextColor file://.../AdobeRGB1998.icc 1.0,1.0,1.0,1.0' />
```

Notice that all these encodings have four values: `Red`, `Green`, `Blue`, and `Alpha`. WPF natively supports an alpha channel for all colors that lets us specify the opacity of the color: zero is transparent, and 255 is completely opaque. Color profiles can have different models for encoding alpha (just as they do for color): In sRGB we have 8 bits of alpha (0–255), and in scRGB we have 16 bits (0.0–1.0; scRGB uses the remaining space in the float for work flow). We will delve into the details of alpha and how to use all the opacity-related features in WPF a bit later in the chapter.

Brushes

Although color is interesting, it isn't enough to have only a color to paint with. Brushes instruct the system how to paint the pixels within a particular region. In some cases that region is the fill of a path; in other cases it is the stroke. WPF has six brushes: `SolidColorBrush`, `LinearGradientBrush`, `RadialGradientBrush`, `ImageBrush`, `DrawingBrush`, and `VisualBrush`. The key point to remember here is that anyplace we can specify a color, we have always typed that space as a brush, and we can use any of these rich brushes as the "color" for anything on the screen. When we use just a color reference in markup, a `SolidColorBrush` instance is actually being created.

Gradient Brushes

`LinearGradientBrush` and `RadialGradientBrush` (shown in Figure 5.6) both use a set of gradient stops to define the fill. `LinearGradientBrush`

FIGURE 5.6: Basic attributes of the two types of gradient brushes

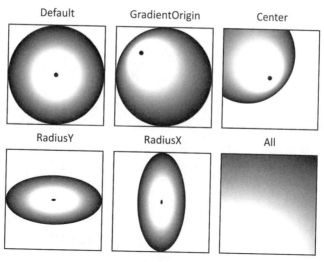

FIGURE 5.7: Effects of adjusting the attributes of RadialGradient

uses an algorithm to blend the colors along a vector. RadialGradientBrush uses an algorithm to blend the colors radiating out from the center of a circle defined by a center point.

RadialGradientBrush is sometimes a bit confusing, involving the interaction of four properties: GradientOrigin, Center, RadiusX, and RadiusY. The last three define an ellipse. Within that ellipse the radial gradient will be applied. The GradientOrigin property is the odd one; it defines where the focus of the gradient should be. We get very odd displays when the origin lies outside the bounds of the ellipse. Figure 5.7 shows the effects of adjusting various properties on RadialGradient. Each example is a rectangle filled with the gradient and stroked with a black brush. The "All" example shows that it is possible for the bounds of the gradient to be outside the bounds of the element.

We have many options for controlling a gradient, but aside from the properties that we've discussed already, the one worth a mention is the SpreadMethod property. SpreadMethod determines what happens when we hit the end of the gradient. The default value, Pad, takes the last gradient stop and paints the rest of the shape with that color. Reflect creates a mirror image of the gradient stops, and Repeat simply repeats the gradient stops. Figure 5.8 (on page 230) shows that we can use SpreadMethod to create complex displays.

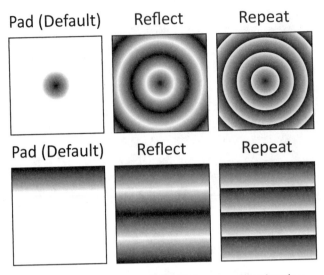

FIGURE 5.8: Effects of SpreadMethod on radial and linear gradient brushes

For all brushes, it is important to understand MappingMode. Using MappingMode, we can either stretch a brush to fill an entire area or keep it at a fixed size. With the Absolute value of MappingMode, the brush will be a fixed size. To stretch the gradient, we use RelativeToBoundingBox; this value means that the bounding box of the fill will define the coordinates. The space is divided by fractions between 0.0 and 1.0. Figure 5.9 shows several MappingMode examples.

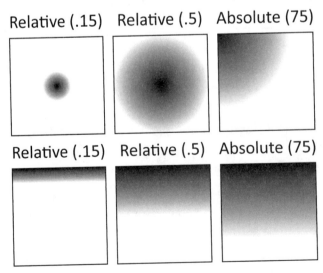

FIGURE 5.9: RelativeToBoundingBox and Absolute mapping modes compared

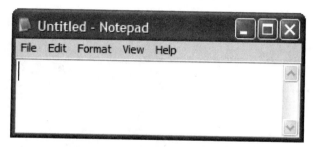

FIGURE 5.10: Close-up of the Windows XP–style border

Gradient brushes have a MappingMode property that controls the overall brush behavior. GradientStop properties are always relative to the area of the gradient fill (similar to RelativeToBoundingBox). To understand why this is important, let's consider creating a Windows XP–style border (Figure 5.10).

The top has a fixed-size gradient and rounded corners. We can use the Border control with LinearGradientBrush to achieve these effects (Figure 5.11):

```
<Border
  CornerRadius='5,5,0,0'
  BorderBrush='#FF0144D0'
  BorderThickness='1'
  >
  <Border.Background>
    <LinearGradientBrush
      MappingMode='Absolute'
      StartPoint='0,0'
      EndPoint='0,24'
      >
      <LinearGradientBrush.GradientStops>
        <GradientStop Offset='0' Color='#FF0058EB' />
        <GradientStop Offset='0.03' Color='#FF3D95FF' />
        <GradientStop Offset='.06' Color='#FF2B90FF' />
        <GradientStop Offset='.4' Color='#FF0055E5' />
        <GradientStop Offset='.6' Color='#FF0055E5' />
        <GradientStop Offset='.9' Color='#FF036EFF' />
        <GradientStop Offset='1' Color='#FF0144D0' />
```

FIGURE 5.11: Using the Absolute mapping mode to create a fixed-size gradient

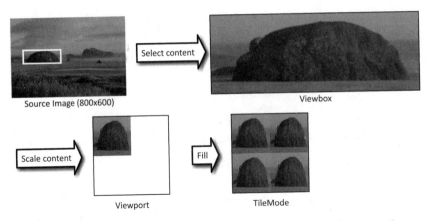

FIGURE 5.12: Using `Viewbox`, `Viewport`, and `TileMode` to create a fill from a portion of an image

```
        </LinearGradientBrush.GradientStops>
      </LinearGradientBrush>
    </Border.Background>
    <Rectangle Fill='White' Margin='2,24,2,2' />
  </Border>
```

Notice that the GradientStop offset is relative to the bounding box of the brush, which was defined using the absolute coordinates of (0,0) to (0,24). This means that the second gradient stop is at 0.03 of the distance from 0 to 24, or about 0.72 pixel from the top.

Tiling Brushes

ImageBrush, DrawingBrush, and VisualBrush are all tiling brushes. They are designed to stretch or repeat a pattern (defined by a raster image, vector drawing, or complete visual tree) in some form to fill an area. Three distinct operations are used with tiling brushes (Figure 5.12): (1) selecting the content to tile (using Viewbox and ViewboxUnits), (2) scaling the content (using Viewport, ViewportUnits, Stretch, AlignmentX, and AlignmentY), and (3) filling the area with the viewport (TileMode).

ImageBrush takes any image as the image source,[9] and DrawingBrush accepts any drawing (we'll cover those next) as the drawing, but probably the most interesting brush is VisualBrush.

---

9. Interestingly, because ImageBrush can take a drawing image as the source, we can use either ImageBrush or DrawingBrush to fill something with a drawing.

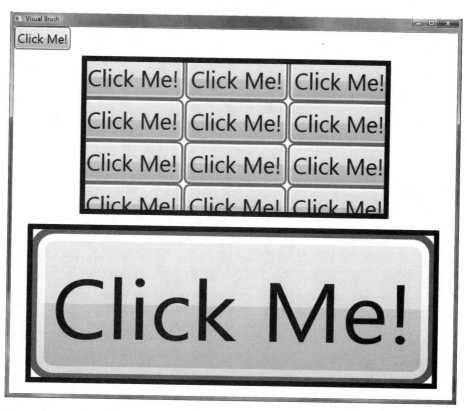

FIGURE 5.13: Using `VisualBrush` to fill several rectangles

`VisualBrush` accepts any control (well, anything deriving from `System.Windows.Media.Visual`) and uses it as the source. Remember that `VisualBrush` uses the display of the controls but doesn't support interactivity. Clicking the rectangle that is filled with an image of a button will not make the button click. This may sound obvious, but when you see the running application (Figure 5.13), it's sometimes hard to remember this!:

```
public class VisualBrushSample : Window {
  public VisualBrushSample() {
    Title = "Visual Brush";

    StackPanel sp = new StackPanel();

    Button theButton = new Button();
    theButton.HorizontalAlignment = HorizontalAlignment.Left;
    theButton.VerticalAlignment = VerticalAlignment.Top;
    theButton.Content = "Click Me!";
    sp.Children.Add(theButton);
```

```
Rectangle rect = new Rectangle();
rect.Margin = new Thickness(5);
rect.Width = 200;
rect.Height = 200;
rect.Stroke = Brushes.Black;
rect.StrokeThickness = 5;
VisualBrush vb = new VisualBrush();
vb.Visual = theButton;
vb.TileMode = TileMode.Tile;
vb.Stretch = Stretch.Uniform;
vb.Viewport = new Rect(0, 0, 50, 20);
vb.ViewportUnits = BrushMappingMode.Absolute;
rect.Fill = vb;
sp.Children.Add(rect);

Rectangle rect2 = new Rectangle();
rect2.Margin = new Thickness(5);
rect2.Width = 500;
rect2.Height = 200;
rect2.Stroke = Brushes.Black;
rect2.StrokeThickness = 5;
VisualBrush vb2 = new VisualBrush();
vb2.Visual = theButton;
rect2.Fill = vb2;
sp.Children.Add(rect2);

Content = sp;
    }
}
```

Notice that we can use the same visual as a source for multiple Visual-Brush objects. In addition, when we run this program we see that moving the mouse over the "real" button highlights all the images of the button correctly. VisualBrush is the most powerful brush, simply because we can use every other feature of WPF to perform the fill.

Pens

Pens are used to "stroke" a geometry—that is, to outline the shape. Pens consist primarily of a brush and a thickness. The brush is used to fill the space defined by the edge of the geometry and the thickness. Because the pen can take any brush, we can combine all the tiling and gradient brushes with the pen to create very complex effects. In addition to the two main properties, we can control how the start and end of a line are drawn, how the joint of a line is drawn, and whether the line contains any dashes.

FIGURE 5.14: Shapes drawn with a pen. Each shape is drawn with three different thicknesses of pens.

In most cases the properties of pens are exposed as properties on the containing element. For example, to adjust how the pen draws a border, we use properties like `BorderBrush` and `BorderThickness`; and for filling in rectangle we use `Stroke`, `StrokeThickness`, `StrokeDashArray`, and other properties.

Points in a geometry are infinitely small; it is only the thickness of the pen that takes up space. The pen thickness is always split half inside and half outside the mathematical line between two geometric points (Figure 5.14).

Notice in Figure 5.14 that, as the pen thickness increases, the acute corners of the triangle at the top begin to project quite far from the original line. To customize this behavior we can adjust `LineJoin` for the pen. The various joins are pretty self-explanatory (Figure 5.15); however, `Miter` has an interesting feature: When we use the miter join, another property, `MiterLimit`, determines when the stroke will be mitered, allowing crisp corners on regular shapes (like the square) and a miter only on out-of-bounds geometries (like acute angles).

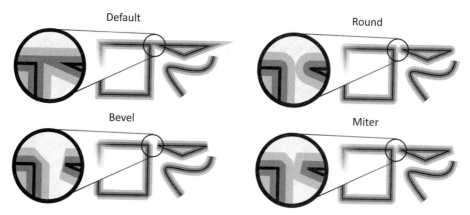

FIGURE 5.15: Shapes with different line joins applied

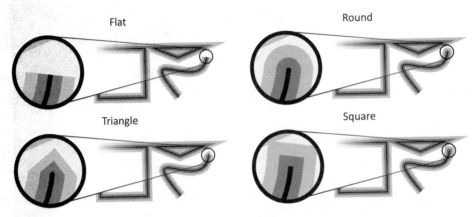

FIGURE 5.16: Shapes with different line caps applied

Although LineJoin controls the shape of the stroke at the connection between two lines (as for the triangle and square), we may also want to customize the look of the start and end points of lines—that is, the line caps (as for the Bezier curve at the bottom right in Figure 5.14). Start-LineCap and EndLineCap let us control what the line caps look like (Figure 5.16).

One more thing that pens can do to customize a shape is apply a dash pattern. Using the DashStyle property on a pen, we can specify the on/off pattern for dashes. We can also use the same line cap model for adjusting the ends of the dashes. Note that the values of this property are relative to the stroke thickness: the thicker the stroke, the farther apart the dashes become (Figure 5.17).[10]

Before we close our discussion of pens, here's one last reminder: Pens are built on top of the brush model that we've already learned about. We can use any brush to stroke in a shape. We can apply a gradient, tiling, or even a visual brush and end up with a stroke that is playing a video!

---

10. Flat and square dash caps look remarkably similar. Comparing the flat and square line caps in Figure 5.16 shows that, as the pen thickness increases, the cap becomes large (effectively making square line caps extend past the last point of the line). The same phenomenon occurs with dash caps: Square dash caps make the dash slightly longer than the flat version. In practice, it is remarkably difficult to tell the difference between the two.

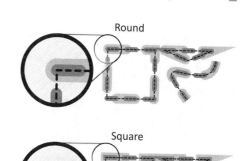

Flat   Round

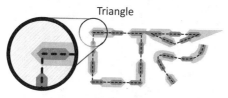

Triangle   Square

FIGURE 5.17: Shapes with different dash caps applied. All the various thicknesses are using the same dash style.

Drawings

With geometries, brushes, and pens safely behind us, we can now move on to how these three concepts can be used to create displays. At the lowest level of the system are drawings. Drawings are the API for directly talking to the low-level composition engine. They are very lightweight wrappers on the drawing instructions that drive the engine. As such, they lack certain features (like input, focus, event routing, layout, etc.), but they have other properties (like sharing) that make them very powerful. Conceptually, all other display features become a series of drawing objects.

Because drawings are designed to be fairly low-level, they lack certain conveniences of shapes. Drawings directly expose the geometry-brush-pen triad that makes up a display. There is no rectangle drawing; rather, we create a drawing and give it a rectangle geometry.

All the concepts that we've discussed so far revolve around the notion of a tree hierarchy. For example, each control can appear in one place in the visual tree, and can have one parent and zero or more children. The drawing introduces a different structure; it is represented in a graph structure. This graph structure allows a single drawing to appear in multiple places in the graph, providing a significant performance benefit.

To demonstrate this sharing model (Figure 5.18 on page 238), we'll define a single geometry and share it using toShare; then we'll define two DrawingGroup objects that both have toShare as a child. The Ellipse-Geometry object (and resulting GeometryDrawing) is defined only once.

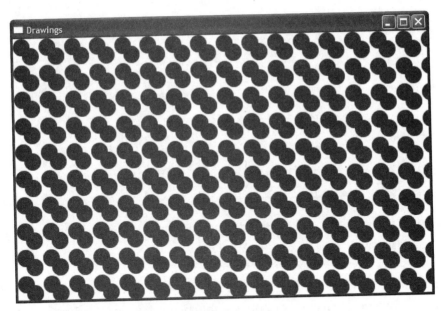

FIGURE 5.18: Using DrawingBrush in combination with GeometryDrawing

It can then be shared in two different contexts, where each DrawingGroup
instance uses the drawing and sets TranslateTransform on it:

```xml
<!-- Drawings.xaml -->
<Window x:Class='EssentialWPF.Drawings'
  xmlns='http://schemas.microsoft.com/winfx/2006/xaml/presentation'
  xmlns:x='http://schemas.microsoft.com/winfx/2006/xaml'
  Title='Drawings'
  >
  <Rectangle Name='_rect' />
</Window>
```

```csharp
// Drawings.xaml.cs
public Drawings() {
  InitializeComponent();

  GeometryDrawing toShare = new GeometryDrawing(Brushes.Red,
    null,
    new EllipseGeometry(new Rect(2, 2, 15, 15)));

  DrawingGroup main = new DrawingGroup();

  DrawingGroup a = new DrawingGroup();
  a.Children.Add(toShare);
  a.Transform = new TranslateTransform(8, 8);

  DrawingGroup b = new DrawingGroup();
  b.Children.Add(toShare);
  b.Transform = new TranslateTransform(0, 0);
```

```
main.Children.Add(b);
main.Children.Add(a);

DrawingBrush brush = new DrawingBrush();
brush.Drawing = main;
brush.Viewport = new Rect(0, 0, 20, 20);
brush.ViewportUnits = BrushMappingMode.Absolute;
brush.TileMode = TileMode.Tile;

_rect.Fill = brush;
}
```

Figure 5.19 shows the graph that is created for this display. The toShare drawing is created only once, enabling very efficient rendering of complex objects. The sharing here is much deeper than just the managed object model exposure; because drawings are a thin wrapper on the composition engine, this sharing is occurring inside of the engine.

WPF has five drawing types: DrawingGroup, GeometryDrawing, GlyphRunDrawing, ImageDrawing, and VideoDrawing. GlyphRunDrawing is a special drawing designed to render text (we'll talk more about text later); ImageDrawing and VideoDrawing are self-explanatory.

Shapes

Shapes bring drawings into the control world. In addition to adding the control features (layout, input, focus, event routing, etc.), shapes provide some easy additional methods for creating common constructs. Ellipse, Line, Path, and Rectangle have one-to-one mappings with their geometry-based brethren. Polygon and Polyline are simple wrappers over constructing a specific path.

Shapes introduce an interesting problem. Drawings have their own coordinate system. Using offsets and transforms, we can render any drawings at

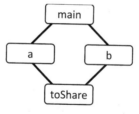

FIGURE 5.19: The drawing graph created to draw the display in Figure 5.18

FIGURE 5.20: Using DrawingBrush to fill a shape with a border

various positions. In the land of controls, however, layout determines position and size. The first way of handling placement is to use Drawing-Brush—effectively applying a geometric transform to the drawing to make it fit in the control. What this means is that strokes are scaled. To see an example, let's try to create a border for a rectangle using an instance of DrawingBrush with a stroked geometry:

```
<Rectangle>
  <Rectangle.Fill>
    <DrawingBrush>
      <DrawingBrush.Drawing>
        <GeometryDrawing Brush='sc# 1,.8,.8,.8'>
          <GeometryDrawing.Pen>
            <Pen Brush='Black' Thickness='1' />
          </GeometryDrawing.Pen>
          <GeometryDrawing.Geometry>
            <RectangleGeometry Rect='0,0,10,10' />
          </GeometryDrawing.Geometry>
        </GeometryDrawing>
      </DrawingBrush.Drawing>
    </DrawingBrush>
  </Rectangle.Fill>
</Rectangle>
```

Figure 5.20 shows that, even though the pen is declared to be 1 pixel wide, it is rendered at one-tenth the size of the rectangle, because the brush is geometrically scaled to fit the fill area:

```
<Rectangle
  Stroke='Black' StrokeThickness='1' Fill='sc# 1,.8,.8,.8'>
</Rectangle>
```

FIGURE 5.21: Using `Rectangle`'s built-in stroke support

Controls typically don't scale by default, so shapes are designed to stretch the associated geometry instead of simply scaling. This stretching allows for nongeometric transformation (for the geeks in the audience):

In Figure 5.21 the stroke is 1 pixel wide regardless of how the rectangle is sized. The difference between these two models is much more exaggerated when we're dealing with paths. In this case the `Stretch` property controls how a path is stretched, and then the shape is sized. The only shape that doesn't support `Stretch` is `Ellipse`, because its sizing behavior is fixed.

Images

In an application of some significance, we will probably want to include images. Before continuing, however, we should define *image.* Images are commonly viewed as either vector or raster (bitmap) data used for rendering. We've already talked a lot about vector data; drawings, shapes, brushes, pens—all of these define vector data.

In WPF-speak, **image** is concretely defined as anything deriving from `ImageSource`; the main distinguishing characteristic is that images have a natural size associated with them, and optionally some metadata. Almost all of WPF's imaging system focuses on raster image formats; this first release of WPF has no formal notion of a vector image file format. However, the `DrawingImage` type offers the ability to use any drawing as an image within an application, which is the very beginning of a full-featured vector-imaging model. For now, let's focus on the raster side of the imaging world.

Basic Imaging

Before delving too deeply into imaging, let's focus on the two simplest and most common ways of accessing raster images. The `Image` class represents a shape that hosts an `ImageSource` object, and `BitmapImage` is the most common type of `ImageSource` for accessing raster images:

```
<!-- markup showing an image -->
<Image Source='some-image.jpg' />

// C# showing an image
Image img = new Image();
img.Source = new BitmapImage(new Uri("some-image.jpg"));
```

The `Image` class is really a viewer for an `ImageSource` object; the meat of the imaging system is hiding in the various `ImageSource` types. All images have a natural size associated with them; for raster images, this is typically the number of pixels in each dimension, divided by the native dpi (dots per inch) in which the image was encoded. When the `Image` control views an image, it must somehow size that image to fit, which is where `Stretch` comes in.

`Stretch` for vector shapes (which we talked about in the previous section) controls how the shape scales the vectors inside of it; the same is true for `Image` with its image content. `Stretch` has two key aspects: direction (do we want to make the image larger or smaller, or allow both?), and type. Typically we can ignore the direction, but the type is interesting. `Stretch` allows for four types (Figure 5.22):

1. `None`. The image is sized to its natural size, and as much as possible is displayed.
2. `Fill`. The image is scaled to fit the entire space.
3. `Uniform`. The image is made to fit in one direction or the other, while maintaining the original aspect ratio.
4. `UniformToFill`. The image is made to fit the entire space, while maintaining the original aspect ratio.

The ImageSource Pipeline

The `Image` control is about adjusting the display of an image; using `Stretch`, `RenderTransform`, `LayoutTransform`, `BitmapEffect` (we'll talk

Source Image

None

Fill

Uniform

UniformToFill

FIGURE 5.22: The `Image` control stretching a raster image. The control is the same size for each example.

about this shortly), and other properties, we can adjust the pixels that are lighted on the screen. But what if we want to control the source of the image?

Suppose we have a very large image (like a 12-megapixel image from a digital camera) and we want to display a small picture of it. If we simply use the `Image` element and point it at the file on disk, the entire image will be loaded into memory and then scaled down for display on the screen. That's not very efficient.[11]

---

11. To be clear, the inefficiency isn't really the poor `Image` control's fault. Because the image may be resized at runtime by the layout, we can't determine the right size for decoding the image. One option would have been to reload the image whenever the display size grew, but that would have introduced lags and jumps as the control was resized. Instead we opted to add `DecodePixelWidth` and `DecodePixelHeight` to `BitmapImage` so that application developers could easily optimize efficiency.

Using several ImageSource objects, we can build a pipeline of commands to be executed on an image as it is decoded. For some formats this approach can do a lot to optimize efficiency (e.g., by reading a different resolution from the file); in other cases we can explicitly inject caching into the pipeline to improve efficiency.

All raster images in WPF are modeled to have one or more frames.[12] Formats like TIFF and GIF natively support multiple frames in a single file, but formats like PNG or BMP will always have only a single frame. To load an image, we can use the Create static function on BitmapFrame:

```
BitmapFrame frame = BitmapFrame.Create(new Uri("test-image.png"));
```

Now suppose we want to crop the bitmap to show only a portion of the picture. We can use the CroppedBitmap class[13] and chain it together with the frame by setting the Source property:[14]

```
CroppedBitmap crop = new CroppedBitmap();
crop.BeginInit();
crop.Source = frame;
crop.SourceRect = new Int32Rect(100, 150, 400, 250);
crop.EndInit();
```

Finally, if we want to convert the image to be just black and white (two colors, not grayscale), we can use the FormatConvertedBitmap class and again set the Source property:

```
FormatConvertedBitmap color = new FormatConvertedBitmap();
color.BeginInit();
color.Source = crop;
color.DestinationFormat = PixelFormats.BlackWhite;
color.EndInit();
```

The final step is to display the image. Because each of the items in this pipeline (BitmapFrame, CroppedBitmap, and FormatConvertedBitmap) derives

---

12. Don't confuse these with frames from HTML, video, or anything else. Each frame in the raster image model is simply a single image. Actually, it would make some sense to confuse this with a video frame because logically video is just a lot of raster image frames.

13. The size passed into SourceRect depends on the image we provide. In this case, the original was an 800×533 pixel image.

14. BeginInit and EndInit are part of the ISupportInitialize interface defined in .NET 1.0. Normally these methods are optional to call, but with WPF imaging they are required.

FIGURE 5.23: Output of an image that has passed through the pipeline

from ImageSource, we can use any of them in an Image control. Here we'll point to the final output (Figure 5.23):

```
Image img =new Image();
img.Source = color;

Window w = new Window();
w.Content = img;
w.Title = "Image Pipeline";
w.Show();
```

Usually we can forgo using the entire pipeline and instead just use BitmapImage, which is an ImageSource class that encapsulates the most common functionality for adjusting images (decode size, rotation, etc.).

Image Metadata

Most image formats today support the association of metadata with the data. The most common case is the inclusion of all sorts of information about photographs taken with a digital camera (Figure 5.24).

Every ImageSource object has a Metadata property that lets us gain access to this information. For all raster images, the Metadata object will return a BitmapMetadata object. This metadata has two views: a simplified view of well-known properties (exposed as direct properties on Bitmap-Metadata, like CameraModel), and a query API (GetQuery) for accessing any piece of information from the metadata store.

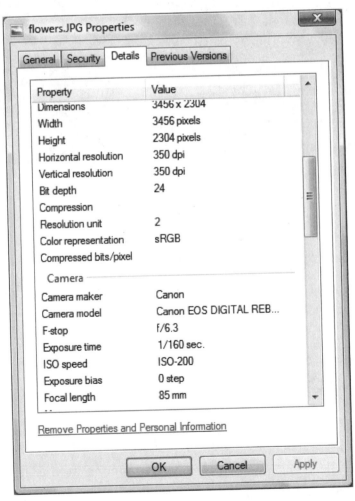

FIGURE 5.24: Windows Vista properties dialog showing metadata about a picture

From a `BitmapFrame` object (in current builds, `BitmapImage` will not return metadata), we can inspect the metadata fairly simply. By enumerating over the metadata, we can get the list of metadata items that the object supports (for some odd reason the API designer in this case decided to make the metadata a collection instead of exposing a property):

```
DumpMetadata(frame.Metadata);

void DumpMetadata(object v) {
  BitmapMetadata md = v as BitmapMetadata;
  if (md != null) {
    foreach (string name in md) {
      Debug.WriteLine(name);
      Debug.IndentLevel++;
      DumpMetadata(md.GetQuery(name));
      Debug.IndentLevel--;
    }
  }
  else {
    Debug.WriteLine("value: " + v.ToString());
  }
}
```

Running this program produces output like this:

```
/app1
    /{uint=0}
        /{uint=271}
            value: Canon
        /{uint=272}
            value: Canon EOS D30
        /{uint=274}
            value: 1
        ...
    /{uint=1}
        /{}
            value: System.Windows.Media.Imaging.BitmapMetadataBlob
        /{uint=259}
            value: 6
        ...
```

Of course, depending on the image, the output may contain more or fewer sections. The cryptic names representing the manufacturer of the camera (`/app1/{uint=0}/{uint=271}`) make it obvious why the simpler API on `BitmapMetdata`—`CameraManufacturer`—is much preferred.

FIGURE 5.25: Rendering a visual into an image, and displaying it (on the right)

In addition, because different formats encode this information differently, BitmapMetadata provides a common abstraction that will work regardless of the format.

Creating Images

Although most images are created by either a camera or a graphic design program, often we want to create images dynamically. Dynamic image creation is useful for two main reasons: (1) to optimize performance (generating a complex image once with vectors and effects, then just showing the bitmap) or (2) to publish an image (e.g., all the images in this book were generated by creating images from WPF applications).

To generate a raster image, we can use either RenderTargetBitmap or WritableBitmap. RenderTargetBitmap allows us to render any visible display to a fixed-size raster image. Once we've created the raster data, we can either save the image using the various image encoders or display it (RenderTargetBitmap also derives from ImageSource). WritableBitmap, on the other hand, allows direct editing of the pixels in a bitmap.

Here we can define a set of elements: a rich text box and button on the left, with an image on the right. When we click the button, we're going to render the rich text box to an image and display it. It is interesting to compare this to the exercise we did earlier with VisualBrush. Although Visual-Brush is a live copy of part of the UI, here we create a static snapshot of the display in a pixel format (Figure 5.25):

```xml
<!-- CreateImages.xaml -->
<Window x:Class='EssentialWPF.CreateImages'
  xmlns='http://schemas.microsoft.com/winfx/2006/xaml/presentation'
  xmlns:x='http://schemas.microsoft.com/winfx/2006/xaml'
  Title='Create Images'
  >
  <Grid>
    <Grid.ColumnDefinitions>
      <ColumnDefinition Width='*' />
      <ColumnDefinition Width='*' />
    </Grid.ColumnDefinitions>
    <DockPanel>
      <Button DockPanel.Dock='Bottom' Click='Copy'>Copy</Button>
      <RichTextBox FontSize='24pt' Name='_textBox' />
    </DockPanel>
    <Image Grid.Column='1' Name='_display' />
  </Grid>
</Window>
```

```csharp
// CreateImages.xaml.cs
void Copy(object sender, RoutedEventArgs e) {
  RenderTargetBitmap bmp =
    new RenderTargetBitmap(
      (int)_textBox.ActualWidth,   // size
      (int)_textBox.ActualHeight,
      96, 96,                      // DPI
      PixelFormats.Pbgra32);       // 32 bits, Alpha+RGB

  // Render _textBox to this image.
  bmp.Render(_textBox);

  _display.Source = bmp;
}
```

If we wanted to then extract the image and save it, we could use an encoder. Here we'll encode the bitmap as a JPEG. Notice that we must add images as frames:

```csharp
void Copy(object sender, RoutedEventArgs e) {
  RenderTargetBitmap bmp =
    new RenderTargetBitmap(
      (int)_textBox.ActualWidth,   // size
      (int)_textBox.ActualHeight,
      96, 96,              // DPI
      PixelFormats.Pbgra32);      // 32 bits, Alpha+RGB

  // Render _textBox to this image.
bmp.Render(_textBox);

  _display.Source = bmp;
```

```
JpegBitmapEncoder encoder = new JpegBitmapEncoder();
encoder.Frames.Add(BitmapFrame.Create(bmp));
using (FileStream o = File.Open(@"c:\out.jpg", FileMode.Create)) {
  encoder.Save(o);
}
}
```

Opacity

Opacity, or transparency, can be accomplished in a variety of ways; certain bitmap formats (like PNG) support an alpha channel in the image, all colors in WPF have an alpha value, and every visual has `Opacity` and `OpacityMask` properties. These four mechanisms can even be combined to create an amazing array of options for creating transparency effects.

Before we continue, here's a word of warning: Anytime we add another layer of transparency, a lot of work must be done somewhere in the system. It's better if the work happens in the video hardware, but there's still a cost. When a complex opacity effect forces the composition to happen in software, a large performance bottleneck will result. Because opacity composition requires reading of the previously rendered display, large portions of an application may be forced into software rendering. That's not fatal, but it's worth noting that transparency effects should be used judiciously, and always remember to profile the performance impact.

All the examples in this section will have a background on the parent element of a grid so that opacity is easy to see. By using the alpha channel of color, we can create brushes that let us see through to the background. All colors in WPF support an alpha value; the standard hex notation for RGB uses the first two characters to denote the alpha value. Here we can fill a rectangle with translucent white (Figure 5.26); because the first two characters are *AA*, the color will have an alpha value of 170 (out of 255), or 66 percent opaque:

```
<Rectangle Width='100' Height='100'
  Fill='#AAFFFFFF' />
```

FIGURE 5.26: Rectangle filled with translucent white, on a checkered background

FIGURE 5.27: Rectangle filled with a gradient, with each stop having an alpha value

Recall from our discussion of color that any color reference in WPF can have an alpha channel, so we can also use the alpha channel when defining any gradient brush (Figure 5.27):

```
<Rectangle Width='100' Height='100'>
  <Rectangle.Fill>
    <LinearGradientBrush EndPoint='0,1'>
      <LinearGradientBrush.GradientStops>
        <GradientStop Offset='0' Color='#FFFF0000' />
        <GradientStop Offset='.33' Color='#9900FF00' />
        <GradientStop Offset='.66' Color='#FF0000FF' />
        <GradientStop Offset='.9' Color='#00FFFFFF' />
      </LinearGradientBrush.GradientStops>
    </LinearGradientBrush>
  </Rectangle.Fill>
</Rectangle>
```

By far the most powerful opacity feature is `OpacityMask`. The opacity mask applies transparency to a tree of visuals. We can use any brush with an alpha channel as the alpha value for a set of visuals. It's easiest to start by looking at an example, so let's use a `RadialGradientBrush` object as our opacity mask. Figure 5.28 shows that a consistent opacity is applied

FIGURE 5.28: Several shapes with an opacity mask applied to their container

to all the content of the Canvas, including the Rectangle objects and the
button:

```
<Canvas Width='100' Height='100' Background='Orange'>
  <Canvas.OpacityMask>
    <RadialGradientBrush GradientOrigin='.5,.3'>
      <RadialGradientBrush.GradientStops>
        <GradientStop Offset='0' Color='#FF000000' />
        <GradientStop Offset='.33' Color='#00000000' />
        <GradientStop Offset='.66' Color='#FF000000' />
        <GradientStop Offset='1' Color='#22000000' />
      </RadialGradientBrush.GradientStops>
    </RadialGradientBrush >
  </Canvas.OpacityMask>
  <Rectangle Canvas.Top='0' Canvas.Left='0' Width='50' Height='50'
    Fill='Red' />
  <Rectangle Canvas.Top='50' Canvas.Left='50' Width='50' Height='50'
    Fill='Blue' />
  <Button Canvas.Top='35' Canvas.Left='15'>Hello World</Button>
</Canvas>
```

The alpha channel of the brush is used to define the alpha value for each
pixel of the display of the visual and its children. Within the visual we can use
any feature (including alpha-valued colors, nesting opacity masks, etc.) to create the display. The opacity mask doesn't affect the interactivity or animation of
any elements within. We can use any brush with an alpha channel as the opacity mask. In addition to the gradients, ImageBrush, DrawingBrush, and Visual-
Brush can also produce very interesting results. Here we try ImageBrush:

```
<Canvas Width='100' Height='100' Background='Orange'>
  <Canvas.OpacityMask>
    <ImageBrush ImageSource='c:\mask.png' />
  </Canvas.OpacityMask>
  <Rectangle Canvas.Top='0' Canvas.Left='0' Width='50' Height='50'
    Fill='Red' />
  <Rectangle Canvas.Top='50' Canvas.Left='50' Width='50' Height='50'
    Fill='Blue' />
  <Button Canvas.Top='35' Canvas.Left='15'>Hello World</Button>
</Canvas>
```

FIGURE 5.29: Several shapes with an image-based opacity mask

FIGURE 5.30: The image used for the opacity mask in Figure 5.29

Figure 5.29 shows how this markup can create interesting "punch out" effects. Remember, with this technique the image must contain an alpha channel, and not just black and white pixels. The mask used here is shown in Figure 5.30.

BitmapEffects

OpacityMask is the first example of a feature that modifies the pixels being produced by the composition engine. The ability to perform pixel-by-pixel operations on the output of visuals is usually supported by the BitmapEffect property on UIElement. These are called **bitmap effects** because they perform an operation on the bitmap (the actual pixels) produced from the composition engine. Some effects may actually run in graphics hardware using the pixel shader support in modern video cards.[15] At this point all BitmapEffect elements force all the content that they affect to render in software, which can cause a significant performance hit, so they should be used judiciously.

---

15. We can build new bitmap effects in managed or unmanaged code; at this time, however, we cannot create new effects that run directly on the graphics hardware (maybe in a future version of WPF).

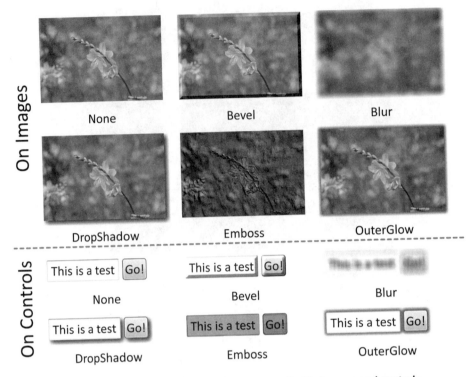

FIGURE 5.31: Selection of `BitmapEffect` elements applied to images and controls

Although all effects can be applied to any element, some (e.g., `DropShadowBitmapEffect`) are well suited to vector content and others (e.g., `EmbossBitmapEffect`) are designed to deal with images. To illustrate vector graphics, Figure 5.31 shows how a few sample effects look when applied to images and controls.

3D Graphics

Let me start this section with a confession: I'm not a 3D programmer. I think 3D is cool, and I've made many failed attempts to play with it, but it always eludes me. However, I don't think a deep understanding of 3D is necessary to use it in software development. With WPF we have taken the approach that 3D should be consistent with 2D. We have tried to limit the number of new concepts and make it simple to integrate the two worlds.

In WPF, 3D is designed to be a form of vector graphics. No physics model, collision detection, or other higher-level services are required for writing a game or fully immersive 3D environment. WPF's 3D is really a stepping-stone to where we want to go in the future. With the building blocks present in WPF today, we can create compelling displays, but it takes a lot of work and understanding of 3D.

In 2D, the split is clear between drawings (as low-level composition objects) and controls, which are a higher-level application programmer concept. For 3D, the current release of WPF has gone partway toward this distinction: Visual3D is the 3D equivalent of Visual, and Model3D is the equivalent of Drawing. 3D lacks a control framework; a known set of shapes, input, and templates; or any of the other more advanced services in WPF; but the beginnings are there.

Hello World, 3D Style

Doing anything in 3D requires an understanding of four basic concepts: models, materials, lights, and cameras.

Models and **materials** have simple corollaries in the 2D world: drawings and brushes. The basic model in 3D is GeometryModel3D, which represents a 3D version of a geometry; it is exactly like GeometryDrawing in 2D. Defining a geometry in 3D space is more complex than defining a 2D geometry; we'll start by building the simplest 3D geometry, a triangle:

```
MeshGeometry3D CreateTriangle() {
    MeshGeometry3D mesh = new MeshGeometry3D();
    mesh.Positions.Add(new Point3D(0, 0, 0));
    mesh.Positions.Add(new Point3D(1, 0, 0));
    mesh.Positions.Add(new Point3D(0, 1, 0));
    mesh.TriangleIndices.Add(0);
    mesh.TriangleIndices.Add(1);
    mesh.TriangleIndices.Add(2);
    return mesh;
}
```

Here we define the three points of the triangle using the Positions property; then, using the TriangleIndices property, we tell the geometry the order of the points to define the triangle. With this geometry we create the model:

```
GeometryModel3D model = new GeometryModel3D();
model.Geometry = CreateTriangle();
```

The 3D equivalent of a brush is `Material`. Materials take a brush to define the color fill, and they may have other properties to control how they reflect light:

```
model.Material = new DiffuseMaterial(Brushes.Red);
```

Now that we have a model with a geometry and material, we can light the scene. Probably the most common error in 3D is not lighting the scene correctly. If the lights are behind the 3D object, too far away, or not powerful enough, only the black outline of a shape will appear. Just as in the real world, there are lots of different types of lights. The simplest is the **point light,** which can be thought of as an exposed lightbulb, projecting light in all directions:

```
PointLight light = new PointLight();
light.Position = new Point3D(12, 12, 12);
light.Color = Colors.White;
light.Range = 150;
light.ConstantAttenuation = 1.0;
```

`Range` defines the "power" of the light (lumens, for the light-oriented geeks out there), `Position` and `Color` are self-explanatory, and `Constant-Attenuation` is one of the properties that control how fast the light "falls off" (we'll dig into this concept deeper later).

At this point we have a model, material, and light. The final step is to create a camera. The **camera** works just like the name implies; it is the device that captures the display and projects it into 2D. By combining a `Camera` object with `Viewport3D`, we can finally see the scene. First we'll set up the camera:

```
PerspectiveCamera viewer = new PerspectiveCamera();
viewer.LookDirection = new Vector3D(0, 0, -1);
viewer.Position = new Point3D(0, 0, 12);
viewer.FieldOfView = 45;
viewer.UpDirection = new Vector3D(0, 1, 0);
```

`FieldOfView` is effectively the "zoom" on the camera, `UpDirection` defines the rotation of the camera (which determines what direction appears as "up" in the display), and `LookDirection` defines the direction

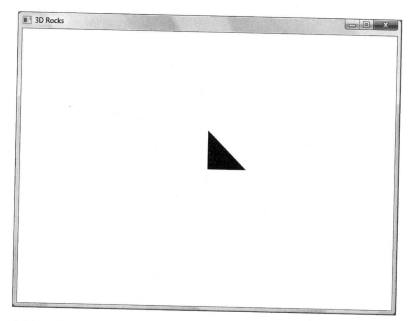

FIGURE 5.32: A simple 3D shape (triangle) being viewed

the camera is looking. Finally, we can wire all this together with the viewport and display it (Figure 5.32):

```
using System;
using System.Windows;
using System.Windows.Controls;
using System.Windows.Data;
using System.Windows.Documents;
using System.Windows.Media;
using System.Windows.Media.Media3D;
using System.Windows.Shapes;

namespace EssentialWPF {
  public class Window3D : Window {
    public Window3D() {
      Title = "3D Rocks";
      Viewport3D viewport = new Viewport3D();

      Model3DGroup group = new Model3DGroup();
      GeometryModel3D model = new GeometryModel3D();
      model.Geometry = CreateTriangle();
      model.Material = new DiffuseMaterial(Brushes.Red);
      group.Children.Add(model);

      PerspectiveCamera viewer = new PerspectiveCamera();
      viewer.LookDirection = new Vector3D(0, 0, -1);
      viewer.Position = new Point3D(0, 0, 12);
```

```
        viewer.FieldOfView = 45;
        viewer.UpDirection = new Vector3D(0, 1, 0);
        viewport.Camera = viewer;

        PointLight light = new PointLight();
        light.Position = new Point3D(12, 12, 12);
        light.Color = Colors.White;
        light.Range = 150;
        light.ConstantAttenuation = 1.0;
        group.Children.Add(light);

        ModelVisual3D scene = new ModelVisual3D();
        scene.Content = group;
        viewport.Children.Add(scene);
        Content = viewport;
    }

    MeshGeometry3D CreateTriangle() {
        MeshGeometry3D mesh = new MeshGeometry3D();
        mesh.Positions.Add(new Point3D(0, 0, 0));
        mesh.Positions.Add(new Point3D(1, 0, 0));
        mesh.Positions.Add(new Point3D(0, 1, 0));
        mesh.TriangleIndices.Add(0);
        mesh.TriangleIndices.Add(1);
        mesh.TriangleIndices.Add(2);
        return mesh;
    }
  }
}
```

Wow, that's a lot of work for just a simple triangle. Before we try to create more interesting shapes, let's review the principles of 3D.

Principles of 3D

Because WPF's support for 3D is limited in the current version, it's best to look at the building blocks that are applied and think about what could be built on top. As mentioned earlier, there are four critical concepts in 3D: models, materials, cameras, and lights.

Models

All 3D objects eventually are decomposed to a set of triangles. The only geometric concept in WPF is the triangle. Note that all of WPF's display is implemented through the 3D pipeline. All text, shapes, controls, drawings—everything—are rendered as 3D triangles. For all the 2D constructs, the decomposition (*tessellation* in 3D parlance) is done behind the scenes.

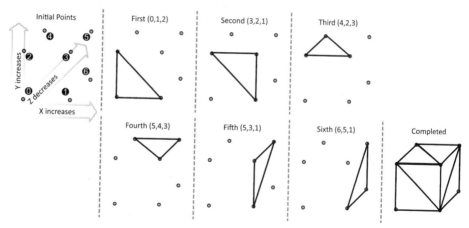

FIGURE 5.33: Partial construction of a 3D cube

For 3D, the author of the model is responsible for creating the triangles. The set of triangles that make up a 3D model is called a **mesh.**

Technically, lights are also models (and in some systems, so are cameras). For this discussion, however, we'll stick with `GeometryModel3D` and `MeshGeometry3D`, which always go hand in hand for creating a model.

To define an instance of `MeshGeometry3D`, we need positions that define a series of points in 3D space. We can then define triangles by picking three points from the position list. We map points to the material by setting the texture coordinates. To understand how these three things are related, let's create a more complex 3D object: most of a cube (we'll walk through the three visible faces; the other three I'll leave as an exercise for the reader).

The `Positions` property defines a series of points.[16] Cubes have eight points, but because we're dealing with only three faces, we need only seven points (Figure 5.33):

```
<MeshGeometry3D>
  <MeshGeometry3D.Positions>
    <Point3D>0,0,0</Point3D>
    <Point3D>1,0,0</Point3D>
    <Point3D>0,1,0</Point3D>
    <Point3D>1,1,0</Point3D>
    <Point3D>0,1,-1</Point3D>
```

---

16. Remember that the camera orientation drastically affects the display. In this case, we are assuming that a positive y value indicates "up." Figure 5.33 shows that z values indicate a direction away from the camera.

```
    <Point3D>1,1,-1</Point3D>
    <Point3D>1,0,-1</Point3D>
  </MeshGeometry3D.Positions>
</MeshGeometry3D>
```

These points don't define any triangles until we tell the mesh the order in which to walk the points (you can follow along in Figure 5.33). Using `TriangleIndices`, we associate three indices to create a triangle. Because we want to create three faces, we need at least six triangles. First we create the lower left of the front face:[17]

```
<MeshGeometry3D>
  <MeshGeometry3D.TriangleIndices>
    <sys:Int32>0</sys:Int32>
    <sys:Int32>1</sys:Int32>
    <sys:Int32>2</sys:Int32>
  </MeshGeometry3D.TriangleIndices>
</MeshGeometry3D>
```

Then we create the upper right (second):

```
<MeshGeometry3D>
  <MeshGeometry3D.TriangleIndices>
    <sys:Int32>3</sys:Int32>
    <sys:Int32>2</sys:Int32>
    <sys:Int32>1</sys:Int32>
  </MeshGeometry3D.TriangleIndices>
</MeshGeometry3D>
```

We repeat this process for each of the remaining four triangles.

The final important piece of information is how the positions map to the material (sometimes called the **texture**). Using the `TextureCoordinate` property, we specify how the bounding-box relative coordinates of the

---

17. WPF uses the right-hand rule for determining the face of a triangle. To understand this rule, curve your right hand around with your thumb pointing up. When you specify the coordinates along the direction of your fingers, the normal of the surface is in the direction of your thumb. Another way to think about this is that, when you're facing a surface, the triangle vertices must be ordered counterclockwise.

FIGURE 5.34: First attempt at using a texture, without texture coordinates

material map to a point. For each position we want to associate a 2D point ranging from (0, 0) to (1, 1) with a point on the material.

Remember that when we define a brush (like `LinearGradientBrush`), we can specify the starting and ending points using bounding-box relative coordinates, which is the same coordinate system that we use for defining the `GradientStop.Offset` properties. Because the material must span multiple triangles and often needs to be rendered multiple times (as with a cube, which has six faces), we need to tell the system how to map the material on each triangle. Because `TriangleIndices` already maps positions to triangles, all we have to do is define the material mapping per position.

By default, the `TextureCoordinate` value for each position is (0, 0). So if we apply `LinearGradientBrush`, only the color at the zero offset is used (Figure 5.34). But if we use the same gradient as the fill for a rectangle, we get a much different result (Figure 5.35):

```
<DiffuseMaterial>
  <DiffuseMaterial.Brush>
    <LinearGradientBrush EndPoint='1,0'>
      <LinearGradientBrush.GradientStops>
        <GradientStop Offset='0' Color='White' />
        <GradientStop Offset='1' Color='Black' />
      </LinearGradientBrush.GradientStops>
    </LinearGradientBrush>
  </DiffuseMaterial.Brush>
</DiffuseMaterial>
```

FIGURE 5.35: The same rectangle, with a texture gradient applied to it

By setting `TextureCoordinates` correctly for the mesh, we can get the same result (bars, lighting, etc.) with a rectangle made up of two triangles:

```
<MeshGeometry3D>
  <MeshGeometry3D.TextureCoordinates>
    <Point2D>0,0</Point2D>
    <Point2D>1,0</Point2D>
    <Point2D>0,1</Point2D>
    <Point2D>1,1</Point2D>
  </MeshGeometry3D.TextureCoordinates>
</MeshGeometry3D>
```

For our three-faced cube, we must determine how the gradient will wrap. We can make the gradient flow from left to right over the cube, leaving the end to be the solid final color. Because the typical model is fairly large, there's also a compact form for noting the various properties. The following compact notation produces the same mesh as the previous examples:

```
<MeshGeometry3D
  TextureCoordinates='0,0 1,0 0,1 1,1 0,0 1,1 1,1 1,1'
  Positions='0,0,0 1,0,0 0,1,0 1,1,0 0,1,-1 1,1,-1 1,0,-1'
  TriangleIndices='0,1,2 3,2,1 4,2,3 5,4,3 5,3,1 6,5,1' />
```

Putting all this together, we can create a markup solution for displaying our first 3D shape (Figure 5.36):

```
<Viewport3D Width='200' Height='200'>
  <Viewport3D.Camera>
    <PerspectiveCamera
      LookDirection='-.7,-.8,-1'
      Position='3.8,4,4'
      FieldOfView='17'
      UpDirection='0,1,0' />
```

```
      </Viewport3D.Camera>
      <ModelVisual3D>
        <ModelVisual3D.Content>
          <Model3DGroup>
            <PointLight
              Position='3.8,4,4'
              Color='White'
              Range='7'
              ConstantAttenuation='1.0' />
            <GeometryModel3D>
              <GeometryModel3D.Geometry>
                <MeshGeometry3D
                  TextureCoordinates='0,0 1,0 0,1 1,1 0,0 1,1 1,1 1,1'
                  Positions='0,0,0 1,0,0 0,1,0 1,1,0 0,1,-1 1,1,-1 1,0,-1'
                  TriangleIndices='0,1,2 3,2,1 4,2,3 5,4,3 5,3,1 6,5,1' />
              </GeometryModel3D.Geometry>
              <GeometryModel3D.Material>
                <DiffuseMaterial>
                <DiffuseMaterial.Brush>
                    <LinearGradientBrush EndPoint='1,0'>
                      <LinearGradientBrush.GradientStops>
                        <GradientStop Offset='0'
                          Color='Black' />
                        <GradientStop Offset='1'
                          Color='White' />
                      </LinearGradientBrush.GradientStops>
                    </LinearGradientBrush>
                </DiffuseMaterial.Brush>
                </DiffuseMaterial>
              </GeometryModel3D.Material>
            </GeometryModel3D>
          </Model3DGroup>
        </ModelVisual3D.Content>
      </ModelVisual3D>
    </Viewport3D>
```

Creating complex models is the true art of 3D graphics. But in much the same way that understanding the mechanics of Bezier curves, gradients,

FIGURE 5.36: A three-faced cube, with a linear gradient texture applied

Diffuse   Specular   Emissive

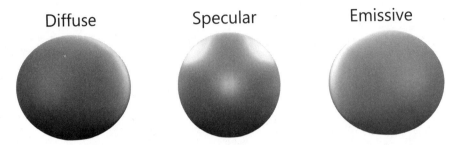

FIGURE 5.37: Spheres with different types of materials applied

and colors doesn't help us make beautiful pictures, understanding triangles and texture coordinates will not enable us to make great art in 3D. 3D models are incredibly complex, consisting of hundreds or thousands of triangles (or hundreds of thousands!). The position and texture coordinate must be specified for each triangle, so obviously people don't do this by hand. Investing in a 3D tool is critical to creating good 3D models.

Materials

Materials are the combination of a brush and a behavior with respect to light. **Diffuse materials** diffuse light, making the object look flat; **specular materials** reflect light, making the object "shiny"; and **emissive materials** emit light. All of these are shown in Figure 5.37. We can combine these materials to create complex materials also. Missing from this version of WPF are bump maps, environment maps, and other more advanced materials.

DiffuseMaterial is probably the most common base material. Typically it is combined with SpecularMaterial to create some reflection on the surface by using MaterialGroup. DiffuseMaterial will take any brush and map it to only a specific model. Figure 5.38 shows several types of brushes

Image   Gradient   Drawing

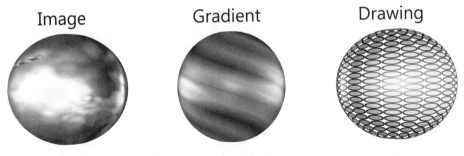

FIGURE 5.38: Spheres with different types of brushes

applied to spheres. Keep in mind that we can use any of the brushes that we've encountered: gradients, tiles, visual brushes—anything!

Lights

Probably the two most common errors that people make when first attempting 3D graphics are forgetting to light the scene (pitch-black scenes tend not to be very visible) and positioning the camera so that it's looking into space. Just as we do when we walk into a room, the first thing we should do with 3D graphics is turn on a light.

WPF supports several lights: `PointLight`, `SpotLight`, `DirectionalLight`, and `AmbientLight` (Figure 5.39). It's easiest to compare each type of light to its real-world counterpart. `PointLight` resembles an incandescent light with no lamp shade around it; it projects light in every direction from a single point. `SpotLight` works like a flashlight; it projects light from a single point in a cone shape. `DirectionalLight` looks like a bank of fluorescent lights infinitely long; a plane of light is projected in one direction. Finally, `AmbientLight` has no real-world counterpart; it projects light from every direction to every direction. Properly lighting a scene generally requires a combination of lights.

Cameras

For projecting a 3D scene into 2D, only one camera is needed. The camera represents the eye of the user looking at the scene. `PerspectiveCamera`, which displays the scene "naturally" (objects farther away are smaller, etc.), is the most common type of camera used. The other two cameras (`MatrixCamera` and `OrthographicCamera`) are fairly deep 3D concepts, which we won't cover here.

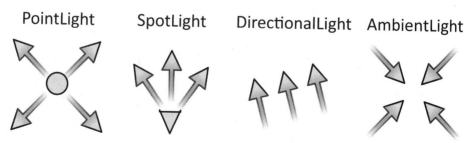

FIGURE 5.39: Types of lights

FIGURE 5.40: `AxisAngleRotation3D`'s two components: a 3D axis and an angle around that axis

`PerspectiveCamera` works just like a real-world camera. There is a position in 3D space for the camera, a direction to point the camera, and a focal length of the lens. Using these three properties, we can move the camera around the scene in a very natural way.

Transforms

2D rendering in WPF is based heavily on transforms; however, they are typically hidden behind layout and simple properties. Fundamentally, the rendering of all 2D images is run through lots of nested matrix transformations to determine their final display location. Remember that, when sharing a drawing, the only way to reposition it is to use `TranslateTransform`. Because the 3D infrastructure is limited to the base-level functionality, transforms are the only game in town.

Translation and scale transforms are pretty straightforward; they just add a third dimension over their 2D counterparts. Rotation, however, is not so simple. There are several models to define rotation in 3D space, but the simplest one to understand is the `AxisAngleRotation3D`. To define a rotation, we need to define a vector (axis) and an angle around that vector (angle), as Figure 5.40 illustrates. Figure 5.41 shows three cones, each

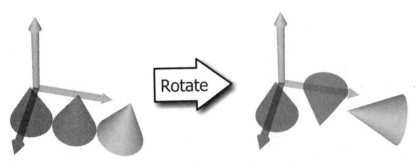

FIGURE 5.41: Effects of rotating a cone in 3D around different axes

rotated 90 degrees around a different axis. From the perspective of the camera, the z axis is the one pointing down in the picture, y is the arrow going up, and x points to the right:

```xml
<!-- rotation around the y axis -->
<RotateTransform3D>
  <RotateTransform3D.Rotation>
    <AxisAngleRotation3D Axis='0,1,0' Angle='90' />
  </RotateTransform3D.Rotation>
</RotateTransform3D>

<!-- rotation around the x axis -->
<RotateTransform3D>
  <RotateTransform3D.Rotation>
    <AxisAngleRotation3D Axis='1,0,0' Angle='90' />
  </RotateTransform3D.Rotation>
</RotateTransform3D>

<!-- rotation around the z axis -->
<RotateTransform3D>
  <RotateTransform3D.Rotation>
    <AxisAngleRotation3D Axis='0,0,1' Angle='90' />
  </RotateTransform3D.Rotation>
</RotateTransform3D>
```

Documents and Text

> *Boiled down to its essence, a book is basically sooty marks on shredded trees. Yet it succeeds in capturing and holding our attention for hours at a stretch. Not only that, but as we read it, the book itself disappears. The "real" book we read is inside our heads; reading is an immersive experience.*
> *What's going on here? What's the magic?*
> BILL HILL, "THE MAGIC OF READING"[18]

Text is the most effective way to present information to humans. Although pictures and graphs can convey a huge volume of information, it is difficult to communicate complex data without eventually resorting to the printed word. In almost every application we build, we'll need to display some amount of text.

---

18. Available online at www.poynterextra.org/msfonts/osprey.doc.

Hello World

FIGURE 5.42: Hello World in text

Hello World, Text Style

So far in this book we've already seen some of the key characteristics of text. The simplest model for targeting text directly is the TextBlock control (Figure 5.42):

```
<TextBlock>
  Hello World
</TextBlock>
```

This may not seem very interesting, but there's a lot going on. Remember that everything is going through the 3D pipeline, so to render this text we have to crack font files, get glyph descriptions, create either bitmap glyphs (for small font size) or complex paths (for larger font sizes), and finally convert all that to 3D triangles for display. Even all that is not very interesting, though, until we move on to the next stage.

WPF has all the standard text elements that we would expect for rich formatting. WPF doesn't support overlapping tags, so we must normalize everything to a tree shape (the same rules apply for RTF and Microsoft Word, so you may already be aware of this):

```
<TextBlock>
  Hello World, <Bold>bold</Bold>, <Italic>italic</Italic>, <Underline>etc.</
Underline>
</TextBlock>
```

The WPF development team decided not to create special tags for every combination of formatting attributes. If we had, we would have ended up with tags like BoldItalic. Instead we favored using attributes to control font rendering. We can re-create the previous code example using the basic Run element:

```
<TextBlock>
  Hello World,
  <Run FontWeight='Bold'>bold</Run>,
  <Run FontStyle='Italic'>italic</Run>,
  <Run TextDecorations='Underline'>etc.</Run>
</TextBlock>
```

こんにちは世界, **bold**, *italic*, <u>etc.</u>

FIGURE 5.43: Hello World, multilingual and multiformat

Text elements belong to one of two families: in-line or block. **In-line elements** can break between lines and flow together; **block elements** must start on a new line and logically occupy a rectangular region of space.

So far so good—if you happen to live in an English-speaking country. One of the big improvements in WPF is that it was built from the ground up with support for Unicode (including complex scripts, etc.). Unicode is a way of representing characters with 16 bits[19] that allows for all characters in all languages to be represented (yes, there are even Klingon characters in Unicode). Let's try switching our example over to Japanese[20] (Figure 5.43).

```
<TextBlock>
    こんにちは世界
  <Run FontWeight='Bold'>bold</Run>,
  <Run FontStyle='Italic'>italic</Run>,
  <Run TextDecorations='Underline'>etc.</Run>
</TextBlock>
```

`TextBlock` is designed to contain a single paragraph. We can turn on word wrapping and stack multiple blocks to simulate paragraphs, but if we really want to go to the next level, we need to move to `FlowDocument`. A pervasive design philosophy in the development of WPF was "pay for play"; we applied this concept to performance, complexity, and anything else we could. With a layered text model, we can have a lighter-weight single-paragraph text control (fewer concepts and better performance) and a richer multiple-paragraph control.

We can switch over to the `FlowDocument` control and add a second paragraph with some more interesting text. `FlowDocument` accepts only

---

19. Originally Unicode was strictly a 16-bit system. There are lots of alternative encodings of the 16-bit values for Unicode, however; one of the more common is UTF-8, which uses 8 bits for the most common values in Western languages. The more recent Unicode specs now contain characters that require two 16-bit values. It is more correct to say that Unicode is a specification of how to represent characters.

20. If you're curious how to type this, install the Japanese language pack for Windows XP. Then install the IME (input method editor) for Japanese, which will let you type Japanese on a keyboard.

こんにちは世界, **bold**, *italic*, <u>etc.</u>

We can switch over to the `FlowDocument` control, and add a second paragraph with some more interesting text.

FIGURE 5.44: Hello World, now with multiple paragraphs

block elements, so we need to surround the initial text with a `Paragraph` element:

```
<FlowDocument>
  <Paragraph>こんにちは世界, <Run FontWeight='Bold'>bold</Run>,
<Run FontStyle='Italic'>italic</Run>, <Run
TextDecorations='Underline'>etc.</Run></Paragraph>

  <Paragraph>We can switch over to the <Run FontFamily='Lucida
Console'>FlowDocument</Run> control, and add a second paragraph
with some more interesting text.</Paragraph>
</FlowDocument>
```

`FlowDocument` is not a display element. To render `FlowDocument`, we must put it in some type of viewer. To start, we'll use the simple `FlowDocumentScrollViewer` which simply displays the document in a scrolling container (Figure 5.44).

Notice in Figure 5.44 that the default font used for the text has changed. Because `TextBlock` is typically used in UI scenarios, while `FlowDocument` caters more to documents, the defaults for the two controls are different. Fonts with serifs (like Times New Roman) are more readable in documents;

こんにちは世界, **bold**, *italic*, <u>etc.</u>

We can switch over to the `FlowDocument` control, and add a second paragraph with some more interesting text.

FIGURE 5.45: Hello World, hosted in the `FlowDocumentReader` control

こんにちは世界, **bold**, *italic*, <u>etc.</u>

We can 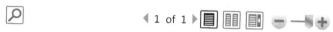 over to the FlowDocument control, and add a second paragraph with some more interesting text.

FIGURE 5.46: Hello World, now with UI controls hosted in-line

sans-serif fonts (like Arial or Tahoma) look better in smaller point sizes for UI display.

Recall from Chapter 3 that there are several document viewer controls that maximize the readability of content. By adding the FlowDocument-Reader controls as the root (Figure 5.45), we can have more control over the display of the document:

```
<FlowDocumentReader>
<FlowDocument>
  <Paragraph>こんにちは世界, <Run FontWeight='Bold'>bold</Run>, <Run
FontStyle='Italic'>italic</Run>, <Run
TextDecorations='Underline'>etc.</Run></Paragraph>
  <Paragraph>We can switch over to the <Run FontFamily='Lucida
Console'>FlowDocument</Run> control, and add a second paragraph
with some more interesting text.</Paragraph>
</FlowDocument>
</FlowDocumentReader>
```

Once hosted in the reader control, the document can be read as either a scrollable bottomless document or a paginated document. WPF's integration theme is also present in the text arena; not only is it simple to host rich documents in the UI, but we can also host any WPF controls directly in the text flow (Figure 5.46):

```
<FlowDocumentReader>
<FlowDocument>
    <Paragraph>こんにちは世界, <Run FontWeight='Bold'>bold</Run>, <Run
FontStyle='Italic'>italic</Run>, <Run
TextDecorations='Underline'>etc.</Run></Paragraph>
  <Paragraph>We can <Button>switch</Button> over to the
<Run FontFamily='Lucida Console'>FlowDocument</Run> control,
and add a second paragraph with some more interesting text.</Paragraph>
</FlowDocument>
</FlowDocumentReader>
```

Now that we have a fully integrated document, the last thing to do is print it out. There are two ways to print the document: (1) by sending the instructions directly to the printer, or (2) by creating a fixed-format document that contains the same information. The new XML Paper Specification (XPS) fixed-format document type creates a static version of the document that can be printed and archived. In fact, some printers support the XPS format as the native spool format.

To print a document to XPS, we need to create a file using the OPC (Open Packaging Conventions) APIs. We can then create an XpsDocument object in the container and write the flow document out to the store:

```
using (Package containerPackage
    = Package.Open(@"c:\test.xps", FileMode.Create))
{
  using (XpsDocument xpsDoc = new XpsDocument(containerPackage))
  {
    XpsDocumentWriter writer
      = XpsDocument.CreateXpsDocumentWriter(xpsDoc);
    writer.Write(
      ((IDocumentPaginatorSource)theDocument).DocumentPaginator);
  }
}
```

Once the document is saved, double-clicking the container from the disk will load the document in a viewer (Figure 5.47). In viewing the document, notice that the button is no longer interactive, because the XPS fixed-format documents are static snapshots that can be exported to any platform, printed, or whatever; they flatten everything to text and basic vectors.

Fonts

Although it may seem odd, there is no Font class in WPF. Instead WPF has a set of attributes that, when bundled together, can be seen as defining a font: FontFamily, FontSize, FontStretch, FontStyle, and FontWeight. Lots of other attributes can change the way text is rendered—for example, TextDecorations to add underline or strikethrough, Capitals to adjust the case of the letters rendered; all told, at least 40 properties affect the shape of the text.

Let's start at the beginning, with FamilyTypeface. The term **typeface** refers to a specific set of character definitions, typically an outline. Typefaces are generally defined in a TrueType or OpenType file (OpenType is

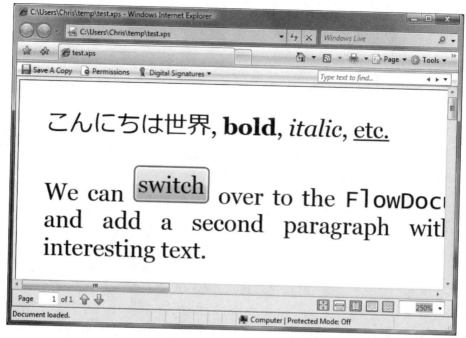

FIGURE 5.47: Hello World, printed as an XPS document being viewed in Internet Explorer

actually a common file format that can contain a typeface defined in one of a number of formats). On most PCs running Windows, the files contained in the `c:\windows\fonts` directory (or wherever the OS is installed) are the typefaces.[21]

Typefaces are grouped into families, which are represented in WPF with the type `FontFamily`. Arial is a font family, which (on my machine) has four typefaces: normal, bold, italic, and bold italic. When we construct a `FontFamily` object, we can pass in any number of comma-delimited values, so we can specify font family names[22] to which we want to bind (this feature lets us define a fallback font in case the one we specify isn't found). Querying the `FamilyNames` property on a constructed `FontFamily` object

---

21. A typeface is basically a program that renders text. It may sound strange, but fonts are a lot like CLR IL (Common Language Runtime Intermediate Language) programs. Each typeface is a specially authored version of the general font for a specific style.

22. In XAML, all family names are listed in the same way: `<Button FontFamily='Arial, Tahoma'/>`.

will tell us which family was found. Family names are indexed by culture so that font vendors can provide localized names for the fonts:

```
XmlLanguage lang =
    XmlLanguage.GetLanguage(CultureInfo.CurrentUICulture.IetfLanguageTag);

FontFamily attempt1 = new FontFamily("Arial");
string name1 = attempt1.FamilyNames[lang];

FontFamily attempt2 = new FontFamily("ChrisFont, Tahoma");
string name2 = attempt2.FamilyNames[lang];
```

After this program is run, typically name1 contains "Arial", and name2 contains "Tahoma" (unless you happen to have a font called *ChrisFont* on your machine).

Once we have a font family, the system will automatically pick a typeface based on the other font-related properties. If a specific typeface is not available (e.g., a particular font might ship with only the normal-weight typeface), then the system will generate the appropriate glyphs. Generated typefaces usually have a lower quality, because they have to use a generic algorithm.

Overall, WPF's treatment of fonts is a bit heavy-handed (a lot of the details of the underlying system tend to shine through), but we have tried to simplify where possible. For example, take FontWeight. Although developers have used the IsBold property to control font weight for a long time, font weight is actually expressed as an integer value from 0 to 900. "Bold" generally maps to 700. FontWeight can be set to any of these values, but to make it easy to control font weight, WPF provides a wrapper type called FontWeights that has a set of well-known values.

Text Layout

Once we've discovered a font and configured it to our liking, we can turn our sights to positioning text on the page or screen. Text layout in a single line is interesting, but eventually text wraps, which brings us to paragraph formatting.

Paragraphs

As all-block elements, paragraphs support a box model for layout. Each block element has Margin, Padding, and BorderThickness properties that

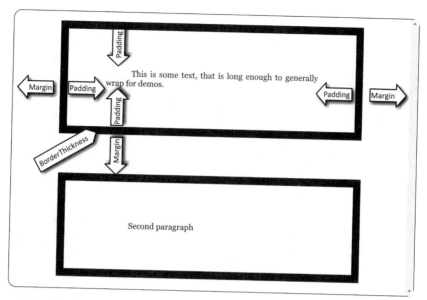

FIGURE 5.48: The block element's box model for layout

control the size of the element. Figure 5.48 shows graphically how the model works. Notice that the margins of the first and second paragraphs collapse to match the margin of the larger paragraph. Notice, too, that the margin for the second paragraph (which is the last paragraph in the document) has been truncated; that is, even though top and bottom margins are defined for both paragraphs, between the two paragraphs there is only one margin.

Beyond the box model, Paragraph supports all the usual suspects for line formatting: TextIndent to control the first-line indent (also shown in Figure 5.48), LineHeight to control line spacing, and so on. In addition, Paragraph has all the needed supports for participating in a paginated world—KeepTogether, KeepWithNext, MinOrphanLines, and MinWidowLines—which control how the paragraph breaks across page boundaries. Figure 5.49 (on page 276) shows the effect of using KeepWithNext on a paginated view; in this case "Heading 2" could have fit in the second column, but because KeepWithNext was set to True, it moved to the third column.

Lists

Beyond basic paragraphs, we often need lists. List is a block element that contains ListItem objects, which are block containers. Note that ListItem

Heading 1

Lorem ipsum dolor sit amet, consectetuer adipiscing elit. Vestibulum fringilla. Class aptent taciti sociosqu ad litora torquent per conubia nostra, per inceptos hymenaeos. Pellentesque varius, mi eget laoreet tincidunt, tortor purus faucibus sem, eget mattis sem sapien dapibus libero. Donec purus enim, facilisis vitae, consequat ut, interdum et, libero. Sed felis arcu, pretium a, rhoncus vitae, aliquet at, neque. Proin venenatis ligula quis dolor. Vestibulum tincidunt. Cum sociis natoque penatibus et magnis dis parturient montes, nascetur ridiculus mus. Nullam vitae orci. Vestibulum ante ipsum primis in faucibus orci luctus et ultrices posuere cubilia Curae; Nullam nisl purus, blandit sit amet, vestibulum semper, commodo a, velit. Mauris ante tortor, nonummy eu, facilisis ut, consequat et, pede. Nullam neque dui, hendrerit eget, eleifend ullamcorper, tristique ut, sapien. Sed tempus. Cras hendrerit cursus arcu. Suspendisse potenti. Morbi vel dui ut nulla consectetuer dictum. Vestibulum ante

ipsum primis in faucibus orci luctus et ultrices posuere cubilia Curae; Aliquam placerat libero ac lectus. Etiam sodales condimentum tellus.

In tincidunt sem sit amet mauris dignissim tincidunt. Morbi id mi a sem vehicula hendrerit. In hac habitasse platea dictumst. Lorem ipsum dolor sit amet, consectetuer adipiscing elit. Nam ipsum. Ut sit amet metus vitae justo pellentesque nonummy. Mauris interdum. Nam imperdiet malesuada lorem. Morbi non sapien ut odio cursus sodales. Curabitur elementum ipsum nec orci. Fusce vitae est. Fusce sem elit, imperdiet ut, suscipit ac, euismod non, nisi. Phasellus mattis pede non erat pretium sodales. Duis nec ligula. Suspendisse vitae sapien in mauris rhoncus aliquet. Sed id nisi. Phasellus magna. Duis vulputate vestibulum augue. Maecenas ornare diam sed libero.

Heading 2

Lorem ipsum dolor sit amet, consectetuer adipiscing elit. Vestibulum fringilla. Class aptent taciti sociosqu ad litora torquent per conubia nostra, per inceptos hymenaeos. Pellentesque varius, mi eget laoreet tincidunt, tortor purus faucibus sem, eget mattis sem sapien dapibus libero. Donec purus enim, facilisis vitae, consequat ut, interdum et, libero. Sed felis arcu, pretium a, rhoncus vitae, aliquet at, neque. Proin venenatis ligula quis dolor. Vestibulum tincidunt. Cum sociis natoque penatibus et magnis dis parturient montes, nascetur ridiculus mus. Nullam vitae orci. Vestibulum ante ipsum primis in faucibus orci luctus et ultrices posuere cubilia Curae; Nullam nisl purus, blandit sit amet, vestibulum semper, commodo a, velit. Mauris ante tortor, nonummy eu, facilisis ut, consequat et, pede. Nullam neque dui, hendrerit eget, eleifend ullamcorper, tristique ut, sapien. Sed tempus. Cras hendrerit cursus arcu. Suspendisse potenti. Morbi vel dui ut nulla consectetuer dictum. Vestibulum ante

⊮ ◂ 1 of 2 ▸ ⊯

FIGURE 5.49: `KeepWithNext` prevents column and page breaks immediately following a heading.

can contain only block elements, and not text directly, which means that each `ListItem` object typically contains one or more `Paragraph` objects.

Here we'll show a list with several items, including a nested list. `MarkerStyle` controls the appearance of the bullet before each item in a bulleted list (Figure 5.50), and `StartIndex` controls the numbering of items

Here is a simple list:

- Item 1
- Item 2
  - Subitem 1
  - Subitem 2

Lists can use a variety of markers:

1. Item 1
2. Item 2
   - Subitem 1
   - Subitem 2

◂ 1 of 1 ▸

FIGURE 5.50: Two lists with different markers

in a numbered list (the current version of WPF does not allow the creation of custom markers):

```
<FlowDocument>
  <Paragraph>Here is a simple list:</Paragraph>
  <List>
    <ListItem><Paragraph>Item 1</Paragraph></ListItem>
    <ListItem>
      <Paragraph>Item 2</Paragraph>
      <List Margin='0'>
        <ListItem><Paragraph>Subitem 1</Paragraph></ListItem>
        <ListItem><Paragraph>Subitem 2</Paragraph></ListItem>
      </List>
    </ListItem>
  </List>
  <Paragraph BreakColumnBefore='True'>Lists can use a variety of markers:
  </Paragraph>
  <List MarkerStyle='Decimal'>
    <ListItem><Paragraph>Item 1</Paragraph></ListItem>
    <ListItem>
      <Paragraph>Item 2</Paragraph>
      <List Margin='0' MarkerStyle='Box'>
        <ListItem><Paragraph>Subitem 1</Paragraph></ListItem>
        <ListItem><Paragraph>Subitem 2</Paragraph></ListItem>
      </List>
    </ListItem>
  </List>
</FlowDocument>
```

Tables

Lists and paragraphs are the basic building blocks of text layout; the granddaddy of all layouts is Table. Table layout has been a mainstay of the Web community for years, as the only real layout beyond flowing text. With more modern HTML, people have moved to using DIV elements with margins and absolute positioning, but table layout still stands as a marvel of complexity and power.

WPF's Table control allows for table layout as we would expect to find in HTML, Word, or most typography programs. As we saw with List, the object model is restricted to ensure that Table contains TableRowGroup objects, TableRowGroup contains TableRow objects, TableRow contains TableCell objects, and TableCell is a block container, so typically it would contain one or more paragraphs.

Because Table, TableRowGroup, TableRow, and TableCell all derive from BlockElement, they each support the box layout model (just like

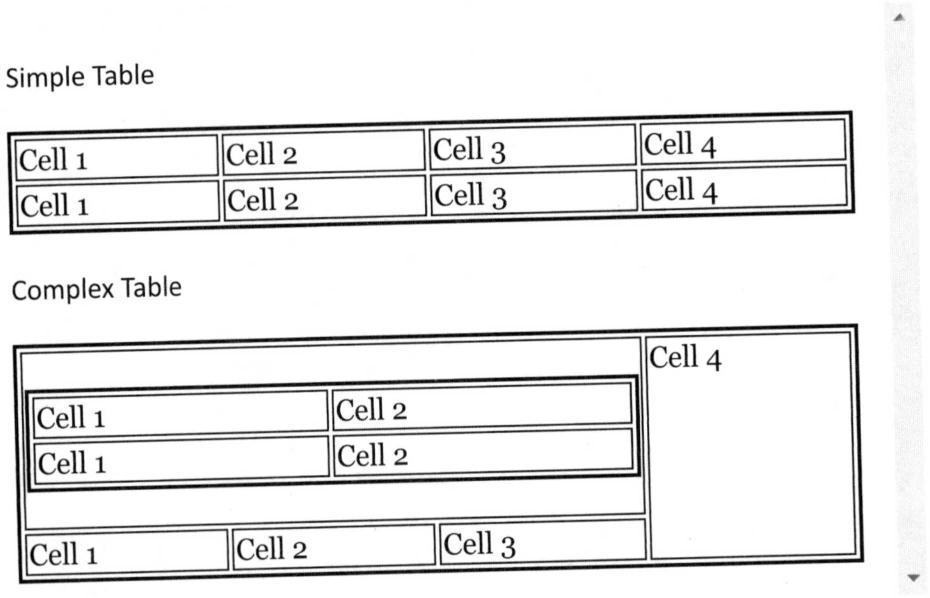

Simple Table

Cell 1	Cell 2	Cell 3	Cell 4
Cell 1	Cell 2	Cell 3	Cell 4

Complex Table

FIGURE 5.51: Two tables with thick borders added around each table and thin borders around cells

Paragraph with Margin, Padding, and BorderThickness), providing a tremendous amount of layout flexibility. In addition, Table contains a collection of TableColumn objects that allow us to apply formatting to an entire column.

Let's look at a couple of tables (Figure 5.51). The first shows the basic structure of a table; the second demonstrates some more advanced features: RowSpan, ColumnSpan, and a nested table:

```
<FlowDocument>
  <Paragraph>A simple table</Paragraph>
  <Table>
    <TableRowGroup>
      <TableRow>
        <TableCell><Paragraph>Cell 1</Paragraph></TableCell>
        <TableCell><Paragraph>Cell 2</Paragraph></TableCell>
        <TableCell><Paragraph>Cell 3</Paragraph></TableCell>
        <TableCell><Paragraph>Cell 4</Paragraph></TableCell>
      </TableRow>
      <TableRow>
        <TableCell><Paragraph>Cell 1</Paragraph></TableCell>
        <TableCell><Paragraph>Cell 2</Paragraph></TableCell>
        <TableCell><Paragraph>Cell 3</Paragraph></TableCell>
```

```
        <TableCell><Paragraph>Cell 4</Paragraph></TableCell>
      </TableRow>
    </TableRowGroup>
  </Table>

  <Paragraph>A complex table</Paragraph>
  <Table>
    <TableRowGroup>
      <TableRow>
        <TableCell ColumnSpan='3'>
          <Table>
            <TableRowGroup>
              <!-- more table cells -->
            </TableRowGroup>
          </Table>
        </TableCell>
        <TableCell RowSpan='2'>
          <Paragraph>Cell 4</Paragraph>
        </TableCell>
      </TableRow>
      <TableRow>
        <TableCell><Paragraph>Cell 1</Paragraph></TableCell>
        <TableCell><Paragraph>Cell 2</Paragraph></TableCell>
        <TableCell><Paragraph>Cell 3</Paragraph></TableCell>
      </TableRow>
    </TableRowGroup>
  </Table>
</FlowDocument>
```

Figures and Floaters

Most "real" documents contain figures (take this book, for example; there are lots of figures!) and floaters. Figures and floaters are both said to be **anchored** blocks, which means that they are relative to a specific point in the normal flow of the text. In markup, we encode this relationship by placing the figure or floater in-line with the text.

Figures and floaters are very similar, with two exceptions: **Figures** can span columns and can be positioned relative to the page on which they're placed (using the HorizontalAnchor and VerticalAnchor properties). **Floaters,** as the name implies, are much more like floating boxes that just accompany the content to which they're anchored. Both are shown in Figure 5.52 (on page 280).

To see how to use these elements, let's create a section of a document with a floater. We will embed an image with a caption right after the heading. The floater is a block container element (like Section) that contains

Heading 1

Lorem ipsum dolor sit amet, consectetuer adipiscing elit. Vestibulum fringilla. Class aptent taciti sociosqu ad litora torquent per conubia nostra, per inceptos hymenaeos. Pellentesque varius, mi eget laoreet tincidunt, tortor purus faucibus sem, eget mattis sem sapien dapibus libero. Donec purus enim, facilisis vitae, consequat ut, interdum et, libero. Sed felis arcu, pretium a, rhoncus vitae, aliquet at, neque. Proin venenatis ligula quis dolor. Vestibulum tincidunt. Cum sociis natoque penatibus et magnis dis parturient montes, nascetur ridiculus mus. Nullam vitae orci. Vestibulum ante ipsum primis in faucibus orci luctus et ultrices posuere cubilia Curae; Nullam nisl purus, blandit sit amet, vestibulum semper, commodo a, velit. Mauris ante tortor, nonummy eu, facilisis ut, consequat et, pede. Nullam neque dui, hendrerit eget, eleifend ullamcorper, tristique ut, sapien. Sed tempus. Cras hendrerit cursus arcu. Suspendisse potenti. Morbi vel dui ut nulla consectetuer dictum. Vestibulum ante

ipsum primis in faucibus orci luctus et ultrices posuere cubilia Curae; Aliquam placerat libero ac lectus. Etiam sodales condimentum tellus.

In tincidunt sem sit amet mauris dignissim tincidunt. Morbi id mi a sem vehicula hendrerit. In hac habitasse platea dictumst. Lorem ipsum dolor sit amet, consectetuer adipiscing elit. Nam ipsum. Ut sit amet metus vitae justo pellentesque nonummy. Mauris interdum. Nam imperdiet malesuada lorem. Morbi non sapien ut odio cursus sodales. Curabitur elementum ipsum nec orci. Fusce vitae est. Fusce sem, imperdiet ut, suscipit ac, euismod non, Phasellus mattis pede non erat pretium. Duis nec ligula. Suspendisse viverra in in mauris rhoncus aliquet. Sed id ante. Phasellus magna. Duis vulputate vestibulum augue. Maecenas ornare diam sed libero.

Heading 2

Lorem ipsum dolor sit amet, consectetuer

adipiscing elit. Vestibulum fringilla. Class aptent taciti sociosqu ad litora torquent per conubia nostra, per inceptos hymenaeos. Pellentesque

Image Floater

varius, mi eget laoreet tincidunt, tortor purus faucibus sem, eget mattis sem sapien dapibus libero. Donec purus enim, facilisis vitae, consequat ut, interdum et, libero. Sed felis arcu, pretium a, rhoncus vitae, aliquet at, neque. Proin venenatis ligula quis dolor. Vestibulum tincidunt. Cum sociis natoque penatibus et magnis dis parturient montes, nascetur ridiculus mus. Nullam vitae orci. Vestibulum ante ipsum primis in faucibus orci luctus et ultrices posuere cubilia Curae; Nullam nisl purus, blandit sit amet, vestibulum semper, commodo a, velit. Mauris ante tortor, nonummy eu, facilisis ut, consequat et, pede. Nullam neque dui, hendrerit eget, eleifend ullamcorper, tristique ut, sapien. Sed tempus. Cras hendrerit cursus arcu. Suspendisse potenti. Morbi vel dui ut nulla consectetuer dictum. Vestibulum ante ipsum primis in faucibus orci luctus et ultrices

Figure Anchor

Floater Anchor

A figure, consisting of text in a paragraph.

◁ 1 of 2 ▷

FIGURE 5.52: Figures and floaters positioned in a paginated document, with marks for their anchors

only other block elements. To host our image, we use `BlockUIContainer`, which allows us to embed any UI control in a document:

```
<Paragraph FontSize='24pt' KeepWithNext='True'>Heading 2</Paragraph>
<Paragraph>
  <Floater Width='200'>
    <BlockUIContainer>
      <StackPanel>
        <Image Source='c:\test-image.png' />
        <TextBlock FontWeight='Bold'>Image Floater</TextBlock>
      </StackPanel>
    </BlockUIContainer>
  </Floater>
  Lorem ipsum ... </Paragraph>
<Paragraph>In tincidunt ... </Paragraph>
```

Columns and Page-Level Formatting

The final level of text layout is applied at the document level. `FlowDocument` offers a set of properties to control how columns are applied and pages are formatted. The basic controls are all there—column rules (the lines between columns) and column width—but the most interesting one is `IsColumn-WidthFlexible`, which allows the system to automatically size the columns according to the area in which the document is displayed (Figure 5.53).

Heading 1

Lorem ipsum dolor sit amet, consectetuer adipiscing elit. Vestibulum fringilla. Class aptent taciti sociosqu ad litora torquent per conubia nostra, per inceptos hymenaeos. Pellentesque varius, mi eget laoreet tincidunt, tortor purus faucibus sem, eget mattis sem sapien dapibus libero. Donec purus enim, facilisis vitae, consequat ut, interdum et, libero. Sed felis arcu, pretium a, rhoncus vitae, aliquet at, neque. Proin venenatis ligula quis dolor. Vestibulum tincidunt. Cum sociis natoque penatibus et magnis dis parturient montes, nascetur ridiculus mus. Nullam vitae orci. Nullam ante ipsum primis in faucibus orci luctus et ultrices posuere cubilia Curae; Nullam nisl purus, blandit sit amet, vestibulum semper, commodo a, velit. Mauris ante tortor, nonummy eu, facilisis ut, consequat et, pede. Nullam neque dui, hendrerit eget, eleifend ullamcorper, tristique ut, sapien. Sed tempus. Cras hendrerit cursus arcu. Suspendisse potenti. Morbi vel dui ut nulla consectetuer dictum. Vestibulum ante ipsum primis in faucibus orci luctus et ultrices posuere cubilia Curae; Aliquam placerat libero ac lectus. Etiam sodales condimentum tellus.

A figure, consisting of text in a paragraph.

Resize →

Heading 1

Lorem ipsum dolor sit amet, consectetuer adipiscing elit. Vestibulum fringilla. Class aptent taciti sociosqu ad litora torquent per conubia nostra, per inceptos hymenaeos. Pellentesque varius, mi eget laoreet tincidunt, tortor purus faucibus sem, eget mattis sem sapien dapibus libero. Donec purus enim, facilisis vitae, consequat ut, interdum et, libero. Sed felis arcu, pretium a, rhoncus vitae, aliquet at, neque. Proin venenatis ligula quis dolor. Vestibulum tincidunt. Cum sociis natoque penatibus et magnis dis parturient montes, nascetur ridiculus mus. Nullam vitae orci. Vestibulum ante ipsum primis in faucibus orci luctus et ultrices posuere cubilia Curae; Nullam nisl purus, blandit sit amet, vestibulum semper, commodo a, velit. Mauris ante tortor, nonummy eu, facilisis ut, consequat et, pede. Nullam neque dui, hendrerit eget, eleifend ullamcorper, tristique ut, sapien. Sed tempus.

Cras hendrerit cursus arcu. Suspendisse potenti. Morbi vel dui ut nulla consectetuer dictum. Vestibulum ante ipsum primis in faucibus orci luctus et ultrices posuere cubilia Curae; Aliquam placerat libero ac lectus. Etiam sodales condimentum tellus.

In tincidunt sem sit amet mauris dignissim tincidunt. Morbi id mi a sem vehicula hendrerit. In hac habitasse platea dictumst. Lorem ipsum dolor sit amet, consectetuer adipiscing elit. Nam ipsum. Ut sit amet metus vitae justo pellentesque nonummy. Mauris interdum. Nam imperdiet malesuada porro. Morbi non sapien ut odio cursus sodales. Curabitur elementum ipsum nec orci. Fusce vitae est. Fusce sem elit, imperdiet ut, suscipit ac, euismod non, nisi. Phasellus mattis pede non erat pretium sodales. Duis nec ligula. Suspendisse vitae sapien in mauris rhoncus aliquet. Sed id nisi. Phasellus magna. Duis vulputate vestibulum augue. Maecenas ornare diam sed libero.

A figure, consisting of text in a paragraph.

FIGURE 5.53: Using document-level formatting, including automatic sizing, to control columns

Using the page size properties for a document, we can determine a range of valid page sizes (based on minimum and maximum page width and height) and specify padding for the page.[23] We can also lock the size of the page by using the `PageWidth` and `PageHeight` properties, if we don't want the document to support a range of sizes.

Advanced Typography

ty•pog•ra•phy The art of displaying text, including selection of fonts, sizes, and layout, to make an attractive and readable display.

Document designers have long lamented the weak support for real typography in the Windows platform. The ability to create great-looking documents always required additional software (like Microsoft Word or Adobe PageMaker). WPF, however, has an entirely new font engine, and a world-class page layout engine has been integrated into the core platform. All the features that we've covered up to now (tables, columns, pagination, etc.) are made possible by this new engine.

We can now leverage the advanced OpenType features that some fonts support. Fonts such as Palatino Linotype support alternate character forms to make text look better in different scenarios. Figure 5.54 shows some of

---

23. *Padding* is an odd term to use; typically this feature would be called *margins,* but we consistently use *padding* to describe insets.

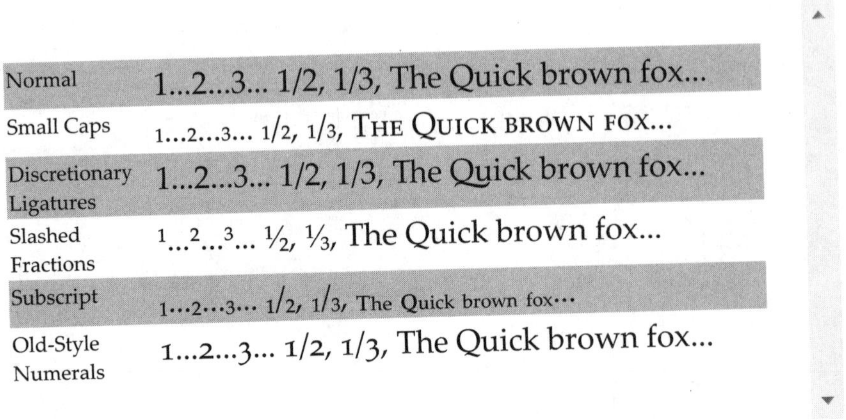

Normal	1...2...3... 1/2, 1/3, The Quick brown fox...
Small Caps	1...2...3... 1/2, 1/3, THE QUICK BROWN FOX...
Discretionary Ligatures	1...2...3... 1/2, 1/3, The Quick brown fox...
Slashed Fractions	1...2...3... ½, ⅓, The Quick brown fox...
Subscript	1...2...3... 1/2, 1/3, The Quick brown fox...
Old-Style Numerals	1...2...3... 1/2, 1/3, The Quick brown fox...

FIGURE 5.54: A demonstration of several alternative forms of Palatino Linotype

these features. The most interesting example is probably the notion of discretionary ligatures. Ligatures are joining marks between characters that help them fit together better. In the example that follows (shown as the third example in Figure 5.54), the joining of the T and h and the extension of the Q under the u are examples of discretionary ligatures. Most of the OpenType features are exposed by means of the Typography class:

```
<Paragraph Typography.DiscretionaryLigatures='True'>
  1..2..3.. 1/2, 1/3, The Quick brown fox...
</Paragraph>
```

Two other advanced features are hyphenation and justification. One of the difficulties in creating a document is balancing the white and dark space. The jagged edge on the right may include large blank spaces because of long words. Hyphenation and justification (illustrated in Figure 5.55) can

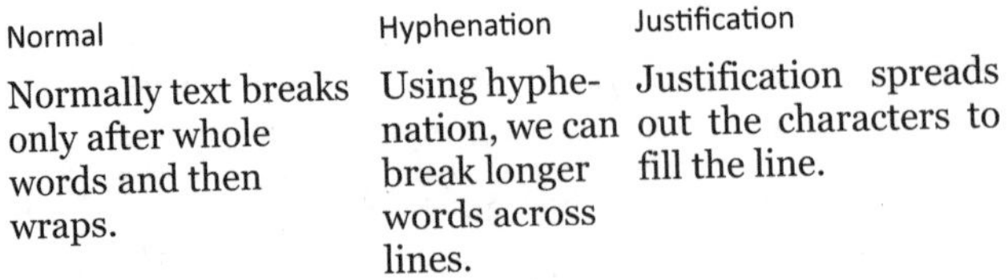

Normal	Hyphenation	Justification
Normally text breaks only after whole words and then wraps.	Using hyphenation, we can break longer words across lines.	Justification spreads out the characters to fill the line.

FIGURE 5.55: Hyphenation and justification control the way in which words are broken and positioned in a paragraph.

help minimize this problem. Hyphenation (IsHyphenationEnabled) uses a language-specific dictionary to correctly break words and automatically add hyphens; justification (TextAlignment = 'Justify') spreads out the white space and character placement to make the text fill the entire line. The two features are commonly used together.

With text under our belts, we can now move beyond the static visuals of 2D, 3D, and documents and into the dynamic world of animation and media.

Animation

Animation can be defined as the modification of a value based on time. Any instance in which function is evaluated over time we can think of as a type of animation. Let's start simply.

Animation as the New Timer

To understand animation, let's start by building some animation the hard way. Suppose we want to animate the increase in font size of a button from 9.0 to 18.0 at a constant rate over the span of 5 seconds. We'll start by hooking up a timer and adjusting the value. With each tick of the timer, we compute the new value for FontSize. We store the start time in the variable _start; then we can use the delta value from _start to determine the percentage of the addition per second (we want to increase the font by 9.0 over 5 seconds). We need to do some bounds checking, and then disable the timer:

```
<Window x:Class='EssentialWPF.Animations'
  xmlns='http://schemas.microsoft.com/winfx/2006/xaml/presentation'
  xmlns:x='http://schemas.microsoft.com/winfx/2006/xaml'
  Title='EssentialWPF'
  >
  <Button
    Name='_button1'
    HorizontalAlignment='Center' VerticalAlignment='Center'
    FontSize='9pt'>
    Hello World
  </Button>
</Window>

public partial class Animations : Window {
```

```
public Animations(){
  InitializeComponent();

  DispatcherTimer timer = new DispatcherTimer();
  timer.Interval = TimeSpan.FromMilliseconds(50);
  _start = Environment.TickCount;
  timer.Tick += timer_Tick;
  timer.IsEnabled = true;
}

long _start;

void timer_Tick(object sender, EventArgs e) {
  long elapsed = Environment.TickCount - _start;
  if (elapsed >= 5000) {
    _button1.FontSize = 18.0;
    ((DispatcherTimer)sender).IsEnabled = false;
    return;
  }
  _button1.FontSize = 9.0 + (9.0 / (5000.0 / elapsed));
}
}
```

We've hard-coded several things in this example: duration of the animation, initial value, and target value. We've also hard-coded something more subtle: the frame rate. Before we tackle the frame rate, we should identify the values of each of these variables:

```
long _start;

double _duration = 5000;
double _from = 9.0;
double _to = 18.0;

void timer_Tick(object sender, EventArgs e) {
  long elapsed = Environment.TickCount - _start;
  if (elapsed >= _duration) {
    _button1.FontSize = _to;
    ((DispatcherTimer)sender).IsEnabled = false;
    return;
  }
  double increase = _to - _from;
  _button1.FontSize = _from + (increase / (_duration / elapsed));
}
```

Now we have a general-purpose function for calculating the value of the font size from given starting and ending points. (I'll leave supporting a shrinking font size as an exercise for the reader.) This model obviously has a lot of problems (even excluding the frame rate problem). For starters, every time we create a property that we want to animate, we have to write this code again. In addition, we end up either creating a timer for each animation, or we have to create a central location to store all the animation information.

Enter animations.

Animations provide a common way to encapsulate time-based values for properties. The functions of tracking frame rate, calling back to calculate a value, and providing an object model for creating reusable animations are all centralized in one place. We can convert our code to define an animation by creating a new type, MyFontAnimation:

```
public class MyFontAnimation : AnimationTimeline {
  double _from = 9.0;
  double _to = 18.0;

  public double From { get { return _from; } set { _from = value; } }
  public double To { get { return _to; } set { _to = value; } }

  public MyFontAnimation() {}

  public override Type TargetPropertyType {
    get { return typeof(double); }
  }

  public override object GetCurrentValue(object defaultOriginValue,
              object defaultDestinationValue,
              AnimationClock animationClock) {
    TimeSpan? current = animationClock.CurrentTime;
    double increase = _to - _from;
    return _from +
      (increase /
      ((double)Duration.TimeSpan.Ticks /
      (double)current.Value.Ticks));
  }

  protected override Freezable CreateInstanceCore() {
    return new MyFontAnimation();
  }
}
```

This example shows that we need a few things to represent an animation: the starting value (From), the ending value (To), a fixed amount of time to move from the starting value to the end value (Duration), and a timer to help change the current value as time elapses (behind the scenes this is AnimationClock).

We can then modify our code to use this animation instead of the timer:

```
public partial class Animations : Window {
  public Animations() {
    InitializeComponent();

    MyFontAnimation animation = new MyFontAnimation();
    animation.Duration = TimeSpan.FromMilliseconds(5000);
    _button1.BeginAnimation(Button.FontSizeProperty, animation);
  }
}
```

This is our first glimpse at the animation system—specifically, the notion of the animation clock. MyFontAnimation is defining an algorithm for animating a double value, and the instance, animation, is adjusting properties associated with the animation. Another entity, AnimationClock, tracks the current state of each running animation.

The call to BeginAnimation takes as a parameter the property that we want to animate. Changing MyFontAnimation to derive from Animation-Timeline and giving it some parameters has made it a general-purpose animation for any double value. Included in WPF are predefined animations for all the common data types. The final step in implementing our animation is to remove it entirely and switch to using the built in Double-Animation type:

```
public partial class Animations : Window {
  public Animations() {
    InitializeComponent();

    DoubleAnimation animation = new DoubleAnimation();
    animation.From = 9.0;
    animation.To = 18.0;
    animation.Duration = TimeSpan.FromMilliseconds(5000);
    _button1.BeginAnimation(Button.FontSizeProperty, animation);
  }
}
```

The simple code that we wrote for MyFontAnimation lacked a lot of the features that DoubleAnimation introduces. All of the built-in animations for WPF support a common set of features[24]—one of which is the notion of animation that can be specified from the current value (we don't set the From value). With this feature we can change the code so that it omits the From value and still works correctly:

```
public partial class Animations : Window {
  public Animations() {
    InitializeComponent();

    DoubleAnimation animation = new DoubleAnimation();
    animation.To = 18.0;
    animation.Duration = TimeSpan.FromMilliseconds(5000);
    _button1.BeginAnimation(Button.FontSizeProperty, animation);
  }
}
```

Now that we've covered the basics of how animations work, we can look at how to control them. Instead of having the animation automatically start when the window is displayed, let's have it start when the mouse is over the control. To do that, instead of setting up the animation in the constructor, we'll do it in the event handler for MouseEnter:

```
public partial class Animations : Window {
  public Animations() {
    InitializeComponent();

    _button1.MouseEnter += Button1_MouseEnter;
  }

  void Button1_MouseEnter(object sender, MouseEventArgs e) {
    DoubleAnimation animation = new DoubleAnimation();
    animation.To = 18.0;
    animation.Duration = TimeSpan.FromMilliseconds(5000);
    _button1.BeginAnimation(Button.FontSizeProperty, animation);
  }
}
```

---

24. You may notice as you dig through the various types in the System.Windows.Media namespace that they sometimes have common patterns, but not common base types. To build all the strongly typed collections, animations, and other patterns, the WPF team used a code generation template. This common template (which isn't visible in the actual product) is what ensures that all animations have the same properties and methods, even though they are defined independently.

The common behavior for these rollover effects is to revert the effect if the mouse leaves the control. We could write a reverse animation that animates back to 9.0, although it would be nice if we could just have a "restore" animation. One of the benefits of not specifying the From value for the "enter" animation is that, if the initial font size in the markup was changed, the animation would still work correctly. For this scenario, animations support a mode in which we don't specify the From or To values. The assumption here is that the animation extends from the current value of the property and to the nonanimated value of the property:

```
public partial class Animations : Window {
  public Animations() {
    InitializeComponent();

    _button1.MouseEnter += Button1_MouseEnter;
    _button1.MouseLeave += Button1_MouseLeave;
  }

  void Button1_MouseEnter(object sender, MouseEventArgs e) {
    DoubleAnimation animation = new DoubleAnimation();
    animation.To = 18.0;
    animation.Duration = TimeSpan.FromMilliseconds(5000);
    _button1.BeginAnimation(Button.FontSizeProperty, animation);
  }
  void Button1_MouseLeave(object sender, MouseEventArgs e) {
    DoubleAnimation animation = new DoubleAnimation();
    animation.Duration = TimeSpan.FromMilliseconds(5000);
    _button1.BeginAnimation(Button.FontSizeProperty, animation);
  }
}
```

This is looking pretty good, but there's a problem. One of the principles of WPF is to allow for the separation of UI definition and behavior. All of this imperative code for hooking up animations is much better than the original timer-based approach, but it would be better to have more of this UI definition in the markup. A higher-level concept of animations, called storyboards, makes that possible.

Storyboards are conceptually like a movie storyboard used in Hollywood. In one location we can write all the various actions that we want, and then we yell "Action" and everything happens in order.

In our example, the enter effect is one storyboard, and the leave effect is another. To define a Storyboard instance, we must supply one or more animations, and for each animation we must specify the object and property that will be affected:

```
public partial class Animations : Window {
  Storyboard _enter;
  Storyboard _leave;

  public Animations() {
    InitializeComponent();

    DoubleAnimation animation1 = new DoubleAnimation();
    animation1.To = 18.0;
    animation1.Duration = TimeSpan.FromMilliseconds(5000);
    Storyboard.SetTargetName(animation1, _button1.Name);
    Storyboard.SetTargetProperty(animation1,
         new PropertyPath(Button.FontSizeProperty));
    _enter = new Storyboard();
    _enter.Children.Add(animation1);

    DoubleAnimation animation2 = new DoubleAnimation();
    animation2.Duration = TimeSpan.FromMilliseconds(5000);
    Storyboard.SetTargetName(animation2, _button1.Name);
    Storyboard.SetTargetProperty(animation2,
         new PropertyPath(Button.FontSizeProperty));
    _leave = new Storyboard();
    _leave.Children.Add(animation2);

    _button1.MouseEnter += Button1_MouseEnter;
    _button1.MouseLeave += Button1_MouseLeave;
  }

  void Button1_MouseEnter(object sender, MouseEventArgs e) {
    _enter.Begin(this);
  }
  void Button1_MouseLeave(object sender, MouseEventArgs e) {
    _leave.Begin(this);
  }
}
```

At this point we're very close. Now that we have a variable made up of property definitions, we can move it into the markup. Because Storyboard objects aren't controls, we need to put them in the resource section for the window. Resources will be covered in depth in Chapter 6, but for now, all we need to know is that we can specify a key to associate with the resource, and we can retrieve that resource using FindResource:

```xml
<Window x:Class='EssentialWPF.Animations'
  xmlns='http://schemas.microsoft.com/winfx/2006/xaml/presentation'
  xmlns:x='http://schemas.microsoft.com/winfx/2006/xaml'
  Title='EssentialWPF'
  >
<Window.Resources>
  <Storyboard x:Key='_enter'>
    <DoubleAnimation
      To='18.0'
      Duration='0:0:5'
      Storyboard.TargetName='_button1'
      Storyboard.TargetProperty='FontSize' />
  </Storyboard>
  <Storyboard x:Key='_leave'>
    <DoubleAnimation
      Duration='0:0:5'
      Storyboard.TargetName='_button1'
      Storyboard.TargetProperty='FontSize' />
  </Storyboard>
</Window.Resources>
<Button
  Name='_button1'
  HorizontalAlignment='Center' VerticalAlignment='Center'
  FontSize='9pt'>
  Hello World
</Button>
</Window>
```

With our animations safely defined in the markup, we can patch the code to find the resource and activate the correct Storyboard instance:

```csharp
public partial class Animations : Window {
  public Animations() {
    InitializeComponent();
    _button1.MouseEnter += Button1_MouseEnter;
    _button1.MouseLeave += Button1_MouseLeave;
  }

  void Button1_MouseEnter(object sender, MouseEventArgs e) {
    ((Storyboard)FindResource("_enter")).Begin(this);
  }
  void Button1_MouseLeave(object sender, MouseEventArgs e) {
    ((Storyboard)FindResource("_leave")).Begin(this);
  }
}
```

To review, we started with a simple timer to perform a hard-coded animation. We wrote a custom animation and then discovered that we could use the built-in `DoubleAnimation` instead. Using the features of the built-in animation, we created a simple rollover effect by creating animations that use implicit `From` and `To` values. Finally, we declared those animations in markup and used a storyboard to control them.

We have one final transition to make: The association between the event (`MouseEnter` and `MouseLeave`) and the action (starting `Storyboard`) is still locked away in the code file. If we really want the markup to declare all of the display, we need to move this last bit of information into the markup.

This final transition requires the introduction of one new concept: triggers. Triggers will be covered in depth in Chapter 7, but the concept is important enough for animations that it's worth mentioning here. **Triggers** allow us to declaratively associate an action with an event or property value.

For this example we will associate `MouseEnter` with a `BeginStoryboard` action. Instead of defining the storyboard in the window's resources section, we can put it right inside of the `BeginStoryboard` tag, to have it invoked directly. We can make the same change for `MouseLeave`:

```xml
<Window x:Class='EssentialWPF.Animations'
  xmlns='http://schemas.microsoft.com/winfx/2006/xaml/presentation'
  xmlns:x='http://schemas.microsoft.com/winfx/2006/xaml'
  Title='EssentialWPF'
  >
<Button
  Name='_button1'
  HorizontalAlignment='Center' VerticalAlignment='Center'
  FontSize='9pt'>
  <Button.Triggers>
    <EventTrigger RoutedEvent='Button.MouseEnter'>
      <EventTrigger.Actions>
        <BeginStoryboard>
          <Storyboard>
            <DoubleAnimation
              To='18.0'
              Duration='0:0:5'
              Storyboard.TargetName='_button1'
              Storyboard.TargetProperty='FontSize' />
          </Storyboard>
        </BeginStoryboard>
      </EventTrigger.Actions>
    </EventTrigger>
```

```
        <EventTrigger RoutedEvent='Button.MouseLeave'>
          <EventTrigger.Actions>
            <BeginStoryboard>
              <Storyboard>
                <DoubleAnimation
                  Duration='0:0:5'
                  Storyboard.TargetName='_button1'
                  Storyboard.TargetProperty='FontSize' />
              </Storyboard>
            </BeginStoryboard>
          </EventTrigger.Actions>
        </EventTrigger>
      </Button.Triggers>
      Hello World
    </Button>
  </Window>
```

With that, we're done. We moved from a completely code-based approach with hard-coded timers all the way to a fully declarative approach, to animation using the built-in animation system. We've seen how the animation system can be extended while still including most of the common operations. Now let's drill into some of the major concepts behind what we just saw.

Time and Timelines

The first and most critical thing to understand about animation is time. Time in the real world is simple; it started eons ago and moves forward at a constant rate. Time in animation is not so simple.

Time in animations is always relative to a timeline. **Time zero** is defined as the start of the timeline, and "30 seconds" always means 30 seconds after the timeline started. Timelines are always hierarchical, and their start and end points are defined relative to the start of the parent timeline. At the top of the timeline hierarchy is the "global" timeline that is defined as starting at the creation of the process.

To understand this relative timeline, suppose we have a double animation with a start time of 0:0:2, or 2 seconds. This animation will start 2 seconds after the storyboard containing it starts. If the animation lasts 0:0:5, it will end 7 seconds after the storyboard begins:

```
<Storyboard>
  <DoubleAnimation BeginTime="0:0:2" Duration="0:0:5" />
</Storyboard>
```

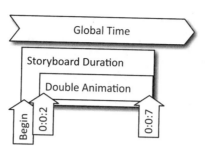

FIGURE 5.56: A time hierarchy, with a double animation starting at 2 seconds and lasting 5 seconds

Figure 5.56 illustrates this example. The duration of the storyboard isn't set in this example, so its duration will be the longest of its child timelines—in other words, 7 seconds. There is no way in WPF to declare an animation with respect to global time.

Time in WPF is measured in hours, minutes, seconds, and milliseconds. This may sound obvious, but the other common way to measure time in animation systems is by frame count. WPF automatically chooses a frame rate for each application, so on some machines (or in some scenarios) we may get 120 frames per second (fps) and on others perhaps only 12 fps. In all cases the animation's duration will be based on the real time elapsed.

The final point we should understand about time is that it is mutable. In WPF we can adjust the speed ratio on any timeline to speed up or slow down time. We can also move time forward and backward on Animation-Clock (the object that tracks the current time for a specific animation). Designer tools for creating animations often want us to manipulate time in the scene so that we can adjust property values at specific times.

Defining an Animation

With time on our side, we can move to the definition of the animation. Animation is a little like a gradient: We can define a starting point (stop at offset 0), a number of intermediate points (the rest of the stops), and what happens when we reach the end. In animation terms, we have the starting point (From), a number of intermediate points (either defined through key frames or specified by To), and what happens when the end is read (FillBehavior, RepeatBehavior, AutoReverse).

To understand how all these interact, let's define an animation for adjusting the size of an ellipse. We will need to define two animations, one for width and one for height. A From/To animation would be the simplest way to animate these two. In this example we want to animate an ellipse with the name _target:

```
<Storyboard>
  <DoubleAnimation
    From='5' To='45'
    Duration='0:0:12'
    Storyboard.TargetName='_target'
    Storyboard.TargetProperty='Width' />
  <DoubleAnimation
    From='5' To='45'
    Duration='0:0:12'
    Storyboard.TargetName='_target'
    Storyboard.TargetProperty='Height' />
</Storyboard>
```

This animation (run through any of the mechanisms we've already discussed) runs for 12 seconds, smoothly animating the width and height of the ellipse from 5 to 45 each. When the animation completes, the ellipse is the larger size. Now let's make this animation run forever, as background. Setting RepeatBehavior on Storyboard applies to the entire animation defined by Storyboard, so the child animations will also repeat forever:

```
<Storyboard RepeatBehavior='Forever'>
  <DoubleAnimation
    From='5' To='45'
    Duration='0:0:12'
    Storyboard.TargetName='_target'
    Storyboard.TargetProperty='Width' />
  <DoubleAnimation
    From='5' To='45'
    Duration='0:0:12'
    Storyboard.TargetName='_target'
    Storyboard.TargetProperty='Height' />
</Storyboard>
```

RepeatBehavior controls how long or for how many iterations the animation repeats. Forever is a special instance of RepeatBehavior that will cause the animation to run, not surprisingly, forever. When this code runs, the animation jumps from 45 to 5 when it repeats. If AutoReverse is also

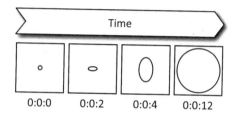

Time

0:0:0   0:0:2   0:0:4   0:0:12

FIGURE 5.57: Key frames for two animations: the width and height of an ellipse

set, Storyboard will reverse all the child animations (taking the full 12 seconds to reverse) and then repeat:

```
<Storyboard AutoReverse='True' RepeatBehavior='Forever'>
  <DoubleAnimation
    From='5' To='45'
    Duration='0:0:12'
    Storyboard.TargetName='_target'
    Storyboard.TargetProperty='Width' />
  <DoubleAnimation
    From='5' To='45'
    Duration='0:0:12'
    Storyboard.TargetName='_target'
    Storyboard.TargetProperty='Height' />
</Storyboard>
```

Now the animation is running smoothly and reversing. Let's do one more thing: define a set of key frames for the animation. Key frames allow us to specify several key points in time and the values that we'd like at those points. Instead of animating with a single speed from start to end, we can define several "mini-animations." We can change from animating the width and height at constant rates to something more like what's illustrated in Figure 5.57, where the width and height move at different rates. Instead of using the base DoubleAnimation, we can use DoubleAnimation-UsingKeyFrames, which lets us define a series of key frames:

```
<Storyboard AutoReverse='True' RepeatBehavior='Forever'>
  <DoubleAnimationUsingKeyFrames
    Storyboard.TargetName='_target'
    Storyboard.TargetProperty='Width'>
    <LinearDoubleKeyFrame KeyTime='0:0:0' Value='5' />
    <LinearDoubleKeyFrame KeyTime='0:0:2' Value='10' />
    <LinearDoubleKeyFrame KeyTime='0:0:4' Value='15' />
    <LinearDoubleKeyFrame KeyTime='0:0:12' Value='45' />
  </DoubleAnimationUsingKeyFrames>
```

```
<DoubleAnimationUsingKeyFrames
    Storyboard.TargetName='_target'
    Storyboard.TargetProperty='Height'>
    <LinearDoubleKeyFrame KeyTime='0:0:0' Value='5' />
    <LinearDoubleKeyFrame KeyTime='0:0:2' Value='5' />
    <LinearDoubleKeyFrame KeyTime='0:0:4' Value='25' />
    <LinearDoubleKeyFrame KeyTime='0:0:12' Value='45' />
</DoubleAnimationUsingKeyFrames>
</Storyboard>
```

WPF's animation system has many more features that are hinted at in the preceding illustrations. For example, in addition to `LinearDoubleKeyFrame` are several other types of key frames. Animation definitions can be extremely rich and complex; and just like good 2D graphics or 3D graphics, a good tool makes all the difference in defining a realistic animation.

In our ellipse animation, two animations are defined under a single storyboard; that is, `Storyboard` derives from not only `Timeline` but also `TimelineGroup`. The notion of composition that we've seen in the control world is also present in the animation world. Using timeline composition, we can nest and order animations to create a desired effect.

Animation Integration

Before we finish up with animation, let's briefly talk a little about integrating animation with the rest of the system. Any property of any value type can be animated, but there are a few more places where animation plugs into the system.[25]

With Control Templates

Animations are great for building media content, but probably more interesting from the view of an application developer is the ability to embed animations into controls. Imagine that we want a button whose border, when we mouse over the button, changes thickness and color (Figure 5.58). Instead of making this a hard transition or hard-coding it into the control, we can define a storyboard as part of `ControlTemplate`.

Using concepts that we've already seen, we can set the `Control-Template.Triggers` property to contain two `EventTrigger` objects. If

---

25. Although we can animate any property *type*, only properties implemented by the `DependencyProperty` system can be animated.

Default   Mouseover

FIGURE 5.58: Using animation in a template to create an interactive button

BeginStoryboard is associated with the correct storyboard, the animation will
be associated with the templated control. Also notice that we can name parts
of the visual tree in ControlTemplate and refer to them by name in
Storyboard:

```
<Button>
  <Button.Template>
    <ControlTemplate TargetType='{x:Type Button}'>
      <Border
        Name='_border'
        CornerRadius='4'
        BorderBrush='Black'
        BorderThickness='1'>
        <ContentPresenter
          HorizontalAlignment='Center'
          VerticalAlignment='Center' />
      </Border>

      <ControlTemplate.Triggers>
        <EventTrigger RoutedEvent='Button.MouseEnter'>
          <EventTrigger.Actions>
            <BeginStoryboard>
              <Storyboard>
                <ColorAnimation
                  To='Red'
                  Storyboard.TargetName='_border'
                  Storyboard.TargetProperty=
                    'BorderBrush.Color' />
                <ThicknessAnimation
                  To='5'
                  Storyboard.TargetName='_border'
                  Storyboard.TargetProperty=
                    'BorderThickness' />
              </Storyboard>
            </BeginStoryboard>
          </EventTrigger.Actions>
        </EventTrigger>
        <EventTrigger RoutedEvent='Button.MouseLeave'>
          <EventTrigger.Actions>
            <BeginStoryboard>
              <Storyboard>
                <ColorAnimation
```

```
                        Storyboard.TargetName='_border'
                        Storyboard.TargetProperty=
                          'BorderBrush.Color' />
                      <ThicknessAnimation
                        Storyboard.TargetName='_border'
                        Storyboard.TargetProperty=
                          'BorderThickness' />
                    </Storyboard>
                  </BeginStoryboard>
                </EventTrigger.Actions>
              </EventTrigger>
            </ControlTemplate.Triggers>
          </ControlTemplate>
        </Button.Template>

        Hello World
      </Button>
```

With Text

Further experimentation with animation might lead to an interesting problem: how to target individual characters in a run of text. Because of the intricacies of text layout (hyphenation, glyph shaping, etc.), text cannot be laid out character by character, so we can't simply break text up into character-sized Span elements. WPF supports character-by-character layout with the help of a text feature: TextEffects. TextEffects is a property on all text elements that allows a developer or designer to target a transform at individual characters. Each TextEffect object contains instances of Transform, PositionStart, and PositionCount, which determine the characters affected.

To see how to combine animation with text, let's write a program that will cause any text in a text block to bounce up and down. To start, we'll define the UI in markup. We could define the effects in markup also, but since we want each character to move at a different time, it's easiest to create the animations programmatically:

```
<Window x:Class='EssentialWPF.TextEffectTest'
  xmlns='http://schemas.microsoft.com/winfx/2006/xaml/presentation'
  xmlns:x='http://schemas.microsoft.com/winfx/2006/xaml'
  Title='TextEffects'
  >
  <TextBlock FontSize='72pt' Name='_text' >
    This is animated text
  </TextBlock>
</Window>
```

Next we need to build the basic structure of the program. We want to iterate over each character in the text block because we'll need to create an effect for each one:

```
public partial class TextEffectTest : Window {
  public TextEffectTest() {
    InitializeComponent();

    for (int i = 0; i < _text.Text.Length; i++) {
      ...
    }
  }
}
```

First we can build the TextEffect objects. With each effect we'll associate a start and count of the characters to affect, and we'll give it a transform that we can animate:

```
public partial class TextEffectTest : Window {
  public TextEffectTest() {
    InitializeComponent();

    _text.TextEffects = new TextEffectCollection();

    for (int i = 0; i < _text.Text.Length; i++) {
      TextEffect effect = new TextEffect();
      effect.Transform = new TranslateTransform();
      effect.PositionStart = i;
      effect.PositionCount = 1;
      _text.TextEffects.Add(effect);
    }
  }
}
```

Finally, we'll create a storyboard that targets the transforms inside of the various TextEffect objects that we've created:

```
public partial class TextEffectTest : Window {
  public TextEffectTest() {
    InitializeComponent();

    Storyboard perChar = new Storyboard();

    _text.TextEffects = new TextEffectCollection();
```

```
for (int i = 0; i < _text.Text.Length; i++) {
    TextEffect effect = new TextEffect();
    effect.Transform = new TranslateTransform();
    effect.PositionStart = i;
    effect.PositionCount = 1;
    _text.TextEffects.Add(effect);

    DoubleAnimation anim = new DoubleAnimation();
    anim.To = 5;
    anim.AccelerationRatio = .2;
    anim.DecelerationRatio = .2;
    anim.RepeatBehavior = RepeatBehavior.Forever;
    anim.AutoReverse = true;
    anim.Duration = TimeSpan.FromSeconds(2);
    anim.BeginTime = TimeSpan.FromMilliseconds(250 * i);
    Storyboard.SetTargetProperty(anim,
        new PropertyPath("TextEffects[" + i + "].Transform.Y"));
    Storyboard.SetTargetName(anim, _text.Name);

    perChar.Children.Add(anim);
}

perChar.Begin(this);
}
}
```

What we end up with is shown in Figure 5.59.

Media

When we talked about images, we had the interesting problem of defining the term *image*. For media we have the same problem. The simple definition of **media** for WPF is "a stream of timed data." With this simple definition, any animation that we've seen is technically a piece of media. For this discussion, though, let's talk about the two most common types of external

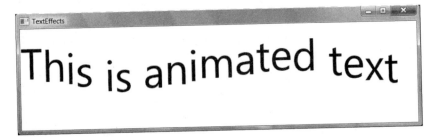

FIGURE 5.59: TextEffects allows targeting of animation to individual characters.

media: audio and video. Audio files contain many waveforms organized by time; video files contain many raster images organized by time. But how do we play these files?

Audio

Audio and video files share a common implementation: MediaTimeline. Representing a piece of media as a timeline might seem weird, but "timeline" is the abstract definition of an animation, which is the essence of any audio or video file. When we want to play a piece of media, we need MediaClock. Remember from our discussion of animation that a distinction is made between the definition of the animation (Timeline) and the state of a single run of that animation (Clock).

To play an audio file, first we need to create an instance of MediaTimeline and set the Source property to point at the media:

```
public class MediaAudio : Window {
  MediaTimeline _audioTimeline;

  public MediaAudio() {
    _audioTimeline = new MediaTimeline();
    _audioTimeline.Source =
      new Uri(@"C:\...\Beethoven's Symphony No. 9 (Scherzo).wma");
  }
}
```

We store the timeline in a member variable to make sure it isn't collected as garbage. Because video elements are typically displayed in the element tree, we don't need to worry about this for video, but for audio, it's important to hold on to the objects!

Now that we have a timeline, we need to create a clock that we can run. For normal animation, a clock is all we need; for media files, however, we also need MediaPlayer, which manages the state of the running media:

```
public class MediaAudio : Window {
  MediaTimeline _audioTimeline;
  MediaClock _audioClock;

  public MediaAudio() {
    _audioTimeline = new MediaTimeline();
    _audioTimeline.Source =
      new Uri(@"C:\...\Beethoven's Symphony No. 9 (Scherzo).wma");
```

```
    _audioClock = _audioTimeline.CreateClock();

    MediaPlayer player = new MediaPlayer();
    player.Clock = _audioClock;
  }
}
```

With our media player and clock in hand, we're ready to play some music. The object model for MediaPlayer might tempt us to call the Play method, but that would be wrong. MediaPlayer supports two modes: bound and unbound. When MediaPlayer is bound to a clock, the clock is in charge and the media player simply watches the clock. We must control the media by calling methods on the clock's controller instead of the player. In unbound mode, MediaPlayer internally tracks a clock and can be used directly (as we'll see later).

To view something in the book, let's hook the CurrentTimeInvalidated event to the clock and update the Window.Title property to indicate where we are in the music (Figure 5.60):

```
public class MediaAudio : Window {
  MediaTimeline _audioTimeline;
  MediaClock _audioClock;

  public MediaAudio() {
    _audioTimeline = new MediaTimeline();
    _audioTimeline.Source =
      new Uri(@"C:\Users\Public\Music\Sample Music\Symphony_No_3.wma");

    _audioClock = _audioTimeline.CreateClock();

    MediaPlayer player = new MediaPlayer();
    player.Clock = _audioClock;

    _audioClock.CurrentTimeInvalidated += TimeChanged;
    _audioClock.Controller.Begin();
  }
  void TimeChanged(object sender, EventArgs e) {
    Title = _audioClock.CurrentTime.ToString();
  }
}
```

These three basic objects—timeline, clock, and player—are common to any media scenario. WPF hides these details using the MediaElement wrapper type:

```
<MediaElement
    Source='C:\Users\Public\Music\Sample Music\Symphony_No_3.wma' />
```

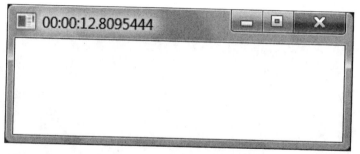

FIGURE 5.60: Music playing (You didn't think that would require a picture, did you?)

MediaElement provides access to the player through the Player property, which lets us control many of the properties of the playback. For more advanced media control (like the CurrentTimeInvalidated event), we have to create the timeline and clock in code.

Video

Playing video is as easy as using the same MediaElement that we just saw. Since MediaElement is actually a visual element (which is little odd for playing music), it can easily display video (Figure 5.61 on page 304):

```
<Window ... Title='Media Video'>
  <MediaElement
    Source='C:\Windows\Help\Windows\en-US\mouse.wmv' />
</Window>
```

Let's briefly flash back to the beginning of this chapter, where we said that one of the design principles for WPF was integration. If the Image control really is a way to display image data, which in turn is represented as a brush, which we can then use as a fill for any stroke or fill of a shape, or even the material of a 3D object, then the same should be true of video.

With VideoDrawing, we can display any video as part of any drawing. Because DrawingBrush allows us to use a drawing as the fill for anything, we can then map the video to make it the fill for the foreground of a rich text box (Figure 5.62 on page 304):

```
<!-- MediaVideo.xaml -->
<Window ... Title='Media Video'>
  <RichTextBox
    FontSize='148pt'
    FontFamily='Arial'
```

FIGURE 5.61: Playing a video using MediaElement

FIGURE 5.62: Using video as the foreground for a rich text box

```
              FontWeight='Bold'
              Background='Yellow'
              Name='_text'>
        <RichTextBox.Document>
          <FlowDocument>
            <Paragraph>
              Welcome to Video!
            </Paragraph>
          </FlowDocument>
        </RichTextBox.Document>
      </RichTextBox>
    </Window>


    // mediavideo.xaml.cs
    public partial class MediaVideo : Window {
      MediaTimeline _videoTimeline;
      MediaClock _videoClock;

      public MediaVideo() {
        InitializeComponent();

        _videoTimeline = new MediaTimeline();
        _videoTimeline.Source =
          new Uri(@"C:\Windows\Help\Windows\en-US\mouse.wmv");

        VideoDrawing v = new VideoDrawing();
        v.Player = new MediaPlayer();
        v.Rect = new Rect(0, 0, 1, 1);
        v.Player.Clock = _videoClock = _videoTimeline.CreateClock();
        _text.Foreground = new DrawingBrush(v);
      }
    }
```

WHERE ARE WE?

In this chapter we've looked at how the displays for controls are created. We've seen how applications are built out of controls, positioned by layout, and displayed using visuals. All the systems of WPF are designed to work together, building on each other.

⊓ 6 ∎
Data

WINDOWS PRESENTATION FOUNDATION differs from many UI frameworks in how it treats data. The old User32-based UI model was fairly data-agnostic. Controls contained data, and displaying something required transforming the data into something the control understood. Other frameworks, like Java's Swing library, had a strict data model that required separation between data and control. In WPF we wanted a separation between data and UI to be possible but not required.

Although WPF enables the mixing of data and UI, generally data-driven models provide more flexibility and ability to integrate the work of both developers and designers.

Data Principles

Most applications are built to display or create some type of data. Whether that data is a document, database, or drawing, applications are fundamentally about displaying, creating, and editing data. There are as many ways of representing data as there are applications. When .NET was first launched, it introduced a standard data model that significantly changed the way that frameworks handled data.

The .NET Data Model

A **data model** describes the contract between a source of data and the consumer of that data. Historically, every framework introduced a new data model: Visual Basic had DAO (Data Access Objects), RDO (Remote Data Objects), and finally ADO (ActiveX Data Objects), before moving on to .NET. With .NET, there was a significant change away from API-specific data models to using a common data model across the framework.

.NET has an object model, with classes, interfaces, structs, enums, delegates, and so on. Beyond that, though, .NET introduced a very basic data model. Lists in .NET are represented by `System.Collection` interfaces: `IEnumerable` and `IList`. Properties are defined either with the built-in CLR properties or by the implementation of `ICustomTypeDescriptor`. This basic data model has remained constant even as new data access technologies have come about, and even through major new language changes like the language-integrated query that is being discussed for the next major release of .NET.

.NET also included several concrete ways of dealing with data: ADO.NET (`System.Data` namespace), XML (`System.Xml` namespace), data contract (`System.Runtime.Serialization` namespace), and markup (`System.Windows.Markup` namespace), to name a few. The important thing is that all of these are built on the basic .NET data model.

Because all of WPF's data operations are based on the fundamental .NET data model, WPF controls can retrieve data from any CLR object:

```
ListBox listBox1 = new ListBox();
listBox1.ItemsSource = new string[] { "Hello", "World" };
```

Namita Gupta, a program manager on the WPF team, used a great phrase to describe this functionality: "Your data, your way." As long as data can be accessed through the CLR, it can be visualized in WPF.

Pervasive Binding

Of all the major innovations in WPF, probably the most significant to the programming experience is the complete integration of binding throughout the system. Control templates utilize template bindings, resources are loaded via resource bindings, and even the base model for controls like `Button` and `ListBox` are based on the "content model," which leverages data binding heavily. The notion of binding properties to data sources, tracking dependencies, and automatically updating the display is inherent in every part of WPF.

Binding in WPF goes by many names. Normally the reason we chose to use a different name was that the flavor of binding had a limitation or behavior that was very specific to the scenario. For example, template bindings use the {TemplateBinding} markup instead of the standard {Binding} notation for data binding. Template bindings work only in the context of a template, and they can bind only to properties of the templated control. This limitation makes template bindings very efficient—a specialization that was necessary because so many controls are bound to templates in WPF.

Binding provides the ability to synchronize two pieces of data. In WPF, that means binding a data item (i.e., a property of a data source) to a property on a UI element. Binding works great as a way to keep two objects in sync, but it begins to have problems when the data types of these objects don't match up perfectly. To make binding truly pervasive in the framework, it was necessary to provide ways to transform data.

Data Transformation

In a framework with pervasive binding, accessing any data is possible only if that data can be transformed anywhere that binding is supported.[1]

WPF supports two main types of transformation: value conversion and data templates. Value converters are just as advertised: They convert values from one format to another (e.g., converting the string value "Red" into Brushes.Red). This is a powerful capability because the converter can take either representation and convert it (a two-way transformation of data). Data templates, on the other hand, allow for controls to be created on the fly to represent data (this is similar in concept to the XSLT, or Extensible Stylesheet Language Transformations, model). In the data template model, the controls have access back to the data model through bindings, which allow for read and (potentially write) access back to the source of the data.

---

1. The only case in which the WPF development team decided not to support transformation with a binding was resources. The rationale for this decision was that resources are defined in the domain of the presentation, so there is no need for further transformation.

Transformations allow any data to be transformed into a compelling display. To start the tour of data in WPF, we can begin with one of the more common data sources: resources.

Resources

Generally the first place that people encounter the separation of display and data is with the use of resources. Every element has a Resources property, which is a simple dictionary.[2] Resources provide a simple hierarchy lookup of a value via a key. Theming, styling, and data binding all leverage this simple technique.

When writing code in C#, we can easily define a variable for later use. Often we do this for code readability; sometimes we do it for sharing:

```
public class Window1 : Window {
  public Window1() {
    Title = "Resources";

    Brush toShare = new SolidColorBrush(Colors.Yellow);

    Button b = new Button();
    b.Content = "My Button";
    b.Background = toShare;

    Content = b;
  }
}
```

In markup this is a harder problem. The XAML model for parsing requires that all created objects be set as properties of something else. If we wanted to create a brush and share it with two buttons, we would have to create some type of control to control binding, which seemed like a big leap just to create a variable. Instead, the WPF team created a common property—Resources—which can hold a list of objects with a name. These variables can then be used by any child element. Here we

---

2. Specifically, anything deriving from FrameworkElement, FrameworkContentElement, or Application has a Resources property.

FIGURE 6.1: Overriding resources in the element hierarchy

define a brush in the window's Resources property, and use it in the button:

```
<Window
  Text='Resources'
  xmlns='http://schemas.microsoft.com/winfx/2006/xaml/presentation'
  xmlns:x='http://schemas.microsoft.com/winfx/2006/xaml'>
  <Window.Resources>
    <SolidColorBrush x:Key='toShare'>Yellow</SolidColorBrush>
  </Window.Resources>

  <Button Background='{StaticResource toShare}' >
    My Button
  </Button>
</Window>
```

With element composition, we wanted this lookup to be hierarchical. If an element's direct parent doesn't contain a variable, then the next parent up is used, and so on.

In this example we will override a resource at multiple levels of the element tree. First we define the value toShare at the root Window element, just like before. Then we can override the resource at the nested Stack-Panel object by creating a resource with the name toShare. The various buttons will all reference toShare and will get the correct value according to their location in the tree (Figure 6.1):

```xml
<Window
  x:Class='EssentialWPF.Resources'
  Title='Resources'
  Visibility='Visible'
  xmlns='http://schemas.microsoft.com/winfx/2006/xaml/presentation'
  xmlns:x='http://schemas.microsoft.com/winfx/2006/xaml'>

  <Window.Resources>
    <SolidColorBrush x:Key='toShare'>Yellow</SolidColorBrush>
  </Window.Resources>

  <StackPanel Margin='10'>
    <Button Background='{StaticResource toShare}'>
      Level 1
    </Button>
    <StackPanel Margin='10'>
      <StackPanel.Resources>
        <LinearGradientBrush x:Key='toShare' ...>
          <GradientStop Offset='0' Color='sc# 1,1,1,1' />
          <GradientStop Offset='1' Color='sc# 1,.6,.6,.6' />
        </LinearGradientBrush>
      </StackPanel.Resources>
      <Button Background='{StaticResource toShare}'>
        Level 2
      </Button>
    </StackPanel>

    <Button Background='{StaticResource toShare}'>
      Level 1
    </Button>

  </StackPanel>
</Window>
```

The lookup path for resources is slightly more complicated than just the element hierarchy. The process also looks at the application object, system theme, and default theme for types. The order is

1. Element hierarchy
2. Application.Resources
3. Type theme
4. System theme

Themes will be covered in more detail in Chapter 8, but the important thing to note here is that resource references can get data from many locations. For an application author, the ability to define resources at the application level is probably the most interesting aspect to this functionality.

In Chapter 2 we learned about the `Application` object. The `Application` object also has a `Resources` property that lets us define resources global to the application:

```
<Application x:Class='EssentialWPF.MyApp'
  xmlns='http://schemas.microsoft.com/winfx/2006/xaml/presentation'
  xmlns:x='http://schemas.microsoft.com/winfx/2006/xaml'
  >
  <Application.Resources>
    <SolidColorBrush x:Key='toShare'>Purple</SolidColorBrush>
  </Application.Resources>
</Application>
```

This technique allows us to share resources among pages, windows, and controls. At any level in the application we can override the default value of the resource, as we saw earlier. In general, it is best to define resources in the lowest level of scoping: If a resource will be used only within a single panel, it should be defined at that panel. If the resource will be used in several windows, it should be defined at the application level.

When we define a resource, it is important to remember that it may be used in more than one location. Because elements in WPF can appear in only one location in the tree, we cannot reliably use an element as a resource:

```
<Window
  x:Class='EssentialWPF.Resources'
  Title='Resources'
  xmlns='http://schemas.microsoft.com/winfx/2006/xaml/presentation'
  xmlns:x='http://schemas.microsoft.com/winfx/2006/xaml'>

  <Window.Resources>
    <TextBox x:Key='sharedTextBox' />
  </Window.Resources>

  <Button Content='{StaticResource sharedTextBox}'/>
</Window>
```

This markup will work fine, provided that `sharedTextBox` is referenced only once. If we try to use the resource a second time, the application will fail at runtime:

```
<Window
  x:Class='EssentialWPF.Resources'
  Title='Resources'
  xmlns='http://schemas.microsoft.com/winfx/2006/xaml/presentation'
  xmlns:x='http://schemas.microsoft.com/winfx/2006/xaml'>
```

```
<Window.Resources>
  <TextBox x:Key='sharedTextBox' />
</Window.Resources>

<StackPanel>
  <!-- this will fail! -->
  <Button Content='{StaticResource sharedTextBox}'/>
  <Button Content='{StaticResource sharedTextBox}'/>
</StackPanel>
</Window>
```

In Chapter 3 we learned about the fix for cases in which a resource needs to be used more than once: FrameworkElementFactory. For elements in control templates, we create a factory instead of creating the elements directly. Most visual objects (brushes, pens, meshes, etc.) don't require a factory, because they support multiuse by virtue of deriving from Freezable.[3]

You may be asking yourself, "Why are we talking about resources in a chapter about data binding?" When using static resource references, we are effectively performing a variable assignment, just as in the first C# example we saw. Once a variable is used, there is no connection to the original variable. Consider the following C#:

```
Brush someBrush = Brushes.Red;
Button button1 = new Button();
button1.Background = someBrush;
someBrush = Brushes.Yellow;
// button1.Background would be red here
```

When using resources, we can either perform this static assignment style of binding, or create a dynamic binding:

```
<Window
  Title='Resources'
  xmlns='http://schemas.microsoft.com/winfx/2006/xaml/presentation'
  xmlns:x='http://schemas.microsoft.com/winfx/2006/xaml'>
  <Window.Resources>
    <SolidColorBrush x:Key='toShare'>Yellow</SolidColorBrush>
  </Window.Resources>
```

---

3. Freezable objects support sharing by having a "frozen" mode, in which they cannot be changed. The frozen mode allows for a single instance to be used by multiple objects, without consumers having to watch for changes in the object.

```
<Button Background='{DynamicResource toShare}' >
    My Button
    </Button>
</Window>
```

Because we used a dynamic resource binding this time, we can update the color of the button by modifying the window's `Resources` property:

```
<!-- window1.xaml -->
...
    <Button Background='{DynamicResource toShare}' Click='Clicked'>
    My Button
    </Button>
...


// window1.xaml.cs
...
void Clicked(object sender, RoutedEventArgs e) {
  Brush newBrush = new SolidColorBrush(Colors.Blue);
  this.Resources["toShare"] = newBrush;
}
...
```

This functionality is very powerful. Combined with the hierarchical scoping of resources, it can be used to cause updates across all the windows or pages in an application. To perform a dynamic resource binding in code, we use the `FrameworkElement.SetResourceReference` API:

```
button1.SetResourceReference(
    Button.BackgroundProperty,
    "toShare");
```

Using dynamic resource references does introduce some performance overhead because the system must track changes in the resources. In building the resource model, the design goal was to create something that the system could use broadly for resource discovery, without introducing a large performance overhead. For this reason, resources are optimized for coarse-grained changes.

When any resource is changed, the entire tree is updated. Therefore, static and dynamic resource references can be used in many places without a cost per reference being incurred. What this means is that we should not make frequent changes of resources to update the UI. It also means that we should not worry about using lots of resource references.

Resources are a specialized form of data binding, optimized for a high number of bindings with low update frequency. Generally, data binding is optimized for a moderate number of bindings with high update frequency (including two-way binding). This more general type of data binding got the simple name; it is called just *binding* in WPF.

Binding Basics

Binding is simply keeping two data points in sync with each other. **Data point** is an abstract concept, the idea of a single "node" of data. A data point can be described in a variety of ways; generally it is a data source and query. For example, a property data point would be an object and a property name. The property name determines the property on the source object from which data should be retrieved.

In WPF the Binding class represents a data point. To construct a binding, we provide it a source (the data source) and path (the query). In this case we can create a data point that references the Text property of a TextBox object:

```
Binding bind = new Binding();
bind.Source = textBox1;
bind.Path = new PropertyPath("Text");
```

We need a second data point to keep in sync with this first one. Because WPF binding is limited to binding data only to and from the element tree, we must use the SetBinding method to define one of the data points. We call SetBinding on the data source, and we bind the data to the query[4] (ContentControl.ContentProperty in this example):

```
contentControl1.SetBinding(ContentControl.Content, bind);
```

This example will bind the Text property from textBox1 to the Content property on contentControl1. We could write exactly the same code using XAML (Figure 6.2):

---

4. Be very careful that the dependency property you're passing is defined on the same type as the object from which SetBinding is called. For example, if you call SetBinding with TextBlock.TextProperty instead of TextBox.TextProperty when binding against Text-Box, your code will compile and run just fine, except that the binding will not work.

```
<Window ... Title='EssentialWPF'>
  <StackPanel>
    <TextBox x:Name='textBox1' />
    <ContentControl Margin='5' x:Name='contentControl1'
      Content='{Binding ElementName=textBox1,Path=Text}' />
  </StackPanel>
</Window>
```

Bindings declared in markup can use the ElementName property to specify the source of the binding.

Given all that we learned about content controls in Chapter 3, it should come as no surprise that we can use data binding to bind the Text property (which is a string) from TextBox to the Content property (which is an object). What might be surprising is that we can bind the Text property to something completely different, like the FontFamily property (which is not a string):

```
<Window ... Title='EssentialWPF' >
  <StackPanel>
    <TextBox x:Name='textBox1' />
    <TextBox x:Name='textBox2' />
    <ContentControl
      Margin='5'
      Content='{Binding ElementName=textBox1,Path=Text}'
      FontFamily='{Binding ElementName=textBox2,Path=Text}'
      />
  </StackPanel>
</Window>
```

FIGURE 6.2: Binding from TextBox to ContentControl

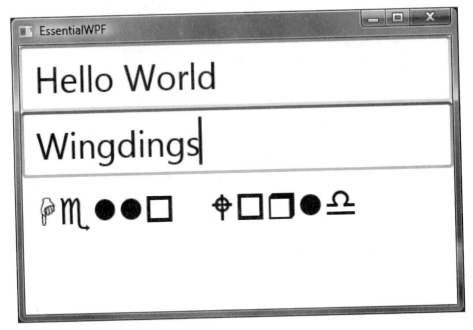

FIGURE 6.3: Binding TextBox to FontFamily

Figure 6.3 shows that the value is being transformed from a string into an instance of FontFamily. There are two base mechanisms for value conversion: TypeConverter, which is a base mechanism that has been in .NET since version 1.0; and the new IValueConverter. In the case of FontFamily, TypeConverter is associated with the FontFamily type, which makes the transformation occur automatically.

We can use value converters associated with a binding to perform any value transformation that we want (Figure 6.4). In this case we will take the source (a string from the Text property) and convert it into a custom object, which we'll use in the destination (the Content property).

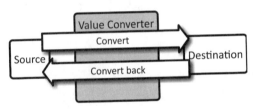

FIGURE 6.4: The conceptual model of binding using a value converter

We will start by creating a small custom type:

```
public class Human {
  private string _name;

public string Name {
    get { return _name; }
    set { _name = value; }
  }
}
```

This could really be any type—a built-in type, a custom type, anything. The idea is that we want to convert the Text property into a particular type. To write the converter, we derive from IValueConverter and implement the two methods:

```
public class HumanConverter : IValueConverter {
  public object Convert(object value, Type targetType,
                        object parameter, CultureInfo culture) {
    Human h = new Human();
    h.Name = (string)value;
    return h;
  }

  public object ConvertBack(object value, Type targetType,
                            object parameter, CultureInfo culture) {
    return ((Human)value).Name;
  }
}
```

In more complex examples it may not be possible to implement both directions of transformation. The final step for using the value converter is wiring it up to the binding:

```
<ContentControl
  Margin='5'
  FontFamily='{Binding ElementName=textBox2,Path=Text}'>
  <ContentControl.Content>
    <Binding
      ElementName='textBox1'
      Path='Text'>
      <Binding.Converter>
        <l:HumanConverter xmlns:l='clr-namespace:EssentialWPF' />
      </Binding.Converter>
    </Binding>

</ContentControl.Content>
</ContentControl>
```

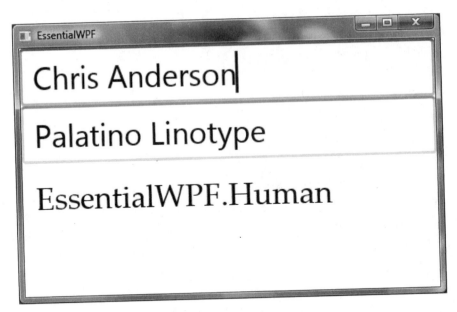

FIGURE 6.5: Binding using a value converter

Value transformation is one part of the story, but in this example (shown in Figure 6.5), it would be nice to generate a complete display for our custom type. In Chapter 3 we saw that content controls support many ways of visualizing data. The most powerful of these is to use a data template to define a transformation from a piece of data into a display tree.

Data templates take a piece of data (described by the DataType property) and build a display tree. Within that display tree, we can bind to parts of the piece of data. In this case we will build a simple template for our Human type and bind data to the Name property:

```
<DataTemplate
  xmlns:l='clr-namespace:EssentialWPF'
  DataType='{x:Type l:Human}'>

  <Border Margin='5' Padding='5' BorderBrush='Black'
    BorderThickness='3' CornerRadius='5'>
    <TextBlock Text='{Binding Path=Name}' />
  </Border>
</DataTemplate>
```

We can associate this template with ContentControl in a variety of ways (via resources, for example). Here we'll set it directly on the Content-Template property (Figure 6.6):

```
<ContentControl
  Margin='5'
  FontFamily='{Binding ElementName=textBox2,Path=Text}'>
  <ContentControl.Content>
    <Binding ... />
  </ContentControl.Content>
  <ContentControl.ContentTemplate>
    <DataTemplate
      xmlns:l='clr-namespace:EssentialWPF'
      DataType='{x:Type l:Human}'>
      ...
    </DataTemplate>
  </ContentControl.ContentTemplate>
</ContentControl>
```

A close look at the data template we built reveals that no data source is specified for our binding:

```
<TextBlock Text='{Binding Path=Name}' />
```

This is possible because WPF allows an ambient data context to be associated with elements. With data templates, the data context is automatically

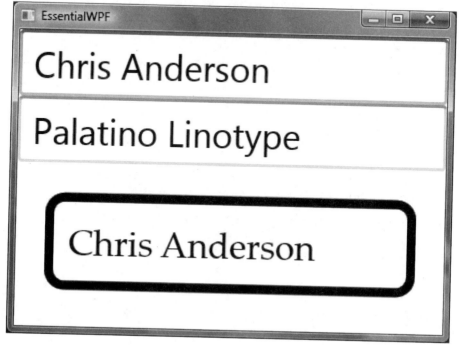

FIGURE 6.6: Binding with a data template

set to be the data that the template is transforming. We can explicitly set the
`DataContext` property on any element, and that data source will be used for
any bindings on that element (or its children).

Data points and transformation are the two fundamental constructs of
binding. Now that we've seen all the basic ingredients of data, we can drill
into the details of binding against CLR objects, XML, and then into the
depths of the data template system.

Binding to CLR Objects

As we have seen, we bind data to CLR objects via properties and lists (the
latter defined as any type implementing `IEnumerable`).

Binding establishes a relationship between a source and a target. In
the case of object binding, the selected item for the source is determined
by a property path, which is a series of named properties or indexes sep-
arated by dots. I choose my words very carefully here: Initially the property path associated with binding can often be confused with C# syntax
because in the basic form it is very similar. The syntax for the binding
property path is the same syntax that we saw in the discussion of storyboards in Chapter 5, and we'll see more of it in Chapter 8 when we talk
about styles.

The property name identifier for object binding has two forms: one for
simple CLR properties and another for WPF's `DependencyProperty`-based
properties. To understand the difference between these two models, let's
start with a simple example:

```
<Window
  xmlns='http://schemas.microsoft.com/winfx/2006/xaml/presentation'
  xmlns:x='http://schemas.microsoft.com/winfx/2006/xaml'
  >
  <StackPanel>
    <TextBox Name='text1'>Hello</TextBox>
    <TextBox Text='{Binding ElementName=text1, Path=Text}' />
  </StackPanel>
</Window>
```

Here we bind the `Text` property of one `TextBox` object to the `Text` property of another. We saw a very similar example earlier. Because `Text` is a
dependency property, this first example is the same as the following:

```
<Window
  xmlns='http://schemas.microsoft.com/winfx/2006/xaml/presentation'
  xmlns:x='http://schemas.microsoft.com/winfx/2006/xaml'
  >
  <StackPanel>
    <TextBox Name='text1'>Hello</TextBox>
    <TextBox Text='{Binding ElementName=text1, Path=(TextBox.Text)}' />
  </StackPanel>
</Window>
```

In this second case we are using the "class-qualified" form of property identifier. Behaviorally, these examples will produce the same effect, but the second will avoid using CLR reflection to resolve the name "Text" in the binding expression. This optimization is useful for two reasons: first, to avoid the performance impact of using reflection; and second, to enable binding to attached properties.[5]

To gain a better understanding of how the property path works, we can use a slightly more complex object. In this case we will define a Person object that has complex Address and Name values (Figure 6.7 on page 324).

These three classes—Person, Name, and Address—provide a small amount of object model but demonstrate a number of interesting challenges with binding. First let's create a small display for a person (Figure 6.8 on page 325):

```
<!-- Window1.xaml -->
<Window ... Title='Object Binding'>
  <StackPanel>
    <ContentControl Content='{Binding Path=Name}' />
    <TextBlock Text='{Binding Path=Addresses[0].AddressName}' />
    <TextBlock Text='{Binding Path=Addresses[0].Street1}' />
    <TextBlock Text='{Binding Path=Addresses[0].City}' />
    <TextBlock Text='{Binding Path=Addresses[0].State}' />
    <TextBlock Text='{Binding Path=Addresses[0].Zip}' />
  </StackPanel>
</Window>

// Window1.xaml.cs
public partial class Window1 : Window {
  public Window1(){
    InitializeComponent();
```

---

5. For example, if we wanted to bind to the Grid.Row property from a TextBox object, we would say, <SomeControl SomeProperty='{Binding ElementName=text1, Path=(Grid.Row)}' />.

```
DataContext = new Person(
  new Name(
    "Chris",
    "Anderson"),
  new Address(
    "Work",
    "One Microsoft Way",
    "Redmond",
    "WA",
    "98053"));
  }
}
```

This example illustrates simple property binding (Path=Name) and more complex paths (Path=Addresses[0].AddressName). Using square

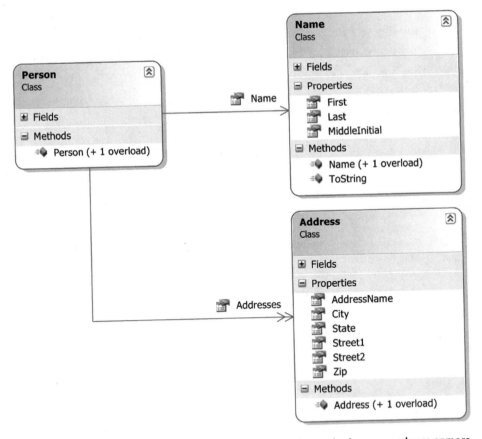

FIGURE 6.7: The object model of a Person object. Person has a single name and zero or more addresses.

FIGURE 6.8: Complex binding paths

brackets—[and]—allows us to access items in a collection. Notice also that we can compose an arbitrarily complex path by combining property and list accessors.

We bind to a list in the same way that we bind to a property. The property path needs to result in an object that supports IEnumerable, but otherwise the process is identical to property binding. We could replace displaying a single address by adding a list box to the display and binding to ItemsSource (of course, we could then define a data template for address type):

```
<ListBox
    ItemsSource='{Binding Path=Addresses}' />
```

Up to now we have focused on the display of data. If a property to which we bind has a setter, then two-way binding is possible.

Editing

To edit values, we must have a way to know when the value has been updated. In addition to supporting a property setter, several interfaces allow an object or list to broadcast change notifications. It is important for data sources to provide change notification (i.e., a signal that their values have changed) to allow the binding system to respond when the data is modified. To enable our `Person` object model to support change notification, we have three options: (1) implement `INotifyPropertyChanged`, (2) add events that report changes to properties, or (3) create `Dependency-Property`-based properties.

The pattern of using events to report property changes was first introduced in .NET 1.0, and it is supported by Windows Forms and ASP.NET data binding. `INotifyPropertyChanged` was introduced in .NET 2.0. This interface is optimized for data-binding scenarios; it has better performance characteristics and is easy for the object author and data-binding system to use. However, `INotifyPropertyChanged` is somewhat harder for normal change notification scenarios.

Using a `DependencyProperty`-based property is relatively straightforward, and it allows the object to benefit from having sparse storage and plug into other services in WPF (dynamic resource binding and styling, for example). Creating objects with `DependencyProperty`-based properties is covered in detail in the appendix.

In the end, all three techniques provide the same runtime behavior. Generally, when creating data models we should implement `INotify-PropertyChanged`. Using `DependencyProperty`-based properties adds the requirement of deriving from `DependencyObject`, which in turn ties the data object to an STA thread. Events for reporting property changes bloat the object model and generally should be implemented only for the properties that developers would commonly listen to:

```
public class Name : INotifyPropertyChanged {
  ...
  public string First {
    get {
      return _first;
    }
    set {
      _first = value;
      NotifyChanged("First");
    }
  }
}
  ...

  public event PropertyChangedEventHandler PropertyChanged;
  void NotifyChanged(string property) {
```

```
      if (PropertyChanged != null) {
        PropertyChanged(this,
          new PropertyChangedEventArgs(property));
      }
    }
  }
```

Once we apply the same pattern to each of the three data objects, we can update the UI to leverage the newly updatable objects. We can use two read-only text fields (TextBlock) to display the current name, and two TextBox objects to edit the values. Because Name supports INotifyPropertyChanged, when the values are updated the binding system will be notified, causing it to update the TextBlock objects (Figure 6.9 on page 328):

```
<Window ... Text='Object Binding'>
  <StackPanel>
    <TextBlock Text='{Binding Path=Name.First}' />
    <TextBlock Text='{Binding Path=Name.Last}' />
    <Grid>
      <Grid.RowDefinitions>
        <RowDefinition />
        <RowDefinition />
      </Grid.RowDefinitions>
      <Grid.ColumnDefinitions>
        <ColumnDefinition />
        <ColumnDefinition />
      </Grid.ColumnDefinitions>
      <Label Grid.Row='0' Grid.Column='0'>First</Label>
      <TextBox Grid.Row='0' Grid.Column='1'
        Text='{Binding Path=Name.First}' />
      <Label Grid.Row='1' Grid.Column='0'>Last</Label>
      <TextBox Grid.Row='1' Grid.Column='1'
        Text='{Binding Path=Name.Last}' />
    </Grid>
  </StackPanel>
</Window>
```

Typing in either text box updates the appropriate display. Notice that we have to tab out of the text box to see the update. By default, TextBox updates the data when it loses keyboard focus. To change this setting, we can specify that the binding should update whenever the property changes value, using the UpdateSourceTrigger property on the binding:

```
<TextBox Grid.Row='1' Grid.Column='1'
  Text='{Binding Path=Name.Last,UpdateSourceTrigger=PropertyChanged}' />
```

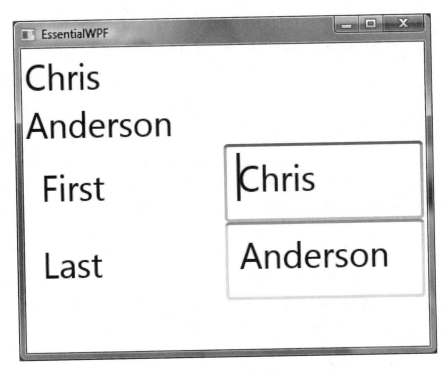

FIGURE 6.9: Editing an object using two-way data binding

Lists are more complicated than just property changes. For efficient bind-ing we need to know when items are added or removed to the list. For this pur-pose WPF has INotifyCollectionChanged. INotifyCollectionChanged offers a single event, CollectionChanged, which has the following event arguments:

```
public class NotifyCollectionChangedEventArgs : EventArgs {
  public NotifyCollectionChangedAction Action { get; }
  public IList NewItems { get; }
  public int NewStartingIndex { get; }
  public IList OldItems { get; }
  public int OldStartingIndex { get; }
}
public enum NotifyCollectionChangedAction {
  Add,
  Remove,
  Replace,
  Move,
  Reset,
}
```

In this sample object model, we might want to support the dynamic addition and removal of addresses from a person's record. The simplest way to accomplish this is to use `ObservableCollection<T>`, which derives from the common `Collection<T>` class and adds support for `INotify-CollectionChanged`:

```
public class Person : INotifyPropertyChanged
{
  IList<Address> _addresses = new ObservableCollection<Address>();
  ...
}
```

We can then modify our little application to display all the addresses in a list box, and provide some UI for creating new addresses and adding them to the list:

```xml
<!-- window1.xaml -->
<Window ... Text='Object Binding'>
  <StackPanel>
    <StackPanel.Resources>

  <!-- template for displaying the list of addresses -->
      <DataTemplate x:Key='addressTemplate'>
        <StackPanel Orientation='Horizontal'>
          <TextBlock Text='{Binding Path=Street1}' />
          <TextBlock Text=',' />
          <TextBlock Text='{Binding Path=City}' />
          <TextBlock Text=',' />
          <TextBlock Text='{Binding Path=State}' />
          <TextBlock Text=',' />
          <TextBlock Text='{Binding Path=Zip}' />
        </StackPanel>
      </DataTemplate>
    </StackPanel.Resources>

  <!-- name of person -->
    <TextBlock Text='{Binding Path=Name.First}' />
    <TextBlock Text='{Binding Path=Name.Last}' />

  <!-- list of addresses -->
    <TextBlock Margin='5' FontSize='14pt'>Addresses:</TextBlock>
    <ListBox ItemsSource='{Binding Path=Addresses}'
      ItemTemplate='{DynamicResource addressTemplate}' />

  <!-- add new address UI -->
    <TextBlock Margin='5' FontSize='14pt'>Add New Address:</TextBlock>
    <Grid Margin='5'>
      <Grid.RowDefinitions>
        <RowDefinition />
        <RowDefinition />
        <RowDefinition />
```

```
          <RowDefinition />
          <RowDefinition />
      </Grid.RowDefinitions>
      <Grid.ColumnDefinitions>
        <ColumnDefinition Width='Auto' />
        <ColumnDefinition Width='*' />
      </Grid.ColumnDefinitions>

      <Label Grid.Row='0' Grid.Column='0'>Street</Label>
      <TextBox  Grid.Row='0' Grid.Column='1' Name='_street' />
      <Label Grid.Row='1' Grid.Column='0'>City</Label>
      <TextBox  Grid.Row='1' Grid.Column='1' Name='_city' />
      <Label Grid.Row='2' Grid.Column='0'>State</Label>
      <TextBox  Grid.Row='2' Grid.Column='1' Name='_state' />
      <Label Grid.Row='3' Grid.Column='0'>Zip</Label>
      <TextBox  Grid.Row='3' Grid.Column='1' Name='_zip' />
      <Button Click='Add' Grid.Row='4'>Add</Button>
    </Grid>
  </StackPanel>
</Window>

// window1.xaml.cs
void Add(object sender, RoutedEventArgs e) {
  Address a = new Address();
  a.Street1 = _street.Text;
  a.City = _city.Text;
  a.State = _state.Text;
  a.Zip = _zip.Text;
  ((Person)DataContext).Addresses.Add(a);
}
```

Running this example yields something like Figure 6.10.

New information can be typed into the text boxes, and pressing **Add** will update the list of addresses. Because the Addresses property implements INotifyCollectionChanged, the data-binding engine is notified of the additional item and updates the UI correctly.

Binding to CLR objects is mostly automatic. By adding support for INotifyPropertyChanged and INotifyCollectionChanged, we can create richer data sources. WPF binding also has built-in support for binding to XML.[6]

---

6. For the more adventurous, it is possible to use ICustomTypeDescriptor to enable WPF binding to work against any specialty object model. In combination with the .NET 2.0 Type-DescriptorProvider feature, existing specialty object models can work seamlessly with WPF binding. Implementing ICustomTypeDescriptor is, alas, beyond the scope of this book.

FIGURE 6.10: Editing a list using two-way binding

Binding to XML

WPF's XML support is rooted in the Document Object Model (DOM) provided in the System.Xml namespace. We can bind to part of an XML document using any XmlDocument, XmlElement, or XmlNode object as the source. Properties can be bound only to an attribute or to the content of an element; lists can be bound to any set of elements.

XPath 101

If you aren't familiar with XPath, it's worth spending a few minutes to become familiar with the syntax because WPF's binding relies heavily on it. Effectively, XPath is a query language for filtering a subsection of an XML document. We can filter down to a set of elements, a single element, or even a single attribute on an element.

The first and most common operator in XPath is the/operator. This operator allows us to build a path to the element that we want. Let's consider the following XML document:

```
<Media>
    <Book Author='John' Title='Fish are my friends' />
    <Book Author='Dave' Title='Fish are my enemies' />
    <Book Author='Jane' Title='Fish are my food' />
    <CD Artist='Jane' Title='Fish sing well' />
    <DVD Director='John' Title='Fish: The Movie'>
        <Actor>Jane</Actor>
        <Actor>Dave</Actor>
    </DVD>
</Media>
```

Using the/operator, we can build a path to any element. To select the CD element, we would use Media/CD as the path. By default, any text name in the path refers to the local name of elements. For complex XML documents, we need to include the XML namespace, but for this basic tutorial we'll stick with basic documents. XPath's Media/CD actually says, "Select all the elements with the element name 'CD' that are direct children of any elements named 'Media'." To see this more clearly, let's look at what is generated when Media/Book is selected:

```
<Book Author='John' Title='Fish are my friends' />
<Book Author='Dave' Title='Fish are my enemies' />
<Book Author='Jane' Title='Fish are my food' />
```

All the Book elements were selected. The idea that XPath can produce either a list of nodes or a single node is very important as we progress into XML binding.

In XML, elements and attributes are both considered XML nodes. XPath actually works by selecting nodes, not just elements. To refer to an attribute name instead of an element name, we use the @ operator. So the XPath Media/DVD/@Title will return "Fish: The Movie". Again, just as with element name selection, we can get a list of attributes. If we use Media/Book/@Title, we will get the following:

```
Title='Fish are my friends'
Title='Fish are my enemies'
Title='Fish are my food'
```

The data type of each node returned in this case is `XmlAttributeNode` (which will be important a little farther down the line). Using the XPath operator *, we can get any named nodes (attributes or elements).

The final basic XPath concept is the [ ] operator. With this operator we can select a node either by position or by attribute. All the concepts we've learned so far apply, but now we can qualify any name. Note that XPath indexes are one-based, not zero-based like CLR collections. The simplest usage is by position—for example, `Media/Book[1]`:

```
<Book Author='John' Title='Fish are my friends' />
```

The other common usage is to select by attribute—for example, `Media/Book[@Author = "Jane"]`:

```
<Book Author='Jane' Title='Fish are my food' />
```

Of course, we can combine all of these to create complex queries across heterogeneous data. `*/*[@Title = "Fish: The Movie"]` will pick any element with the appropriate title—in this case, the DVD. Table 6.1 (on page 334) lists the common XPath queries and provides examples from our sample document.

XML Binding

Now that we understand the basics of XPath, we can return to XML binding. We can begin by binding to the same XML document as earlier. We'll start without using any real "binding" to speak of (Figure 6.11 on page 335):

```
public class Window1 : Window {
  public Window1() {
    XmlDocument doc = new XmlDocument();
    doc.LoadXml(@"
<Media xmlns=''>
  <Book Author='John' Title='Fish are my friends' />
  <Book Author='Dave' Title='Fish are my enemies' />
  <Book Author='Jane' Title='Fish are my food' />
  <CD Artist='Jane' Title='Fish sing well' />
  <DVD Director='John' Title='Fish: The Movie'>
    <Actor>Jane</Actor>
    <Actor>Dave</Actor>
  </DVD>
</Media>");
    ListBox list = new ListBox();
    list.ItemsSource = doc.SelectNodes("/Media/Book/@Title");
    Title = "XML Binding";
    Content = list;
  }
}
```

TABLE 6.1: Results of Using Various XPath Queries against an XML Document

XPath	Description	Example	Results
/	Selects from the root	/	``` <Media xmlns=""> <Book Author="John" Title="Fish are my friends" /> <Book Author="Dave" Title="Fish are my enemies" /> <Book Author="Jane" Title="Fish are my food" /> <CD Artist="Jane" Title="Fish sing well" /> <DVD Director="John" Title="Fish: The Movie"> <Actor>Jane</Actor> <Actor>Dave</Actor> </DVD> </Media> ```
//NAME	Matches the tag NAME in any descendant	//Book	``` <Book Author="John" Title="Fish are my friends" /> <Book Author="Dave" Title="Fish are my enemies" /> <Book Author="Jane" Title="Fish are my food" /> ```
@NAME	Matches the attribute NAME	//Book/@Author	``` Author="John" Author="Dave" Author="Jane" ```
*	Matches any tag	//*/@Author	``` Author="John" Author="Dave" Author="Jane" ```
@*	Matches any attribute	//Book/@*	``` Author="John" Title="Fish are my friends" Author="Dave" Title="Fish are my enemies" Author="Jane" Title="Fish are my food" ```
NAME	Matches the tag NAME	/Media	``` <Media xmlns=""> <Book Author="John" Title="Fish are my friends" /> <Book Author="Dave" Title="Fish are my enemies" /> <Book Author="Jane" Title="Fish are my food" /> <CD Artist="Jane" ```

XPath	Description	Example	Results
			Title="Fish sing well" /> <DVD Director="John" Title="Fish: The Movie"> <Actor>Jane</Actor> <Actor>Dave</Actor> </DVD> </Media>
[]	Selects child tag by position or attribute	//Book[1]	<Book Author="John" Title="Fish are my friends" />
		//Book[@Author = "Jane"]	<Book Author="Jane" Title="Fish are my food" />

The important point here is that binding is an integrated part of WPF. The model for list and content controls natively supports displaying arbitrary data. Data binding is really a way to move the imperative code just displayed into a more tool-friendly declarative form. If we switch this code

FIGURE 6.11: Selecting nodes from an XML document

over to using binding, it looks very similar (in fact, Figure 6.11 shows exactly what this looks like):

```
public class Window1 : Window {
  public Window1() {
    XmlDocument doc = new XmlDocument();
    doc.LoadXml(...);
    XmlDataProvider dataSource = new XmlDataProvider();
    dataSource.Document = doc;
    Binding bind = new Binding();
    bind.Source = dataSource;
    bind.XPath = "/Media/Book/@Title";
    ListBox list = new ListBox();
    list.SetBinding(ListBox.ItemsSourceProperty, bind);
    Title = "XML Binding";
    Content = list;
  }
}
```

An important difference between the two examples is that, once we begin using binding, we can track changes. If we update or modify the XmlDataProvider object, ListBox will automatically be updated. In addition, by not basing the selection on imperative code, we have moved it into a regular object with known semantics, improving the support that tools can provide and reducing the number of concepts that a developer must understand.

The markup version of the same code is relatively straightforward:

```
<Window ... Title='XML Binding'>
  <Window.Resources>
    <XmlDataProvider x:Key='dataSource'>
      <x:XData>
        <Media xmlns=''>
          <Book Author='John' Title='Fish are my friends' />
          <Book Author='Dave' Title='Fish are my enemies' />
          <Book Author='Jane' Title='Fish are my food' />
          <CD Artist='Jane' Title='Fish sing well' />
          <DVD Director='John' Title='Fish: The Movie'>
            <Actor>Jane</Actor>
            <Actor>Dave</Actor>
          </DVD>
        </Media>
      </x:XData>
    </XmlDataProvider>
```

```
    </XmlDataProvider>
  </Window.Resources>
  <ListBox
    ItemsSource =
  '{Binding XPath=/Media/Book/@Title,Source={StaticResource dataSource}}'
      />
</Window>
```

XmlDataProvider serves two purposes: It is a markup-friendly way to build an XmlDocument object and apply an XPath (we can filter directly on the data source), and it is a common way of moving XML data into a data source (later we'll see other data source types). Often we can simply use an XmlDocument or XmlElement object as the source for binding, with no need to create the XmlDataProvider object.

Note the following important detail: The Source property of the binding is set via StaticResource. The Binding object itself isn't an element, so we cannot set its properties using a dynamic resource. If the data source must be determined dynamically (either with a dynamic resource reference, or via binding to determine the data source), we can alternatively use the DataContext property (which has the added benefit of simplifying the binding expression):

```
<Window x:Class='BookScratch.Window1'
  xmlns='http://schemas.microsoft.com/winfx/2006/xaml/presentation'
  xmlns:x='http://schemas.microsoft.com/winfx/2006/xaml'
  Text='XML Binding'
  DataContext='{DynamicResource dataSource}'
  >
  <Window.Resources>
    <XmlDataProvider x:Key='dataSource'>
      ...
    </XmlDataProvider>
  </Window.Resources>
  <ListBox
    ItemsSource= '{Binding XPath=/Media/Book/@Title}' />
</Window>
```

Now that we've reviewed object and XML binding, the next major thing to investigate is data templates, which provide us with the ability to visualize our data. In all the examples so far, we've been using data templates, though sometimes undetectably.

Data Templates

As we've already seen, data templates allow us to define how a piece of data will appear. In this section we'll use XML binding, but everything we do here can be applied to binding to any type of data.

To understand data templates, let's jump back to the code example that we had for binding. Instead of binding directly to the `Title` attribute, we'll bind to the elements:

```
public class Window1 : Window {
  public Window1() {
    XmlDocument doc = new XmlDocument();
    doc.LoadXml(...);
    XmlDataProvider dataSource = new XmlDataProvider();
    dataSource.Document = doc;
    Binding bind = new Binding();
    bind.Source = dataSource;
    bind.XPath = "/Media/Book";
    ListBox list = new ListBox();
    list.SetBinding(ListBox.ItemsSourceProperty, bind);
    Title = "XML Binding";
    Content = list;
  }
}
```

This markup produces an apparently empty list box that, in reality, contains three empty elements, as clicking inside the list reveals. Because no template is associated with `XmlElement`, the system simply calls `ToString` on it, which returns an empty string because there are no child elements under "Book".

The `DataTemplate` type resembles `ControlTemplate` quite a bit. They both leverage `FrameworkElementFactory` to define the display tree. `Control-Template` defines a display tree for a control, within which we use template binding to wire up display properties to control properties. `DataTemplate`, however, defines a display tree for a data item, within which we use data binding to wire up display properties to data properties. `DataTemplate` also automatically sets the data context of the display tree to be the template data item.

To build our first template in code, let's create a simple text display with the title of the book. We create a `DataTemplate` object associated with `XmlElement` as the data type:

```
DataTemplate template = new DataTemplate();
template.DataType = typeof(XmlElement);
```

Next we have to create the visual tree for the template:

```
FrameworkElementFactory textFactory =
  new FrameworkElementFactory(typeof(TextBlock));
```

We need to bind the Text property so that TextBlock will be the correct XPath statement:

```
Binding bind = new Binding();
bind.XPath="@Title";
textFactory.SetBinding(TextBlock.TextProperty, bind);
```

Notice that there is no need to declare a data source. The DataContext property for the instantiated visual tree is automatically set to the item to which the template is being applied. We can now associate the factory with the template:

```
template.VisualTree = textFactory;
```

The last step is to set the ItemTemplate property on ListBox to reference our newly defined template. Putting all this together, we have a simple application that displays the book titles:

```
public Window1() {
  XmlDocument doc = new XmlDocument();
  doc.LoadXml(...);

  DataTemplate template = new DataTemplate();
  template.DataType = typeof(XmlElement);
  Binding bind = new Binding();
  bind.XPath="@Title";
  FrameworkElementFactory textFactory =
    new FrameworkElementFactory(typeof(TextBlock));
  textFactory.SetBinding(TextBlock.TextProperty, bind);
  template.VisualTree = textFactory;

  XmlDataProvider dataSource = new XmlDataProvider();
  dataSource.Document = doc;
  bind = new Binding();
  bind.Source = doc;
  bind.XPath = "/Media/Book";
```

```
ListBox list = new ListBox();
 list.ItemTemplate = template;
 list.SetBinding(ListBox.ItemsSourceProperty, bind);

Title = "XML Binding";
 Content = list;
}
```

DataTemplate and ControlTemplate have very similar functionality and usage, and they use many of the same patterns. These resource references are often used to bind the ItemTemplate property of a list to the template instead. All of the code we just wrote would have been much simpler if we had written it using XAML instead:

```
<Window ...
   xmlns:sx='clr-namespace:System.Xml;assembly=System.Xml'
   Title='XML Binding'
   DataContext='{DynamicResource dataSource}'
   >
   <Window.Resources>
     <XmlDataProvider x:Key='dataSource'>
       ...
     </XmlDataProvider>
     <DataTemplate x:Key='template' DataType='{x:Type sx:XmlElement}'>
       <TextBlock Text='{Binding XPath=@Title}' />
     </DataTemplate>
   </Window.Resources>
   <ListBox
     ItemsSource= '{Binding XPath=/Media/Book }'
     ItemTemplate='{DynamicResource template}' />
</Window>
```

Templates are an extremely powerful mechanism for visualizing data. In addition to building complex templates, we can also create multiple templates and switch between then dynamically.

Template Selection

Typically we associate a template with a specific piece of data, but often we want to dynamically determine what template to use—on the basis of either a property value (although in Chapter 7 we'll learn about triggers, which help with this) or a global state. When we really need to replace the template wholesale, we can use DataTemplateSelector.

DataTemplateSelector provides a single method, SelectTemplate, that allows us to perform any logic we want to determine which template to return. We can find the template in the contained element (i.e., ListBox) and return some hard-coded templates, or even dynamically create a template for each item.

We can start by creating a class that derives from DataTemplateSelector and performs some logic to select among several templates. In this case we'll just look at the LocalName property of XmlElement and retrieve a resource with that name from the container:

```
public class LocalNameTemplateSelector : DataTemplateSelector {
    public override DataTemplate SelectTemplate(object item,
                        DependencyObject container) {

        XmlElement data = item as XmlElement;
        if (data != null) {
          return ((FrameworkElement)container).FindResource(data.LocalName)
             as DataTemplate;
        }
        return null;
    }
}
```

To initialize all the templates, we will build three templates: brown rectangles for books, silver circles for CDs, and blue circles for DVDs. Because the template selector will look at the local name of the XmlElement object, we need to set x:Key for each template:

```
<DataTemplate x:Key='Book' DataType='{x:Type sx:XmlElement}'>
  <StackPanel Orientation='Horizontal'>
    <Rectangle Margin='2' Width='14' Height='14' Fill='Brown' />
    <TextBlock VerticalAlignment='Center'
      Text='{Binding XPath=@Title}' />
  </StackPanel>
</DataTemplate>

<DataTemplate x:Key='CD' DataType='{x:Type sx:XmlElement}'>
  <StackPanel Orientation='Horizontal'>
    <Ellipse Margin='2' Width='14' Height='14' Fill='Silver' />
    <TextBlock VerticalAlignment='Center'
      Text='{Binding XPath=@Title}' />
  </StackPanel>
</DataTemplate>

<DataTemplate x:Key='DVD' DataType='{x:Type sx:XmlElement}'>
  <StackPanel Orientation='Horizontal'>
    <Ellipse Margin='2' Width='14' Height='14' Fill='Blue' />
    <TextBlock VerticalAlignment='Center'
```

```
                  Text='{Binding XPath=@Title}' />
              </StackPanel>
            </DataTemplate>
```

The remaining change is to associated the template selector with the list box instead of with the static template (and we'll select all media, not just books):

```
<Window ...
   xmlns:sx='clr-namespace:System.Xml;assembly=System.Xml'
   Title='XML Binding'
   DataContext='{DynamicResource dataSource}'
   >
   <Window.Resources>
     <XmlDataProvider x:Key='dataSource'>
       ...
     </XmlDataProvider>
     <DataTemplate x:Key='Book' DataType='{x:Type sx:XmlElement}'>
       ...
     </DataTemplate>
     <DataTemplate x:Key='CD' DataType='{x:Type sx:XmlElement}'>
       ...
     </DataTemplate>
     <DataTemplate x:Key='DVD' DataType='{x:Type sx:XmlElement}'>
       ...
     </DataTemplate>
   </Window.Resources>
   <ListBox
     ItemsSource= '{Binding XPath=/Media/*}'>
     <ListBox.ItemTemplateSelector>
       <l:LocalNameTemplateSelector
         xmlns:l='clr-namespace:EssentialWPF' />
     </ListBox.ItemTemplateSelector>
   </ListBox>

</Window>
```

This markup yields something like Figure 6.12.

Advanced Binding

Hierarchical Binding

So far, the data that we've examined has all been relatively flat: lists of customers or media. Data is often hierarchical, like a generic XML tree or file system. Because WPF supports element composition, our first thought might be to simply leverage element composition to build a tree of elements.

FIGURE 6.12: Binding using a template selector

To try this out, we can start by querying the file system. We need to define a simple template, and we will populate the data into a list box. Because `ItemsSource` expects a collection, we will take our initial directory and wrap it in an array:

```xml
<!-- filebrowser.xaml -->
<Window ... Title='EssentialWPF'>
  <ListBox
    ItemsSource='{Binding}'>
    <ListBox.ItemTemplate>
      <DataTemplate>
        <TextBlock Text='{Binding Path=Name}' />
      </DataTemplate>
    </ListBox.ItemTemplate>
  </ListBox>
</Window>
```

```csharp
// filebrowser.xaml.cs
public partial class FileBrowser : Window {

public FileBrowser() {
   InitializeComponent();

DataContext =
   new DirectoryInfo[] { new DirectoryInfo("c:\\windows") };
 }
}
```

FIGURE 6.13: A list box displaying our one directory

Running this code will produce the rather uninteresting results shown in Figure 6.13. What we really want to do is drill into the directory structure.

The System.IO.DirectoryInfo class doesn't have a handy property for retrieving the child items from the directory, so we will create a value converter to retrieve the necessary data:[7]

```
public class GetFileSystemInfosConverter : IValueConverter {
    public object Convert(object value, Type targetType,
                          object parameter, CultureInfo culture) {

        try {
          if (value is DirectoryInfo) {
            return ((DirectoryInfo)value).GetFileSystemInfos();
          }
        }
        catch {}
        return null;
    }

    public object ConvertBack(object value, Type targetType,
                              object parameter, CultureInfo culture) {
        throw new NotImplementedException();
    }
}
```

---

7. If you're curious, the try/catch method around the implementation is to (poorly) handle the cases in which we are denied access to directories that we don't have permission to access.

Now we can switch from binding to just the `Name` property of `Directory-Info`, to getting the child items of the directory. Inside of our data template we will nest a list box, within which we will define another data template (yes, it's getting that weird!):

```
<Window ... xmlns:l='clr-namespace:EssentialWPF' >
  ...
  <ListBox ItemsSource='{Binding}'>
    <ListBox.ItemTemplate>
      <DataTemplate>
        <StackPanel>
          <TextBlock Text='{Binding Path=Name}' />
          <ListBox Height='75'>
            <!-- ItemsSource for the inner ListBox
                 is going to be the collection of
                 child items. -->
            <ListBox.ItemsSource>
              <Binding Path='.'>
                <Binding.Converter>
                  <l:GetFileSystemInfosConverter />
                </Binding.Converter>
              </Binding>
            </ListBox.ItemsSource>

            <!-- The items inside of the inner ListBox
                 get to be just TextBlocks. -->
            <ListBox.ItemTemplate>
              <DataTemplate>
                <TextBlock Text='{Binding Path=Name}' />
              </DataTemplate>
            </ListBox.ItemTemplate>
          </ListBox>
        </StackPanel>
      </DataTemplate>
    </ListBox.ItemTemplate>
  </ListBox>
</Window>
```

Now we have the hierarchy shown in Figure 6.14 (on page 346).

We still aren't quite there. To get the entire structure of the document, we need to add more and more copies of the template for each level of hierarchy that we want to display. Copying this a couple more times will yield the display shown in Figure 6.15 (on page 346).

Although this approach does work, it has some problems. First, no control has knowledge of the hierarchy. Think about a control like `TreeView` or `Menu` that has inherent hierarchy; to work correctly, the control needs to see

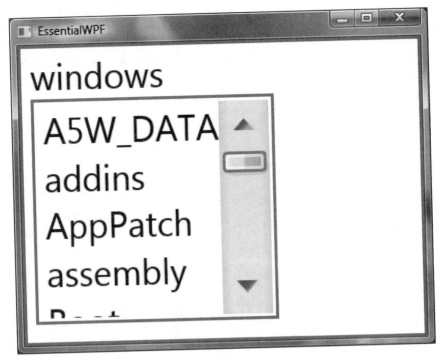

FIGURE 6.14: Simple hierarchical binding using nested data templates

the hierarchy. Second, the template must be copied for each level of hierarchy that we want to support.

To start, let's fix the copy problem. Instead of defining the template with ListBox, we can pull the definition out as a resource and then use a

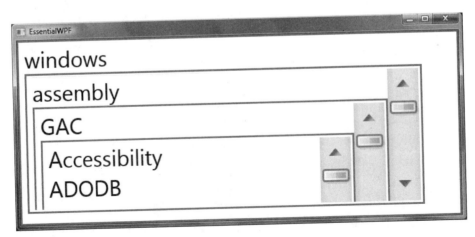

FIGURE 6.15: More hierarchy using more nested data templates

resource reference to introduce recursion (this is just like having a function that calls itself):

```
<Window ... xmlns:io='clr-namespace:System.IO;assembly=mscorlib'>
  <Window.Resources>
    <DataTemplate DataType='{x:Type io:DirectoryInfo}'>
      <StackPanel>
        <TextBlock Text='{Binding Path=Name}' />
        <ListBox>
          <ListBox.ItemsSource>
            <Binding Path='.'>
              <Binding.Converter>
                <l:GetFileSystemInfosConverter />
              </Binding.Converter>
            </Binding>
          </ListBox.ItemsSource>
        </ListBox>
      </StackPanel>
    </DataTemplate>
  </Window.Resources>
  <ListBox ItemsSource='{Binding}' />
</Window>
```

Wait! Where is the recursion? Remember that data templates can be discovered by the DataType property. This means that when ListBox sees an item of type DirectoryInfo, it will automatically find the template that we just defined. Within that template is a nested list box that will do the same thing. Voilà! The application will look identical to Figure 6.15, but we avoided the manual cloning of the template.

For a control, like TreeView or Menu, that natively supports hierarchy, we don't want to nest dozens of control objects together. To expose the hierarchical nature of some data to the control, we can use Hierarchical-DataTemplate. This is really just an instance of DataTemplate with an added set of properties, as we would expect on an ItemsControl object:

```
public class HierarchicalDataTemplate : DataTemplate {
  public BindingBase ItemsSource { get; set; }
  public DataTemplate ItemTemplate { get; set; }
  public DataTemplateSelector ItemTemplateSelector { get; set; }
}
```

In the case of a simple recursive template, as we have with the file system, we can use the fact that data templates are automatically associated to a type and create an incredibly simple template:

```
<Window ... >
  <Window.Resources>
    <HierarchicalDataTemplate DataType='{x:Type io:DirectoryInfo}'>
      <HierarchicalDataTemplate.ItemsSource>
        <Binding Path='.'>
          <Binding.Converter>
            <l:GetFileSystemInfosConverter />
          </Binding.Converter>
        </Binding>
      </HierarchicalDataTemplate.ItemsSource>
      <TextBlock Text='{Binding Path=Name}' />
    </HierarchicalDataTemplate>
  </Window.Resources>

  <TreeView ItemsSource='{Binding}'/>
</Window>
```

At first blush this is a bit confusing: The content of Hierarchical-DataTemplate is the template for the item. This is what we want displayed for each directory. The ItemsSource property tells the template how to retrieve the child items that should be displayed. Because the children are also DirectoryInfo objects, the data-binding system will automatically apply the same template. Figure 6.16 shows the result.

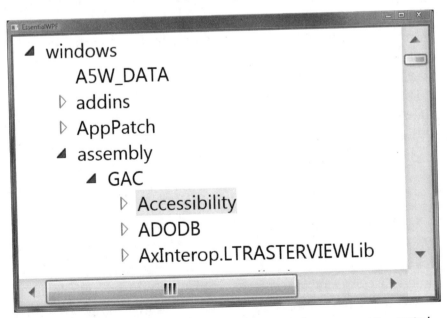

FIGURE 6.16: Using HierarchicalDataTemplate to provide data to a TreeView control

We can use `HierarchicalDataTemplate` even when the data is not uniform. For each type in the hierarchy, we can define a different template (instead of reusing the same one).

Collection Views

Up to now we have talked about three objects in play to perform binding: the data source, the binding, and the target element. With list binding there is actually a fourth player: the collection view. This view is responsible for keeping track of the current item (*currency management*), as well as filtering, sorting, and grouping the data. We can think of the collection view as a lightweight wrapper on the underlying data that allows us to have multiple "views" on top of the same data. For small lists, like the ones used in this book, this isn't so important, but with larger data sets it becomes increasingly important not to load the data into memory more than once.

Currency Management

The most important service that a collection view supplies is **currency management,** tracking the current item in a list. Whenever we bind to a list of data, a default collection view is created behind the scenes to track the current item. The simplest way to see how currency management works is to use the `IsSynchronizedWithCurrentItem` property on a list control. This property synchronizes the list selection with the current item in the view.

Typically we bind a collection to a collection-valued property (like `ItemsSource`). We can bind the entire collection, an indexed element from the collection, or a property of the current item. We've already seen the entire collection and indexed element binding; to bind to a property of the current item, we simply name the property. The current item is implied by the lack of square brackets:

```
public class AdvancedBinding : Window {
  public AdvancedBinding() {
    StackPanel sp = new StackPanel();

    Person[] names = new Person[] {
      new Person(new Name("Chris", "Anderson")),
      new Person(new Name("Don", "Box")),
```

```
      new Person(new Name("Chris", "Sells")),
  };

  ListBox list = new ListBox();
  list.IsSynchronizedWithCurrentItem = true;
  list.DisplayMemberPath = "Name";
  list.ItemsSource = names;

  TextBlock selected = new TextBlock();
  selected.FontSize = 24;
  Binding text = new Binding();
  text.Source = names;
  text.Path = new PropertyPath("Name");
  selected.SetBinding(TextBlock.TextProperty, text);

  sp.Children.Add(list);
  sp.Children.Add(selected);

  Content = sp;
  }
}
```

The window that is displayed will look something like Figure 6.17, and as we select an item in the list box, the text block will update.

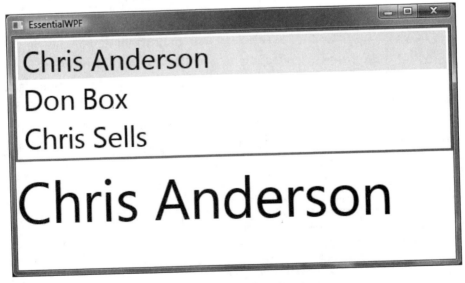

FIGURE 6.17: Using ListBox to show currency management

In this case we are using the default view for the names collection. We can access this view to programmatically manipulate it using the GetDefaultView static method of the CollectionViewSource type:

```
public class AdvancedBinding : Window {
  public CollectionViews() {
    StackPanel sp = new StackPanel();
    ...

    WrapPanel commands = new WrapPanel();
    Button prev = new Button();
    prev.Content = "<";
    prev.Click +=
      delegate {
        ICollectionView view =
          CollectionViewSource.GetDefaultView(names);
        view.MoveCurrentToPrevious();
      };
    commands.Children.Add(prev);

    Button next = new Button();
    next.Content = ">";
    next.Click +=
      delegate {
        ICollectionView view =
          CollectionViewSource.GetDefaultView(names);
        view.MoveCurrentToNext();
      };
    commands.Children.Add(next);

    sp.Children.Add(commands);
    ...
  }
}
```

Currency management is the most important thing that a collection view does. The remaining features focus more on providing a virtual view over the data. This virtual view allows for controls (like a grid) to provide some default features (like clicking a column header to sort).

Filtering, Sorting, and Grouping

Filtering is the simplest of the view features: We provide a delegate callback that determines whether an item should be visible to the controls. As with any of the view features, we can either modify or use the default view, or we can create a new view. To make it apparent how items are

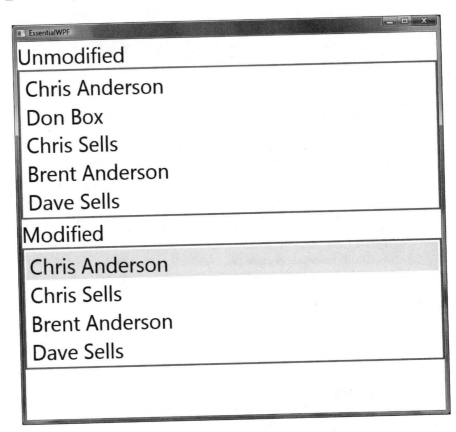

FIGURE 6.18: Filtering items out of a view

being handled, here we will have two lists: one with the default view (unmodified) and the other having a custom view with tweaks.

First let's create the custom view, filtering out anyone named Don:

```
ICollectionView view = new ListCollectionView(names);
view.Filter =
  delegate(object item) {
    return ((Person)item).Name.First != "Don";
  };
```

To display the view, we can use it as the `ItemsSource` property for a list. Figure 6.18 shows that, as a result, only one entry is removed from the list:

```
public class CollectionViews : Window {

  public CollectionViews() {
    StackPanel sp = new StackPanel();
```

```
Person[] names = new Person[] {
  new Person(new Name("Chris", "Anderson")),
  new Person(new Name("Don", "Box")),
  new Person(new Name("Chris", "Sells")),
  new Person(new Name("Brent", "Anderson")),
  new Person(new Name("Dave", "Sells")),
};

sp.Children.Add(new TextBlock(new Run("Unmodified")));

ListBox list = new ListBox();
list.DisplayMemberPath = "Name";
list.ItemsSource = names;
sp.Children.Add(list);

sp.Children.Add(new TextBlock(new Run("Modified")));

ListBox modified = new ListBox();
ICollectionView view = new ListCollectionView(names);
view.Filter =
  delegate(object item) {
    return ((Person)item).Name.First != "Don";
  };
modified.DisplayMemberPath = "Name";
modified.ItemsSource = view;
sp.Children.Add(modified);

Content = sp;
  }
}
```

Sorting is also very easy. By adding one or more SortDescription objects, we can sort the list by any number of properties. Here we'll sort by last name and then first name (Figure 6.19 on page 354):

```
view.SortDescriptions.Add(
  new SortDescription("Name.Last", ListSortDirection.Ascending));

view.SortDescriptions.Add(
  new SortDescription("Name.First", ListSortDirection.Ascending));
```

The final feature of collection views, **grouping,** requires support from both the collection view and the control that is binding to the data. On the collection view side, grouping is handled almost exactly like sorting: We add one or more GroupDescription objects to define how the data will be translated into groups:

```
view.GroupDescriptions.Add(new PropertyGroupDescription("Name.Last"));
```

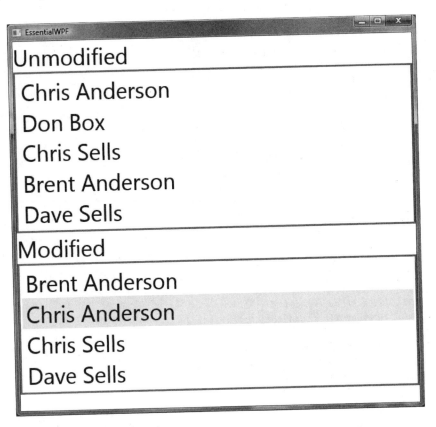

FIGURE 6.19: Sorting items in a view

One the control side, we need to provide a way to visualize the groups. All the WPF list controls support a `GroupStyle` property for this purpose (Figure 6.20):

```
GroupStyle style = new GroupStyle();

style.HeaderTemplate = new DataTemplate();
style.HeaderTemplate.VisualTree =
  new FrameworkElementFactory(typeof(TextBlock));
style.HeaderTemplate.VisualTree.SetBinding(
  TextBlock.TextProperty, new Binding("Name"));
style.HeaderTemplate.VisualTree.SetValue(
  TextBlock.BackgroundProperty, Brushes.Silver);

modified.GroupStyle.Add(style);
```

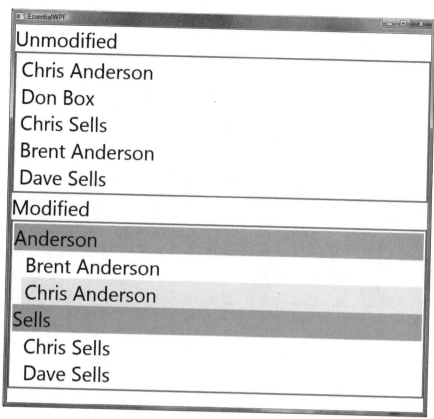

FIGURE 6.20: Grouping items in a view

This example uses the PropertyGroupDescription class, which determines grouping on the basis of a property value. It is relatively easy to create custom grouping logic by deriving from GroupDescription and overriding the GroupNameFromItem method.

Converting this into markup is relatively straightforward, but there are some interesting gotchas. To describe a collection view in markup, we must use the CollectionViewSource type:

```
<Window ...
    Title='EssentialWPF'
    >
  <Window.Resources>
    <CollectionViewSource x:Key='customView' />
  </Window.Resources>
</Window>
```

To wire up data to the collection view source, we need to set the `Source` property. In the spirit of the original example, we will describe the source as an array of `Person` objects. We will also set the data context on the window:

```
<Window ...
    xmlns:l='clr-namespace:EssentialWPF'
    Title='EssentialWPF'
    DataContext='{DynamicResource dataSource}'
    >
  <Window.Resources>
    <x:Array Type='{x:Type l:Person}' x:Key='dataSource'>
      <l:Person>
        <l:Person.Name>
          <l:Name First='Chris' Last='Anderson' />
        </l:Person.Name>
      </l:Person>
      <!-- rest of people -->
    </x:Array>
    <CollectionViewSource x:Key='customView'
      Source='{StaticResource dataSource}' />
  </Window.Resources>
</Window>
```

We must use `StaticResource` to set `Source` because it is not a dependency property. We must use `DynamicResource` to set `DataContext` on the window in this case because the definition for `dataSource` is provided inside of the window (`DynamicResource` enables this type of forward referencing).

Filtering on `CollectionViewSource` uses an event instead of a simple delegate callback, so we need to update the C# definition of our filter slightly:

```
public void NotDon(object sender, FilterEventArgs e) {
  e.Accepted = ((Person)e.Item).Name.First != "Don";
}
```

Adding the filter then becomes as simple as wiring up an event handler to `CollectionViewSource`:

```
<CollectionViewSource x:Key='customView'
  Filter='NotDon'
  Source='{StaticResource dataSource}' />
```

Sorting is complicated only by the fact that `SortDescription` is defined in the namespace `System.ComponentModel`, which isn't included in the normal WPF xmlns:

```
<CollectionViewSource x:Key='customView'
  xmlns:cm='clr-namespace:System.ComponentModel;assembly=WindowsBase'
  Filter='NotDon'
  Source='{StaticResource dataSource}'>

  <CollectionViewSource.SortDescriptions>
    <cm:SortDescription PropertyName='Name.Last'
      Direction='Ascending' />
    <cm:SortDescription PropertyName='Name.First'
      Direction='Ascending' />
  </CollectionViewSource.SortDescriptions>
</CollectionViewSource>
```

Grouping is trivial, and exactly how we would expect:

```
<CollectionViewSource x:Key='customView' ... >
  ...
  <CollectionViewSource.GroupDescriptions>
    <PropertyGroupDescription PropertyName='Name.Last' />
  </CollectionViewSource.GroupDescriptions>
</CollectionViewSource>
```

We wire up the list box to the collection view source using the standard `ItemsSource` property. Notice that, although a collection view can be used directly as the `ItemsSource` property, we must use a `Binding` object to wire up the collection view source:

```
<ListBox DisplayMemberPath='Name'
  ItemsSource='{Binding Source={StaticResource customView}}'>

  <ListBox.GroupStyle>
    <GroupStyle HeaderTemplate='{StaticResource groupHeader}' />
  </ListBox.GroupStyle>
</ListBox>
```

Collection views enable efficient sharing of data, as well as multiple views for the user. Although it isn't necessary to use collection views in every binding scenario, effective use of views can greatly increase the performance of an application.

Data-Driven Display

For most applications, people build a simple UI, create a data model, and wire up the two using data binding. One of the more powerful things we can do with WPF is to reverse the typical relationship: The data can be the center of an application, and the UI can be secondary. The power of this reversed relationship is that we can build rich data visualizations independent of the usage. Three classes—`ContentControl`, `ItemsControl`, and `DataTemplate`—are the key to this model.

Let's begin with a simple data model: an image. In Chapter 5, we saw that there are two primary data types for dealing with images: the `Image` control and the `ImageSource` class hierarchy (including `BitmapImage`, which is used frequently). The `Image` control is a typical UI first model for dealing with images. The simplest usage is to set the `Source` property to a URI:

```
<Image Source='c:\data\book\images\flowers.jpg' />
```

`Source` is really a property of type `ImageSource`, and we can directly specify `BitmapImage` if we want to control detail-loading properties (like decode resolution):

```
<Image>
  <Image.Source>
    <BitmapImage UriSource='c:\data\book\images\flowers.jpg' />
  </Image.Source>
</Image>
```

Now we can reverse the model: Instead of using the `Image` control and populating it with data, let's start with the data (the image) and figure out how to display it. Because this is only one image, we will use `ContentControl`:

```
<ContentControl>
  <ContentControl.Content>
    <BitmapImage UriSource='c:\data\book\images\flowers.jpg' />
  </ContentControl.Content>
</ContentControl>
```

Running this code produces something like Figure 6.21—relatively uninteresting.

What happened here is that the default logic for `ContentControl` saw a piece of data, in this case the bitmap data, and called `ToString` to produce a display. By adding a date template, we can make this look much more interesting. To start, we will define a simple template that uses an `Image` control to display the image (Figure 6.22):

```
<DataTemplate DataType='{x:Type BitmapImage}'>
  <Image Source='{Binding}' />
</DataTemplate>
```

FIGURE 6.21: Displaying a bitmap image with `ContentControl`

As Figure 6.22 shows, the display is now more interesting. Effectively, though, this is identical to our original use of the Image element. We can make this more interesting by adding a richer display (Figure 6.23 on page 360):

```
<DataTemplate DataType='{x:Type BitmapImage}'>
  <Border>
    <Border
      HorizontalAlignment='Center'
      VerticalAlignment='Center'
```

FIGURE 6.22: Displaying a bitmap image with a more interesting template

FIGURE 6.23: Displaying a bitmap image with more chrome

```
            Margin='4'
            BorderThickness='1'
            BorderBrush='Black'
            Padding='4'
        Background='White'>
            <Border.BitmapEffect>
              <DropShadowBitmapEffect Softness='.2' ShadowDepth='1'/>
            </Border.BitmapEffect>
            <Image Source='{Binding}' />
        </Border>
      </Border>
    </DataTemplate>
```

FIGURE 6.24: More complex chrome, including actions and additional binding

We could take this even further, adding panning controls or other types of adornments (Figure 6.24).

The key thing to note here is that the data model for the image has not changed. Imagine for a moment that, instead of using BitmapImage as the data, we were using a Customer object. We could create the data model for that customer, with the correct properties, behavior, and so on. Then we could build various user interfaces to interact with that data.

The great thing about building a UI from the data up is that rich views of the data can be reused everywhere in the application. We can use this technique of "data first" programming on many levels. For example, suppose we wanted to display a list of images. At first, we might be tempted to use a list box and hard-code the list of images. This is relatively simple for the first place that we want to display a list of images, but if we plan to display a list in multiple places, we might want to reuse the definition of how we display the list. We might want a list box that scrolls horizontally or vertically, or maybe a list view instead, with column details. If we start by defining a new type for the image list, we can create a template for it just as we did for a single image:

```
using System.Collections.ObjectModel;

public class ImageList : ObservableCollection<BitmapImage> {}
```

As we've already seen in this chapter, ObservableCollection is a list implementation that supports change notification and the necessary patterns for working easily in markup. We can now set the content of our window to be simply a list of images:

```
<Window ...>
  <l:ImageList>
    <BitmapImage ... />
    <BitmapImage ... />
    <BitmapImage ... />
  </l:ImageList>
</Window>
```

To specify how this list will appear (Figure 6.25), we do exactly what we did for the single image:

```
<DataTemplate DataType='{x:Type l:ImageList}'>
  <ListBox ItemsSource='{Binding}' />
</DataTemplate>
```

By moving to a data-driven model for defining the display of an application, we create a clear separation between the data model and the UI model of the program. As a result, it is much easier to change the look of the application. Having an explicit contract between the data model and UI model also makes it easier to understand when we make a change that might break the UI display.

FIGURE 6.25: Reusing a complex template in a list

WHERE ARE WE?

In this chapter we have looked at how WPF deals with data in an application. WPF's data-binding system is deeply integrated in the platform, and with the proper model we can create applications with a completely data-driven approach.

7

Actions

I N CHAPTER 6 WE looked at how to include data in an application and visualize it in interesting ways. Up to now we have focused on the output side of the platform, looking at how an application is built up from controls that use visuals to display and layout to position everything. Now we can start to look at the input side of the platform.

Often we want an application to respond in some way when a user moves the mouse, clicks a button, presses a key, or draws with a pen. Windows Presentation Foundation has three common ways of dealing with actions: events, commands, and triggers. We will look at the principles that apply to all three of these mechanisms, and then dig into the details about each one.

Action Principles

For actions, WPF operates on three principles, which are actually continuations of principles we have seen already: element composition, loose coupling, and declarative actions. To allow actions to work with the way that WPF builds the display tree, with many elements that may be further composed of other elements, requires the use of element composition. The fact that controls can completely change their display introduces a problem if the source of an event and the code that handles it are tightly coupled, so the ability for loose coupling is necessary. And finally, because declarative programming should extend to all aspects of the system, WPF must support handling actions in a declarative fashion also.

Element Composition

As we saw in Chapter 3, a button is actually made up of several elements. This composition introduces an interesting problem for handling events. Remember the three principles of the control model: element composition, rich content everywhere, and simple programming model.

To start, from the simple programming model we know that we want the code for listening to a click event to be simple and familiar to developers. We should have to do nothing more than attach a handler to the `Click` event:

```
Button b = new Button();
b.Content = "Click Me";
b.Click += delegate { MessageBox.Show("You clicked me!"); };
```

This appears to work great, but let's look at what is actually happening. It's not the button itself that's being clicked, but rather the elements that make up the display of the button. To make all this work seamlessly, WPF introduces the concept of a routed event that lets events traverse the elements. We can see this by changing the preceding example to include a second button as content; clicking on either the inner or the outer button will cause the event to be raised:

```
Button b = new Button();
b.Content = new Button();
b.Click += delegate { MessageBox.Show("You clicked me!"); };
```

The resulting display tree is pictured in Figure 7.1, which also shows that we must concern ourselves with more than just the two buttons. Even in the simple scenario of a single button, event composition is necessary for routing the mouse events to the button.

Element composition affects all aspects of action handling, not just events.

Loose Coupling

The events published by `Button` show that it supports both direct mouse events (`MouseUp`, `MouseDown`, etc.) as well as the `Click` event. `Click` is an abstraction at a much higher level than mouse events. In fact, `Click` will be

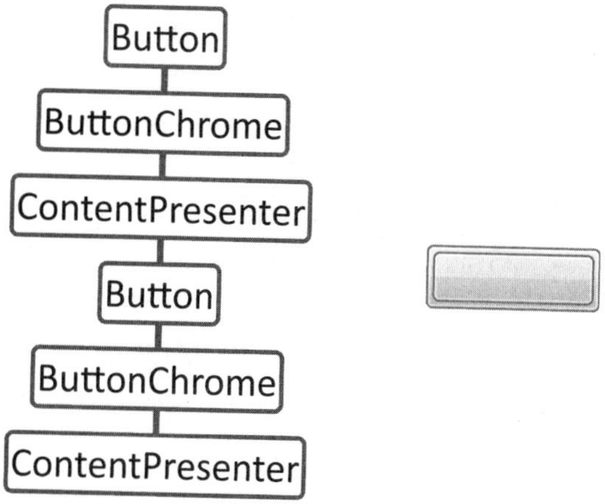

Button

ButtonChrome

ContentPresenter

Button

ButtonChrome

ContentPresenter

FIGURE 7.1: Display tree (left) of a button containing another button (right)

raised if the user presses the space bar (when the button has keyboard focus) or **Enter** (when the button is the default button in a window). Click is a *semantic event*, and mouse events are *physical events*.

Writing code against the Click event has two advantages: (1) We don't tie ourselves to a specific input gesture (mouse versus keyboard), and (2) we don't tie ourselves to a button. CheckBox, RadioButton, Button, and Hyperlink all support clicking. Code written against the Click event depends only on a component that can be clicked. This decoupling of code to the action produced allows for more flexibility in the implementation of handlers.

Events themselves, though, suffer from a form of coupling that requires the method implementation to be of a specific signature. For example, the delegate for Button.Click is defined as follows:

```
public delegate void RoutedEventHandler(object sender,
                                        RoutedEventArgs e);
```

One of the goals in WPF is to allow a spectrum of actions (Figure 7.2), ranging from tightly coupled physical events (like MouseUp) all the way to

FIGURE 7.2: Examples illustrating the spectrum of coupling actions

completely semantic notifications (like the `ApplicationCommands.Close` command that signals that a window should be closed).

By allowing for loose coupling, we are able to write templates that dramatically change a control. For example, by adding a button wired to the `Close` command, we can write a template for a window that adds chrome for closing the window:

```
<ControlTemplate TargetType='{x:Type Window}'>
  <DockPanel>
    <StatusBar DockPanel.Dock='Bottom'>
      <StatusBarItem>
        <Button
          Command='{x:Static ApplicationCommands.Close}'>
          Close
        </Button>
      </StatusBarItem>
    </StatusBar>
    <ContentPresenter />
  </DockPanel>
</ControlTemplate>
```

We can then make the window close when any component issues the `Close` command by adding a command binding to the window:

```
public MyWindow() {
  InitializeComponent();

  CommandBindings.Add(
    new CommandBinding(
      ApplicationCommands.Close,
      CloseExecuted
    )
  );
}

void CloseExecuted(object sender, ExecuteRoutedEventArgs e) {
  this.Close();
}
```

Commands represent the most loosely coupled action model in WPF. Loose coupling provides a complete abstraction from the action source (in this case, the button) and the action handler (in this case, the window). Leveraging this loose coupling, we could change the window style to use a totally different control and not break anything.

Declarative Actions

With the introduction of commands and loose coupling, we can start to see that WPF is moving toward a model in which software declares its intent (e.g., "I want the window to close when you issue this command") instead of its implementation (e.g., "Call `Window.Close()` when you click this button").

A major foundation of WPF is the notion of declarative programming. In addition to visuals and UI layout, much of application logic can be specified in markup. Declarative logic is extremely useful in that, around a declarative format, we can often provide a better experience in providing tools for the user, and potentially provide more advanced services in the system.

The various ways of handling actions have different levels of support for declarative programming. Events allow us to declare the target function in markup, but the handler must be implemented in code. Commands are specifically designed for declarative use, providing the best abstraction between the action source and consumer. Triggers provide probably the richest declarative support, but their lack of extensibility makes them difficult to use for complex tasks.

All of the mechanisms for dealing with actions support some amount of all of these principles. Let's start by digging into the one that's probably the most familiar: events.

Events

In WPF, events behave exactly as they do in any other .NET class library. Each object exposes a set of events to which we can attach a listener using a delegate. As discussed earlier, WPF has an additional set of features around routed events that allow events to propagate through the tree of elements.

There are three types of routed events: direct, bubbling, and tunneling events. **Direct events** are simple events that fire on a single source; these are nearly identical to standard .NET events, with the exception that they are registered with the WPF routed-event system.[1] Certain features in the platform (triggers, for example) require an event to be registered to be used.

---

1. The routed-event system is the part of WPF that is responsible for routing events through the element tree. This system is mostly hidden, with only small parts of it, like `EventManager.RegisterRoutedEvent`, visible.

Bubbling and tunneling events are really two sides of the same coin: **Tunneling events** travel from the root of the element tree to a target element, and **bubbling events** do the opposite. Typically, these two types of events are paired, and the tunneling version is prefixed with *Preview*. Most input events (keyboard, mouse, and pen) have bubbling and tunneling versions of each event—for example, `MouseRightButtonDown` and `PreviewMouseRightButtonDown`, respectively.

If we write a small sample that creates a hierarchy of elements and listens to some events, we can see how bubbling and tunneling versions relate. Here we will create a window with a group box and some buttons:

```
<Window ...
   PreviewMouseRightButtonDown='WindowPreviewRightButtonDown'
   MouseRightButtonDown='WindowRightButtonDown'
  >
  <GroupBox
    PreviewMouseRightButtonDown='GroupBoxPreviewRightButtonDown'
    MouseRightButtonDown='GroupBoxRightButtonDown'
   >
   <StackPanel>
     <Button>One</Button>
     <Button
       PreviewMouseRightButtonDown='ButtonTwoPreviewRightButtonDown'
       MouseRightButtonDown='ButtonTwoRightButtonDown'
      >
      Two
     </Button>
   </StackPanel>
  </GroupBox>
</Window>
```

In the event handler for each, we can dump the name of the event:

```
void ButtonTwoPreviewRightButtonDown(object sender,
                                     MouseButtonEventArgs e) {
  Debug.WriteLine("ButtonTwo PreviewRightButtonDown");
}

void ButtonTwoRightButtonDown(object sender, MouseButtonEventArgs e) {
  Debug.WriteLine("ButtonTwo RightButtonDown");
}

void GroupBoxPreviewRightButtonDown(object sender,
                                    MouseButtonEventArgs e) {
  Debug.WriteLine("GroupBox PreviewRightButtonDown");
}
```

```
void GroupBoxRightButtonDown(object sender, MouseButtonEventArgs e) {
    Debug.WriteLine("GroupBox RightButtonDown");
}

void WindowPreviewRightButtonDown(object sender, MouseButtonEventArgs e) {
    Debug.WriteLine("Window PreviewRightButtonDown");
}

void WindowRightButtonDown(object sender, MouseButtonEventArgs e) {
    Debug.WriteLine("Window RightButtonDown");
}
```

Running this code reveals the order of events:

1. `Window PreviewMouseRightButtonDown`
2. `GroupBox PreviewMouseRightButtonDown`
3. `Button PreviewMouseRightButtonDown`
4. `Button MouseRightButtonDown`
5. `GroupBox MouseRightButtonDown`
6. `Window MouseRightButtonDown`

As further illustration, Figure 7.3 shows the two phases of event routing.

Any default behavior for a control should always be implemented in the bubbling version of a given event. For example, `Button` creates the `Click` event in the `MouseLeftButtonUp` event. This pattern of never using the preview events allows application developers to use preview events to hook in logic or cancel the default behavior of a control. At any point during an event route we can set the `Handled` property on the event arguments to block any more event handlers from being invoked.

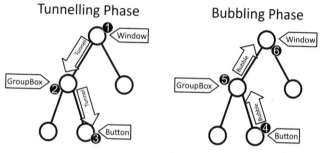

FIGURE 7.3: Event tunneling and bubbling in an element tree

To see this in action, we can listen to the `PreviewMouseLeftButtonDown` event on `Window`. By setting `Handled` to `true`, we can prevent any elements from being clicked:

```
public Window1() {
    ...
    this.PreviewMouseRightButtonDown += WindowPreviewRightButtonDown;
}

void WindowPreviewRightButtonDown(object sender,
                                  MouseButtonEventArgs e) {

    e.Handled = true;
}
```

The `Handled` property is one of several interesting properties that all routed events share. All event arguments for routed events derive from the common type `RoutedEventArgs`:

```
public class RoutedEventArgs : EventArgs {
    public bool Handled { get; set; }
    public object OriginalSource { get; }
    public RoutedEvent RoutedEvent { get; set; }
    public object Source { get; set; }
}
```

`OriginalSource` and `Source` are very useful in dealing with routed events. `Source` maps to the sender of the event; that is, it represents the object on which we are listening to the events. `OriginalSource` represents the originator of the event. In the preceding examples, the originator of the event is actually `ButtonChrome`, the display element that is used in the button's template. Because mouse events are physical events, their original source will always be the actual element over which the mouse was hovering when the event was created. The original source for more abstract events, like `Click`, will be the element that created the event.

To see this directly, we can write some code that listens to the left-button up and down events, as well as click events. Building a structure similar to what we already have, we get output like this:

```
Window PreviewMouseLeftButtonDown,Source=Button,Original=ButtonChrome
GroupBox PreviewMouseLeftButtonDown,Source=Button,Original=ButtonChrome
ButtonTwo PreviewMouseLeftButtonDown,Source=Button,Original=
    ButtonChrome
```

```
ButtonTwo Click, Source=Button, OriginalSource=Button
GroupBox Click, Source=Button, OriginalSource=Button
Window Click, Source=Button, OriginalSource=Button
```

Notice that the MouseLeftButtonDown events are not visible. The reason is that the button handles the Button events to generate the Click event.

Tunneling and bubbling work great for events that are built into every control, like mouse events; however, any event can tunnel or bubble (as the preceding Click example illustrates). To allow for both tunneling and bubbling, WPF supports attached events. In much the same way that the property system allows for properties to be attached to any element, we can attach an event handler to any element.

If we want to be notified when any button in a window is clicked, we can simply call AddHandler. Every event that uses the event system in WPF has a RoutedEvent field on the defining object, just like the Dependency-Property field that is used for the property system. To attach a handler, we call AddHandler and pass to it the RoutedEvent object and the delegate to be invoked:

```
this.AddHandler(Button.ClickEvent,
    (RoutedEventHandler)delegate { MessageBox.Show("Clicked"); });
```

WPF extends the basic .NET event model to include the notion of routing to events, which enables element composition. The other action-processing features are all built on top of this base event-routing model.

Commands

Most events in WPF are tied to implementation details about each control—selection changed, element clicked, mouse moved down, and so on. Events are great when we're wiring up a specific section of code to a notification from a control, but often we want to deal with things more abstractly.

Suppose we want to add the ability to quit a program (something most programs should support!). For starters, we know that we want to have a menu for exiting the program. We will first define the menu in the markup file:

```
<MenuItem Header='_File'>
  <MenuItem Header='E_xit' Click='ExitClicked' />
</MenuItem>
```

In the code behind, we can implement the event handler:

```
void ExitClicked(object sender, RoutedEventArgs e) {
  Application.Current.Shutdown();
}
```

This works fine, but now let's also add a text section that includes a hyperlink to exit the application:

```
<TextBlock>
  Welcome to my program. If you are bored, you can
  <Hyperlink Click='ExitClicked'>exit</Hyperlink>.
</TextBlock>
```

Here's where it starts to get a little weird. We're making a lot of assumptions about the implementation of ExitClicked—for example, that the signature is compatible with the Hyperlink.Click event, and that the implementation is, in fact, just exiting the application. In addition, we now have arbitrary methods in the code behind baked into the markup file, so a graphic designer trying to build the UI for this application would have no idea what event handlers to bind to.

Commands exist to help solve this problem. They allow us to provide a single name to signify the action that we want. To start using commands, we must do three things: (1) define a command, (2) define the implementation of that command, and (3) create a trigger for the command.

The basis for the command system in WPF is the relatively simple ICommand interface:

```
public interface ICommand {
  event EventHandler CanExecuteChanged;

  bool CanExecute(object parameter);
  void Execute(object parameter);
}
```

CanExecute is used to determine whether the command is in a state that it can execute. Typically, UI controls use CanExecute to enable or disable themselves; that is, a button will become disabled when the associated command returns False from CanExecute. This shared notion of "enabled" allows multiple controls being wired to the same command to have a consistent enabled state.

Execute is the key thing for a command; when called, it triggers execution of the command. The implementation for Button (or any other command-enabled control), would include a section that looked roughly like this:

```
protected virtual void OnClick(RoutedEventArgs e) {
  if (Command != null && Command.CanExecute(CommandParameter)) {
    Command.Execute(CommandParameter);
  }
  // ... rest of implementation
}
```

To define a new command, we can implement the ICommand interface. Because we want ICommand to close after being invoked, we can call the Shutdown method on the current application:

```
public class Exit : ICommand {
  public bool CanExecute(object parameter) {
    return true;
  }

  public event EventHandler CanExecuteChanged;

  public void Execute(object parameter) {
    Application.Current.Shutdown();
  }
}
```

To bind a menu item or hyperlink to the shutdown of the application, we can wire the Command property to the Exit command:

```
<MenuItem Header='_File'>
  <MenuItem Header='E_xit'>
    <MenuItem.Command>
      <l:Exit />
    </MenuItem.Command>
  </MenuItem>
</MenuItem>
...
<Hyperlink>
  <Hyperlink.Command><l:Exit /></Hyperlink.Command>
  ...
</Hyperlink>
```

Because it is common to use a command from more than one location, it is also common to create a static field with a command instance:

```
public partial class Window1 : Window {
  public static readonly ICommand ExitCommand = new Exit();
  ...
}
```

This has the added benefit of allowing us to make the implementation of Exit completely private by making ICommand the type of the field. We can now mark Exit as a private class and switch our markup to bind to the static field:

```
<MenuItem Header='_File'>
  <MenuItem Header='E_xit' Command='{x:Static 1:Window1.ExitCommand}' />
</MenuItem>
</MenuItem>
```

Now our window can publish a set of functionality by exposing commands. There is an interesting problem here, though. Right now Exit is implemented in global terms: We can call it anywhere, and it will shut down the application. Suppose, instead, that we wanted "exit" to be equivalent to closing the current window. In this case, similar to what we do with events, we would want to separate the implementation of exit from its definition.

The simplest way to achieve this separation is to leverage the event system. We can define a new event on the command and use the event-routing system to notify components:

```
class Exit : ICommand {
  public static readonly RoutedEvent ExecuteEvent =
    EventManager.RegisterRoutedEvent(
      "Execute",
      RoutingStrategy.Bubble,
      typeof(RoutedEventHandler),
      typeof(Exit));

  ...
}
```

Because this event is defined with the Bubble strategy, it will bubble from the source of the event. To raise the event, we can update our implementation of Execute to find the current element (we will use Keyboard.FocusedElement in this example, but we could use any mechanism to track "current") and then raise the appropriate event:

```
public void Execute(object parameter) {
  RoutedEventArgs e =
    new RoutedEventArgs(Exit.ExecuteEvent, Keyboard.FocusedElement);
  Keyboard.FocusedElement.RaiseEvent(e);
}
```

This introduces the concept of **command binding,** the ability to separate the implementation of a command from the identity of that command. We need to go back to our Window1 implementation and add the implementation of the command:

```
public partial class Window1 : Window {
  ...

  public Window1() {
    InitializeComponent();

    AddHandler(Exit.ExecuteEvent, ExitExecuted);
  }
  void ExitExecuted(object sender, RoutedEventArgs e) {
    this.Close();
  }
}
```

You may be a little confused at this point. Remember, the command's purpose is to provide an abstract notion of what should happen. What is happening is that a control (like MenuItem) is triggering the command in response to an event (like Click). In this case, the Exit command will raise an Execute event on the element tree so that Window can listen to that event and act (Figure 7.4 on page 378):

1. A menu item is clicked.
2. MenuItem calls Execute on the command.
3. The Exit implementation raises the Exit.Execute event on the focused element (the MenuItem object, in this case)
4. That event bubbles up the tree.
5. Window receives the Exit.Execute event.
6. Window runs the implementation of the event (closing the window).

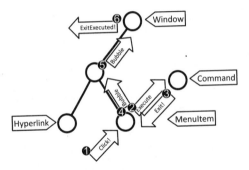

FIGURE 7.4: Execution flow of a command using an event to route notifications

We could continue down this path, enhancing the base `ICommand` model to support input bindings (to handle keyboard, mouse, and stylus input), parameters, and other features.[2] However, the framework has a built-in utility class—`RoutedCommand`—that handles most of this already.

Routed commands completely separate the implementation of the command from the identity of the command. The pattern for defining a new command is similar to `RoutedEvent` and `DependencyProperty`. The definition of the command is static; it is really just a unique token to provide an identity for the command:

```
public partial class Window1 : Window {
    public static readonly ICommand ExitCommand =
            new RoutedCommand("Exit", typeof(Window1));

    ...
}
```

To make something happen when a command is executed, we need to bind handling code to the command (similar to when we used an event in the previous example). Routed commands bubble (just like events), so we can add a command binding on the root window and see all commands. Command bindings take two pieces of data—the command to listen to, and the code to run when the command is triggered:

---

2. The common reason for creating a custom version of command routing is that a route is not tied to the element tree. It's very easy to imagine a system with a document and project structure in which we would want the command route to follow the logical structure, not the display tree.

```
public Window1() {
  InitializeComponent();

  CommandBindings.Add(new CommandBinding(ExitCommand, ExitExecuted));
}
void ExitExecuted(object sender, ExecutedRoutedEventArgs e) {
  this.Close();
}
```

Command bindings allow us to specify the logic for determining whether the command should be enabled, and they also map input gestures[3] using the InputBindings property:

```
<Window x:Class='EssentialWPF.Window1'
  xmlns='http://schemas.microsoft.com/winfx/2006/xaml/presentation'
  xmlns:x='http://schemas.microsoft.com/winfx/2006/xaml'
  xmlns:l='clr-namespace:EssentialWPF'
  Title='EssentialWPF'
  >
  <Window.InputBindings>
    <KeyBinding Key='A' Modifiers='Control'
      Command='{x:Static l:Window1.ExitCommand}' />
  </Window.InputBindings>
  ...
</Window>
```

The other main feature is the notion of "secure" commands. Certain commands, like cut, copy, and paste, have security ramifications. To ensure that the system performs these operations only when requested by a user (or when digital rights management permits), the RoutedCommand class can track whether a command was initiated by a user.

Using a command cleanly separates the display from the behavior. By having a single name that signifies the semantic action we want, we avoid many of the tight coupling problems that can occur when we're trying to wire up multiple controls to a single event handler. Generally, application logic should always be implemented in terms of commands, not event handlers. Many of the common cases of needing to wire directly to event handlers are better handled with triggers, which we will cover shortly.

---

3. Input gestures include mouse, keyboard, and stylus input. Input gestures are covered in detail in the appendix.

Commands and Data Binding

One of the most compelling and powerful features of using commands is the integration to data binding. Because both Command and CommandParameter are properties on elements, they can have data bound to them. Therefore, we can use the shape of the data that we're binding to determine the action that should happen. In Chapter 6 we talked about data-driven UIs; now with commands we can also have data-driven logic.

To see how this comes together, we will start with an application that displays all the files in the c:\ drive. We'll start by defining a simple dialog with a list box, and a data template to display the name of each file:

```
<Window x:Class='EssentialWPF.DataAndCommands'
  xmlns='http://schemas.microsoft.com/winfx/2006/xaml/presentation'
  xmlns:x='http://schemas.microsoft.com/winfx/2006/xaml'
  Title='Data and Commands'
  >
  <ListBox Margin='2' Name='_files'>
    <ListBox.ItemTemplate>
      <DataTemplate>
        <TextBlock Text='{Binding Path=Name}' />
      </DataTemplate>
    </ListBox.ItemTemplate>
  </ListBox>
</Window>
```

In the code behind, we can then populate the ItemsSource property to contain the list of files:

```
public partial class DataAndCommands : Window {
  public DataAndCommands() {
    InitializeComponent();

    FileInfo[] fileList = new DirectoryInfo("c:\\").GetFiles("*.*");
    _files.ItemsSource = fileList;
  }

}
```

Running this program will produce something like Figure 7.5.

Great! Now we want to add a button to display the file. However, we don't want to allow arbitrary applications to run, so we want to provide

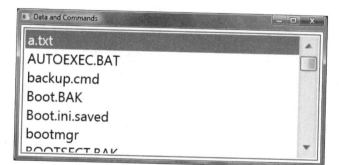

FIGURE 7.5: Displaying the list of files

some type of filter on the files that we load. We will have two commands, Open and Blocked:

```
public partial class DataAndCommands : Window {
    public static readonly RoutedCommand OpenCommand =
        new RoutedCommand("Open", typeof(DataAndCommands));

    public static readonly RoutedCommand BlockedCommand =
        new RoutedCommand("Blocked", typeof(DataAndCommands));

    ...
}
```

Also we need to provide some type of handler for these commands:

```
public partial class DataAndCommands : Window {
    public DataAndCommands() {
        InitializeComponent();

        CommandBindings.Add(new CommandBinding(OpenCommand,
            delegate (object sender, ExecutedRoutedEventArgs e) {
                Process.Start("notepad.exe", (string)e.Parameter);
            }));
        CommandBindings.Add(new CommandBinding(BlockedCommand,
            delegate (object sender, ExecutedRoutedEventArgs e) {
                MessageBox.Show((string)e.Parameter, "Blocked");
            }));
    }
}
```

With our two commands defined, we can update the data template for our files to include a button. We can use data binding for the command parameter (the file name). For the command itself, because we want some items to use OpenCommand and others to use BlockedCommand, we will use IValueConverter to go from the file name to ICommand:

```
<DataTemplate>
  <WrapPanel>
    <TextBlock Text='{Binding Path=Name}' />
    <Button
      CommandParameter='{Binding Path=FullName}'>
      <Button.Command>
        <Binding>
          <Binding.Converter>
            <l:FileToCommandConverter />
          </Binding.Converter>
        </Binding>
      </Button.Command>
      Show
    </Button>
  </WrapPanel>
</DataTemplate>
```

The converter can perform any logic based on the data to determine what command to execute. For this example, we will check the file extension:

```
public class FileToCommandConverter : IValueConverter {
  public object Convert(object value,
    Type targetType, object parameter, CultureInfo culture) {

    string ext = ((FileInfo)value).Extension.ToLowerInvariant();

    if (ext == ".txt") {
      return DataAndCommands.OpenCommand;
    }
    return DataAndCommands.BlockedCommand;
  }

  ...

}
```

When we run the program (Figure 7.6), we can see that only .txt files will show their contents.[4] This example is a bit trivial; we could easily

---

4. This example should not be misinterpreted as a secure way to implement filtering. Any filtering done on file extension is very easy to spoof. I just wanted a simple example, instead of actually trying to sniff the bytes or doing something really secure.

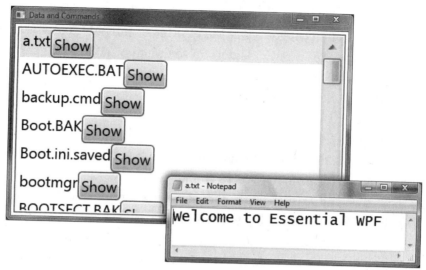

FIGURE 7.6: Running the program with data-bound commands

accomplish a similar behavior by using the CanExecute method and disable the command for "bad" files. However, the important point here is that we could have returned any command. We can use any logic based on the data to determine the behavior of any element displayed.

Commands allow for a loose coupling between the UI and the behavior. Commands also enable a much more data-driven approach to defining the behavior of an application. There is a set of behavior that is not really application logic, but rather just manipulation of the display state. For example, when a user moves the mouse over a button, we want that button to be highlighted. This display logic can be implemented with command or event handlers, but once that behavior is moved into code it is very difficult to provide good tools for it, and we have reintroduced a tight coupling of the display to the behavior. Triggers are designed to solve this exact problem.

Triggers

In Chapter 5 we had our first taste of triggers, using them to declaratively start an animation in conjunction with a control template. Triggers are signaled by three things: (1) the state of a display property (Trigger), (2) the state of a data property (DataTrigger), or (3) an event (EventTrigger).

All three trigger types cause a set of actions when they are signaled. There are also two collection trigger types: MultiTrigger and MultiDataTrigger.

Triggers can be used only inside of a template or style.[5] Trigger and EventTrigger can be used inside of a control template or style; DataTrigger can be used only within a data template.

Adding Triggers to Data

In building a data template, there are two options for binding a display element to part of a data model. We've already seen how to use a binding to accomplish this, and we can optionally use a value converter to translate the data model value into something that the display elements can consume.

DataTrigger provides a declarative way to specify a set of actions that should be performed for specific data model values. In this way, DataTrigger is effectively a simple value converter in markup. DataTrigger uses a binding to get a value from the data model, and a series of Setter and EventSetter objects that should be used when the value matches a specified value.

To illustrate, let's take the last example from the section on commands (see Figure 7.6) and switch from using a value converter to using DataTrigger. Instead of using a value converter on the binding for the button's Command property, we specifically bind it to the default value for the property (in this case, BlockedCommand):

```
<DataTemplate>
  <WrapPanel>
    <TextBlock Text='{Binding Path=Name}' />
    <Button
       Command='{x:Static 1:DataAndTriggers.BlockedCommand}'
       CommandParameter='{Binding Path=FullName}'>
       Show
    </Button>
  </WrapPanel>
</DataTemplate>
```

---

5. Don't let the Triggers properties on FrameworkElement and FrameworkContentElement fool you. They are like the appendix in the human body: They have very little value and can be removed if they start causing problems. In all seriousness, triggers are implemented through the property system and work only in templates and styles. The local Triggers property is there as a placeholder, and hopefully will work directly in a future release of WPF.

Next we want to set up a data trigger that will be implemented when the file extension is ".txt":

```
<DataTemplate>
  <WrapPanel>
    <TextBlock Text='{Binding Path=Name}' />
    <Button
      Command='{x:Static 1:DataAndTriggers.BlockedCommand}'
      CommandParameter='{Binding Path=FullName}'>
      Show
    </Button>
  </WrapPanel>
  <DataTemplate.Triggers>
    <DataTrigger Binding='{Binding Path=Extension}' Value='.txt'>
    </DataTrigger>
  </DataTemplate.Triggers>
</DataTemplate>
```

When the extension matches ".txt", we want to set the Command property to OpenCommand. To accomplish this, we need to add a setter to the trigger. A setter sets a property to a certain value. In this case we must also specify a target for the property, because we don't want to set the property on the data model:

```
<DataTemplate>
  <WrapPanel>
    <TextBlock Text='{Binding Path=Name}' />
    <Button
      x:Name='_showButton'
      Command='{x:Static 1:DataAndTriggers.BlockedCommand}'
      CommandParameter='{Binding Path=FullName}'>
      Show
    </Button>
  </WrapPanel>
  <DataTemplate.Triggers>
    <DataTrigger Binding='{Binding Path=Extension}' Value='.txt'>
      <Setter
        TargetName='_showButton'
        Property='Command'
        Value='{x:Static 1:DataAndTriggers.OpenCommand}' />
    </DataTrigger>
  </DataTemplate.Triggers>
</DataTemplate>
```

Because DataTrigger supports a set of Setter objects, we can easily perform multiple actions in response to the data value. Here we will add a

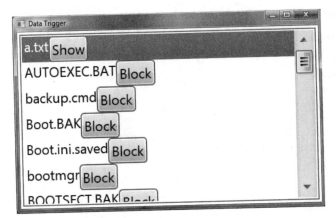

Figure 7.7: Using `DataTrigger` to replace a value converter, and setting multiple properties

second setter that displays the command to be executed (Figure 7.7). The order in which setters are applied is not guaranteed, although currently they are applied in the order that they're declared:

```
<DataTemplate>
  <WrapPanel>
    <TextBlock Text='{Binding Path=Name}' />
    <Button
      x:Name='_showButton'
      Command='{x:Static l:DataAndTriggers.BlockedCommand}'
      CommandParameter='{Binding Path=FullName}'
      Content='Block'
      />
  </WrapPanel>
  <DataTemplate.Triggers>
    <DataTrigger Binding='{Binding Path=Extension}' Value='.txt'>
      <Setter
        TargetName='_showButton'
        Property='Command'
        Value='{x:Static l:DataAndTriggers.OpenCommand}' />
      <Setter
        TargetName='_showButton'
        Property='Content'
        Value='Show' />
    </DataTrigger>
  </DataTemplate.Triggers>
</DataTemplate>
```

When using `DataTrigger`, we are limited to simple value equality: The data value must exactly match the value we specify. The preceding example differs from the value converter version in one small but important way:

The original value converter always called ToLowerInvariant to handle different cases in the file name. To deal with file name variations, we can create a simple value converter that does the conversion:

```
public class ToLowerInvariantConverter : IValueConverter {

    public object Convert(object value, Type targetType,
                object parameter, CultureInfo culture) {
      return ((string)value).ToLowerInvariant();
    }

    public object ConvertBack(object value, Type targetType,
                object parameter, CultureInfo culture) {
      return value;
    }
}
```

It's then trivial to attach the converter to the trigger:

```
<DataTrigger Value='.txt'>
  <DataTrigger.Binding>
    <Binding Path='Extension'>
      <Binding.Converter>
        <l:ToLowerInvariantConverter />
      </Binding.Converter>
    </Binding>
  </DataTrigger.Binding>
  <Setter
    TargetName='_showButton'
    Property='Command'
    Value='{x:Static l:DataAndTriggers.OpenCommand}' />
  <Setter
    TargetName='_showButton'
    Property='Content'
    Value='Show' />
</DataTrigger>
```

By using DataTrigger, we could move all the UI-dependent logic (binding of the correct command) into the markup and leave the minimal amount of code (the string conversion) in the code. This approach allows for the majority of the logic to be in the markup, improving our ability to create tools for the display, and providing a cleaner separation between the UI and application logic.

Adding Triggers to Controls

Although data triggers provide the ability to move more logic out of value converters, the design for Trigger and EventTrigger was inspired by the desire to have all view-dependent logic of a control declared in the markup. The goal of `ControlTemplate` was to allow the display of a control to be completely replaceable, with no change to the control logic:

```
<ControlTemplate TargetType='{x:Type Button}'>
  <Border x:Name='border'>
    <ContentPresenter />
  </Border>
  <ControlTemplate.Triggers>
    <Trigger Property='IsPressed' Value='true'>
      <Setter TargetName='border' Property='Background' Value='Red' />
    </Trigger>
  </ControlTemplate.Triggers>
</ControlTemplate>
```

`DataTrigger` takes us partway there: We can perform data transformation and binding declaratively. For the display of a control, however, we often need more flexibility. `Trigger` builds on the functionality of `DataTrigger` by adding `EnterActions` and `ExitActions`. Consequently, we can have animations start and stop in response to the transition of a property from one state to another (as we saw in Chapter 5).

`EventTrigger`, on the other hand, is signaled from an event (like `MouseEnter` or `Loaded`) and lets us control a set of animations.

Two interesting observations can be made about triggers at this point. First, two classes of "actions" can happen in response to a trigger: storyboard control actions, and setters. Setters support property and event wire-up; storyboard control actions allow us to play, stop, pause, and perform other actions on a storyboard. `EventTrigger` and the enter and exit actions of `Trigger` all work only with the storyboard control actions.

The second interesting observation is that the list of triggers and actions that triggers can wire up to cannot be extended in version 1.0 of WPF. However, it is possible to stretch triggers pretty far using complex triggers and combining them in interesting ways.

Triggers as the New "if"

Triggers are a simple form of rules engine. They let us express a condition (through the value) and an action (the list of setters or enter and exit actions). If we think about this in C# terms, triggers let us write code like

```
if (IsPressed) {
  border.Background = Brushes.Red;
}
```

Because we can have multiple conditions, using either MultiTrigger or MultiDataTrigger, we can write a trigger like this:

```
if (IsPressed && IsMouseOver) {
  border.Background = Brushes.Red;
}
```

This would actually be written with MultiTrigger (assuming the control template example we just saw):

```
<ControlTemplate TargetType='{x:Type Button}'>
  <Border x:Name='border'>
    <ContentPresenter />
  </Border>
  <ControlTemplate.Triggers>
    <MultiTrigger>
      <MultiTrigger.Conditions>
        <Condition Property='IsPressed' Value='true' />
        <Condition Property='IsMouseOver' Value='true' />
      </MultiTrigger.Conditions>
      <Setter TargetName='border' Property='Background' Value='Red' />
    </MultiTrigger>
  </ControlTemplate.Triggers>
</ControlTemplate>
```

If no trigger applies, then the value specified on the element will be used. Effectively this means that the else clause of the if statement is found on the element. Here we'll make the background blue if no trigger applies:

```
<ControlTemplate TargetType='{x:Type Button}'>
  <Border x:Name='border' Background='Blue'>
    <ContentPresenter />
  </Border>
  <ControlTemplate.Triggers>
    <MultiTrigger>
      <MultiTrigger.Conditions>
        <Condition Property='IsPressed' Value='true' />
        <Condition Property='IsMouseOver' Value='true' />
      </MultiTrigger.Conditions>
      <Setter TargetName='border' Property='Background' Value='Red' />
    </MultiTrigger>
  </ControlTemplate.Triggers>
</ControlTemplate>
```

WHERE ARE WE?

In this chapter we have looked at how to add behavior in response to an event, from either the user or the system, using the various action models: events, commands, or triggers.

■8■
Styles

O VER THE PRECEDING six chapters we have looked at all the pieces that we need to build an application in Windows Presentation Foundation. We've seen how an application is constructed out of controls that can be positioned with layout, visualized, and integrated with data, and finally perform a set of actions. The final concept to understand is styles.

Styles are a set of properties and actions to associate with an element. Styles are the aggregators of all customizations; they support all the concepts we've learned about so far: changing templates, animations, bindings, commands, and all other features exposed by WPF. Styles can be combined with other resources and packaged into a theme. **Themes** provide a consistent way for designers to interact with developers to create applications. Using themes, we can define a completely different look and behavior for an application.

Style Principles

The notion of creating a separate definition of the style or theme for a "thing" has been around a long time. Microsoft Word afforded me my first experience with styles and themes many years ago. Word has a notion of named bundles of formatting information: Heading 1, Heading 2, Normal, and so on. The Web world's first dabbling in styles consisted of the notion of basic semantic markup: things like H1, H2, and EMPHASIS. These semantic tags would then be rendered by a browser with a specific style.

With the advent of Cascading Style Sheets (CSS), the document author could define a custom style for each of these named tags or, in fact, for any tag using a specialized query language.

For WPF we knew we wanted to support some type of styling, the ability to reuse style information across multiple elements. Styling would enable consistent UIs and support the designer/developer work flow by allowing for a clean separation of the designer's style and the developer's UI structure. Having a single model to span UI, documents, and media was critical. Three principles drove the development of the WPF style system: (1) embrace element composition, (2) provide a unified model for customization, and (3) optimize for the tools experience.

Element Composition

As we've seen in the rest of this book, WPF relies heavily on element composition, which introduces some interesting questions for the styling system. First, how should styles be associated with elements? Initially the WPF team thought of having a single style at the root of the element tree and using some type of query language for applying styles to elements deep in the tree. Imagine something like this:

```
<Window ...>
  <Window.Styles>
    <!-- Apply this style to any Button inside
         of a StackPanel... (of course, this is not
         the actual syntax). -->
    <Style ApplyTo='StackPanel - Button'> ... </Style>
  </Window.Styles>
</Window>
```

This model, however, did not work well with element composition and deep hierarchies. The fact that the document structure must be encoded into the ApplyTo clause breaks encapsulation. In a deeply nested document structure these clauses also become very large and unwieldy.

What we really wanted was a style for any container element, so that styles could be associated with the document structure without the large ApplyTo clauses. We also wanted to be able to put the style definitions close to the elements; if we have a set of styles that we want to apply to only a section of the display tree, we don't want to have to define a scope for every rule.

Instead of this notion of global styles, we opted to define a scope for each style. So we can define a new style at any point in the tree:

```
<Window ...>
  <Window.Style>
    <Style>...</Style>
  </Window.Style>

  <StackPanel>
    <StackPanel.Style>
      <Style>...</Style>
    </StackPanel.Style>

  </StackPanel>
</Window>
```

In addition, because of how resource references work, we can leverage the resource system to scope named and type-based styles to the tree as well:

```
<Window ...>
  <Window.Resources>
    <Style x:Key='someStyle'>...</Style>
  </Window.Resources>

  <StackPanel>
    <StackPanel.Resources>
      <Style x:Key='someStyle'>...</Style>
    </StackPanel.Resources>

    <!-- Anything contained in this StackPanel
         will get "someStyle" from the StackPanel,
         not the Window definition. -->
  </StackPanel>
</Window>
```

Because the rest of WPF relies so heavily on element composition, the style system must also be optimized for composition. Beyond basic composition is also the overall goal of unifying UI, documents, and media. Styling, too, should apply uniformly.

Unified Model for Customization

For WPF, unification came in two flavors: (1) being able to apply styles to any of the presentation domains (UI, documents, and media) and (2) being able to customize anything in the system (properties, actions, display, etc.). One of the big benefits we got from building a unified presentation platform was that the ability to use styles across the entire platform did not cost anything, provided that the styling system gave access to all the features of the platform.

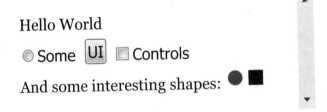

FIGURE 8.1: Using property setters to apply styles to UI, documents, and media

We needed styles to be able to do only two things: set properties and listen to events. If we could support these two functionalities, then everything else in the system would be accessible.

Here we'll build a set of styles that apply to any type of element: paragraphs, buttons, shapes, and so on (Figure 8.1):

```
<FlowDocumentScrollViewer
  xmlns='http://schemas.microsoft.com/winfx/2006/xaml/presentation'
  xmlns:x='http://schemas.microsoft.com/winfx/2006/xaml'
  >
  <FlowDocument>
    <FlowDocument.Resources>
      <Style TargetType='{x:Type Paragraph}'>
        <Setter Property='FontFamily' Value='Georgia' />
        <Setter Property='Margin' Value='3' />
      </Style>
      <Style TargetType='{x:Type Button}'>
        <Setter Property='FontFamily' Value='Tahoma' />
        <Setter Property='Margin' Value='3' />
      </Style>
      <Style TargetType='{x:Type RadioButton}'>
        <Setter Property='FontFamily' Value='Tahoma' />
        <Setter Property='Margin' Value='3' />
      </Style>
      <Style TargetType='{x:Type CheckBox}'>
        <Setter Property='FontFamily' Value='Tahoma' />
        <Setter Property='Margin' Value='3' />
      </Style>
      <Style TargetType='{x:Type Ellipse}'>
        <Setter Property='Fill' Value='Red' />
        <Setter Property='Margin' Value='3' />
      </Style>
      <Style TargetType='{x:Type Rectangle}'>
        <Setter Property='Fill' Value='Blue' />
        <Setter Property='Margin' Value='3' />
```

```
        </Style>
      </FlowDocument.Resources>
      <Paragraph>Hello World</Paragraph>
      <Paragraph>
        <RadioButton>Some</RadioButton>
        <Button>UI</Button>
        <CheckBox>Controls</CheckBox>
      </Paragraph>
      <Paragraph>And some interesting shapes:
        <Ellipse Width='15' Height='15' />
        <Rectangle Width='15' Height='15' />
      </Paragraph>
    </FlowDocument>
  </FlowDocumentScrollViewer>
```

Nothing is ever quite that easy, so we'll see some places where the styling system exposes implementation details of the core WPF engine. For example, the simple way to apply triggers to an element would be to use a simple property setter against the Triggers property on an element:

```
<Style TargetType='{x:Type Button}'>
    <!-- this doesn't work -->
    <Setter Property='Triggers'>
        <Setter.Value>
            <Trigger Property='IsMouseOver' Value='True'>
                ...
            </Trigger>
        </Setter.Value>
    </Setter>
</Style>
```

However, because of some implementation details having to do with how triggers are applied, we end up with a slightly more specialized model with the Style.Triggers property:

```
<Style TargetType='{x:Type Button}'>
    <Style.Triggers>
        <Trigger Property='IsMouseOver' Value='True'>
            ...
        </Trigger>
    </Style.Triggers>
</Style>
```

The principle is still present, even if the object model is a bit archaic; if something can be done to an element, it can be done in a style. We hope that most developers won't have to spend all their days in markup, though, so tool support is critical.

Optimization for Tools

Providing great tool support is probably the single most difficult task with styles. CSS has an amazing power to apply multiple rules to a given element using a specialized query language. Within this very powerful language is support for declaring rule precedence, hierarchical selection, tag name selection, identified element selection, and so on. CSS provides an incredibly powerful, but extremely difficult, tool model.

One problem with the CSS rules-based approach for style selection is that the process is one-way. Given a set of rules, we can determine the elements that it affects; but given a change to a property on an element, it is effectively impossible to determine what style should "own" the property value. Suppose we want a visual designer to update the style definition when we change a property value, so that it can be shared with other elements. The only real way to do this with a complex rules system is to enforce some simplifications: In CSS it is common to have a model in which all styles are identified by CSS class names.

WPF very intentionally limits the power of style selection; each element has exactly two styles affecting it at any given time, only one of which can be customized by the developer using the element (the other style is the "default" style associated by the element author). There are only two ways to determine the style to use: by direct reference from the element to a named resource, or via the type of the element. This is basically a hybrid model of Word styles and CSS.

In addition to the simplicity of the model, there is now no need to build a query language for determining which elements a style should affect. In addition, designers and developers find it much easier to determine which elements will be affected by a change to a style.

The final big decision regarding tool support came down to the actual encoding of the style definition in the markup. If you are familiar with CSS, you have probably seen styles defined by name/value pair combinations:

```
Button {
  Background = Red;
  FontSize = 24pt;
}
```

This is a very nice, compact syntax, but it suffers from two problems. The first is predominantly a tool problem: We now have a way of parsing and handling styles that is completely different from anything else in the system (everything else is XML). This adds a lot of complexity to the tool. For WPF we decided to bet on XML, so we chose to encode styles using XAML notation:

```
<Style TargetType='{x:Type Button}'>
  <Setter Property='Background' Value='Red' />
  <Setter Property='FontSize' Value='24pt' />
</Style>
```

The second problem has more to do with composition: There is no good way to nest complex values in the CSS style notation. Using XAML property element syntax, we can specify arbitrarily complex values:

```
<Style TargetType='{x:Type Button}'>
  <Setter Property='Background'>
    <Setter.Value>
      <LinearGradientBrush ...>
        ...
      </LinearGradientBrush>
    </Setter.Value>
  </Setter>
  <Setter Property='FontSize' Value='24pt' />
</Style>
```

With the principles of element composition, unified styling, and optimization for tools, we can begin looking at the details of how the style system works.

Beginning Styles

Styles are composed of three things: setters, triggers, and resources. To see the progression of using styles, we will start with a simple button that uses a local property set to make the background red:

```
<Button Background='Red'>
  Hello, Red World!
</Button>
```

We can start by moving the property set into a style. When we create a new style, we need to tell the style (using the TargetType property) what type of object we want to associate the style with:

```
<Style TargetType='{x:Type Button}'>

</Style>
```

To set the background to be red, we need to specify a property setter using a `Setter` object. There are two types of setters: property setters and event setters. Property setters allow us to set a property value for all objects that use the style. Event setters allow us to connect an event handler to any objects to which the style is applied. Generally it is better to use commands to connect behavior to controls, so event setters are infrequently used.

The property name is scoped by the target type of the style; thus "Background" is known to refer to `Button.BackgroundProperty`:

```
<Style TargetType='{x:Type Button}'>
  <Setter Property='Background' Value='Red' />
</Style>
```

When the model for styles was created, there was a lot of debate about whether a special syntax should be developed for handling property and event setters. One idea was to have an "as used" syntax—that is, something more akin to the following:

```
<Style>
  <!-- this doesn't work! -->
  <Button Background='Red' />
</Style>
```

Recall that one of the main tenets for all of WPF was the notion that markup and the object model should be as similar as possible. In this case, the normal rules for processing markup would say that this example would create a new button and set the background to be red. For styles, obviously this isn't what we really wanted to happen. Instead, styles are actually a customization script. The style allows us to adjust properties, events, triggers, and resources for an object.

With the setter syntax for a style, the markup is explicit that it is a customization script and completely in sync with the object model. To associate the style with the type, we need to set the `Style` property:

```
<Button>
  <Button.Style>
    <Style TargetType='{x:Type Button}'>
      <Setter Property='Background' Value='Red' />
    </Style>
  </Button.Style>
  Hello, Red World!
</Button>
```

As we learned in Chapter 6, we can use a resource reference to share the definition of the style:

```
<Window ...>
  <Window.Resources>
    <Style x:Key='myStyle' TargetType='{x:Type Button}'>
      <Setter Property='Background' Value='Red' />
    </Style>
  </Window.Resources>

  <StackPanel>
    <Button Style='{DynamicResource myStyle}'>
      Hello, Red World!
    </Button>

    <Button Style='{DynamicResource myStyle}'>
      Another button!
    </Button>
  </StackPanel>
</Window>
```

In Chapter 6 we saw that we can associate data templates with a type by using DataTemplateKey instead of directly referencing the template. We can do the same thing with styles, by specifying the key to be the type object for associating with the style; therefore, we can automatically apply a style to all objects of the specified type. If we change the key in our example to {x:Type Button}, any button contained within the window will be red:

```
<Window ...>
  <Window.Resources>
    <Style x:Key='{x:Type Button}' TargetType='{x:Type Button}'>
      <Setter Property='Background' Value='Red' />
    </Style>
  </Window.Resources>

  <Button>
    Hello, Red World!
  </Button>
</Window>
```

The key for a style defines how it will be retrieved from the resource dictionary. The target type of a style defines the type to which the style will be applied. All this can be confusing, since often the key and target type are the same.[1] However, we saw earlier that we may want to create multiple named styles for the same target type.

---

1. This can become even more confusing: If we do not specify a key for a style in a resource dictionary, then the target type is automatically used. I don't recommend using this trick, and it makes the markup much harder to read.

Beyond the basic setter functionality of styles, we can associate triggers and resources with a style. Triggers work exactly as they do for control and data templates. We can adjust the background of the button by attaching a property trigger to the IsMouseOver property:

```
<Style x:Key='{x:Type Button}' TargetType='{x:Type Button}'>
  <Setter Property='Background' Value='Red' />
  <Style.Triggers>
    <Trigger Property='IsMouseOver' Value='True'>
      <Setter Property='Background' Value='Blue' />
    </Trigger>
  </Style.Triggers>
</Style>
```

At this point you might be asking, What is the difference between ControlTemplate.Triggers and Style.Triggers? Remember that the control template affects the display tree for the control. In the case of adjusting the button's background color, the style appears to affect the display tree, but really the button's Background property is being set and the default template for Button binds the Background property to an element in the display tree.

To see the distinction between these two, we can add another trigger for the IsPressed property:

```
<Style x:Key='{x:Type Button}' TargetType='{x:Type Button}'>
  <Setter Property='Background' Value='Red' />
  <Style.Triggers>
    <Trigger Property='IsMouseOver' Value='True'>
      <Setter Property='Background' Value='Blue' />
    </Trigger>

    <Trigger Property='IsPressed' Value='True'>
      <Setter Property='Background' Value='Yellow' />
    </Trigger>
  </Style.Triggers>
</Style>
```

If we run this example, we'll find that when we move the mouse down on the button, it does not become yellow. The reason is that the default template for Button does not bind the background property to any element in the display tree when the button is pressed. To understand this, let's look at a simplified version of Button's default control template:

```
<ControlTemplate TargetType='{x:Type Button}'>
  <Border Background='{TemplateBinding Background}' x:Name='border'>
    <ContentPresenter />
```

```
        </Border>
    <ControlTemplate.Triggers>
      <Trigger Property='IsPressed' Value='True'>
        <Setter
          Property='Background'
          Value='Red'
          TargetName='border' />
      </Trigger>
    </ControlTemplate.Triggers>
  </ControlTemplate>
```

Because the default template for `Button` removes the background template binding (by explicitly making the border's background red), our style trigger has no impact. The reason for this type of feature is that control templates can affect only the properties on visual tree elements, whereas styles can affect only the control's properties.

Models, Display, and Styles

The overlap between `Style` and `ControlTemplate` brings us to the issue of the split between display and behavior. There are several well-known patterns for object-oriented design, one of which is called model-view-controller (MVC). In this pattern, objects are divided into three parts: (1) a *model* that defines the data structures, (2) a *view* that defines the data display, and (3) a *controller* that defines the interaction. Although WPF doesn't strictly conform to this pattern, it is useful to think about MVC when looking at styles and templates.

WPF's control types, such as `Button`, define both a data model and an interaction model for the control. The display of the control is completely determined by the template. WPF then allows us to provide data through the content model, which was covered in Chapter 3. With the content model, we now have a basic MVC style pattern without all the usual complexity.

The reason why it's interesting to think about this split of data (model), template (view), and control (controller) is that styles provide a simple way to connect all these. Controls provide customization through properties, which styles support setting. Templates provide customization through property and resource bindings, which styles support setting. And data is wired to controls through the control's properties, which styles support setting. Not only do styles participate in adjusting each of these three parts, but they connect the parts; using a style, we can associate a template with a control, and a data source with the control.

We can now look in more depth at the relationship between styles and templates. We'll begin with a simple template for a button:

```
<ControlTemplate
  x:Key='simpleButtonTemplate'
  TargetType='{x:Type Button}'>
  <Border>
    <ContentPresenter
      HorizontalAlignment='Center'
      VerticalAlignment='Center' />
  </Border>
</ControlTemplate>
```

At first glance, it may not be obvious that this template supports any additional customization; the template contains no references to any properties on the element. In Chapter 3 we saw that ContentPresenter implicitly binds to the Content property of the templated control. For this reason we could set the Content property and the template control and see the results.

We can bind more properties to the template using the TemplateBinding feature, which we learned about in Chapter 7:

```
<ControlTemplate
  x:Key='simpleButtonTemplate'
  TargetType='{x:Type Button}'>
  <Border
    Background='{TemplateBinding Property=Background}'>
    <ContentPresenter
      HorizontalAlignment='Center'
      VerticalAlignment='Center' />
  </Border>
</ControlTemplate>
```

Now the template for the button has a parameter that is a property on the button itself, so we style the button using the Background property and have that style affect the display:

```
<Button Template='{DynamicResource simpleButtonTemplate}'>
  <Button.Style>
    <Style TargetType='{x:Type Button}'>
      <Setter Property='Background' Value='Red' />
    </Style>
  </Button.Style>
  Hello, Red World!
</Button>
```

Using this approach, we can create a template that has quite a bit of flexibility, but we are limited to customizing the properties that the control author anticipated needing (e.g., Background and Foreground properties). If we want more levers of control in customization—for example, to offer a "highlight" color in a template—we have three options: (1) to create a new control with the additional property, (2) to create an attached property that applies to the control that we're customizing, or (3) to use a well-known named resource.

Generally, creating a new control to enable styling is overkill. Ideally we'd like to be able to apply styles and templates to existing elements. The options of creating attached properties and using named resources are very similar; however, attached properties are seen more as "programmatic" access than as style access. Attached properties are generally seen as ways of influencing behavior, but named resources work more naturally in styles.

To define a named resource we need to create a unique key, which we do by creating a static instance of ComponentResourceKey[2]:

```
public static class SimpleButton {

    public static readonly ComponentResourceKey RingBrush =
        new ComponentResourceKey(typeof(SimpleButton), "RingBrush");
}
```

Now we have a globally unique identifier for this custom property, which we can use in the template. Here we will wire up the Border.BorderBrush property to the named resource:

```
<ControlTemplate
  x:Key='simpleButtonTemplate'
  TargetType='{x:Type Button}'>
  <Border
    BorderBrush=
      '{DynamicResource {x:Static l:SimpleButton.RingBrush}}'
    BorderThickness='5'
```

---

2. ComponentResourceKey isn't necessarily required here, but it provides a convenient way to create a globally unique value. The combination of type plus string provides a unique namespace (strong, named CLR type) and a domain of names (the string). The only requirement is that the key is unique and implements GetHashCode and Equals correctly.

```
    Background='{TemplateBinding Property=Background}'>
    <ContentPresenter
      HorizontalAlignment='Center'
      VerticalAlignment='Center' />
  </Border>
</ControlTemplate>
```

In the style for `Button`, we can now adjust this resource, as well as any local properties:

```
<Button Template='{DynamicResource simpleButtonTemplate}'>
  <Button.Style>
    <Style TargetType='{x:Type Button}'>
      <Style.Resources>
        <SolidColorBrush
          x:Key='{x:Static l:SimpleButton.RingBrush}'
          Color='Red' />
      </Style.Resources>
      <Setter Property='Background' Value='Red' />
    </Style>
  </Button.Style>
  Hello, World!
</Button>
```

Notice that the style now has some type of dependency on the template. The style refers to a named resource that has impact only if the template is binding to it. For this reason, it is very common to have the style implement the association with the template:

```
<Button>
  <Button.Style>
    <Style TargetType='{x:Type Button}'>
      <Style.Resources>
        <SolidColorBrush
          x:Key='{x:Static l:SimpleButton.RingBrush}'
          Color='Red' />
      </Style.Resources>
      <Setter Property='Background' Value='Red' />
      <Setter Property='Template'
        Value='{DynamicResource simpleButtonTemplate}' />
    </Style>
  </Button.Style>
  Hello, World!
</Button>
```

If we think about all of these bits together—templates, styles, and resources—we can begin to see that there is an interesting packaging that defines a complete look and feel for a control. This bundling effectively defines a single control *theme*.

Themes

WPF has been built with themes in mind; however, most of the APIs in WPF are focused around styles and resources. The only place where themes are mentioned in the object model is a single assembly attribute called `ThemeInfoAttribute`. A theme is actually just a resource dictionary. Although you may not think that you've seen the type up to now, `ResourceDictionary` is the type of all the `Resources` properties that we've seen on controls, templates, and styles.

To define a custom theme, the easiest starting point is to create a new XAML file in a project and define a `ResourceDictionary` object (for this example we will call the file myTheme.xaml):

```
<ResourceDictionary
  xmlns='http://schemas.microsoft.com/winfx/2006/xaml/presentation'
  xmlns:x='http://schemas.microsoft.com/winfx/2006/xaml'
  >
  <Style x:Key='...' TargetType='...'>
    ...
  </Style>
  <ControlTemplate x:Key='...' TargetType='...'>
    ...
  </ControlTemplate>
  <SolidColorBrush x:Key='...'>
    ...
  </SolidColorBrush>
  ...
</ResourceDictionary>
```

Wherever we want to apply this new style, we can do so using the `MergedDictionaries` property on `ResourceDictionary`:

```
<Window
  xmlns='http://schemas.microsoft.com/winfx/2006/xaml/presentation'
  xmlns:x='http://schemas.microsoft.com/winfx/2006/xaml'
  >
  <Window.Resources>
    <ResourceDictionary>
      <ResourceDictionary.MergedDictionaries>
        <ResourceDictionary Source='myTheme.xaml' />
      </ResourceDictionary.MergedDictionaries>
```

```
    </ResourceDictionary>
  </Window.Resources>
  ...
</Window>
```

In this usage, a theme definition is merged into the standard resource lookup hierarchy. Recall from Chapter 6 that we retrieve resources by looking up the element tree, then the application object, and finally the system resources. When we merge a dictionary into the tree, those resources become available at that location. We can use this technique to make a different theme active for portions of a UI.

Style lookup generally follows the standard resource lookup pattern, with one notable exception: ThemeInfoAttribute allows a type author to tell the system where the default theme for the type will be located. When retrieving a style, the system uses a particular default for a theme if no information for that type is found in the control tree, application object, or system resources. This default enables control authors to create themes for their controls.

Defining a new control that we want to be theme-aware takes three steps: First we must set DefaultStyleKey to associate the type with a theme:

```
public class MyCustomControl : FrameworkElement {

  public static MyCustomControl() {

    DefaultStyleKeyProperty.OverrideMetadata(
      typeof(MyCustomControl),
       new FrameworkPropertyMetadata(typeof(MyCustomControl)));
  }
}
```

The next step is to specify the theme discovery policy for the assembly using ThemeInfoAttribute:

```
[assembly: ThemeInfo(
   ResourceDictionaryLocation.SourceAssembly,
   ResourceDictionaryLocation.SourceAssembly)]
```

Finally, we must create one or more themes for the control. Each theme must be added to the application with the correct name (detailed in Table 8.1), and marked as a page in the project file (remember from Chapter 2 that we compile XAML files into a project by using the Page item type).

TABLE 8.1: Operating System Themes and the Names to Use for the Theme Resource Dictionary

Theme	Color	Resource Dictionary Name

Windows XP Style	Blue
	Olive green
	Silver
		`themes\luna.normalcolor.xaml`
		`themes\luna.homestead.xaml`
		`themes\luna.metallic.xaml`

Windows XP Media Center Edition; Windows XP Tablet PC Edition		`themes\royale.normalcolor.xaml`
Windows Vista Style		`themes\aero.normalcolor.xaml`
Classic		`themes\classic.xaml`
Anything else (fallback)		`themes\generic.xaml`

Using this technique, we can create a control that has a different default appearance for each operating system theme. The list of operating system themes cannot be extended at this time. Microsoft occasionally adds new themes (the "royale" theme was added for the Media Center and Tablet PC editions of Windows XP), but there is no public way for third parties to create new themes.[3]

Skinning

People often confuse two related concepts: themes and skins. Typically, a **theme** is defined as a collection of data used to customize the look and feel of an application, and **skinning** is generally the *end user customizability* of that theme. Microsoft Office, for example, has a rich theme for its UI but provides no skinning support. Windows Media Player, on the other hand, has great support for skinning, including allowing end users to build custom themes.

---

3. There are several third-party solutions for adding themes to Windows—most notably "ThemeXP." These options work by modifying core parts of Windows and they compromise the security of the system, so I strongly recommend not using them. Personally, I wish that Microsoft would make the theming model open and allowed third-party extensibility, but until that happens, I think it's best to live with the built-in themes.

WPF ships with rich support for themes, enabling both a control and an application author to have an amazing degree of flexibility in controlling their look and feel. WPF, however, does not ship with any intrinsic ability for skinning an application.

To implement skinning is a trivial matter, though, if we understand how styles and themes work. If themes are nothing more than merging a resource dictionary into a global collection, then it seems we can implement skinning with a small amount of code to adjust the collection of resources at the application, window, or container level.

To demonstrate, we can create a simple window that has a check box (to toggle the skin) and two buttons (to show the skin):

```
<Window
    x:Class='Styles.Skinning'
    xmlns='http://schemas.microsoft.com/winfx/2006/xaml/presentation'
    xmlns:x='http://schemas.microsoft.com/winfx/2006/xaml'
    Title='Styles'
    >

    <StackPanel>
        <CheckBox>
            Use custom buttons?
        </CheckBox>
        <Button
          Margin='2'
          HorizontalAlignment='center'>
          A button
        </Button>
        <Button
          Margin='2'
          HorizontalAlignment='center'>
          Another button
        </Button>
    </StackPanel>

</Window>
```

Running this application right now will produce the expected display (Figure 8.2).

We can then define two different themes using `ResourceDictionary`. The first theme will be a boring theme that does nothing. This boring theme will allow us to return easily to the default look of the application:

```
<!-- DefaultButtons.xaml -->
<ResourceDictionary
    xmlns='http://schemas.microsoft.com/winfx/2006/xaml/presentation'
    xmlns:x='http://schemas.microsoft.com/winfx/2006/xaml'
    >
    <Style x:Key='{x:Type Button}' TargetType='{x:Type Button}'>
    </Style>
</ResourceDictionary>
```

The second theme will apply a custom template to any button used in the application:

```
<!-- CustomButtons.xaml -->
<ResourceDictionary
  xmlns='http://schemas.microsoft.com/winfx/2006/xaml/presentation'
  xmlns:x='http://schemas.microsoft.com/winfx/2006/xaml'
  >
  <Style x:Key='{x:Type Button}' TargetType='{x:Type Button}'>
    <Setter Property='Template'>
      <Setter.Value>
        <ControlTemplate TargetType='{x:Type Button}'>
```

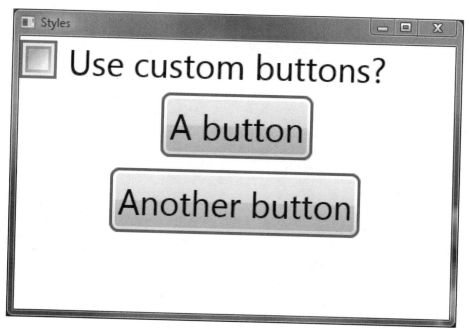

FIGURE 8.2: Our skinning application with no skin applied

```
<Border
  CornerRadius='10,2,10,2'
  BorderThickness='1'
  BorderBrush='Black'
  Padding='2'>
  <Border.Background>
    <LinearGradientBrush>
      <GradientStop Offset='0' Color='#FFFFFFFF' />
      <GradientStop Offset='1' Color='#FFCCCCCC' />
    </LinearGradientBrush>
  </Border.Background>
  <ContentPresenter
    HorizontalAlignment='Center'
    VerticalAlignment='Center' />
</Border>
        </ControlTemplate>
      </Setter.Value>
    </Setter>
  </Style>
</ResourceDictionary>
```

To toggle between the styles, we will hook up the CheckBox.Checked and CheckBox.Unchecked events to a single function that does the work. We also need to provide a name for the check box so that we can later check its value:

```
<Window ... >

    ...
    <CheckBox
        x:Name='_check1'
        IsChecked='False'
        Checked='ButtonChecked'
        Unchecked='ButtonChecked'>
        Use custom buttons?
    </CheckBox>
    ...
</Window>
```

To load the appropriate resource, we can use Application.LoadComponent, which will take a URI and return the resource dictionary:

```
ResourceDictionary theme = Application.LoadComponent(
                    new Uri("DefaultButtons.xaml",
                            UriKind.Relative)
                ) as ResourceDictionary;
```

Using the MergedDictionaries property on ResourceDictionary, we can add the theme resources to the window's resources. MergedDictionaries allows us to keep all the locally defined resources and merge in the theme.

To do this, we need to clone the resource dictionary from the window:

```
ResourceDictionary rd = new ResourceDictionary();

foreach (DictionaryEntry t in this.Resources)
{
    rd[t.Key] = t.Value;
}
```

Putting all this together, we can see the implementation of merging in a custom theme and associating it with the window:[4]

```
void ButtonsChecked(object sender, RoutedEventArgs e)
{
    ResourceDictionary rd = new ResourceDictionary();

    foreach (DictionaryEntry t in this.Resources)
    {
        rd[t.Key] = t.Value;
    }

    if (_check1.IsChecked ?? false)
    {
        ResourceDictionary theme = Application.LoadComponent(
                            new Uri("DefaultButtons.xaml",
                                    UriKind.Relative)
                            ) as ResourceDictionary;
        rd.MergedDictionaries.Add(theme);
    }
    else
    {
        ResourceDictionary theme = Application.LoadComponent(
                            new Uri("CustomButtons.xaml",
                                    UriKind.Relative)
                            ) as ResourceDictionary;
        rd.MergedDictionaries.Add(theme);
    }
    this.Resources = rd;
}
```

Running this application will produce a display something like Figure 8.3 (on page 412).

---

4. The ?? operator is a C# 2.0 feature that works on Nullable<T>. In this case, if _check1.IsChecked returns null, then false will be used for the value of this expression.

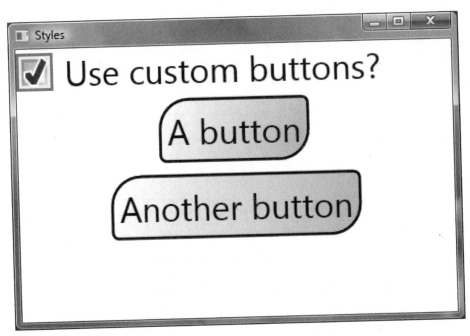

FIGURE 8.3: Our skinning application with a custom skin applied

This logic could easily be keyed off of a registry or configuration setting. In addition, we could replace the LoadComponent call with a direct call to XamlReader, which would allow us to load the XAML definition of the theme from anywhere (LoadComponent is limited to loading resources that are included in the application's manifest).

Style Inheritance

WPF's controls are all heavily based on styles and templates. The general design philosophy is that the controls themselves may not contain any hard-coded property values, defaults, or visuals, because we want graphic designers and theme authors to have complete control over the defaults for the controls. The various examples of customizing controls in this chapter have shown that, within a style, we can adjust only a few properties, so where are the rest of the values coming from?

Every property in WPF has a notion of value precedence (Figure 8.4). All the features we've seen so far—styling, data binding, inheritance, and so on—are applied in a strict order. The interesting thing about styles is that actually two are applied to any given element. When we use a control, it appears that

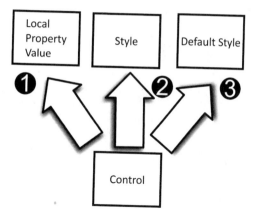

there is only one style because the second one is reserved for the control author. In all scenarios, local property values will trump any style-specified value.

In addition to this basic precedence is the ability to create a base style from which multiple styles can inherit. Styles are allowed to have only one parent style (no multiple inheritance, you C++ fans), but a base style can apply to multiple types of child styles. This changes the picture from Figure 8.4 by introducing hierarchy to styles, as Figure 8.5 (on page 414) shows.

Suppose we want to create a base style for use in all of our controls that defines some common font properties. We can do this by defining a style with a target type of a common base type that has all the properties we want to adjust and giving the style a name:

```
<Style x:Key='baseControls' TargetType='{x:Type Control}'>
    <Setter Property='FontSize' Value='14pt' />
    <Setter Property='FontFamily' Value='Corbel, Arial' />
    <Setter Property='Margin' Value='2' />
</Style>
```

We can then associate this base type with multiple control types using a normal style definition and setting the BasedOn property:[5]

---

5. Notice the use of StaticResource in the code that follows. Because the Style object itself doesn't use the dependency property system, we can't use binding, styling, or dynamic resources to set properties of the style object. By using StaticResource, we can apply a resource exactly once—which has the negative effect that the style's BasedOn property will not be updated if we modify ResourceDictionary.

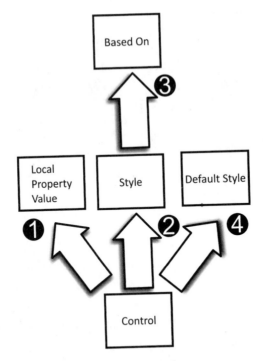

FIGURE 8.5: Property value precedence with base styles

```
<Style
    x:Key='{x:Type TextBox}'
    TargetType='{x:Type TextBox}'
    BasedOn='{StaticResource baseControls}' />
```

To really see the power here, we can create a couple of styles for different control types. In addition, for this example we will say that we want buttons to be bold, no matter what the base font is:

```
<Window x:Class='Styles.StyleInheritence'
    xmlns='http://schemas.microsoft.com/winfx/2006/xaml/presentation'
    xmlns:x='http://schemas.microsoft.com/winfx/2006/xaml'
    Title='Styles'
    >
    <Window.Resources>
        <Style x:Key='baseControls' TargetType='{x:Type Control}'>
            <Setter Property='FontSize' Value='14pt' />
            <Setter Property='FontFamily' Value='Corbel, Arial' />
            <Setter Property='Margin' Value='2' />
        </Style>

        <Style
            x:Key='{x:Type Button}'
```

```
            TargetType='{x:Type Button}'
            BasedOn='{StaticResource baseControls}'>

            <Setter Property='FontWeight' Value='Bold' />
        </Style>

        <Style
            x:Key='{x:Type CheckBox}'
            TargetType='{x:Type CheckBox}'
            BasedOn='{StaticResource baseControls}' />

        <Style
            x:Key='{x:Type TextBox}'
            TargetType='{x:Type TextBox}'
            BasedOn='{StaticResource baseControls}' />
    </Window.Resources>
    <StackPanel>
        <CheckBox>Hello World</CheckBox>
        <TextBox>Hello World</TextBox>
        <Button>Hello World</Button>
        <Button>Hello World</Button>
    </StackPanel>
</Window>
```

Running this code shows that all three control types get their font family and size from the `baseControls` style, and that all buttons are bold as well (Figure 8.6 on page 416).

We've now seen all the basic features of styles. Probably the most important thing about styles, though, is how to use them to improve an application, not break it.

Using Styles for Good, Not Evil

The inclusion of styles, and more generally the complete customizability of WPF, is probably one of the biggest changes over previous presentation technologies. On the WPF team we often compare what we're doing to the original Macintosh that introduced average users to a rich set of fonts and typography. We, the humans of the world, had to endure a decade of ransom note–style documents until people figured out how to use fonts responsibly to communicate information in a better fashion.

The same rigor is needed when we're thinking about styles. People define custom styles for three primary reasons: (1) to share property sets across two or more instances, (2) to move all customizations to a single point in an application, or (3) to define a distinctive look for an application.

FIGURE 8.6: Using a BasedOn style to apply common properties to multiple styles

Using styles for the first two purposes is great, and I highly encourage it. Provided that we have guidelines for how to do this (just like we should have coding guidelines for the code), using styles can boost productivity quite a lot. Whether we move these style definitions into a separate file or not is really just a matter of personal coding style.

It is for this last type of style—the definition of a custom look for an application—that I provide three notes of caution:

1. Never build just a style to try to create a custom look. Think about this as a holistic theme for the application.

2. Encompass enough of the common controls in a theme that the application feels consistent, because consistency is king.

3. Have a point.

Build Themes, Not Styles

Custom themes tend to get big quickly. The definition of a few custom gradients and shapes for controls can consume hundreds of lines of markup. In addition, we begin to introduce dependencies between templates and styles and resources and templates (notice the circular dependency?). Often rich themes may involve custom code for value converters or additional control behavior. Consequently, generally the best practice is to think of a theme as a "thing" rather than just a collection of styles at the root window in the application.

The first piece of concrete advice I would give is to move the definition of the theme into a separate file and use the merged-dictionaries feature to bind the theme into the application. Even better, move the theme definition to a separate assembly and use a cross-assembly reference to load the style (/<assemblyName>;component/<resourceName>):

```
<Application.Resources>
    <ResourceDictionary>
        <ResourceDictionary.MergedDictionaries>
            <ResourceDictionary
                Source='/StyleLibrary;Component/theme.xaml' />
        </ResourceDictionary.MergedDictionaries>
    </ResourceDictionary>
</Application.Resources>
```

This practice clearly isolates the theme from the application, makes it easier for us to hand off the theme to a designer, and forces us to think about the theme as a separate component.

Consistency Is King

When building a custom look and feel for an application, it is important to make it consistent across all the controls that will be used. One of the goals of WPF was to make every control customizable so that we wouldn't get the "Frankenstein" applications often seen with older forms packages (appearing as if the UI had been stitched together using parts of other applications). Of course, this powerful functionality raises the bar for developing custom themes, but it increases the quality of the user experience.

Probably the simplest way to approach creating a consistent design is to pick a theme ("metallic," "flat," etc.). Consider the "evil" set of controls

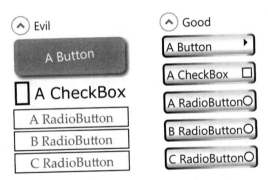

FIGURE 8.7: Consistency in a theme is critical to building a usable application.

shown in Figure 8.7. Here the font choices and sizes are all different, colors are different, even the angle of the text is different. The top button might be a great style for creating a game UI or whimsical survey-type interface, and the radio buttons are in a simple typographic style that might be nice for a Web application. Although I won't claim to be a good graphic designer, the controls under "good" are at least consistent. They use a common UI style, font choice, and so on.

Beyond basic consistency is the idea of creating a full suite of controls. When most people start building a theme, they pick a few common and simple controls to style, like the various buttons. But then they try to build a real application and run into all types of controls that may require more complex styles, or again they end up with a different, but equally bad, type of Frankenstein UI (Figure 8.8). One of the very common errors in this area is forgetting to style scrollbars. In Figure 8.8, the buttons have a "cool" theme, but the slider and tab controls lack any customization.

If we create a style that is consistent both in the look and in the breadth of controls, we need to have something that ties the entire theme together.

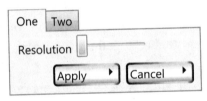

FIGURE 8.8: Consistency applies also to using a custom theme for all the controls, or at least matching the existing ones.

Have a Point

Custom themes allow us to differentiate one application from others. Creating a custom theme is potentially expensive, in terms of both design and implementation. The key thing is that a custom theme should convey something to the user. Maybe the message in the theme is a company brand, or an "extreme" styling to convey how cool an application is. The important thing is that we should be able to say what that message is, ideally in a single sentence. An example that the WPF team often banters around is the Xbox theme that we might imagine creating. Xbox has a very distinctive look for its hardware, software, and even Web presence. Creating a custom theme that matched the Xbox look would be a great message to send; it would clearly distinguish Xbox applications from the rest of Windows.

In general, if an application is a utility or a standard type of business application, it is unlikely that a custom theme will really add a lot of value to that offering. Even in these scenarios, though, it may be interesting to use themes to enforce good usability guidelines.

WHERE ARE WE?

In this chapter we've covered how styles and themes work in WPF. We've seen how to define and use styles, and how to package them into themes, and we've learned some best practices for using styles. With this final piece of the puzzle, we can see how styles plug into the data system, using resources and templates. All the parts of WPF come together in styling.

▪ Appendix ▪
Base Services

Syncategorematic: \Syn*cat`e*gor`e*mat"ic\ ... *Not capable of being
used as a term by itself;—said of words, as an adverb or preposition.*
Source: *Webster's Revised Unabridged Dictionary*, © 1996,
1998 MICRA, Inc.

W INDOWS PRESENTATION FOUNDATION provides a very rich and deep
set of services. The goal of this book was to cover the major concepts
of the platform in the previous eight chapters. There is, however, a set of
services that are often useful and may help us understand how the system
is built and hangs together. This appendix reviews some of my favorite
WPF services and describes how they might be used in an application.

Threading and Dispatchers

At the outset, one of the WPF development team's goals was to remove the
antiquated dependency on the single-threaded apartment (STA) model of
threading. Many ActiveX controls and other COM-based services require
the STA threading model, which states that only one thread at a time will
ever be executing against our code, and it will always be the same thread.
For any Windows UI programming today, the code is almost always running in an STA model.

The problem with STA is that all objects are tied to a single thread and
can't move between threads. Enforcing a single thread of execution in a
given body of code is a very effective simplification, but tying execution to

a specific instance of a thread seems too limiting. Alas, as "Longhorn" became Vista, we came to the realization that, for WPF to work together with almost any existing service (Clipboard, Internet Explorer, etc.), we would have to support STA, so we decided to create a single threading model instead of supporting many threading models.

So it is with great apology that I report that WPF requires STA threading. The first place we run into this requirement is when we write a typical Hello World application; it has the STAThread attribute on the entry point function:

```
using System;
using System.Windows;

class Program {
  [STAThread]
  static void Main() {
    Application app = new Application();
    Window w = new Window();
    w.Show();
    app.Run();
  }
}
```

Most WPF objects derive from a common base type: DispatcherObject. Partly because of the original intent to move away from STA, we tie objects not to the thread, but to a single dispatcher. A dispatcher is an object that receives messages (*events* in the CLR world, *messages* in the User32 world) and dispatches them to the correct object. Most of the types related to the dispatcher and WPF's threading model are located in the System.Windows. Threading namespace.

True shared memory concurrency (multithreading) is almost impossible to program correctly with today's mainstream programming languages. The problem has to do with the complex rules of locking and concurrency management: If we don't lock correctly, we quickly run into race conditions, deadlocks, livelocks, and memory corruption. The most successful model for doing more than one thing at a time is to have a loose coupling between the two tasks and use an asynchronous messaging model for communicating between the two threads.

One of the changes to the threading support that shipped in the .NET Framework 2.0 was the introduction of SynchronizationContext. This class lets a platform, like WPF, tell the system how to deal with concurrency management. In the case of WPF, it pushes a reference to the dispatcher into the context, so any asynchronous callbacks from components (like System.Net.WebClient) can be posted back to the UI thread. This happens automatically, so we can ignore any threading issues.

To see this in action, let's write a simple program that downloads an HTML page from a Web site. The simplest way to write this program is to use the WebClient class and call DownloadStringAsync:

```
<Window x:Class='ThreadingExample.Window1'
  xmlns='http://schemas.microsoft.com/winfx/2006/xaml/presentation'
  xmlns:x='http://schemas.microsoft.com/winfx/2006/xaml'
  Title='ThreadingExample'
  >
  <StackPanel>
    <TextBox x:Name='_text'
      Height='150'
      HorizontalScrollBarVisibility='Auto'
      VerticalScrollBarVisibility='Auto' />
    <Button Click='DownloadNormally'>Download</Button>
  </StackPanel>
</Window>

using System;
...


namespace ThreadingExample {
  public partial class Window1 : Window {
    public Window1() {
      InitializeComponent();
    }

    void DownloadNormally(object sender, RoutedEventArgs e) {
      WebClient wc = new WebClient();
      wc.DownloadStringCompleted +=
        delegate(object sender2,
            DownloadStringCompletedEventArgs e2)
        {
          _text.Text = e2.Result;
        };
      wc.DownloadStringAsync(new Uri("http://www.msn.com"));
    }
  }
}
```

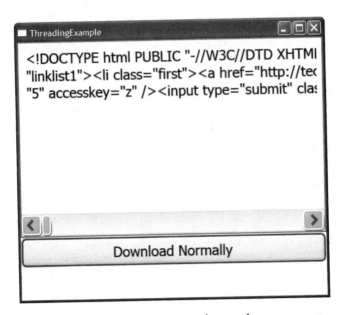

FIGURE A.1: Downloading some HTML content asynchronously

Running this program just works, as Figure A.1 illustrates. What happens is that the WebClient type retrieves SynchronizationContext, which it then uses to post events (an action that results in the callback delegates being invoked on the UI thread). This model works well for doing asynchronous programming without introducing the complexity of multithreading.

Sometimes we really do want to do explicit multithreading—for example, to create a background thread for a long-running process. In such cases we have two ways to handle communication with the UI thread. If we're creating a reusable component that may be used outside of a WPF application (as in a Windows Forms or ASP.NET application), then we should manage the callbacks using SynchronizationContext just as WebClient does. If, instead, we're implementing application logic that is tied to a program, we can directly use the dispatcher associated with the UI thread. By talking to the dispatcher directly, we gain more control over how the messages are processed, but we no longer post callbacks to the correct context in Windows Forms or ASP.NET.

Regardless of the style of component we build, the pieces are the same. We need to create an object to represent a task and an object to represent the result "message." Here we'll create a task that calculates the sum of numbers from 0 to $(n-1)$. The result message will be an EventArgs-derived type that contains the result value:

```
class SumCompletedEventArgs : EventArgs {
  int _result;

  public int Result {
    get { return _result;}
    set { _result = value;}
  }
}
```

The task object needs only a simple object model, which should follow the asychronous component pattern. We will have a <DoSomething> Async method and a <DoSomething>Completed event:

```
class Sum {
  public Sum() { ... }

  public event EventHandler<SumCompletedEventArgs> SumCompleted;

  public void SumAsync(int value) { ... }
}
```

In this case we'll use SynchronizationContext to manage the callbacks, so in our constructor we will capture the current context:

```
class Sum {
  SynchronizationContext _context;

  public Sum() {
    _context = SynchronizationContext.Current;
  }
  ...
}
```

To make this task run on a background thread we will need to define two functions. The first is the implementation of the background thread execution, which we will call BackgroundTask. The second function is the callback that will happen on the UI thread, which we will call Completed. Notice that we don't touch any state on the object from the background thread, thereby ensuring that there are no conflicts. To avoid subtle threading bugs, all the data will be accessed only from the UI thread. We must copy any data we need into the arguments that we pass to the background thread:

```
class Sum {
  SynchronizationContext _context;

  public Sum() {
    _context = SynchronizationContext.Current;
  }

  public event EventHandler<SumCompletedEventArgs> SumCompleted;

  public void SumAsync(int value) {
    Thread background = new Thread(BackgroundTask);
    background.IsBackground = true;
    background.Start(value);
  }

  void BackgroundTask(object parameter) {
    int value = (int)parameter;
    int result = 0;

    for (int i = 0; i <= value; i++) {
      result += i;
      Thread.Sleep(10);
    }

    _context.Post(Completed, result);
  }

  void Completed(object result) {
    if (SumCompleted != null) {
      SumCompletedEventArgs e = new SumCompletedEventArgs();
      e.Result = (int)result;
      SumCompleted(this, e);
    }
  }
}
```

This type works exactly like the WebClient type. We create it, hook up a listener to the event, and then call SumAsync:

```
void RunTask(object sender, RoutedEventArgs e) {
  Sum t = new Sum();
  t.SumCompleted +=
    delegate(object sender2, SumCompletedEventArgs e2) {
      _text.Text = e2.Result.ToString();
    };
  t.SumAsync(250);
}
```

The primary benefit of using the WPF dispatcher instead of SynchronizationContext is the ability to express the priority of the callback to the UI thread. The System.Windows.Threading.DispatcherPriority enum defines the 12 priorities that we can associate with a callback to the UI thread. It is simpler, though, to use the BackgroundWorker component that is included in .NET, which leverages SynchronizationContext.

Properties

When designing types, we often talk about their PMEs: properties, methods, and events. These three concepts define the developer's view of an object. The previous big component model from Microsoft, COM, really supported only methods. Properties were barely supported, with a bit of metadata in the interface definition to tag put_ and get_ methods so that tools like VB could present a property-based model; events were implemented straight out instead of with makeshift callback sinks.

One of the design goals for .NET was to natively support these concepts. Events and properties were given special billing in both the runtime and almost all the major languages targeting .NET. WPF is built from the ground up in managed code. The WPF team made the decision early on to follow .NET conventions and patterns, and use native features of the runtime. So why on earth is there a WPF property system?

.NET Properties

While we are here at the base of the WPF system, looking at the lowest-level services, it is interesting to think about what we're going to build on top. We want to build a dynamic, data-driven, declarative, composited presentation system.

Let's start with the beginning—a CLR property on a fictitious type:

```
public class Widget {
  Widget _parent;
  Color _background;
  public Color Background {
    get { return _background; }
    set { _background = value; }
  }
  public Widget Parent {
```

```
      get { return _parent; }
      set { _parent = value; }
    }
  }
```

We have defined two properties: Background and Parent. The first challenge we hit is that, when Background changes, we want to cause Widget to repaint. Of course, other developers may want to know that the background changed, so we will make the change notification public:

```
public class Widget {
  Widget _parent;
  Color _background;

  public event EventHandler BackgroundChanged;

  public Color Background {
    get { return _background; }
    set {
      if (_background != value) {
        _background = value;
        OnBackgroundChanged(EventArgs.Empty);
      }
    }
  }

  public Widget Parent { get { ... } set { ... } }

  protected virtual void OnBackgroundChanged(EventArgs e) {
    if (BackgroundChanged != null) {
      BackgroundChanged(this, e);
    }
    RepaintWidget();
  }
}
```

Simple! The next thing we probably want is the ability to have the background match the parent:

```
public class Widget {
  Widget _parent;
  bool _isBackgroundSet = false;
  Color _background;

  public event EventHandler BackgroundChanged;

  public Color Background {
    get {
      if (!isBackgroundSet && Parent != null) {
```

```
      return Parent.Background;
    }
    return _background;
  }
  set {
    if (_background != value) {
      _background = value;
      _isBackgroundSet = true;
      OnBackgroundChanged(EventArgs.Empty);
    }
  }
}

public Widget Parent { get { ... } set { ... } }

protected virtual void OnBackgroundChanged(EventArgs e) {
  ...
}
}
```

We aren't quite out of the woods yet. We have missed two critical things: First, when the parent changes and the background isn't set, we need to fire the change notification. Second, we need to provide a mechanism for resetting the background to its default (inherited) value:

```
public class Widget {
  Widget _parent;
  bool _isBackgroundSet = false;
  Color _background;

  public event EventHandler BackgroundChanged;
  public event EventHandler ParentChanged;

  public Color Background { get { ... } set { ... } }

  public Widget Parent {
    get { ... }
    set {
      if (_parent != value) {
        _parent = value;
        OnParentChanged(EventArgs.Empty);
      }
    }
  }

  public void ResetBackground() {
    _isBackgroundSet = false;
    OnBackgroundChanged(EventArgs.Empty);
  }
```

```
protected virtual void OnBackgroundChanged(EventArgs e) {
  ...
}

protected virtual void OnParentChanged(EventArgs e) {
  if (ParentChanged != null) {
    ParentChanged(this, e);
  }
  if (!_isBackgroundSet) {
    OnBackgroundChanged(EventArgs.Empty);
  }
}
}
```

Here we already begin to see a lot of duplicate code. Remember, though, that a key part of the dynamic, data-driven, declarative system is the notion of styling. To facilitate better code reuse, WPF enables a single object to be defined that can apply property values to multiple other objects; this capability is comparable to the use of styles inside of Microsoft Word or CSS styles in HTML. Of course, we want our widget to support this functionality:

```
public class Widget {
  Style _style;
  Widget _parent;
  bool _isBackgroundSet = false;
  Color _background;

  public event EventHandler BackgroundChanged;
  public event EventHandler ParentChanged;
  public event EventHandler StyleChanged;

  public Color Background {
    get {
      if (!isBackgroundSet) {
        if (Style != null) {
          return Style.Background;
        }
        return Parent.Background;
      }
      return _background;
    }
    set { ... }
  }
  public Widget Parent { get { ... } set { ... } }
  public Style Style { get { ... } set { ... } }
```

```
public void ResetBackground() { ... }
protected virtual void OnBackgroundChanged(EventArgs e) {
  ...
}
protected virtual void OnParentChanged(EventArgs e) { ... }
protected virtual void OnStyleChanged(EventArgs e) { ... }
}
```

In this example we have added a lot more boilerplate code for the Style property, and some interesting code inside of the get method for Background. We have many more features to add to properties (animation, default values, etc.) to match all the functionality that WPF will require, but before we get too far, let's look at the design that we're producing.

To start, any inherited property must be defined on the base type. Because we have a hard-coded lookup from a given widget to its parent, at compile time of the base type we have to know every property that may need to be inherited. The same is true for styles: Because the definition for Style needs to be updated for each property, the only properties that can be styled are the ones we know about in advance. We are duplicating a lot of code for change notifications. We had to hard-code the dependencies between properties; specifically, we had to write code in the parent change notification to fire the background change notification. We had to allocate a local field on the type for every property. The list goes on.

Property System 101

Boiling all this down, the WPF team pinpointed three essential services in a property system:

1. Change notification
2. Dependency tracking
3. Expressions

Initially these may not seem like enough, but the logic works something like this: If we have the ability to know when a property changes, and we understand the properties affected by that change, we can then implement complex expressions that enable many features (inheritance, styles, etc.). Using these three concepts, we can model all the other services in the property system; the only one that's not documented anywhere is expressions. Expressions are an internal-only concept in the first version of WPF. Instead, WPF exposes a richer set of built-in functionality:

1. Sparse storage
2. Styling
3. Animation
4. Binding
5. Attached properties

To facilitate all this is a base class that encapsulates this behavior in a generic way:

```
public class DependencyObject : DispatcherObject {
    public DependencyObject();
    public void ClearValue(DependencyProperty dp);
    public object GetValue(DependencyProperty dp);
    protected virtual void OnPropertyChanged
        (PropertyChangedEventArgs e);
    public void SetValue(DependencyProperty dp, object value);
    // many methods omitted for the reader's sanity
}
```

There are basically three functions (get, set, and clear), and a callback (change notification). DependencyProperty is an object that represents the identity of the property; it is the programmatic name of the property.

DependencyObject provides sparse storage. This is important: Properties defined using the property system incur no cost per instance unless they are set to something other than a default value. Sparse storage was a big goal in defining the property system because we knew that the framework would heavily utilize properties (there are more than 40 just to control text rendering!), and any per-instance cost would destroy performance. The source for DependencyObject looks something like this:

```
public class DependencyObject : DispatcherObject {
    IDictionary<DependencyProperty,object> _values =
        new Dictionary<DependencyProperty, object>();
    public DependencyObject();
    public void ClearValue(DependencyProperty dp) {
        _values.RemoveValue(dp);
```

```
      }
    public object GetValue(DependencyProperty dp) {
      if (_values.ContainsKey(dp)) return _values[dp];
      return dp.DefaultValue;
    }
    public void SetValue(DependencyProperty dp, object value) {
      _values[dp] = value;
    }
  }
```

The logic is more complex than this, but this simplified version shows that there is now a fixed overhead per object of a dictionary, and we can have any number of properties. This flexibility doesn't come without a cost; if most of the properties are set locally (instead of with a style, inheritance, or default value), we'll have worse performance than if we used only local values.

Converting our widget code over to using the property system is trivial:

```
public class Widget : DependencyObject {
  public static readonly DependencyProperty StyleProperty =
    DependencyProperty.Register("Style",
                typeof(Style),
                typeof(Widget));
  public static readonly DependencyProperty BackgroundProperty =
    DependencyProperty.Register("Background",
                typeof(Color),
                typeof(Widget));
  public static readonly DependencyProperty ParentProperty =
    DependencyProperty.Register("Parent",
                typeof(Widget),
                typeof(Widget));
}
```

However, it would be rude (and break most tools!) if we left it at this. Remember that WPF had a premise to follow .NET conventions, and that includes using the property system built into .NET. The dependency property system is designed to be an addition to the .NET system, not a replacement:

```
public class Widget : DependencyObject {
  public static readonly DependencyProperty StyleProperty = ...;
  public static readonly DependencyProperty BackgroundProperty = ...;
  public static readonly DependencyProperty ParentProperty = ...;

  public Style Style {
    get { return (Style)GetValue(StyleProperty); }
    set { SetValue(StyleProperty, value); }
  }
```

```
public Color Background {
  get { return (Color)GetValue(BackgroundProperty); }
  set { SetValue(BackgroundProperty, value); }
}
public Widget Parent {
  get { return (Widget)GetValue(ParentProperty); }
  set { SetValue(ParentProperty, value); }
}
}
```

Metadata

.NET already has a notion of metadata: We can declare a custom attribute on any member, type, or assembly. The system has limitations, one of which is performance. For the dependency property system it was absolutely critical to enable high-performance operations and discovery of certain aspects of the property, which is one reason why declaring a dependency property requires telling the property system what the type of the property is (so that we don't have to reflect against the type and find the CLR wrapper to find the property type).

The dependency property system stores metadata in two ways. First, a set of information is stored on the dependency property itself. This information includes the name and type of the property, as well as the type that declared the property (the owner). Property names must be unique for each owner type.

The second store for metadata in the dependency property system is the PropertyMetadata object. Although the information in Dependency Property is fixed, we are free to define new properties on our own derived type of PropertyMetadata. PropertyMetadata allows us to control additional behavioral metadata (DefaultValue and IsReadOnly), globally listen to change notifications (PropertyChangedCallback), and apply value coercion (CoerceValueCallback).

DefaultValue determines what value should be returned when the property isn't set. Most properties should specify such a default. The norm is to return the default value for the given data type (null for any reference type, 0 for numerics, false for booleans, etc.). IsReadOnly, as the name implies, forces the property to be read-only. In .NET, read-only fields are enforced at a low level by the intermediate-language verifier, ensuring that all read-only fields are assigned exactly once by the time the constructor is run. In the dependency property system, the guarantee around read-only is looser, ensuring only that the owning type (or an instance of that owning type) assigns to the property.

Global change notification for a property is pretty simple to understand, but the value coercion is worth looking at a bit more in depth. The simplest way to understand value coercion is to think about the Slider control. Slider supports three properties: Minimum, Maximum, and Value. The design requires that Value return a value between Minimum and Maximum, but we also know that properties may be set in any order. To make sure that no values violate the minimum and maximum constraints, while allowing the flexibility of setting properties in any order desired, we want to support *storing* any value in the Value property but constrain that value between Minimum and Maximum when we *get* the value.

The first step to leveraging value coercion is to define our properties:

```
public class Slider : DependencyObject {
  public static readonly DependencyProperty MinimumProperty =
    DependencyProperty.Register("Minimum",
      typeof(int),
      typeof(Slider),
      new PropertyMetadata(0));

  public static readonly DependencyProperty MaximumProperty =
    DependencyProperty.Register("Maximum",
      typeof(int),
      typeof(Slider),
      new PropertyMetadata(100));

  public static readonly DependencyProperty ValueProperty =
    DependencyProperty.Register("Value",
      typeof(int),
      typeof(Slider),
      new PropertyMetadata(50));

  public int Minimum {
    get { return (int)GetValue(MinimumProperty); }
    set { SetValue(MinimumProperty, value); }
  }
  public int Maximum {
    get { return (int)GetValue(MaximumProperty); }
    set { SetValue(MaximumProperty, value); }
  }
  public int Value {
    get { return (int)GetValue(ValueProperty); }
    set { SetValue(ValueProperty, value); }
  }
}
```

Because we always want Value to be bounded by Minimum and Maximum, we will introduce a new static method that performs the coercion and add it to the metadata for Value:

```
public class Slider : DependencyObject {
  public static readonly DependencyProperty MinimumProperty =
    ...;

  public static readonly DependencyProperty MaximumProperty =
    ...;

  public static readonly DependencyProperty ValueProperty =
    DependencyProperty.Register("Value",
      typeof(int),
      typeof(Slider),
      new PropertyMetadata(50, null, ConstrainValue));

  static object ConstrainValue(DependencyObject target,
                object baseValue) {
    int min = (int)target.GetValue(MinimumProperty);
    int max = (int)target.GetValue(MaximumProperty);
    int value = (int)baseValue;

    return Math.Min(Math.Max(value, min), max);
  }

  public int Minimum { get { ... } set { ... } }
  public int Maximum { get { ... } set { ... } }
  public int Value { get { ... } set { ... } }
}
```

Here's where it gets a little tricky. One main advantage of the property system is that it attempts to understand all dependencies between properties to efficiently cache values and communicate changes. This coercion has introduced a new dependency. Because there is no general extensibility mechanism for adding dependencies, instead we need to manually drive the property system to deal with change notifications. We can add a global property change handler for Maximum and Minimum, and invalidate the Value property whenever either changes:

```
public class Slider : DependencyObject {
  public static readonly DependencyProperty MinimumProperty =
    DependencyProperty.Register("Minimum",
      typeof(int),
      typeof(Slider),
      new PropertyMetadata(0, ValueDependencyChanged));
```

```
public static readonly DependencyProperty MaximumProperty =
    DependencyProperty.Register("Maximum",
        typeof(int),
        typeof(Slider),
        new PropertyMetadata(100, ValueDependencyChanged));

public static readonly DependencyProperty ValueProperty =
    ...;

static void ValueDependencyChanged(DependencyObject target,
            DependencyPropertyChangedEventArgs e) {
    target.InvalidateProperty(ValueProperty);
}

static object ConstrainValue(DependencyObject target,
            object baseValue) { ... }

public int Minimum { get { ... } set { ... } }
public int Maximum { get { ... } set { ... } }
public int Value { get { ... } set { ... } }
}
```

Beyond the basic `PropertyMetadata` type, there is an important derived type, `FrameworkPropertyMetadata`, that allows customization of a property's behavior with respect to the higher-level features of WPF, such as binding, styles, and inheritance.

Keyboards, Mice, and Styluses

Back in the early days of User32, the general model for handling special keys (like **Ctrl+S** for save) was either to use an accelerator table[1] or to handle `WM_KEYDOWN` and `WM_KEYUP`. In Visual Basic it was common to handle KeyDown/KeyUp events because there was no way to build a custom accelerator table. There are two big problems with doing anything in direct response to keyboard input: First, sytems with input method editors (Japanese, Korean, Chinese, etc.) tend to break; and second, the ability to let the user rebind the keystrokes to other behavior is lost.

In some scenarios we do need to talk to a device directly—listening to the stylus in a paint program, for example—but in most cases we want to bind to commands. The binding from input events to commands is fairly

---

1. Accelerator tables in User32 would translate from key strokes into `WM_COMMAND` messages.

powerful by default, but it is completely extensible, such that we can implement our own rules for when to raise a command.

By structuring an application with input bindings as a separate concept, we can easily allow end users to customize bindings to suit their needs. In Chapter 7 we touched briefly on input bindings, but let's take a closer look.

InputBinding

InputBinding has two interesting properties: Gesture and Command. Gesture maps to any input gesture that we want to map to a given command. Both InputGesture (the data type of the Gesture property) and ICommand (the data type of the Command property) are extensible, allowing us to map any gesture to any command. By default, WPF supports two types of gestures: key and mouse gestures. These allow the common set of accelerators and behaviors needed to build basic applications.

A more advanced type of gesture is something we commonly see in development tools: key chords. **Key chords** consist of a set of key inputs that are uninterrupted, allowing for combinations of keys to have special meanings (e.g., in Emacs, the binding to **Ctrl+X, S** to mean "save"). To show the extensibility of the binding system, let's add support to WPF for binding to key chords.

The gesture we want to support is really a collection of key gestures. The built-in KeyGesture type in WPF doesn't support keys without any modifier presses (control, shift, etc.), but in a key-chord scenario, it is common for the second key to be neutral. The first step is to define a new Key-ChordItemGesture object, which will map to one "note" in the key chord. InputGesture has only one important method, Match, which determines whether a given gesture maps to an input event:

```
public class KeyChordItemGesture : InputGesture {
  Key _key;
  ModifierKeys _modifiers;

  public Key Key {
    get { return _key; }
    set { _key = value; }
  }


  public ModifierKeys Modifiers {
```

```
      get { return _modifiers; }
      set { _modifiers = value; }
    }

  public override bool Matches(
    object targetElement, InputEventArgs inputEventArgs) {

    KeyEventArgs e = inputEventArgs as KeyEventArgs;
    if (e != null)
    {
      return e.Key == Key && Keyboard.Modifiers == Modifiers;
    }
    return false;
  }
}
```

We can now create the KeyChordGesture type, which contains a collection of input gestures that must be matched in order. A queue of gestures
to match is maintained, and as each gesture is matched it is removed. If the
user presses an incorrect key, the queue is drained:

```
[ContentProperty("Gestures")]
public class KeyChordGesture : InputGesture {
  InputGestureCollection _gestures = new InputGestureCollection();
  Queue<InputGesture> _chords = new Queue<InputGesture>();

  public KeyChordGesture() {
  }

  public InputGestureCollection Gestures { get { return _gestures; } }

  public override bool Matches(
    object targetElement, InputEventArgs inputEventArgs) {

    if (_chords.Count == 0) {
      foreach (InputGesture k in _gestures) {
        _chords.Enqueue(k);
      }
    }
    if (_chords.Peek().Matches(targetElement, inputEventArgs)) {
      _chords.Dequeue();
      return _chords.Count == 0;
    }
    else if (inputEventArgs is KeyEventArgs) {
      KeyEventArgs unmatched = (KeyEventArgs)inputEventArgs;
      if (unmatched.Key != Key.None
        && unmatched.Key != Key.LeftCtrl
        && unmatched.Key != Key.RightCtrl
        && unmatched.Key != Key.LeftShift
```

```
            && unmatched.Key != Key.RightShift
            && unmatched.Key != Key.LeftAlt
            && unmatched.Key != Key.RightAlt)
        {
          _chords.Clear();
        }
      }
      return false;
    }
  }
}
```

The final step is to define an input binding. We have no custom object model to add to our binding, but the base `InputBinding` type has no public constructor, so we need to define a type simply to make it usable in markup:

```
public class KeyChordBinding : InputBinding {
  public KeyChordBinding() {
  }
}
```

This binding can now be used on any control in the `InputBindings` collection:

```
<Window.InputBindings>
  <l:KeyChordBinding
    xmlns:l='clr-namespace:InputExample'
    Command='...some command...'>
    <l:KeyChordBinding.Gesture>
      <l:KeyChordGesture>
        <l:KeyChordItemGesture Key='X' Modifiers='Control' />
        <l:KeyChordItemGesture Key='S' Modifiers='Control' />
      </l:KeyChordGesture>
    </l:KeyChordBinding.Gesture>
  </l:KeyChordBinding>
</Window.InputBindings>
```

By defining custom binding types, we can avoid ever having hard-coded dependencies between logic (command handlers) and user input. Avoiding such dependencies is valuable in making an application configurable, and in making sure that we can work against any type of input.

WPF's philosophy is to move to more declarative programming of input devices, so features like input bindings are made to be much closer to the surface, and talking to the devices themselves is somewhat obscured. If we do need to talk to the input devices, WPF has a rich object model.

Input Device Communication

The object models for all input devices are structured in the same way. There is one static service class (Keyboard, Mouse, Stylus, or Tablet) and a device class (KeyboardDevice, MouseDevice, etc.). The static service class provides global functionality (like attaching to direct input events and retrieving the devices), and the device classes provide device-specific functionality. The most common properties for the primary instance of a given device are generally promoted to the static service class.

To firm up this concept of communication, let's consider the keyboard. In the earlier KeyChordItemGesture implementation, you may have noticed that we retrieved the current state of the modifier keys by looking at the Keyboard class:

```
public override bool Matches(
  object targetElement, InputEventArgs inputEventArgs) {

  KeyEventArgs e = inputEventArgs as KeyEventArgs;
  if (e != null) {
    return e.Key == Key && Keyboard.Modifiers == Modifiers;
  }
  return false;
}
```

Keyboard.Modifiers is a static property that is implemented as a call to Keyboard.PrimaryDevice.Modifiers. The system allows only one keyboard and only one mouse. For stylus input, however, multiple tablets (digitizers) may be attached to the system, and each tablet may have one or more styluses associated with it. Tablet.TabletDevices will return the enumeration of all the tablets currently recognized by the system.

With mouse and stylus input, the location of the mouse or stylus determines the target, or focused, control. Using Capture, we can lock the device to a specific control for a period of time, but generally the focus simply travels along with the pointer. Keyboard focus is a different story.

Keyboard Focus

Only one control can have keyboard focus at a time. There are two interesting types for dealing with focus: KeyboardNavigation and FocusManager. KeyboardNavigation is responsible for dealing with how keyboard focus will move around elements when various keys are pressed, and the FocusManager is responsible for tracking the keyboard focus. FocusManager can largely be ignored because all the interesting events and properties that it exposes are available in more convenient places (like Keyboard and UIElement).

KeyboardNavigation, on the other hand, provides a way for controls to determine how they want to deal with keyboard focus commands. Probably the most commonly used properties are IsTabStop and TabIndex. The most common way for users to move the keyboard focus around a set of controls (besides using the mouse) is by using the **Tab** key. The **Tab** key is designed to move the keyboard focus to the next logical element into which the user can type.

WHERE ARE WE?

In this appendix we have looked at a few of the base services provided by WPF. Although typically you won't have to interact with these services directly, it is often useful to understand some of them so that you know better what is available to build on.

Index

Symbols

* operator, XPath, 333, 334
/ operator, XPath, 332, 334
@ operator, XPath, 332–333, 334
[ ] operator, XPath, 333, 335

A

Absolute mapping mode, 230–231
Actions, 365–389
  commands, 373–379
  commands and data binding, 380–383
  declarative, 369
  element composition and, 366–367
  events, 369–372
  loose coupling and, 366–368
  triggers. *See* Triggers
Activated event, Window, 72
Active X DocObjects, 109
Actual size, two-phase layout, 175
AddHandler, 373
Algorithmic layout, 208–214
  arranging children in, 211–214
  calculating desired size of, 209–210
  example of, 208
  fitting into available size, 210–211
Alpha channel of color, 228, 250–253
AmbientLight, 265
Anchored blocks, 279–280
AnimationClock, 286, 293
Animations, 283–300
  AnimationClock, 286
  defined, 283

defining, 293–296
  with DoubleAnimation, 286–287
  encapsulating time-based values for
    properties, 285–286
  hard way of building, 283–285
  integration and, 34–37, 296–300
  predefined, 286
  roll-over effects for, 287–288
  storyboards for, 288–290
  summary of, 290–292
  time and timelines in, 292–293
  triggers in, 291
Anti-aliasing, 220
Application manifest, browser-hosted
  applications, 105
Application object, 52–71
  building program using markup,
    19–20
  configuration state, 61–64
  content state, 64–71
  controlling lifetime of process, 55–56
  creating scalable applications, 45–46
  definition, 53–55
  Document state, 71
  error handling, 57–59
  informed about all windows, 78–80
  invoking Run method, 52–53
  managing state, 59–60
  open packaging conventions, 68–69
  starting WPF application with, 17
Application-scoped settings, Configuration
  state, 62
Application.Current property, 53

443

Applications
  Application object. *See* Application object
  desktop style, 50–52
  hosting in browser. *See* XBAPs (XAML
      Browser Application)
  navigation. *See* Navigation
  overview of, 43
  passing state between pages, 89–94
  principles of creating, 43–44
  scalable, 44–48
  tools for building, 39–41
  user controls, 80–83
  Web style, 48–50
  windows. *See* Windows
ApplicationSettingsBase, Configuration
    state, 61
Application.StartupUri, 104–105
Application.Windows property, 79
ArcSegment, 223
Arrange phase, two-phase layout, 175
ArrangeOverride, 185
ASP.NET, 10–11
assemblyIdentity tag, browser hosting, 108
Attached properties, 16–17, 186
Attributes
  defining fonts, 272–274
  defining text, 268–269
  name of XML, 332–333
Audio, 301–303
Author time, 64
Automatic sizing, 177
AutoReverse, Storyboard, 294
Available size, two-phase layout, 175
AxisAngleRotation3D, 266–267

B

BarrelButton, 157
Base services, 421–442
  dispatchers, 427
  input device communication, 441
  InputBinding, 438–440
  keyboard focus, 441–442
  keyboard, mice and styluses, 437–442
  metadata, 434–437
  .NET properties, 427–431
  property system, 431–434
  threading, 421–426
BasedOn property, 413–414
BeginStoryboard, 291–292, 297–298

BezierSegment, 223
Binding
  collection views. *See* Collection views
  commands, 377–383
  controls, 27–30
  defined, 316
  hierarchical, 342–349
  to objects, editing, 325–331
  to objects, overview of, 322–325
  overview of, 316–322
  pervasiveness throughout system, 308–309
  resources, 314–315
  templates, 126–127
  to XML, 331–337
Bitmap effects, 2D graphics, 253–254
BitmapImage
  adding richer display to, 359–361
  displaying with ContentControl, 358–359
  displaying with interesting template, 359
  encapsulating functionality for images, 245
BitMapMetadata, 246–248
Block elements
  defined, 269
  text containment rules for, 147–148
  in text layout in paragraphs, 274–275
  in text layout in tables, 277–279
Blocked command, 381
Boilerplate code, 54–55
Border control
  creating template for controls with, 125
  with LinearGradientBrush, 231
  overview of, 165–166
  as render control, 121
BorderLayout class, 191
Bottom property, Canvas, 186–187
Browser-based applications
  adding navigation to, 48–51
  converting to desktop applications, 46–47
Browser hosting, 103–111
  HelloBrowser, 103–109
  loose markup and, 111
  overview of, 103–104
  PresentationHost view and, 109–110
Brushes, 228–234
  3D equivalent of, 256
  combining with pens, 234–237
  defined, 218
  gradient, 228–232
  overview of, 228
  tiling, 232–234

Bubbling events, 370–371
Built-in layout, 185–186
Button control
  as content control, 121
  hierarchy, 129–130
  overview of, 129–130
  setting content of, 116–117
  stack panel layout for, 22
  supporting clicking, 368, 373
  template binding in, 126–127
  templates in, 122–125
  three principles of, 114–116
  toolbar, 141–142
  in window, 21
ButtonChrome, 116–117

C

C#
  compiler, 18–19
  partial types, 24–25
  Visual C# Express, 39
Cameras, 3D graphics
  creating, 256–258
  defined, 265–266
  overview of, 265–266
CanExecute method, 374–375, 382–383
CanGoBack property, 97
Canvas, 186–189
Caret, 150–151
CaretPosition, 151
Cascading Style Sheets. *See* CSS (Cascading
  Style Sheets)
Center property, 229
CER (constrained execution region), 57
CheckBox control, 129–130, 367
Child/children
  Border control containing, 165–166
  controlling in layout with Visibility, 176
  defined, 120
  effects of z-index on layout of controls,
    183–184
  ScrollViewer and, 167–168
  Viewbox control stretching, 169–170
Circle layout, 208–214
  arranging children in, 211–214
  calculating desired size of, 209–210
  example of algorithmic layout as, 208
  fitting into available size, 210–211
ClearType, 220

Click events, 140, 366–368
Clipping
  GDI and User32 based on, 219
  layout patterns and, 180
  overview of, 4
Clocks, 293, 301–302
Closed events, Window, 72–74
Closing events, Window, 72–74, 94
CLR objects
  binding to, editing, 325–331
  binding to, overview of, 322–325
  naming components authored in XAML,
    69–71
  retrieving data from, 308
Code-behind files, 24–27
Collection-based text object model, 146–148
Collection trigger types, 384
Collection views, 349–357
  currency management, 349–351
  describing in markup, 355–356
  filtering, 351–353
  grouping, 353–355
  overview of, 349
  sorting, 353
CollectionViewSource, 351, 355–356
Color, 2D graphics, 225–228
ColumnDefinitions property, Grid, 196,
  202–203
Columns, 280–281
COM, 68
CombinedGeometry, 224–225
CombineGeometry, 224
ComboBox, 131–135
Command property
  data-bound commands, 380–383
  DataTriggers, 385
  InputBinding, 438
CommandParameter, 380–383
Commands, 373–379
  command binding, 377–379
  data binding and, 380–383
  defining with ICommand interface, 374–377
  naming desired action with, 374
  routed, 378–379
  secure, 379
Community technology preview. *See* CTP
  (community technology preview)
ComponentResourceKey, 403
Composite rendering, 2D graphics, 218–219
Compositing system, 219

Concurrency management, 432–434
Configuration file bindings, setup, 62
Configuration state settings
  configuration file bindings for, 62–63
  defining object model for, 61–62
  running application using, 63–64
ConstantAttenuation property, light, 256
Constrained execution region (CER), 57
Constraints, layout, 177
Containers, 7, 143–144
Content controls
  binding TextBox to, 317
  binding with data templates, 320–322
  defined, 81
  displaying bitmap image with, 358–359
  overview of, 121
  supporting templates. See Templates
Content model, 116–121
  Children and Child of, 120
  content controls of, 121
  ContentPresenter of, 117–119
  creating Window template, 127–128
  function of, 27
  Items of, 119–120
  layout controls of, 121
  overview of, 116–117
  render controls of, 121
Content state (resources), 64–71
  adding to application, 65–67
  applications and, 312–314
  configuring, 65–66
  defined, 64, 310–311
  loading, 68–69
  lookup path for, 312
  Open Packaging Conventions and, 68–69
  overriding in element hierarchy, 311–312
  overview of, 28–29
  static assignment or dynamic binding of,
    314–315
  styles and, 400, 403
  types of, 65
  using more than once, 314
ContentPresenter, 116–120, 402
ContentRendered event, Window, 72
ContentTemplate property, 118, 320–321
ContentTemplateSelector, 118
Context menus, displaying, 139
Control library, 128–161
  buttons, 129–130
  containers, 143–144

document viewers, 160
Frame, 160–161
menus, 138–140
overview of, 128–129
ranges, 144–145
toolbars, 138–143
Control library, editors, 145–159
  ink data, 154–158
  overview of, 145–146
  text data, 146–150
  using InkCanvas, 158–159
  using RichTextBox, 150–154
  using TextBox, 154
Control library, lists, 130–138
  creating with templates, 137–138
  ListBox and ComboBox, 131–135
  ListView, 135–137
  overview of, 130–131
  TreeView, 137
Controls, 113–171. See also Control library
  as 2D drawings, 31–33
  as 3D shapes, 33–35
  adding styles to, 37–39, 401, 418
  adding triggers to, 387–388
  binding, 27–30
  Border, 165–166
  bubbling events for, 371
  code interacting with, 24–27
  content model for, 116–121
  creating themes for, 406–407
  customizing appearance of. See Templates
  keyboard focus for, 441–442
  layout of. See Layout
  overview of, 113
  Popup, 167
  ScrollViewer, 167–169
  three principles of, 113–116
  Thumb, 163–165
  ToolTip, 161–163
  user, 80–83
  Viewbox, 169–170
ControlTemplate
  adding triggers to controls with,
    388, 400
  animation integration with, 296–298
  customizing ListBox with, 134
  DataTemplate vs., 338–340
  defined, 123
  defining new, 123–125
  integrating animation with, 296–298

CopyToOutputDirectory, 65
CroppedBitmap class, 244
CS_PARENTDC, 219
CSS (Cascading Style Sheets)
  customizing controls in HTML using, 122
  customizing style for tags using, 392
  encoding styles using, 396–397
CTP (community technology preview), 41
Currency management, collection view, 349–351
CWnd, 71

D

DashStyle property, pens, 236–237
Data, 307–364
  adding triggers to, 384–387
  binding. *See* Binding
  data-driven display, 357–362
  .NET data model, 307–308
  pervasive binding, 308–309
  resources, 310–316
  transformation, 309–310
  working with, 27–30
Data-driven display
  data models in, 361
  example of, 358–362
  reusing rich views in, 361–362
  reversed relationships in, 357–358
Data model, .NET, 307–308, 361
Data point, 316
Data templates
  adding content to display tree, 118
  adding triggers to data, 384–387
  binding with, 320–322, 338–340
  data-bound commands, 381–382
  data-driven display. *See* Data-driven
    display
  defined, 309
  defining, 123
  in hierarchical binding, 342–349
  selecting, 340–342
DataTemplateKey, 399
DataTemplateSelector, 340–343
DataTrigger
  adding triggers to controls, 388
  adding triggers to data, 384–387
  defined, 383–384
DataType property, 347
Deactivated event, Window, 72

Declarative actions, 369
Declarative programming, 10, 54
DeclareChangeBlock, 153–154
DefaultValue, metadata, 434
DependencyObject, 432–434
DependencyProperty system, 326, 432–434
Deployment, scalable, 47–48
Deployment tag, browser hosting, 106–108
Desired size, two-phase layout, 175
Desktop applications
  adding navigation to, 48–50
  converting browser applications to, 46–47
  deploying, 48
  overview of, 50–52
Dialogs
  displaying modal, 74–75
  preventing user from dismissing, 94
  with scroll view, 168–170
  windowing model for, 51
Diffuse materials, 264–265
Direct events, 369
DirectionalLight, 265
DirectoryInfo, 344–345
Dispatchers, 422, 427
DispatcherUnhandledException event, 58–59
DispatcherUnhandledExceptionEventArgs, 58
Display, and styles, 401–405
Display tree
  adding content to, 118
  binding with data templates, 320–322
  ControlTemplate vs. DataTemplate, 338
  defined, 116–117
  ListBox, 120
  templates creating, 123–124
Display, windows, 74–77
Dock property, 191
DockPanel, 139–140, 190–193
DocObjects, Active X, 109
Document property, 150
Document state, 71
Document viewers, 160
Documents and text, 267–283
  advanced typography, 281–283
  columns and page-level formatting, 280–281
  figures and floaters, 279–280
  fonts, 272–274
  Hello World, text style, 268–272
  lists, 275–277
  paragraph formatting, 274–275
  tables, 277–279

DoubleAnimation, 36, 286–288, 295–296
DoubleAnimationUsingKeyFrames, 295–296
Drawing attributes, Stroke, 156–157
Drawing instructions, 218
DrawingBrush, 232–234, 303
DrawingGroup, 239
DrawingImage type, 241
Drawings, 218, 237–239
Dynamic resource binding, 314–315
DynamicResource, 356

E

Editing
  binding to CLR objects, 325–331
  two-way data binding for, 327–328
Editors, 145–159
  ink data, 154–158
  overview of, 145–146
  text data, 146–150
  using InkCanvas, 158–159
  using RichTextBox, 150–154
  using TextBox, 154
Element composition
  for actions, 366–367
  for controls, 114, 116–117
  for styles, 392–393
  for templates, 126
ElementName property, 317
Ellipse control, 121
EmbeddedResource, 65–67
Emissive materials, 264–265
Error handling, 57–59
Event handlers
  linking markup to code-behind files, 25–27
  setting new control template, 124–125
Event setters, 398
Events
  loose coupling and, 367–368
  overview of, 369–372
  reporting property changes with, 326–327
EventTrigger
  adding to controls, 387–388
  defined, 383–384
  integrating animation with
    ControlTemplate, 296–298
Exception-handling, 57–59
Exceptions, unrecoverable, 57
Execute, commands, 375–376
Exit command, 375–377

Expander control, 143–144
Expression Blend, 41
Extensible Application Markup Language.
  See XAML (Extensible Application
  Markup Language)

F

FamilyNames property, fonts, 273–274
FamilyTypeface, 272–273
FieldOfView, 256–258
Figures, 279–280
FillRule property, 224
Filtering, in collection view, 351–353, 356
FindResource, 289–290
Flexible sizing models, Grid, 197–199
Floaters, 279–280
FlowDocument
  controlling column layout, 280–281
  overview of, 269–271
  TextBox allowing editing of single, 150
FlowDocumentPageViewer control, 160
FlowDocumentReader control, 160, 271
FlowDocumentScrollViewer control, 160, 270
FocusManager, 441–442
Fonts
  FontFamily, 273, 317–318
  overview of, 272–274
Forever, RepeatBehavior, 294
Form, in Windows Forms, 71
FormatConvertedBitmap class, 244
Formatting, of arbitrary ranges, 149
Frame, 160–161
FrameworkContentElement, 384
FrameworkElement
  controlling layout constraints, 177
  defined, 176
  triggers properties on, 384
  using layout properties of, 185
FrameworkElementFactory, 124, 314, 338
FrameworkElement.SetResourceReference
  API, 315
FrameworkPropertyMetadata type, 437
Freezable objects, 314
Fully qualified file path, 64–65
Functional navigation, 97–103
  building Welcome page, 99–100
  call to SayHello, 100–101
  creating UI to display to user, 99–100
  defined, 98

implementing, 98–99
implementing flow of, 101–102
implementing GetName, 102–103
overview of, 97–98

G

GDI coordinate system, 219
Geometries
2D graphics, 222–225
3D graphics, 255
basic, 218
outlining shape with pens, 234–236
GeometryCombineMode, 224–225
GeometryDrawing, 239, 255
GeometryGroup, 224
GeometryModel3D, 255, 259
Gestures
InkCanvas recognizing, 158–159
InputBinding, 438
GetContentStream, 68
GetDefaultView static method, 351
GetName event, 101, 102–103
GetName.Return event, 101
GetRemoteStream, 68
GetResourcesStream, 68, 69
GlyphRunDrawing, 239
GoBack method, 97
Gradient brushes, 228–232
GradientOrigin property, 229
Graphics
effects of painter's algorithm on, 5–6
power of integration for, 30–37
stretch for, 242–243
vector vs. raster, 5–6
Gravity, and RichTextBox, 151
Grid, 196–207
editing at runtime with GridSplitter, 205–207
flexible sizing models in, 197–199
layout, 202–306
overview of, 196
with shared sizing, 199–202
UniformGrid, 194–195
GridSplitter, 205–207
GridView, 135–137
GroupBox control, 143–144
Grouping
in collection view, 353–355, 357
shared size, 200–202
Gupta, Namita, 308

H

Handled flag, 58
Handled property, routed events, 372
HeaderedContentControl, 144
HeaderedItemsControl, 138, 140
Headers, toolbar, 141–142
Height property
controlling window size, 77–78
layout constraints, 177
Hello World
in 3D graphics, 255–258
requiring STA threading, 422
in text style, 268–272
in User32, 1–2
in Windows Forms, 3
in WPF, 3–4
writing scalable applications, 44–46
HelloBrowser, 104–109
Hierarchical binding, 342–349
fixing copy problem in, 346–347
using HierarchicalDataTemplate, 347–349
using nested data templates, 342–346
HierarchicalDataTemplate, 347–349
Hierarchy, TreeView display, 137
HorizontalAlignment property, layout
patterns, 178–180
HostInBrowser attribute, 46–47, 104–105
Hosting
with document viewers, 160
with Frame, 160–161
scalable, 48
Hosting in browser, 103–111
HelloBrowser, 103–109
loose markup, 111
overview of, 103–104
PresentationHost view, 109–110
HTML
customizing appearance of controls in,
121–122
popularizing navigation, 83–84
XAML vs., 8–11
HWND, User32, 71
Hyperlinks
adding to page, 86
binding to shutdown of application, 375
creating between Welcome page and
SayHello, 100–101
supporting clicking, 368
Hyphenation, 282–283

I

ICC (International Color Consortium) color
profiles, 227–228
ICommand interface, 374–376
ICustomTypeDesciptor, 328, 330
Image control, 242–243, 358
ImageBrush, 232–234
ImageDrawing, 239
Images, 241–250
  in 2D graphics. *See* Images
  basics of, 242
  creating, 248–250
  data-driven display of. *See* Data-driven
    display
  defined, 241
  ImageSource and, 242–245
  metadata, 246–248
  overview of, 241
ImageSource
  basic imaging, 242–243
  data-driven display and, 358
  images deriving from, 241
  Metadata property of, 246–248
  overview of, 242–245
In-line text elements, 147–148, 269
Incremental customization, 127
Inheritance, style, 412–415
InitializeComponent, 25, 69–71
Ink data, 154–158
Ink serialized format (ISF), 154
InkCanvas control
  defined, 146
  overview of, 158–159
  working with, 155–156
INotifyCollectionChanged, 328, 330
INotifyPropertyChanged, 326–327, 329–330
Input device communication, 441
Input events, 370
InputBinding, 438–440
Integrated hosting, 161
Integration
  animation, 296–300
  WPF features for, 30–37
InternalChildren property, 208
International Color Consortium (ICC) color
  profiles, 227–228
IsChecked property, 129
ISF (ink serialized format), 154
Isolated hosting, 160–161
IsReadOnly property, 434–435

IsSharedSizeScope property, 201
IsSynchronizedWithCurrentItem property,
  349–351
IsThreeState property, 129
IStorage, 68
IStream, 68
Items property
  adding data to lists with, 131
  overview of, 119–120
  TreeView using, 137
ItemsPanel, 132–134
ItemsPanelTemplate, 132–134
ItemsPresenter, 120
ItemsSource property
  binding to list, 325
  in collection view, 357
  filling list controls using, 131
  in hierarchical binding, 343, 345, 347–348
  ListBox and ComboBox using, 131–135
  TreeView using, 137
ItemTemplate property, 339–340
IValueConverter
  binding using, 318–320
  data-bound commands using, 382
  value conversion using, 318

J

Java, with docking, 191
Joins, pen, 235
Journal
  controlling, 96–97
  defined, 84
  implementing with InkCanvas control,
    158–159
  querying, 97
Justification, 282–283

K

KeepAlive property, 101
KeepWithNext, Paragraph, 275–276
Key chords, 438
Key frames, animation, 295–296
Keyboard
  focus, 441–442
  input device communication in, 441
  structuring in WPF, 437–438
  structuring with InputBinding, 438–440
KeyboardNavigation, 441–442
KeyGesture type, 438–440

L

Layout
  contract, 174–176
  controls, 121
  Grid. *See* Grid
  panel, 22–23
  writing custom, 207–214
Layout library, 186–195
  Canvas, 186–189
  DockPanel, 190–193
  StackPanel, 189–190
  UniformGrid, 194–195
  WrapPanel, 194
Layout principles
  implementing consistent, 185
  layout constraints, 177
  layout contract, 174
  no built-in layout, 185–186
  size to content, 174
  slot model, 178–181
  transforms, 181–183
  two-phase layout, 174–176
  Z-index, 183–184
LayoutTransform property, 181–183
Left property
  Canvas, 186–187
  window position and size, 78
Library, layout. *See* Layout library
Lifetime, controlling process, 55–56
Ligatures, 282
Light, 3D graphics, 265
Light point, 3D graphics, 256–258
LinearDoubleKeyFrame, 296
LinearGradientBrush, 228–232
LineHeight, Paragraph, 275
LineJoin, pens, 235–236
LineSegment, 222
List controls, 130–138
  creating with templates, 137–138
  ListBox and ComboBox, 131–135
  ListView, 135–137
  in .NET, 308
  overview of, 130–131
  TabControl as, 144
  TreeView, 137
ListBox
  binding to, 325
  containing strings and display tree, 119–120
  as content control, 121
  currency management in, 349–350

ListView deriving from, 135–137
  making into radio button list, 137–138
  overview of, 131–135
ListItem, 275–277
ListOpenWindows event handler, 80
ListView, 135–137
LoadCompleted event, 93–94
LoadComponent, 69
Loaded event, window, 72–73, 95–96
Logical pixels, 220
LookDirection, 256–257
Lookup path, for resources, 312
Loose coupling, 368, 422
Loose markup, 111

M

Mapping Mode, for brushes, 230–231
Margins, 178–180, 187
MarkerStyle, lists, 275–276
Markup
  associating code with, 24–25
  building program using, 19–21
  declaring bindings in, 317
  defining application in, 54–55
  deploying, 47
  describing collection views in, 355–356
  loose XAML hosted in browser, 111
  templates and, 124
  writing simple WPF applications in, 44–46
Markup extensions, XAML, 13, 15
Materials, 3D, 255–256, 264–265
MatrixCamera, 265
MaxHeight property
  circle layout, 208–209
  Grid layout, 203
  layout constraints, 177
  for user interactivity with window, 77–78
Maximum property, 144–145
MaxWidth property
  circle layout, 208–209
  Grid layout, 203
  layout constraints, 177
  for user interactivity with window, 77–78
MDIs (multiple-document interfaces), 51–52
Measure phase, two-phase layout, 175
MeasureOverride, 185
Media
  audio, 301–303
  defined, 300–301
  video, 303–305

MediaClock, 301–302
MediaElement
   playing audio, 302–303
   playing video, 303–305
MediaPlayer, 301–302
MediaTimeline, 301
Memory gates, 57
MenuItem controls, 138–140
Menus
   binding to shutdown of application, 375
   overview of, 138–140
   toolbars vs., 139
MergedDictionaries property, Resource
      Dictionary, 405–406
Mesh, 259
MeshGeometry3D, 259–260
Metadata
   base services, 434–437
   image, 246–248
Microsoft
   Expression Blend, 41
   Presentation Foundation. *See* WPF
         (Windows Presentation Foundation)
   Windows. *See* Windows
   Windows Explorer, 191–193
   Windows Forms. *See* Windows Forms
   Windows Software Development Kit, 39
   Windows XP, 132–133, 155–156
Microsoft Foundation Classes (MFC), 71
MinHeight property
   Grid layout, 203
   layout constraints, 177
   for user interactivity with window, 77–78
Minimum property, 144–145
MinWidth property
   Grid layout, 203
   layout constraints, 177
   for user interactivity with window, 77–78
Miter joins, pens, 235
Model-view-controller (MVC) pattern, 400
Models
   3D, creating complex, 258–264
   3D, defined, 255
   and styles, 401–405
Mouse
   events, 366–367
   input device communication, 441
   overview of, 437–438
   roll-over effects for animation, 287–288
   structuring with InputBinding, 438–440

MouseEnter, 287–288, 291
MSBuild project file, 18–19
MultiDataTrigger, 384, 389
Multiple-document interfaces (MDIs),
      51–52
Multithreading, 422
MultiTrigger, 384, 389
MVC (model-view-controller) pattern, 400
MyFontAnimation, 285–286

N

Named resources, and styles, 403
Namespaces, XAML, 11–12, 14–15
Naming conventions
   code-behind files, 24–27
   components authored in XAML, 69
Navigable content (Page), 84, 86
NavigateUri property, 88
Navigating events
   adding validation to page, 95–96
   canceling navigation with, 94
Navigation
   adding hyperlink to page for, 86–88
   controlling, 94–96
   functional, 97–103
   hosting applications in browser. *See* XBAPs
         (XAML Browser Application)
   HTML popularizing, 83–84
   initial display of, 87
   journal, 88, 96–97
   NavigationWindow as host for, 84–85
   passing state between pages, 89–94
   SDI (single-document interface), 51
   Web style, 48–50
navigation-State argument, 93
NavigationService
   adding hyperlink to page, 86
   adding validation to page, 95–96
   controlling journal, 97
   passing state between pages, 93
   preventing user from dismissing
         dialogs, 94
NavigationWindow, 84–88
Nesting
   toolbars vs. menus, 140–141
   WPF composition engine for, 7
.NET Framework
   3.0 Extensions for Visual Studio, 41
   data model, 307–308

online resource for, 39
properties, 427–431
simple programming model in, 114
.NET properties, 427–431
NewWindowClicked event handler, 80
Nodes, XML, 332–333, 335
NormalPressure property, ink data, 157

O

Object binding
    editing values, 325–331
    to list, 325
    overview of, 322
    with property path, 322–324
Object model, for ContentPresenter,
        117–118
ObservableCollection<T>, 131, 329
Offsets, RichTextBox and, 151–153
Opacity (transparency)
    in 2D graphics, 250–253
    color, 228
OpacityMask, 251–253
OPC (Open Packaging Convention),
        68–69
Open Packaging Convention (OPC),
        68–69
OpenCommand, 381, 385
OpenType file, 272–273, 281–282
Orcas, 41
Orientation property, StackPanel, 189–190
OriginalSource, in routed events, 372
OrthographicCamera, 265
OutOfMemoryException, 57
Overflow menu, 142
Overlapping controls, 4–5
Owner property, in window, 75–76

P

Packages, OPC model, 68–69
Page build type, compiled markup, 21
PageFunction
    building Welcome page, 99–100
    creating for SayHello, 100–102
    navigation innovation of, 103
Pages
    adding validation to, 95–96
    functional applications and, 97–103
    passing state between, 89–94
    sizing for documents, 280–281

Painter's algorithm, 5–6, 180
Panel, layout, 121, 207
Paragraphs
    FlowDocument model for, 269–270
    formatting, 274–275
    text containment rules for, 147–148
    text layout for, 274–275
    TextBlock designed for single, 269
Partial types feature, 24–25
Parts, OPC model, 69
PasswordBox control, 146
PathGeometry, 222–225
Pens, 218, 234–237
Percentage sizing, 177, 197–199
Performance
    cost of using dynamic resource references,
        315
    customizing layout for, 207
PerspectiveCamera, 265–266
Petzold, Charles, 1
Pixel snapping, 220–221
Pixels, 219–221
Player, 302–303
Point light, 256–258
PointLight, 265
Popup, 167
Positions property, lighting in 3D, 255
Positions property, MeshGeometry3D,
        259–260
PresentationHost, 109–110
Preview, 370
Primitives namespace, 167, 194–195
Printing, documents and text, 272
ProgressBar control, 144–145
Project files, signing manifests for, 46
Properties
    base services, 431–434
    binding between controls, 29–30
    controlling layout constraints, 177
    customizing appearance of controls
        using, 122
    layout implementation with attached, 186
    setting new control template, 124
Properties dictionary, 89
Properties property, 59–60
Property path, binding to, 322–324
Property setters
    applying to styles, 394–395
    setting styles with, 397–398
PropertyMetadata type, 434–437

Q

QuadraticBezierSegment, 223
Queries, XPath, 334–335

R

RadialGradientBrush, 228–232
RadioButton control, 129–130, 368
RadioButtonList, 131, 137
RadiusX property, 229
RadiusY property, 229
Range controls, 144–145, 149
Range property, light, 256
Raster graphics
  basic imaging, 242–243
  generating image, 248–249
  overview of, 5–6
  supporting frames, 244
Reader control, FlowDocumentReader,
    160, 271
Rectangle, as render control, 121
Relationships, OPC model, 69
RelativeToBoundingBox, 230–231
RemoveBackEntry, 97
Render controls, 121, 165
RenderTargetBitmap, 248–249
RenderTransform property, 181–182
RepeatBehavior, 294
RequestNavigate event, 89
ResizeBehavior, 207
ResizeDirection, 206
ResizeMode property, 77–78
Resolution independence, in 2D graphics,
    219–221
Resource binding, 28–29
Resource references
  overview of, 49–50
  for state determined at author time, 64–65
  for styles, 398–399
ResourceDictionary, 405–406, 408–409
Resources (content state), 64–71
  adding to application, 65–67
  applications and, 312–314
  configuring, 65–66
  defined, 64, 310–311
  loading, 68–69
  lookup path for, 312
  Open Packaging Conventions and, 68–69
  overriding in element hierarchy, 311–312
  overview of, 28–29

static assignment or dynamic binding of,
    314–315
  styles and, 400, 403
  types of, 65
  using more than once, 314
Rich content, 114, 126
RichEdit control, Win32, 114
RichTextBox control
  displaying documents with, 160
  TextBox vs., 146
  video as foreground for, 303–305
  working with, 150–154
Right property, 78, 186–187
Root browser window, 111
RotateTransform, 181–182, 221
RoutedCommand, 378–379
RoutedEvent field, 373
RowDefinitions property, Grid, 196,
    202–203
Run method, 52–53, 55–56

S

SayHello, 100–101
Scalable applications, 44–48, 169–170
ScaleTransform, 181, 221
Scope named styles, 392–393
scRGB, 227–228
Script programming, 10
ScrollBar control, 144–145, 418
ScrollViewer control, 167–170, 190
SDI (single-document interface)
  overview of, 50
  windowing model, 51
  windows and dialogs, 71
Security, 109, 379
Selection.End, 151
Selection.Start, 151
SelectTemplate method, 340–342
Server-side programming, 10
SetBinding method, 316
Setters
  adding to triggers, 385–386
  responding to triggers, 388
  types of, 397–398
SettingsBase, Configuration state, 61
Settings.Save method, Configuration state,
    63–64
Shapes
  2D graphics, 239–241
  defined, 218

Shared sizing, Grid, 199–202
SharedSizeGroup property, 201
Shift+F10, 139
Show method, 74–76
ShowDialog method, 74–75
Shutdown method
  calling, 375
  controlling process lifetime, 56
Shutdown property, 79
Simple programming model, 114–116
Single-document interface (SDI)
  overview of, 50
  windowing model, 51
  windows and dialogs, 71
Single-threaded apartment (STA) threading,
  422
Size to content, 77, 174
Sizing
  in Grid, 197–198, 200–202, 205–207
  layout constraints, 177
  in two-phase layout, 174–175
  windows, 77–78
Skinning, 407–412
Slider control, 144–145, 435–436
Slot model, 178–181
Slotless layout panel, Canvas as, 187
SolidColorBrush, 228
Sorting, in collection view, 353, 356–357
Source property
  in binding, 337
  in collection view, 356
  in data-driven display, 358
  in routed events, 372
Sparkle, 41
Sparse storage, 432–434
Specular materials, 264–265
SpotLight, 265
SpreadMethod property, gradient brushes,
  229–230
sRGB, 226–228
STA (single-threaded apartment) threading,
  422
Stack panel, 22
StackOverflowException, 57
StackPanel
  DockPanel vs., 190–191
  as layout control, 121
  overview of, 189–190
Star sizing, Grid, 197–199
StartIndex, lists, 275–276

Startup behavior, window, 77
Startup event, process lifetime, 55–56
StartupUri property, 88
State
  Configuration, 61–64
  Content, 64–71
  Document, 71
  managing, 59–60
  passing between pages, 89–94
STAThread attribute, 422
StaticResource
  in style inheritance, 413–414
  wiring up data to collection view source,
    356
  in XML binding, 337
Storage, sparse, 432–434
Storage, structured, 68–69
Storyboard
  control actions and triggers for, 388
  defining animation with, 294–295
  integrating animation with text, 299–300
  overview of, 288–290
Streaming-based text object model, 146
Stretch, image, 242–243
Stretch property, Viewbox, 169–170
StretchDirection property, Viewbox, 169–170
Stroke, 154–157
Structured storage, 68–69
Styles, 391–419
  cautions when applying, 415–416
  consistency in, 417–418
  conveying something to user, 419
  defined, 391
  element composition and, 392–393
  inheritance, 412–415
  models, display and, 401–405
  optimizing tool, 396–397
  overview of, 37–40
  principles of, 391–397
  skinning and, 407–412
  starting to use, 397–401
  themes vs., 405–407, 417
  as unified model for customization,
    393–395
Style.Triggers, 400
Stylus packets, 156–157
Styluses
  input device communication in, 441
  overview of, 437–438
  structuring with InputBinding, 438–440

SynchronizationContext, 422–424
System.Collection interfaces, 308
System.Collections.IDictionary, 59
System.Configuration APIs, 61
System.IO.Packaging namespace, 69
System.Windows.Window, 71

T

Tab key, for keyboard focus, 442
TabControl control, 143–144
Table element, 147–148
Table layout, 277–279
Tags, in WPF, 268
TargetType property, 398–399
TemplateBinding, 402
Templates, 121–128. *See also* Data templates
    binding with, 126–127, 309
    list controls with, 132–135, 137–138
    overview of, 121–125
    reusing in list of images, 361–362
    styles and, 401–405
    tool tips with, 163–164
    working with, 127–128
Tessellation, 2D constructs, 258
Text
    communicating through, 267
    data for, 146–150
    fonts for, 272–274
    Hello World in, 268–272
    integrating animation with, 298–300
Text layout, 274–283
    advanced typography, 281–283
    challenges of, 173
    columns and page-level, 280–281
    figures and floaters, 279–280
    lists, 275–277
    paragraphs, 274–275
    tables, 277–279
TextBlock control
    adding content to display tree, 118
    containing single paragraph, 269
    defined, 116–117
    StackPanel problems in, 190
    targeting text with, 268
TextBox control
    adding to window, 23
    binding to Content control, 317
    binding to FontFamily, 317–318
    overview of, 146

RichTextBox control vs., 150–154
    updating data in, 327–328
    working with, 154
TextEffects, 298–300
TextIndent, Paragraph, 275
TextPointer objects, 149, 151
TextRange objects, 149
Texture, 260–262
ThemeInfoAttribute, 405–406
Themes
    consistency of, 417–418
    conveying message through, 419
    defined, 391
    isolating from application, 417
    skinning, 407–412
ThreadAbortException, 57
Threading, 421–426
    multithreading vs., 424–426
    STA used in, 421–422
    SynchronizationContext used in, 422–426
    WPF dispatcher for, 422, 427
3D graphics, 255–267
    animating, 34–37
    cameras, 265–266
    Hello World in, 255–258
    lights, 265
    materials, 33–34, 264–265
    models, 258–264
    overview of, 254–255
    transforms, 266–267
Thumb, 163–165
Tiling brushes, 232–234
Time, animation and, 292–293
Time zero, 292
Timelines, 292–293, 301
Toolbars, 139, 140–143
Tools
    for building applications, 39–41
    for styles, 396–397
ToolTips, 161–164
ToolTipService, 161
Top property, Canvas, 186–187
ToString method, 118–119
Transform models, 5–6
Transformations, 5–6, 309–310
TransformGroup, 181
Transforms
    2D graphics, 221, 266
    3D graphics, 266–267
    layout with, 181–183

TranslateTransform
  in 3D graphics, 266–267
  defined, 221
  layout with, 181
Tree hierarchy concept, 237
TreeView control, 137, 138
TriangleIndices property, 255, 260–261
Triangles, 3D, 258–261
Triggers
  adding to controls, 387–388
  adding to data, 384–387
  in animation, 291
  applying styles to, 395, 400
  overview of, 383–384
  summary of, 388–389
Triggers property, 384, 395
TrueType file, 272–273
Tunneling events, 370–371
Two-phase layout model, 174–176
Two-way data binding, 327–331
2Dgraphics, 218–254
  bitmap effects, 253–254
  brushes, 228–234
  color, 225–228
  composite rendering, 218–219
  drawings, 237–239
  geometry, 222–225
  images. See Images
  integration and, 30–31
  opacity, 250–253
  pens, 234–237
  resolution independence, 219–221
  shapes, 239–241
  transforms, 221
TypeConverter, 118, 318
Typefaces, basic, 272–274
Typography, 281–283

U

UIElement, 118, 175
Undo units, 153–154
Unicode support, 269
Unified model, for customizing styles, 393–395
UniformGrid, 194–195, 207
Unrecoverable exceptions, 57
Updates, TextBox data, 327–330
UpdateSourceTrigger property, 327–328

URIs
  referencing resources with, 64–65
  Web-style applications with, 49
  XAML and, 69–71
User controls, 80–83
User-scoped settings, Configuration state, 62
User32, 1–7
  clipping system in, 4, 219
  customizing controls in, 121–122
  display of menus in, 139
  Hello World written in, 1–2
  HWND in, 71
  no container nesting in, 5–6
  Windows Forms and, 3–4
Users
  creating UI to display to, 99–100
  interactivity with window, 77–78

V

Validation, 95–96
Value coercion, leveraging for properties, 435–436
Value conversion, 309, 318–320
Vector graphics
  3D as form of, 254–255
  integrating with layout engine, 30–31
  overview of, 5–6
VerticalAlignment property, 178–180
Video, 303–305
VideoDrawing, 239, 303–305
ViewBase type, 136
Viewbox, 169–170
Viewport, 257
Visibility property, 74–75, 175–176
Visual C# Express, 39
Visual Studio, 41
VisualBrush, 31–32, 232–234
Visuals
  2D graphics. See 2D graphics
  3D graphics. See 3D graphics
  animation. See Animations
  documents and text. See Documents and text
  media, 300–305
  overview of, 217

W

Web
  applications, 48–50
  development, 8–11
  styles, 391

Welcome page, 99–100
Width property, 77–78, 177
Win32, 114, 116
Windowing models, 50–52
windows, 69–71
    Application object and, 78–80
    creating for WPF applications, 17–18
    creating template for, 127–128
    displaying, 74–77
    overview of, 71–74
    sizing and position of, 77–78
    using markup, 20–21
Windows Explorer, 191–193
Windows Forms
    clip-based painting systems and, 4
    customizing controls in, 121–122
    docking support in, 191
    form in, 71
    MDI support in, 52
    nesting problems in, 7
    WPF vs., 3–4
Windows Presentation Foundation). *See* WPF
        (Windows Presentation Foundation)
Windows Software Development Kit, 39
Windows XP, 132–133, 155–156
WindowStartUpLocation property, 77
WPF (Windows Presentation Foundation),
        overview of, 1–41
    composition, 7
    controls, 21–24
    events, 25–27
    getting up and running, 17–19
    integration, 30–37
    layouts, 22–23
    markup, 19–21
    styles, 37–39
    tools for building applications, 39–41
    transformations, 5–6
    User32 and, 1–2
    vector-based graphics of, 5–6
    Web development, 8–11
    working with data, 27–30
    XAML programming model, 11–17
Wrap panel, 23–24

WrapPanel, 194
WritableBitmap, 248–249

X

XAML (Extensible Application Markup
        Language), 11–17
    attached properties in, 16–17
    built-in features of, 14–15
    encoding styles with, 396–397
    HTML vs., 8–11
    importing WPF into, 15–16
    loose, 111
    markup extensions in, 13, 15
    as XML-based instantiation script for CLR,
        11–13
XBAP (XAML Browser Application)
    converting to desktop application, 46–47
    HelloBrowser and, 104–109
    loose markup and, 111
    overview of, 103–104
    PresentationHost in, 109–110
x:Class attribute, 44
XML binding, 331–337
XML namespace, 82
XML Paper Specification (XPS), 272
Xml property, TextRange, 149
XmlAttributeNode, 333
XmlDataProvider, 336–337
XmlDocument, 337
XmlElement, 337
xmlns attribute, 11–12
x:Name attribute, 44
XPath, 331–333, 334–335
XPS (XML Paper Specification), 272
XTilt, 157

Y

YTilt, 157

Z

Z-index, for layout, 183–184
ZipPackage, 69

Microsoft .NET Development Series

**.NET Framework
Standard Library
Annotated Reference**

Volume 1: Base Class Library and
Extended Numerics Library

Brad Abrams

0321154894

**.NET Framework
Standard Library
Annotated Reference**

Volume 2: Networking Library, Reflection Library
and XML Library

Brad Abrams
Tamara Abrams

0321194454

**Essential
Windows Presentation
Foundation**

Chris Anderson

0321374479

.NET Web Services

Architecture and Implementation

Keith Ballinger

0321113594

**Visual Studio Tools
for Office**

Using C# with Excel, Word,
Outlook, and InfoPath

Eric Carter
Eric Lippert

0321334884

**Visual Studio Tools
for Office**

Using Visual Basic 2005 with
Excel, Word, Outlook, and InfoPath

Eric Carter
Eric Lippert

0321411757

**Graphics
Programming
with GDI+**

Mahesh Chand

0321160770

**Framework
Design Guidelines**

Conventions, Idioms, and Patterns
for Reusable .NET Libraries

Krzysztof Cwalina
Brad Abrams

0321246756

**ASP.NET 2.0
Illustrated**

Alex Homer
Dave Sussman

0321418344

**The .NET Developer's
Guide to Directory
Services Programming**

Joe Kaplan
Ryan Dunn

0321350170

Essential C# 2.0

Mark Michaelis

0321150775

**The
Common Language
Infrastructure
Annotated Standard**

James S. Miller
Susann Ragsdale

0321154932

Essential ASP.NET

with Examples in C#

Fritz Onion

0201760401

Essential ASP.NET

with Examples in Visual Basic .NET

Fritz Onion

0201760398

**Building Applications
and Components with
Visual Basic .NET**

Ted Pattison
with Dr. Joe Hummel

0201734958

**.NET
Internationalization**

The Developer's Guide to Building Global
Windows and Web Applications

Guy Smith-Ferrier

0321341384

**The Visual Basic
.NET Programming
Language**

Paul Vick

0321169514